Religious Freedom and Gay Rights

D1526085

Religious Freedom and Gay Rights

Emerging Conflicts in the United States and Europe

EDITED BY TIMOTHY SAMUEL SHAH,
THOMAS F. FARR,
and
JACK FRIEDMAN

WITH AN INTRODUCTION BY MATTHEW J. FRANCK
and
AN AFTERWORD BY ROGER TRIGG

OXFORD
UNIVERSITY PRESS

OXFORD
UNIVERSITY PRESS

Oxford University Press is a department of the University of Oxford. It furthers
the University's objective of excellence in research, scholarship, and education
by publishing worldwide. Oxford is a registered trade mark of Oxford University
Press in the UK and certain other countries.

Published in the United States of America by Oxford University Press
198 Madison Avenue, New York, NY 10016, United States of America.

CIP data is on file at the Library of Congress
ISBN 978–0–19–060060–0 (hbk.); 978–0–19–060061–7 (pbk.)

CONTENTS

ACKNOWLEDGMENTS

Virtually all of the contributions to this volume were originally presented at a conference on "Religious Freedom and Equality: Emerging Conflicts in North America and Europe," which took place at Magdalen College, Oxford on April 12, 2012. The conference was organized by what was then the Religious Freedom Project, and is now the Religious Freedom Research Project, of the Berkley Center for Religion, Peace & World Affairs of Georgetown University.

For their contributions to the success of the conference or to the subsequent organization and completion of this volume, we gratefully acknowledge the following individuals: Kyle Vander Meulen, Roger Trigg, Julia Trigg, Thomas Banchoff, Michael Kessler, Michael Gerson, Peter Petkoff, Christopher McCrudden, Christopher Sugden, Karen Taliaferro, Matthew Quallen, Cynthia Soliman, Cole Durham, Steven Smith, Matthew Franck, Claudia Winkler, and Nicholas Fedyk. We also thank our editor at Oxford University Press, David McBride, and Oxford's two anonymous reviewers for their time and comments.

The John Templeton Foundation deserves a special note of thanks. Of course, as is always the case, the opinions expressed in this publication are those of the authors and do not necessarily reflect the views of the Templeton Foundation or of any of our other supporters. Nonetheless, we wish to take this opportunity to underscore that without the Templeton Foundation's generous funding in 2011, there would have been no Magdalen College conference and no volume of outstanding essays. In fact, there would have been no Religious Freedom Project at all. The decision to bet on the Religious Freedom Project with a major start-up grant ultimately rested with Dr. Jack Templeton, President of the John Templeton Foundation. It was thus a blow to us and to the visionary philanthropy the Templeton Foundation uniquely embodies that he passed away on May 19, 2015 as this volume was being completed. We take this opportunity to record our unpayable debt of gratitude to Dr. Jack Templeton. And we take this opportunity to pray: Eternal rest grant unto him. . . . Long may his work continue.

LIST OF CONTRIBUTORS

Rocco Buttiglione, Professor of Political Science at Saint Pius V University (Rome)

John Finnis, Biolchini Family Professor of Law at Notre Dame University and Professor of Law and Legal Philosophy at Oxford University

Matthew J. Franck, Director of the William E. and Carol G. Simon Center on Religion and the Constitution at the Witherspoon Institute

Richard W. Garnett, Paul J. Schierl/Fort Howard Corporation Professor of Law at the University of Notre Dame

Maarit Jänterä-Jareborg, Professor of Law at Uppsala University (Sweden)

Stephen Law, Senior Lecturer in Philosophy at Heythrop College, University of London

Linda C. McClain, Professor of Law and Paul M. Siskind Research Scholar at Boston University School of Law; Laurance S. Rockefeller Visiting Faculty Fellow, University Center for Human Values at Princeton University, 2016–2017

Andrea Pin, Associate Professor of Comparative Public Law at the University of Padova (Italy)

Steven D. Smith, Warren Distinguished Professor of Law at the University of San Diego School of Law

Archbishop Philip Tartaglia, Archbishop of Glasgow

Roger Trigg, Senior Research Fellow at the Ian Ramsey Centre, University of Oxford

Robin Fretwell Wilson, Roger and Stephany Joslin Professor of Law and Director, Family Law and Policy Program, University of Illinois College of Law.

THE RELIGIOUS FREEDOM
RESEARCH PROJECT

This volume is the fruit of research conceived and supported by the Religious Freedom Research Project (RFRP) of the Berkley Center for Religion, Peace, and World Affairs at Georgetown University. Under the leadership of Director Thomas Farr and Associate Director Timothy Samuel Shah, the Religious Freedom Research Project is the world's only university-based program devoted exclusively to the analysis of religious freedom, a basic human right restricted in many parts of the globe. The RFRP is made possible by significant grants from the John Templeton Foundation, a partnership with Baylor University's Institute for Studies of Religion, and the generous support of numerous other individuals and foundations.

The goal of the RFRP is to deepen scholarly understanding, inform policy deliberation, and educate the wider public concerning the meaning and value of religious freedom. It achieves this goal through publications such as this one, as well as conferences, workshops, media appearances, a vigorous web presence, and a blog, *Cornerstone: A Conversation on Religious Freedom and Its Social Implications*. Find out more at www.berkleycenter.georgetown.edu/rfp.

Introduction

Religious Freedom, Same-Sex Marriage, and the Dignity of the Human Person

MATTHEW J. FRANCK

I.

Like many ideas both good and bad that resonate throughout the entire world today, the idea of religious freedom is a product of that world-colonizing project called western civilization. Other cultures, in their history or at present, may have practiced *toleration* of diverse religious views. But toleration *is* a practice, a gift from the powerful to the powerless—and a revocable gift, at that.

Religious freedom, by contrast, is an idea, or the product of an idea. Or it may be better to say it is invariably the reflection of a principle, and principles, unlike practices, must have an intellectual underpinning. Practices may be based on principles; they may also be wholly unprincipled—mere habits, or mere accommodations reached between necessity and desire. Toleration can be like that, a practice responding to the necessities of power or peace, in competition with the desire to live in a way unfettered by such necessities. Or it can be more, if an attempt is made to articulate an underlying principle—but even then there is likely to be a *more* important principle demarcating and subordinating toleration to itself.

But religious freedom *must* be more than a mere practice, or a gift from the powerful to the powerless.[1] Its very name gives it away. The noun is *freedom*; the adjective *religious* indicates a particular species of the larger genus. What sort of idea is freedom?

The achievement of truly free societies—characterized by limited constitutional government, the rule of law, and popular control of political institutions, with a premium placed on individual liberty—seems to be a relatively recent achievement, if by "recent" we mean the last two or three centuries. Is this achievement therefore to be laid entirely to the credit of modern political philosophy?

One might be forgiven for thinking so. Liberal, constitutional democracy, in theory as in historical reality, seems peculiarly to be the project of modern thinkers such as John Locke and Baruch Spinoza—thinkers who set themselves to varying degrees in opposition to both classical political philosophy and the biblical traditions of Christianity and Judaism, respectively, as those traditions were understood in their day. Both Locke and Spinoza are famously advocates of religious freedom in particular, and both are commonly read by some of their most influential interpreters as impious, even iconoclastic thinkers, if to varying degrees esoteric ones.[2]

Does it follow that the politics of freedom—even or especially the politics of religious freedom—rests on a foundation of impiety or iconoclasm? Or, to put the matter more pointedly, is the free society necessarily the impious, irreligious, or anti-religious society, while the pious society is necessarily the unfree one?

By no means. We may fully acknowledge the contributions of modern political philosophers such as Locke (to take the stronger example where influence on succeeding generations is concerned) to the subsequent development of free institutions as both successful in practice and stable over time. And at the same time we must say that men such as Locke turned their intellects on a subject bequeathed to them by the whole tradition of western thought: the needs and aspirations of the free human person.

As for *that* subject, with all due respect to the Socratic tradition in political philosophy, the free human person is an idea that belongs decisively to the Judeo-Christian tradition. It might even be said to be the theme of that tradition. That is to say, in the famous tension, sometimes fraught and often fruitful, between Athens and Jerusalem in the generation of western culture, the palm must be awarded to Jerusalem—and to Christian Rome—for introducing the idea of the free human person, and of the equal dignity of every human individual.[3]

The dignity of the individual is traceable to the first chapter of the first book of the Hebrew Bible, in which men and women are said to be made in the image of God (Gen. 1:27). And as though it were the opposite bookend, St. Paul's Letter to the Galatians (3:28) tells us that "[t]here is neither Jew nor Greek, there is neither slave nor free, there is neither male nor female, for you are all one in Christ Jesus." The fallen character of all, and the promise of redemption for each: these make for a common denominator more important than any differences of class, tribe, nation, or culture.

Notwithstanding the intellectual liberation achieved by Socratic philosophy, the pagan world remained largely a world of near horizons, bounded by the gods of the hearth, the traditions of the tribe, and the *nomos* of the city. Socrates and his followers may have discovered the idea of natural right, as Leo Strauss argued decades ago.⁴ But it was only in the Christian worldview that every man, not just the philosopher, found it possible to transcend the *nomos* and live in the light of the *logos*. "In the beginning was the Word" or *Logos*, as the Gospel of John opens, and the Word was that same God in whose image we are made.

Like the God who made us, we, though his mere creatures, are beings with *logos*—reason—and a free will. It is given to us, each and every one, to reason about the good, and to choose, and to act. And philosophic wisdom, the light of unaided reason, is from the Christian point of view an untrustworthy guide to our choosing and acting, for most men in most times and places. (Even from the perspective of classical political philosophy, the activity of philosophy is the province of very few.) Faith is thus the sine qua non for the right use of reason in general, and faith is accessible to all, not just to the philosopher. The Christian faith thus democratized the freedom of the will and the range of the intellect, pushing back a near horizon and enabling a longer, farther view, of time and history, of human limitation and possibility, of our relation to eternity and the whole.

Central to the Christian idea of freedom is the freedom of faith itself—religious freedom. From very early in the Christian era, we find thinkers such as Tertullian and Lactantius advancing the view that faith must be free and uncoerced. Our duty to God is identical to our duty to the truth: we must go whither the evidence of reason and faith leads, not according to the will of others, but of our own free will.⁵ We can begin to see, then, how the larger genus "freedom" begets a distinct species called "religious freedom." In order to be truly authentic, religion must be engaged freely and uncoercedly. Freedom is a necessary condition of religion, when religion is understood as the "effort of individuals and communities to understand, to express, and to seek harmony with a transcendent reality of such importance that they feel compelled to organize their lives around their understanding of it, to be guided by it in their moral conduct, and to communicate their devotion to others," both in public and in private.⁶

Thus at the base of our modern, liberal commitments in western (and western-influenced) societies to the freedom of the individual—an individual of dignity and worth equal to every other—is a fundamental Judeo-Christian conception of the free, rational, choosing human person, fallen but redeemable, above all freely answering to the evidence that impels a response to the God who made him. And from this Judeo-Christian conception of the human person we get a comprehensive guiding notion of religious freedom.

Here we encounter the sticking point for the controversy taken up by the various authors in this book: namely, the potential impediments to religious freedom that arise when society conceives and enacts equal rights, especially regarding marriage, for gay and lesbian men and women.

Before it became the subject of this book, this controversy was the focus of a major international conference held at Magdalen College, Oxford University on April 11–13, 2012 and sponsored by the Religious Freedom Research Project of Georgetown University's Berkley Center for Religion, Peace and World Affairs. The conference, entitled "Religious Freedom and Homosexual Equality: Emerging Conflicts in North America and Europe," convened leading scholars, politicians, and religious leaders to explore how the conflicts between gay rights and religious freedom are currently unfolding within the United Kingdom and Ireland, the United States and Canada, and continental Europe.

This book is the product of that April 2012 conference. Its chapters are, almost without exception, the papers initially presented at the conference, revised and updated as much as possible to reflect the cascade of recent developments affecting gay rights and religious freedom in the United Kingdom, the United States, and continental Europe.

The cultural and political landscape has changed dramatically indeed in the period between the April 2012 conference and the completion of this book. In a 2013 case, *United States v. Windsor*,[7] the US Supreme Court ruled it unconstitutional for the federal government to define marriage in a way that excludes those same-sex couples recognized as married in particular states. And in its 2015 *Obergefell v. Hodges*[8] ruling, the Court declared a constitutional right of same-sex marriage nationwide. The controversy surrounding these landmark cases was punctuated by a wave of opposition to religious freedom laws passed in Indiana and Arkansas in spring 2015.

The situation on the other side of the Atlantic has been equally fluid and, in many cases, controversial. In 2013 the UK Parliament passed legislation legalizing same-sex marriage in England and Wales, and the next year the Scottish Parliament followed suit with legislation legalizing same-sex marriage in Scotland. In the courts, religious freedom experienced a setback with *Bull v. Hall* (2013),[9] heard before the UK Supreme Court, and in three of four cases consolidated in *Eweida and Others v. United Kingdom* (2013),[10] decided in the European Court of Human Rights (ECtHR). Among sundry other complex legal and philosophical issues, these cases dealt with balancing freedom of religion and freedom from discrimination, where the courts demonstrated a resolve to protect the latter.

Meanwhile, in continental Europe the ECtHR found in *X. v. Austria* (2013)[11] that Austria cannot withhold from same-sex couples the right to joint adoption of a biological child when that right is available to heterosexual couples. But significantly, the Court upheld the precedent that European states are not obligated to grant a right to same-sex marriage. The ECtHR set a parallel precedent when it ruled in *Oliari and Others v. Italy* (2015)[12] that Italy must offer some form of legal recognition to same-sex couples, even if that recognition does not involve "marriage."

These recent events suggest that the present moment is one of increasing urgency. Today more than ever, there is a need to grapple with tensions between gay rights and religious freedom. Yet despite these rapidly unfolding developments, the substance of the controversy remains essentially unchanged: the conflict between gay rights and religious freedom is but another (yet profound) iteration of the classic tension in political philosophy between equality and liberty. While the modern project of democratic government was inspired by the idea of liberty, it was also imbued with a commitment to the principle of equality. As we have just seen, this dual commitment to liberty and equality reflects a historically prior conception of innate human dignity rooted in a Judeo-Christian theological and philosophical anthropology: to be created in God's image presupposes that all humans possess a fundamental dignity, one that renders them naturally free *and* equal.

Today, however, modern liberalism has engineered a novel reconceptualization of equality, generating a burgeoning field of heretofore-unrecognized rights. Central to this new logic of equality are rights that would extend to homosexuals across different sectors of society, including housing, employment, and private enterprise. Among these, greatest attention has been paid to the prospect of establishing an equal right to marriage—often referred to as "same-sex marriage" or "marriage equality"—that would enable individuals to marry a person of the same sex. Proponents of this right argue that, in order to be fully equal to their heterosexual counterparts, homosexuals must be granted equal access to the institution of marriage. They argue that to deny them this equal access is to discriminate against them unlawfully; it is to withhold from gay couples recognition of their fundamental and equal dignity.

It is important to recognize here that the issue of same-sex marriage does not hinge on a wholesale acceptance or rejection of equality. Opponents of same-sex marriage typically do not object to equality per se, but to a specific understanding of what equality entails. Their underlying premise is that claims to "marriage equality" are based on a claim of identity—regarding sexual orientation—that is factually dubious and morally misleading, and entails a misunderstanding of the nature of marriage. Moreover, such an equality claim threatens to impinge on other fundamental rights, such as religious freedom. At this point we reach a virtual impasse of intractable conflict.

To appreciate why this is so, let us turn again to the core teachings of Christianity that did so much to shape western societies. For the Christian vision of the human person, freely responding in faith to a loving Creator, is a package deal. And part of the package concerns the Christian ethic of marriage and chastity—that is, of sexual relations being licit only within the bonds of marriage, and of marriage being the ground from which family and community spring. This sexual ethic is not an adventitious and dispensable part of Christian humanism. It is, strictly speaking, inseparable from it, and historically has not been even *apparently* separated but by the most strenuous efforts to reinterpret the Christian message in post-liberal, postmodern societies of recent decades, which are the first societies to witness the advent of churches that may properly be called post-Christian.

What looks today, to many, like historic Christianity's bondage to outmoded norms of morality, hopelessly retrograde in our enlightened age, is actually, from the perspective of historic Christianity itself, the mark of an ancient liberation from forms of sexual bondage and degradation that pervaded pagan antiquity.[13] The elite classes, or, to be more precise, elite *men* of the pagan Mediterranean in late antiquity were sexually continent only within the bonds of family and class, with the shame of stained honor being the only powerful restraint on sexual coupling. With slaves and the laboring classes and prostitutes—social groups with extremely permeable boundaries between them—these elite men were libertine exploiters, using the members of both sexes in such "inferior" groups for sexual pleasure without restraint or shame.

In this ancient milieu, the Christians were an astonishing phenomenon. They condemned and abhorred abortion and infanticide, adultery and divorce, and sexual libertinism of every kind. It was not shame (an offense against social norms and class roles) but sin (an offense against God) that moved them to cabin human sexuality entirely within the walls of marriage, and monogamous marriage at that. Sexual relations between persons of the same sex were perforce out of the question, but so too was all premarital and extramarital sex, or the taking of multiple wives.

Nor was this Christian revolution in sexual morality merely a form of reactionary repression. It was understood to be woven inextricably into the fabric of the Christian tapestry of freedom. Christian moral norms regarding sexuality, however imperfectly followed through, attempted to honor the equal dignity of both sexes, however different their familial and social roles; to safeguard the innocence of children and assure their decent upbringing; to distinguish erotic relationships from friendships and partnerships of other kinds; and to do justice to the poor and the marginalized. At bottom, this morality sprang from a recognition that *eros*'s great power in human relationships could only be tamed and made safe by *agapē*—one love being made subject to the sovereignty of the other, greater love.

II.

This Christian moral revolution in the ancient sexual economy was, it must be repeated, inseparable from the larger theme of the free human person. Thus the Christian sexual morality, and the emerging Christian argument for religious freedom, were stalks from a common root. The question today — a strictly empirical question — is whether the second stalk can survive if the first is severed. We are in early days yet in discerning an answer to this question. But the chapters of this book suggest that religious freedom in full may not have an easy time surviving the decline, in law, public policy, and mainstream culture, of Christian sexual morality and the Judeo-Christian conception of human dignity in which it is embedded.

Chapter One—the first of three in Section I on developments in the United Kingdom—underscores this likely reality. In "Equality and Religious Liberty: Oppressing Conscientious Diversity in England," John Finnis details a recent string of judicial rulings in UK courts and the ECtHR in which efforts to root out discrimination (against homosexuals) have instead resulted in discrimination against religious persons. The courts, he argues, have failed to develop a reasonable doctrine of accommodation for individuals who make conscientious religious objections to generally applicable (typically anti-discrimination) laws. Instead, the courts have applied disproportionate restrictions on religious freedom, as when it was ruled that a British Airways employee could not, in violation of company policy, wear a visible religious symbol (a cross), or that the owners and operators of a hotel could not, for religious reasons, deny a single-bedded room to a homosexual couple, even when this rule applied to all unmarried couples.

However, for the next author, Stephen Law, these court rulings represent a justifiable effort to apply anti-discrimination laws equally. In "Gay Rights versus Religious Rights," Law argues that the state should not grant religious exemptions to generally applicable laws. To do so, he insists, would be to confer special privilege upon religious individuals and their religious claims. The crux of the disagreement between Finnis and Law, then, is what a fair balance between competing claims of gay equality and religious freedom looks like. For Law, a fair balance does not involve showing preference to religious objections, however sincere they may be, by virtue of their religious nature and grounding. The implication is that the imperative to promote the equality of homosexuals outweighs the need to accommodate religious objectors.

In Chapter Three, Philip Tartaglia, Archbishop of Glasgow, observes that in recent years religious freedom has been whittled down to an impoverished notion of "freedom of worship" wherein one's religious freedom stops, as it were, at the "door of the temple." The effect has been to restrict a significant field of religious activity—public religious expression, in civil society, in the marketplace, and in the political life of the nation. This constriction of religious freedom to a marginalized sphere of private "worship" has grave implications, he warns, for the role of the democratic state. Properly understood, the state exists to facilitate society's most basic institutions, such as the family and the Church, not to absorb them within its all-encompassing authority.

Section II turns to the tension between gay equality and religious freedom in the United States. It should be noted that because these chapters were written and revised over a period from late 2012 to early 2015, they do not include detailed analyses of the Supreme Court's landmark *Obergefell* decision (released June 2015) establishing a constitutional right to same-sex marriage. In a matter of months, this ruling has given way to a new moral and political calculus centered around fresh and intensified tensions—tensions that figure to define a new era of American life, to which future work must respond with novel insight and solutions. Yet because many of the core issues in these tensions remain essentially unchanged, the four chapters in this section are instructive nevertheless, offering a prospective framework for grappling with religious freedom in a post-*Obergefell* world.

In Chapter Four, Richard W. Garnett proposes that in order to make sense of the tensions between religious freedom and gay equality, we need greater conceptual clarity about "discrimination." Discrimination is not wrong in and of itself, he points out.[14] Rather, *wrongful* discrimination is wrong. And sometimes our most basic freedoms require the latitude to discriminate. This is often the case, he suggests, with the right to religious freedom. Looking at three US Supreme Court cases—*Bob Jones University, Christian Legal Society,* and *Hosanna-Tabor*—Garnett delineates the boundaries between unjust and just discrimination by religious individuals and communities. Discrimination is just, he argues, when a "compelling state interest" is not at stake, or when denying one's ability to discriminate violates one's equal dignity or fundamental rights. For example, in the United States religious institutions are free to discriminate in their internal affairs under the "ministerial exception," such as when the Catholic Church excludes women from the priesthood. To deny religious organizations the freedom to discriminate in this sense is to impose an unjustified burden on their constitutionally guaranteed religious liberty.

In "Civil Marriage for Same-Sex Couples, 'Moral Disapproval', and Tensions between Religious Liberty and Equality," Linda C. McClain observes that objections to same-sex marriage often hinge on the assumption that laws and policies should reflect the religious virtues and values of citizens. There should be a *congruence*, in other words, between civil society and government, between traditional religious conceptions of marriage, on the one hand, and a legal definition of marriage, on the other. When these two are forced out of alignment—as when the Supreme Court struck down same-sex marriage bans in *Obergefell*—it often precipitates a fierce debate about religious liberty versus gay equality. But religious liberty and gay equality need not be at odds, McClain argues, so long as we recognize the distinction between "civil marriage," which obtains in the public sphere of secular law, and "religious marriage," which is limited to the private sphere of moral and religious values. Understood in this binary frame, she suggests that moral disapproval of homosexuality based on private religious values is, by itself, an insufficient basis for enacting and implementing laws that discriminate against homosexuals. Any moral disapproval must correspond to a compelling state interest, a *public* interest, one that is not ultimately reducible to a particular religious doctrine or value. Chronicling constitutional jurisprudence on liberty and equality over the past few decades, McClain observes that this understanding of the role of moral disapproval is, in fact, repeatedly borne out in the courts.

In "The Politics of Accommodation: The American Experience with Same-Sex Marriage and Religious Freedom," Robin Fretwell Wilson urges an approach of mutual accommodation for opponents and supporters of same-sex marriage. Although *Obergefell* took same-sex marriage off the bargaining table, it did not eliminate the urgent need for compromise. On the one hand, those who object to same-sex marriage on religious grounds still seek religious liberty protections. But with same-sex marriage now legal in 50 states, and with public support for marriage equality growing alongside an increasing public acceptance of the lesbian, gay, bisexual, and transgender (LGBT) community, the window for securing these protections may be closing. On the other hand, though same-sex marriage supporters emerged from *Obergefell* victorious, discrimination against members of the LGBT community in housing, employment, and public accommodations is still lawful in most states. To successfully enact bans against such discrimination, Wilson argues, same-sex marriage supporters would be wise to concede religious liberty protections; likewise, to secure religious liberty protections, opponents of same-sex marriage should be willing to concede LGBT nondiscrimination measures. Unpalatable though it may be to both sides, Wilson maintains that only compromise will yield adequate protections for conscientious religious objectors *and* the LGBT community.

To round out the section on religious freedom and gay equality in the United States, "Die and Let Live? The Asymmetry of Accommodation" by Steven D. Smith critiques the "accommodationist" approach advocated by Wilson and others. According to Smith, the approach relies on two mistaken assumptions of symmetry: first, that the negotiated outcomes—such as the legalization of same-sex marriage and accommodations for religious objectors—will be symmetrical in their fairness and balance to both sides; and second, that both sides are equally intransigent and eager to oppress the other side by enforcing their own views. Regarding the first assumption—called "prescriptive symmetry"—Smith argues that the compromise that accommodationists prescribe nevertheless favors same-sex marriage supporters because it privileges their view of marriage as the official position of the state, thereby casting religious objectors as "outsiders" to be "accommodated." Regarding the second assumption—called "critical symmetry"—Smith points out that it presupposes both sides face equally serious threats and thus respond with proportional and equally justified vigor. In reality, however, religious objectors face the far graver dilemma of having to choose between violating their conscience and convictions or being relegated to the margins of society. Their resistance is thus motivated not by intolerance or an impulse to impose their values on others, but by a legitimate fear of being stranded in a subordinate position in which they are at best tolerated, and at worst disadvantaged under a new hegemony.

The volume's final section (Section III) is an appraisal of the situation in continental Europe. In Chapter Eight, Rocco Buttiglione seeks clarification of the central concepts that fuel tensions between gay equality and religious freedom: What is the "nature" and "cause" of homosexuality? What do we mean when we invoke the word "discrimination"? How do we reconcile expanding definitions of tolerance and rights? Buttiglione argues that homosexual relationships, especially marriages, are not the same as heterosexual ones, and advises that we differentiate between the two. This differentiation is not based on animus or a desire to harm, he maintains, but on an understanding of homosexuality as a lifestyle, and of marriage as an institution whose central function is to bring children into the world, and to provide them with a healthy upbringing. Since homosexual couples are incapable of fulfilling this social function, Buttiglione concludes it is necessary and justified to deny them the right of marriage. Although this involves discrimination in the sense of "differentiation," it does not, he insists, involve an *unjust* denial of rights, for our rights derive from our status as human beings, not our sexual orientation. To deny gay couples marriage is thus not to deny the authenticity or significance of their love, but properly to situate their love outside the "social" reality of marriage.

In "Same-Sex Partnership and Religious Exemptions in Italy: Constitutional Textualism versus European Consensus," Andrea Pin criticizes the Italian Constitutional Court for employing a strict originalist reading when it ruled that the Italian constitution does not guarantee same-sex marriage. In so doing, he says, the Court avoided addressing important substantive questions, such as the justification for marriage (religious or otherwise), how to balance conflicting rights, and how properly to conceive of "self-determination." Moreover, Pin argues that religious communities should have a proactive role in the process of crafting gay rights legislation *before* such legislation is introduced. They should not be expected to wait until those rights are enacted before weighing in with their own interests and concerns, such as on the need for "conscientious objection."

In the final chapter, Maarit Jänterä-Jareborg presents a Scandinavian outlook on homosexuality, equal rights, and freedom of religion. She views religious freedom as being free to practice one's religion, but not to assert one's beliefs as a ground for shirking one's civil or legal obligations (as in the case of civil servants who refuse to register same-sex marriages on religious grounds). This view, she argues, enables us to reconcile two competing claims: the religious proscription against same-sex marriage, on the one hand, and the right of equal access to the institution of marriage by same-sex couples, on the other. In any case, Jänterä-Jareborg notes that in Scandinavia today it is individual freedom and rights, not religious values, that dictate legislation. And since there are various concepts of morality, the state must be neutral toward them. In practice, this means that religious beliefs that do not recognize the validity of same-sex partnerships, marriages, and adoptions are outweighed by an individual's right to equality before the law.

Concluding the volume in his Afterword, Roger Trigg inquires into whether much of the conflict's seeming intractability may stem from a widespread opinion that religious belief is "subjective" and therefore subject to marginalization and the ascendancy of other values held to be more objective in nature. If so, Trigg observes, the prospects for accommodation of religious freedom on a principled basis, recognizing its claims in full, are not very good.

III.

As one can see in the descriptions above and the chapters that follow, the contributors to this volume offer an array of different perspectives, reflecting their differing expertise and prior moral and philosophical commitments. Nevertheless, they tend to converge around a forecast in which society—for better or worse depending on which author you ask—increasingly moves *away* from a Christian sexual morality and *toward* a diminished tolerance of religious freedom.

The beginning of understanding this more-than-possible future is in considering the metamorphosis of the notion of dignity. As Ronald Osborn has recently written:

> Even if the language of "rights" was not explicitly or formally used, the New Testament invested every person with a previously unimaginable worth. Instead of struggling to attain *dignitas* as a scarce commodity in competitive rivalry with others, all persons were now summoned to live in generous solidarity with their neighbors as persons of dignity and worth equal to their own. Dignity, in the Christian revaluation of values, could not be earned, because it was bestowed as a gift from God, although the gift could be lost or squandered precisely by transgressing the dignity of the Other, whether through violence or by indifference to the Other's welfare—by denying that that person too was the privileged bearer of the divine image, the divine image now being of a man broken, tortured, and executed by the state.[15]

All men and women, in the Christian teaching, are possessed of an inherent and incalculable dignity inseparable from their humanity itself, which is carried with them from conception until death—and beyond. All are fallen, all are sinners in need of redemption—but no one may claim a superior status to another, by nature or by divine right, for all, as Osborn points out, have the same unearned dignity.

To Osborn's remark on how this inherent dignity may be "lost or squandered precisely by transgressing the dignity of the Other," we may offer a partial demurral and clarification. Neither the transgressor nor his victim, strictly speaking, "loses" his inherent dignity, for that is impossible. The victim of injustice may have his dignity *denied*, but it remains steadfastly his own and is not *lost*. Neither does the perpetrator lose his own dignity through his own unjust actions—but in acting to call into question another's dignity, he succeeds only in revealing his disbelief in *anyone's dignity, including his own* (this may be what Osborn means by "squandered"). The harm he does redounds thus to his own discredit.

Thus much the demurral; now for the clarification. The effective denial of one's own dignity can manifest itself in every kind of sin, even the kind that appears to have no "victim" beyond oneself. (Consider how many of the seven deadly sins may be committed entirely or chiefly in solitude. The person offended by these sins is God Himself.) So the Christian sexual ethic has never turned decisively on questions of violence, coercion, or victimization of another; sins falling under this rubric may involve such open assaults on others' dignity, but may be more subtle in their denial, or even appear to have nothing to do with any other beyond the self. The decisive thing is God's bestowal of dignity upon each of us on His terms, not our own. The willful spoliation of that God-given dignity is evident in the rebellion against God that every sin represents.

Now consider the contrast between this notion of equal dignity and the notion of dignity the US Supreme Court advanced in its recent case proclaiming a constitutional right of same-sex marriage. Justice Anthony Kennedy, writing for the narrow majority in *Obergefell v. Hodges*, makes "dignity" the recurring theme of the Court's opinion. It first appears in this way:

> Until the mid-20th century, same-sex intimacy long had been condemned as immoral by the state itself in most Western nations, a belief often embodied in the criminal law. For this reason, among others, many persons did not deem homosexuals to have dignity in their own distinct identity.[16]

The characterization of what "many persons did not deem" others to have is highly interesting. The common view in predominantly Christian societies (but not only them) that certain sexual acts were immoral—whether the acts were criminalized or not—did not amount to a denial of the dignity of those who engage in such acts. To the contrary, from the Christian (but again, not only the Christian) point of view, the moral norm against such acts was an affirmation of the dignity of the human person. The denial or spoliation of such dignity was constituted by the immoral act, and only by the immoral act.

Justice Kennedy's view here has echoes of what Osborn calls "the very moral and humanistic categories introduced into the West by Christianity itself."[17] But as everyone knows, an echo often carries a significant distortion of the original sound. Here the distortion can be heard in Kennedy's reference to "their own distinct identity." From the Christian perspective, none of us has any "distinct identity" except as an individual, a free human person made in the image of God. There is no *group* identity of any class of persons, and certainly no such "identity" can be "distinct" on the basis of the acts, inclinations, or desires of the members of a self-identified class. But what Christianity has historically denied is plainly affirmed by Justice Kennedy here, when he ties a claim of dignity (as though it were, in Osborn's description of the ancient pagan view, "a scarce commodity in competitive rivalry with others") to a self-assertion of a "distinct identity."

If there were any doubt that for Justice Kennedy "identity" and therefore "dignity" are crafted by the autonomous self, rather than recognized as the gifts of a God who made us in His image, it is dispelled a few pages later in his *Obergefell* opinion. Writing of the protection cast about the individual's liberties by the Due Process Clause of the Constitution's Fourteenth Amendment, he says that "these liberties extend to certain personal choices central to individual dignity and autonomy, including intimate choices that define personal identity and beliefs."[18] It is sometimes difficult to discern Justice Kennedy's meaning, but it seems clear enough here that the real progression of his logic is from autonomy (a power of lawgiving or norm-assertion for oneself) to identity (self-made) to dignity (self-defined and self-asserted). All the work of this self-lawgiving, self-making, self-assertion rests squarely on the shoulders of the individual self, a self that from the perspective of historical Christianity is scandalously independent of (which is to say, rebellious against) God, the proper source of all these things.

Justice Kennedy concludes his opinion by saying, of the petitioners seeking a right of same-sex marriage, "They ask for equal dignity in the eyes of the law. The Constitution grants them that right."[19]

From this as well as much else in Kennedy's rhetoric of dignity, Justice Clarence Thomas, dissenting in *Obergefell*, plausibly inferred that for Kennedy and the majority, dignity is a prize that is in the power of government—or at least the judicial branch—to bestow, as the reward for the self-assertion of the autonomous, identity-making individual. How else is a self-made dignity, suspended as it were in midair with no other basis than the individual's self-legislation for an

identity that is not so much *given* as manufactured, to be made good against others who may be inclined to deny it? The remit of one's self-legislation can extend
no further than one's own reach. To legislate *for others* will require more, and this
is what the Kennedy majority supplied.

Speaking for an older view that was shaped by the Christian revolution in
favor of universal dignity, Justice Thomas said the majority led by Kennedy
"rejects the idea—captured in our Declaration of Independence—that human
dignity is innate and suggests instead that it comes from the Government."[20] He
continued:

> Human dignity has long been understood in this country to be innate.
> When the Framers proclaimed in the Declaration of Independence that
> "all men are created equal," and "endowed by their Creator with cer-
> tain unalienable Rights," they referred to a vision of mankind in which
> all humans are created in the image of God and therefore of inherent
> worth. That vision is the foundation upon which this Nation was built.
>
> The corollary of that principle is that human dignity cannot be taken
> away by the government. Slaves did not lose their dignity (any more
> than they lost their humanity) because the government allowed them to
> be enslaved. Those held in internment camps did not lose their dignity
> because the government confined them. And those denied governmen-
> tal benefits certainly do not lose their dignity because the government
> denies them those benefits. The government cannot bestow dignity,
> and it cannot take it away.[21]

The majority in *Obergefell* had similarly misconstrued liberty, argued Thomas,
when it rested a right of same-sex marriage chiefly on the principle of liberty
in the Due Process Clause. Liberty, said Thomas—again speaking for an older
view—is the realm of free action on the part of individuals: "In the American
legal tradition, liberty has long been understood as individual freedom *from*
governmental action, not as a right *to* a particular governmental entitlement."
But the petitioners in *Obergefell*, already free to act as they will on whatever
notions of autonomy, identity, and dignity they please, answerable only to their
consciences, were insistent on the government's recognition of those notions
in binding new legal norms, so that their fellow citizens could be said to share
them. An inverted idea of liberty, Thomas argued, had been made to serve an
erroneous understanding of dignity.

And the foreseeable future victims of these inversions and errors, Justice
Thomas and his fellow dissenters argued in *Obergefell*, will be those whose consciences cannot countenance their acceptance. In the United States as in the rest
of the western liberal democracies, these will be chiefly (though not exclusively)

Christians who align themselves with the historic teachings of their faith. As Chief Justice John Roberts said in his dissent:

> Today's decision . . . creates serious questions about religious liberty. Many good and decent people oppose same-sex marriage as a tenet of faith, and their freedom to exercise religion is—unlike the right imagined by the majority—actually spelled out in the Constitution.[22]

Likewise Justice Thomas remarked:

> In our society, marriage is not simply a governmental institution; it is a religious institution as well. Today's decision might change the former, but it cannot change the latter. It appears all but inevitable that the two will come into conflict, particularly as individuals and churches are confronted with demands to participate in and endorse civil marriages between same-sex couples.[23]

Last of all the dissenters, Justice Samuel Alito noted that the Court's opinion in *Obergefell* would no doubt be "exploited by those who are determined to stamp out every vestige of dissent," and continued:

> Perhaps recognizing how its reasoning may be used, the majority attempts, toward the end of its opinion, to reassure those who oppose same-sex marriage that their rights of conscience will be protected. . . . We will soon see whether this proves to be true. I assume that those who cling to old beliefs will be able to whisper their thoughts in the recesses of their homes, but if they repeat those views in public, they will risk being labeled as bigots and treated as such by governments, employers, and schools.[24]

These are remarkable warnings from justices of the Supreme Court, in a case that in itself had nothing whatever to do with issues of religious liberty. What can account for this felt sense of urgency about religious liberty on their part? Why indeed did Justice Kennedy feel compelled to offer assurances that there was no threat to religious freedom lurking in the logic of the Court's ruling?

The answer, I think, is that the adoption of same-sex marriage in the laws of the United States and the other western democracies is different in kind from previous developments that had relaxed or abandoned the legal enforcement of Christian (but not uniquely Christian) norms of sexual morality. When most of the Christian churches other than the Roman Catholic abandoned the historic condemnation of artificial contraception beginning some 80 years ago, and the laws gradually followed suit in dropping proscriptions of it, there was no inroad on the freedom of those who clung to the ancient teaching to continue following their consciences, as individuals or in their institutions. (Lately this has changed in the United States, with the Health and Human Services mandate for employer provision of contraception under the Affordable Care Act of 2010.)

Likewise, when adultery was decriminalized, or when sodomy laws fell into desuetude, no one who believed in the sinfulness or immorality of such acts was harmed in his own freedom to live conscientiously by such moral or religious norms. The American people's right of self-government—an underappreciated part of their liberty of acting together in community—was arguably harmed by the Supreme Court's invalidation of all sodomy laws in *Lawrence v. Texas* (2003), but religious freedom as such suffered no blow.

Even *Roe v. Wade* (1973), viewed by all who hold life sacred from conception to natural death as a legal horror, a grievous injustice against basic human rights, was not by the force of its own logic a threat to the religious freedom of the ruling's opponents. To be sure, there were medical institutions and others in need of a shield against any coerced complicity in abortions they conscientiously opposed, but in the main (while there were and still are flashpoints here and there) such a shield was ungrudgingly provided by legislators.

The redefinition of marriage, extending the civil status of the institution by law to same-sex couples, propels us into very different territory. As Justice Thomas noted, the claim that was victorious in *Obergefell* was not really, in the logic of the law, a "liberty" claim at all. It was a demand for government recognition and inclusion in an institution whose definition has always included some and excluded others. And marriage is an institution both civil and religious, as Justice Thomas also noted.

More than that, marriage's meaning permeates civil society generally—the economy, education, the structures and activities of intermediate associations generally, all of which are subject in varying degrees to the law's understanding of marriage and family relations. From schools to hospitals to social service agencies to charitable institutions to workplaces to market transactions of myriad kinds, any modern society presents countless micro-environments where conscience, moral choice, and claims of dignity regarding the meaning of marriage can potentially clash in ways that erupt into litigation, prosecution, and/or public administration of where the right should prevail.

As I have noted above, the chapters that follow do not give us cause to be sanguine that terms of peace acceptable to both sides in the coming struggle can be fashioned. Indeed, the authors who contribute to this book appear, for all their other highly interesting differences, to be mostly in a curious state of agreement about this. Those who express sympathy with the traditional understanding of marriage as the conjugal union of a man and a woman, and wish to defend as well the tradition of religious freedom that grew out of the Christian idea of the dignity of the human person (such as Archbishop Tartaglia and Professors Smith, Finnis, and Buttiglione), are understandably very worried that as the first of these traditions is defeated, the second will fall with it in due course. Even the one author in this camp who powerfully argues that there is no necessary conflict between same-sex marriage and religious freedom "in principle," Professor Garnett, is inclined to take a somewhat dyspeptic view of how things will work out in practice.

On the other side, the authors who are friendly to the cause of gay rights and same-sex marriage range from one, Professor Wilson, who strives to accommodate the rights of conscience within a new legal order whose assumption is that they represent carve-outs from a general principle and have the greatest importance on the wedding day, to those (like Professors McClain, Jänterä-Jareborg, and Law) who are entirely heedless of any claims religious freedom might make to a special status in the law of any democracy committed to modern notions of equality.

Thus we see that the probable failure of religious freedom and same-sex marriage to coexist peaceably in the future, on terms satisfactory to actual claimants on both sides, is a matter of virtual consensus among our authors. What remain of keenest interest are the arguments, in the chapters that follow, regarding the best ways for the American and European democracies to navigate through these inevitable controversies, responding justly to the needs and aspirations, the rights and the dignity, of the human beings caught up in it.

For what appears now to be happening in the western democracies, under the pressure of new understandings of "dignity," is a rapid collapse of the principled case for religious freedom—a case whose construction was the work of many centuries—and a reversion to mere toleration. But the hallmark of toleration, as we remarked at the outset, is that it is at best a halfway house on the way to religious freedom in full, a second-order principle subordinate to something of presumptively greater value. And at worst toleration is unprincipled, a merely arbitrary practice: the granting of space as is felt to be either necessary or convenient by those who occupy the seats of power. If we are witnessing the retrogression of religious freedom into toleration, this would be a momentous change indeed. And the frontier marking the spaces accorded, respectively, to conscience claims and to new-style dignity claims will be contested terrain for years to come.

PART I

THE UNITED KINGDOM

1

Equality and Religious Liberty

Oppressing Conscientious Diversity in England

JOHN FINNIS

When these analyses and reflections were first drafted, in 2012, the stories they focused upon outlined a situation ominous for conscience, religion, and civil liberty. By the time they were supplemented and completed in 2015, the stories had almost all ended badly, and the outlines of an oppressive new settlement had been etched deeply into English law and civil society. Oppression in the name of equality and diversity sharply attacks those very values, even as it deepens the other wounds it inflicts on the substance of our common good and the sustainability of our people.

I. The Situation in 2012: An Employment Vignette

A couple of vignettes from recent litigation in or involving England will take us to the heart of the matter. In July 2011, the Equality and Human Rights Commission, a body (established under the Equality Acts 2006–2010) which, in its self-description, "enforces equality legislation on age, disability, gender reassignment, marriage and civil partnership, pregnancy and maternity, race, religion or belief, sex, [and] sexual orientation, and encourages compliance with the Human Rights Act,"[1] announced that it was seeking to intervene in four cases that had proceeded from English appellate courts toward imminent hearing in the European Court of Human Rights (ECtHR).[2] According to its announcement, the Commission was going to argue, in all four cases, (A) that the English courts were taking too narrow a view of the kinds of restrictions which engage the right to freedom of religion,[3] by holding, for example that the right is *not* engaged at all if the relevant individual's desired manifestation of belief is one

21

not *required* by that person's religion, or is one that others of that faith who are employed in the same business do not insist on being allowed to manifest, or is one that the individual could manifest without restriction by moving to another more accommodating place of employment, or school or other relevant environment; and (B) that where the right is engaged and the question of the restriction's justification is therefore the issue, the courts should—but do not—adopt a principle that where practicable there should be "reasonable accommodation" of manifestations of religious belief, wherever that can be managed with minimal disruption of the relevant operation (business, school, public service, etc.).

The four cases were these: (i) *Eweida*[4] and (ii) *Chaplin*[5] each involved a claim to be allowed to wear a small cross or crucifix on a necklace made visible by British Airways' (BA's) change from high-necked to V-necked female uniform. The claim was in each case refused at the relevant time by BA and the employment tribunals, and in *Eweida* by the appeal courts,[6] but before long was accepted without difficulty by BA under the pressure of newspaper campaigns. (iii) *Ladele*[7] and (iv) *McFarlane*[8] each involved requirements imposed by employers set upon prohibiting discrimination against same-sex couples. Both cases went up to the Court of Appeal, but in every way, *Ladele* is the more significant and revealing—indeed the most important of the whole set of four.

Lillian Ladele was a registrar employed since 2002 in Islington Council's registry of marriages who, when "civil partnerships" were introduced in 2005, was unwilling on Christian religious grounds of conscience to officiate (with or without ceremonies) at the contracting of such partnerships (which are entered upon with a view to or in recognition of same-sex sex acts).[9] The Council did not deny that it could without difficulty have used its other registrars to officiate instead of Ms. Ladele, and have done so without imposing disparate burdens on those other registrars or unfairly lightening her load. But the courts held (in the Equality Commission's accurate summary) that the legitimacy of the Council's aim in imposing a policy of equality for practicing homosexuals "automatically means" that its requirement that she conduct these ceremonies was proportionate; no question of accommodation between homosexuals' non-discrimination rights/interests and Ladele's religious *or other conscience rights*/interests could arise.[10]

The phrase "automatically means" is the Commission's, but it communicates the substance of the court decisions in *Ladele* and *McFarlane*. The Court of Appeal in *Ladele* (per Lord Neuberger MR) put it like this:

> As the Employment Appeal Tribunal said [in this case] in paragraph 111 of Elias J's judgment, "[o]nce it is accepted that the aim of providing the service on a non-discriminatory basis was legitimate . . . it must follow that the council were entitled to require all registrars to perform

the *full* range of services." As the EAT went on to point out, permitting Ms Ladele to refuse to perform civil partnerships "would necessarily undermine the council's clear commitment to" what the EAT described as "their non-discriminatory objectives which [they] thought it important to espouse both to their staff and to the wider community."[11]

Lord Neuberger MR then added:

> [T]he fact that Ms Ladele's refusal to perform civil partnerships was based on her religious view of marriage could not justify the conclusion that Islington should not be *allowed to implement its aim to the full*, namely that all registrars should perform civil partnerships as part of its Dignity for All policy. Ms Ladele was employed in a public job and was working for a public authority; she was being required to perform a purely secular task, which was being treated as part of her job; Ms Ladele's refusal to perform that task involved discriminating against gay people in the course of that job; she was being asked to perform the task because of Islington's Dignity for All policy, whose laudable aim was to avoid, or at least minimize, discrimination both among Islington's employees, and as between Islington (and its employees) and those in the community they served; Ms Ladele's refusal was *causing offence to at least two of her gay colleagues*; Ms Ladele's objection was based on her view of marriage, which was *not a core part of her religion*; and Islington's requirement *in no way prevented her from worshipping as she wished*.[12]

Neither passage even begins to confront either the issue of accommodation, or the "no-more-than-necessary adverse impact" element in the test of the proportionality[13] or reasonableness of the limitation on freedom of religion and conscience, defined in Article 9 of the European Convention on Human Rights (ECHR) as the freedom "in public or private, to manifest [one's] religion or belief, in worship, teaching, practice and observance."[14] Rather: each passage brushes aside the argument for accommodation with languid indifference if not studied tacit contempt.

Gary McFarlane was employed as a relationship counselor for a charity called Relate, and on Christian religious grounds was unwilling to provide psychosexual therapy advice to same-sex couples when that became required; again there was no suggestion that the charity could not have reached a reasonable accommodation with him by using others of its counselors for such couples. But the very senior and scholarly judge who disposed of the final appeal application concluded: "There is no more room here than there was [in *Ladele*] for any balancing exercise in the name of proportionality. To give effect to the applicant's position would necessarily undermine [the charity's] proper and legitimate policy."[15] In short, the corporate aim of having a no-accommodation policy (whether in Islington or within Relate) was treated by the courts as automatically excluding any legal requirement of accommodation.

I return to the Equality and Human Rights Commission and its July 2011 statement of intent to argue in the ECtHR for reasonable accommodation between religious beliefs and gay rights policies.[16] Within six weeks of announcing that intention, the Commission—after who knows what controversies or even internal power struggles—publicly reversed itself and announced that its submissions to the ECtHR in Ladele and McFarlane would now be in support of the English courts' decisions. In fact, when the Commission's submissions were published in September 2011, they were found (A) to argue rightly and effectively (in relation to all four cases) that the English courts were being far too restrictive about when the right to religious freedom is engaged (at stake, in issue). But (B) there was no plea for a doctrine of reasonable accommodation. The Commission almost (but not quite) endorsed the position of the courts that (as the Commission summarized it) "the refusal to accommodate discriminatory religious beliefs would always be proportionate." It put its position thus:

> In the Commission's view, it will generally be proportionate to refuse to make an accommodation in cases where a public sector employee seeks to be exempted from providing a public service on discriminatory grounds. Very strong arguments and evidence are required to prove the employer has acted disproportionately in cases such as these. State services must be provided on an impartial basis and employees cannot expect their public functions to be shaped to accommodate their personal religious beliefs.[17]

(Whether these remarks applied to McFarlane and the private sector was left in shadow.) The real ground of the Commission's stance, and of its September U-turn, is indicated in the immediately preceding paragraph of the Submission:

> In the words of Judge Tulkens in Sahin v Turkey (2007) 44 EHRR 5, §4: "it is necessary to seek to harmonise the principles of secularism, equality and liberty, not to weigh one against the other." Nonetheless, this Court [ECtHR] has recognised that interfering with some rights will require particularly strong justification. The right to equal treatment on the grounds of sexual orientation is one such right.[18]

Thus "gay [equality] rights," unknown to the text or founding intentions of the Convention, were to be ratified[19] as having a weight and claim superior to the rights of conscience and religious freedom written into the heart of the Convention by its founders—freedoms omitted by the Commission from its key quotation from Judge Tulkens's statement[20] of the "principles" that must be harmonized with each other.

To conclude this snapshot of the 2011–2012 position, I need only add that in March 2012 it was reported[21] that the UK government's submissions in the *Eweida* and *Chaplin* cases would not only support the Commission's rejection of accommodation but would also *oppose* the Commission's position (A); the government would maintain that

> [T]he applicants' [employees'] wearing of a visible cross or crucifix was not a manifestation of their religion or belief within the meaning of Article 9, and . . . [*sic*] the restriction on the applicants' wearing of a visible cross or crucifix was not an interference within their rights protected by Article 9.[22]

(And thus it did not need to be justified as a reasonable or proportionate restriction of those rights.) The argument appeared to be that wearing such symbols is not "a generally recognised form of practising the Christian faith" and is not "regarded (including by the applicants) as a requirement of the faith."[23] To the Commission, it seemed (reasonably enough) that such considerations manifestly belong to the Article 9(2) issue of (un)justified limitations and mutual accommodation, not to the Article 9(1) issue of whether the right to manifest one's religious or other conscientious belief is engaged. In relation to Article 9(1), the appropriate issue is simply whether the complainant's religious or other conscientious belief is genuine (sincere), not tactical or factitious, and is being manifested in the practice sought to be restricted. But the position reached by the English courts by 2011–2012 was no accident; they were following a course of ECtHR jurisprudence strongly minimizing the Article 9 right, in part by minimizing, quite implausibly, the scope of Article 9(1). It is true, and important, that in this the English courts have been following also the lead of the British legislature, and of various ministers responsible to the elected legislature in their regulation-making. But the Human Rights Act 1998 requires the courts to test the legislature's, and *a fortiori* the ministers', regulations by the standards of the Convention, and in many *other* contexts the courts are more than ready to do so. In *this* context, however, they treat an equality right judicially constructed out of whole cloth—read into the Convention—as easily trumping a right central to the Convention as it was conceived and drafted by the signatory states.

II. The Situation in 2012: Some Wider Implications

The foregoing vignette happens to concern individuals confronting employers or analogous authorities. But by 2012 the impact of equality law on religious associations, and on associations and enterprises with a religious ethos, was already even more serious, far-reaching, and lopsided.

The negative impact of the UK equality law on freedom of religion and conscience here overlaps with its negative impact on other established common-law constitutional rights such as freedom of association (enshrined in ECHR Article 11), and/or on recognized human rights such as freedom of parents to educate their children toward good forms of life.[24] In each case, the negative impact involves also a substantial shrinking of private life, or invasion of it, by coercive law. The legal requirement that parents who wish to band together to employ professional teachers for their children must, against their wishes, be fully willing and ready to employ as teachers qualified applicants who live openly unchaste lives (according to the conception of chastity accepted by those parents and desired for their children's education) is plainly an interference with their legitimate interest in associational freedom.[25] And it is generally a quite disproportionate interference, given that the only kind of unchastity protected by the equality law is one indulged in by persons sufficiently few that they can readily find equally desirable employment in schools that are uninterested in promoting chastity, or that conception of chastity.[26]

In some jurisdictions in the English-speaking world, anti-discrimination law still exempts from its provisions about homosexuality the employment practices of private schools and the services provided by adoption agencies run by faith-based organizations.[27] But even in those places, people who agitate for repeal of this exemption wrongly call it, as the UK government called it, an arbitrary license to discriminate.[28] In Britain (as earlier in Massachusetts), the disproportionality or needlessness of the refusal to accommodate associational and religious liberties in the new laws against sexual-orientation discrimination in the employment practices of schools was even more vividly manifested by the law prohibiting adoption agencies from continuing to give effect to their judgment—the judgment shared until the other day by everyone, still quite unrefuted in reason and experience, and supported by the religious faith of the agencies and their sponsors—that both the unchastity and the lack of complementarity involved in adoption by same-sex sex partners should count at least *as a negative factor*, if not simply a disqualification, in decisions about adoption. This coercion (resulting in some cases in the agency's withdrawal from providing adoption services at all) was imposed by the British enactments even though would-be same-sex adopters had widely available to them in Britain other competent, and vastly more numerous, adoption agencies willing to cater to them. This imposition, originating in legislation, is similar to the judicially approved administrative impositions in the vignette cases of conscientious objection by employees unwilling to *cooperate with* what they consider unchastity *and injustice to children*, employees whose position could easily have been accommodated without material detriment to the public policies to which they (reasonably, we might add) objected.

And in all these cases, the courts, as we saw in Section I, have proceeded immediately from affirming the legitimacy of an anti-discriminatory aim, and the efficacy of the anti-discrimination policy's means, to concluding that the policy was justified and the conduct it prohibited was discrimination in the genuine sense: *unjustified* differentiation. These courts neglected their duty to consider whether the means (the policy) was not only effective but proportionate, i.e., that it did not affect people's legitimate interest in other recognized rights *more than was needed by* the legitimate aim.[29]

The current discourse—and consequent legal regime—about discrimination, harassment, and victimization effectively suppresses, or at best misframes and distorts, rational discourse and sensible judgment about the interests of children and the conditions of demographic and cultural sustainability, in which all who have a responsible conscience—and religions too—take a keen interest. Thus in England, the law has in two decades been transformed in ways affecting the community's most fundamental social relationships, the familial, a central concern of its long-fundamental religion. In 1988, to maintain the historic judgments of its people, Parliament ruled that *public* authorities should not "promote the teaching . . . of the acceptability of homosexuality as a pretended family relationship."[30] This wholesome and beneficent provision was repealed in 2000 and, by 2007, statutory and judicial rulings had made it unlawful for any public person or body—and moreover for any *private* person or body *employing* anyone or *offering any service* to the public—to make *any use*[31] of the philosophically sound and religiously endorsed criteria of chastity and marital and familial integrity in the course of assessing how employing openly unchaste homosexuals, or how providing a service promoting the acceptability of homosexual sex relationships (and parenting), might affect the long-term well-being of children and their families, and the parental and religious rights of those children's parents.[32] Innumerable bystanders and participants in this revolution assumed that what at stake was no more than the protection of a small minority with a certain inborn predisposition—protection against denials of employment or service *unrelated to* their competence, their conduct,[33] or their proselytizing for an unchaste way of life. The assumption was sadly mistaken.

And as for *religious* associational and conscientious freedom, the guarantee offered by politicians to religious associations in enacting the Human Rights Act 1998 proved to be quite worthless. Section 13 of the Act reads:

Freedom of thought, conscience and religion.
(1) If a court's determination of any question arising under this Act might affect the exercise by a religious organisation (itself or its members collectively) of the Convention right to freedom of thought, conscience and religion, it must have particular regard to the importance of that right.
(2) In this section "court" includes a tribunal.

The courts soon declared that "whilst there is a need to have specific regard to the rights protected by article 9, section 13 of the 1998 Act does not give greater weight to those rights than they would otherwise enjoy under the Convention."[34] The provision has had no effect in any of the cases concerning associational religious liberty and the equality laws.[35]

III. How Should the Questions Be Answered? 2012 Reflections

Other papers in this volume have taken positions on the merits of the issues— that is, on (i) whether religious freedom or belief deserves any special protection at all in law, and (ii) whether there are any rational grounds to object to the laws outlawing (what is defined as) discrimination against people who publicly announce their practice of same-sex sex acts, where the unfavorable treatment of these people, in employment or provision of services, is motivated exclusively by concern to protect children from influential rationalization of unchastity, or to avoid being accessory to (complicit in) acts or public commitment to acts of unchastity, and/or by concern to give witness to truths about chastity and unchastity and their importance for the common good.[36] So I add just a few words on those merits.[37]

As to issue (i): The ground for treating religious conscience as specially important is that it is really of great importance that people should seek and form a responsible judgment about an issue of unsurpassed importance: the truth about the origin, significance, and destiny of the entire universe and of human beings as the only beings, within our experience, who are capable of engaging with reality on this uniquely profound way. Indeed, people have a moral duty to interest themselves in that issue, and to seriously seek the truth about it. A society that fails to acknowledge this duty, at least indirectly, is to that extent both frivolous and truncated, and in a deep, implicit way is undercutting its own claim to be taken seriously and defended (at the defenders' peril) against its enemies. So: acknowledging the right to liberty of religious practice has nothing to do with giving religious people a privilege. Consider one of the examples raised by Stephen Law in Chapter 2 of this volume.[38] To treat a genuine religious objection (such as he postulates) to mixing of races as of no more weight (as he holds) than a quasi-aesthetic prejudice against people of different color is, in my view, misguided. Of course, after giving the religious objection (never supported by mainstream Christianity) due weight, we may well, and quite properly, disqualify its practical application in the field of provision of services, advertised sales, etc., on the ground that its claim to be divinely revealed should not be conceded, and that its content and/or practical application is contrary to an important and reasonable public policy—that is, to an important part of the conceptions of public order and public morality that have long been held in Christendom and its more or less unbelieving successor communities.

For there can be no doubt that claims of religious liberty are properly subject to considerations of public order and public morality, as well as to the genuine rights of others. It has for centuries been contrary to public policy, and thus illegal, for innkeepers (hoteliers in public not private hotels) and "common carriers" to discriminate among would-be customers on grounds unrelated to the safety and salubriousness of their commercial enterprises. So I am not much moved by real and hypothetical cases in which *such* persons are prohibited from discriminating against some of their would-be customers or employees by modern anti-discrimination legislation. But it is objectionable to extend such legislation across the whole fields of "employment" and "provision of services" indiscriminately, regardless of the essentially private character of the employer or provider (even a publicly recognized and financially supported employer or provider) as a person or association legitimately concerned to promote views in circumstances where that promotion would be hindered or frustrated by employment of, or provision of services to, persons likely to give witness to antithetical views. And (generally speaking) it is somewhat more objectionable when that employer's purposes and concerns are religious.[39]

Of course, the special weightiness of sincere religious beliefs has a further consequence which is of great public importance but doubtless is not really under discussion in this volume: if a significant number of citizens hold, and are even conditionally willing to act upon, religious beliefs incompatible with our public and constitutional order—not least with the right to religious liberty itself—we have a special problem that may well require extraordinary solutions.[40]

As to issue (ii): To treat the objections to same-sex "marriage" as discredited because, after a decade or so, "the sky has not fallen" seems to me about as misguided an approach to human and social reality as could be imagined: the sky would not fall if and when polygamy or marriage with domestic pets is introduced, any more than it fell when the Nazis entered Paris and instead of massacre or wide deprivation, a notably diverting four years began for many of the city's inhabitants.[41] Even now, telling married couples, with the voice of the law and state—backed up by the intensive state propaganda that we see being imposed, say, on the Catholic school system in Ontario[42]—that their marital acts are of the same moral quality as masturbation and sodomy, and that their lifelong commitment to complementary parenting is of no more value and importance to children than that of two men or two women purchasing a conception, a gestation, and thus a child whom they will thereby deliberately deprive of the care of its mother or father or both, is conveying a message that—even if countless married people do not now realize it—trashes the "natural and fundamental group unit of society" (as the Universal Declaration of Rights puts it)[43] and, beyond that, demeans married couples. It is an insult to them of unparalleled severity and depth. As for the future, check back in fifty years to see how this legally sponsored and protected pseudogamy panned out, both in accelerated disintegration and even collapse of societies already undergoing visibly rapid, unprecedented cultural and demographic decline, and in miseries for very many of the children who do get born and for the women paid to bear them for far-away "gay" men.[44]

Those remarks are very summary; to see the relevant philosophical arguments, pivoting on the meaningfulness of marital sex acts, one may consult essays which build on the insights of the best philosophers, Plato, Aristotle, and Aquinas, but offer further argumentation—to be assessed on its merits and without appeal to authority, philosophical or religious.[45] The sophisms that have been deployed in and by the US courts,[46] as expounded by Linda McClain in her contribution in Chapter 5 to this volume, essentially take the form of converting the moral critique of kinds of *acts*, acts which can tempt almost everybody (as anyone who has been to single-sex boarding schools, or served at sea, is well aware) and against which children therefore need to be warned, into a mere prejudice or animus against *persons*. The results include blatant discrimination (whether by intention or effect) in favor of same-sex sexual couples as compared to ordinary adulterers or fornicators, who have no legal grounds for complaint when they are excluded from double-bedded rooms in a lodging-house such as the Bulls'[47] out of conscientious religious and moral concern to avoid complicity in wrongdoing and to witness to the importance of marriage.

A final point. What we are considering here are essentially legislative questions.[48] That being so, the issue is generally miscast if presented in terms of "exemptions" to the law. The question rather is, what shape should the law take, given the rights and interests people have in equality, religious liberty, freedom of speech and association, education of their children, and so forth. The Equality Act 2010 (England and Wales) has 218 sections plus 28 Schedules, totaling in all several thousand distinct propositions needed to state what a hostile rhetoric might call "exemptions," but more sensible assessment would call, as the Act does, "exceptions" to general propositions—propositions which if unqualified by these exceptions would be manifestly unjust, intolerable, and contrary to many accepted public policies. The question is not about exemptions in favor of religious and similar interests, but about the extent to which they should have been accommodated[49] in the law's provisions, among and along with those provisions' thousands of other allowances, qualifications, and reasonable differentiations (discriminations).

IV. The Aftermath: Retrospect and Prospect from 2015

In 2013 the ECtHR in Strasbourg gave judgment on the four cases discussed in Section I above, and the UK Supreme Court gave judgment in the *Bull & Bull v. Hall and Preddy* case noted briefly in Section III. These two judgments cover the main litigious contexts for considering the rights of conscience and religious freedom. For in the only important case among the Strasbourg set, *Ladele*, the applicant argued that those rights are being violated by the new laws forbidding "discrimination" against homosexuals—indeed, that the employer's anti-discrimination policy, shaped by those laws, itself constitutes unlawful discrimination on grounds of religion. And in *Bull*, practicing homosexual applicants (Hall and Preddy) claimed the right to be compensated under those laws by defendants (the Bulls) who on grounds of religion and conscience declined to accede to the applicants' demands for services that the defendants judged would make them complicit in wrongful acts of the applicants. In the result, however, whichever side was applicant or defendant, the courts, as we should by now expect, sided effortlessly with the practicing homosexuals and/or with pro-gay anti-discrimination laws and policies; rejected the claims of discrimination on grounds of religion; upheld the claims of discrimination on grounds of sexual orientation; and refused to require of the homosexuals or their allies any accommodation of the religious and conscience interests at stake. The judicial argumentation in each case was at best desultory, and in substance dismally poor. Only a spirited dissent by two of the seven judges in the ECtHR *Ladele* case provided a glimpse, albeit transitory, of sunlight through the clouds.

Eweida (and Ladele)

Under the one name *Eweida and Others v United Kingdom*, the ECtHR decision deals with all four employment cases, rejecting the appeals in *Chaplin, Ladele*, and *McFarlane* but upholding the appeal by *Eweida*. It is important to note that the ECtHR dealt with Eweida's own case not as one about *discrimination* on grounds of religion, but as one about violation of her *freedom* to manifest her religious belief. On that basis it held that the British state's law, as manifested in the British tribunal's and court's disposal of her case, provided insufficient respect for her Article 9 rights. In those judgments,

> [A] fair balance was not struck. On one side of the scales was Ms Eweida's desire to manifest her religious belief. As previously noted, this is a fundamental right: because a healthy democratic society needs to tolerate and sustain pluralism and diversity; but also because of the value to an individual who has made religion a central tenet of his or her life to be able to communicate that belief to others. On the other side of the scales was the employer's wish to project a certain corporate image. The Court considers that, while this aim was undoubtedly legitimate, the domestic courts accorded it too much weight. Ms Eweida's cross was discreet and cannot have detracted from her professional appearance. There was no evidence that the wearing of other, previously authorised, items of religious clothing, such as turbans and hijabs, by other employees, had any negative impact on British Airways' brand or image. Moreover, the fact that the company was able to amend the uniform code to allow for the visible wearing of religious symbolic jewellery demonstrates that the earlier prohibition was not of crucial importance.[50]

In *Chaplin*, on the other hand,

> The Court considers that, as in Ms Eweida's case, the importance for the second applicant of being permitted to manifest her religion by wearing her cross visibly must weigh heavily in the balance. However, the reason for asking her to remove the cross, namely the protection of health and safety on a hospital ward, was inherently of a greater magnitude than that which applied in respect of Ms Eweida. Moreover, this is a field where the domestic authorities must be allowed a wide margin of appreciation. The hospital managers were better placed to make decisions about clinical safety than a court, particularly an international court which has heard no direct evidence.[51]

Before examining the ECtHR's decision in the much more important context of individuals who, like Ladele and McFarlane, sought not affirmative freedom to make a symbolic affirmation of their belief but rather the negative freedom *not* to be required to *participate in* or *promote* activities they judged (on conscientious religious grounds) immoral, it should be noted that in relation to all four cases, the ECtHR largely accepted the argument labeled (A) in the first paragraph of Section I above. That is, it held that the English courts, and to some extent the earlier ECtHR decisions on which the English courts had relied, had been too restrictive in deciding when the right of religious liberty is *engaged* (that is, *prima facie* "interfered with")[52]:

> [T]here is case-law of the Court and Commission which indicates that, if a person is able to take steps to circumvent a limitation placed on his or her freedom to manifest religion or belief, there is no interference with the right under Article 9 § 1 and the limitation does not there-fore require to be justified under Article 9 § 2. . . . However, the Court has not applied a similar approach in respect of employment sanctions imposed on individuals as a result of the exercise by them of other rights protected by the Convention, for example the right to respect for private life under Article 8; the right to freedom of expression under Article 10; or the negative right, not to join a trade union, under Article 11. . . . Given the importance in a democratic society of freedom of religion, the Court considers that, where an individual complains of restriction on freedom of religion in the workplace, rather than holding that the possibility of changing job would negate any interference with the right, the better approach would be to weigh that possibility in the overall balance when considering whether or not the restriction was proportionate.[53]

This was a desirable and long-overdue revision of doctrine or interpretation.[54] But its importance is more theoretical than practical, since in practice the English courts and tribunals have generally—as in these cases—gone ahead with a pro-portionality assessment rather than simply dismissing the religious claims wher-ever an alternative job (or school . . .) could have been found by the person claiming Article 9 protection. Everything, then, turns on that assessment, which is misleadingly called a proportionality "analysis" or "balancing," as if there were objective criteria or weights and measures rather than, as is the case, a parade of incommensurables, and a decision made by a more or less discretionary—arbitrary or, at least, legally quite unguided[55]—prioritizing of some one factor (such as, in *Eweida* itself, BA's own different former and subsequent practice).

How, then, did the ECtHR dispose of *Ladele*? Ladele's counsel had pressed on the Court the necessity for accommodation and for the adoption of a doctrine of accommodation. Indeed, among her junior counsel at the hearing in Strasbourg in September 2011 was Christopher McCrudden, whose explication of the established German roots of that idea (as "practical concordancy" between competing *rights*) I have indicated and illustrated in note 49. That explication was extended to include detailed references to the American and Canadian "reasonable accommodation" doctrine.[56] Ladele's argument went further, stressing not only the ease with which her employer could have provided (and did provide)—without overriding her conscientious objection to herself participating in—the non-discriminatory services it wished to offer to homosexuals, but also the fact that she manifested no prejudice against homosexuals at all, instead objecting only to being made to *participate in* the public performative acts of creating a status relationship she regarded as a wrongful imitation of marriage.[57] She added the argument that if great weight should (as the ECtHR not long ago took to saying) be given to the [Court-created] right not to be discriminated against on grounds of sexual orientation, great weight should similarly be accorded to the [explicit Convention] right not to be discriminated against on grounds of religion.

And the Court did accept that Ladele's employers' application of their non-discrimination policy to her was indeed "indirect discrimination on grounds of religion," discrimination which is unlawful (under the ECHR's anti-discrimination Article 14) unless justified ("proportionate").[58]

Yet the Court held that the religious discrimination against her was *justified*. Why? Here are its reasons, in their entirety:

> It remains to be determined whether the means used to pursue this aim [of the employer maintaining an exceptionless non-discrimination policy in respect of sexual orientation] were proportionate. The Court takes into account that the consequences for the applicant were serious: given the strength of her religious conviction, she considered that she had no choice but to face disciplinary action rather than be designated a civil partnership registrar and, ultimately, she lost her job. Furthermore, it cannot be said that, when she entered into her contract of employment, the applicant specifically waived her right to manifest her religious belief by objecting to participating in the creation of civil partnerships, since this requirement was introduced by her employer at a later date. On the other hand, however, the local authority's policy aimed to secure the rights of others which are also protected under the Convention. The Court generally allows the national authorities a wide margin of appreciation when it comes to striking a balance between

competing Convention rights. . . . In all the circumstances, the Court does not consider that the national authorities, that is the local author- ity employer which brought the disciplinary proceedings and also the domestic courts which rejected the applicant's discrimination claim, exceeded the margin of appreciation available to them. It cannot, there- fore, be said that there has been a violation of Article 14 taken in con- junction with Article 9 in respect of [Ladele].[59]

As is evident, not one of Ladele's specific arguments was even mentioned, let alone "weighed," in this assessment. Not the possibility of and need for a con- cordancy, compromise, or accommodation between competing rights. Nor that objecting to being personally complicit in wrongdoing is quite different from other ways of manifesting religious belief. Nor the need that religious freedom— especially of *conscientious objection to complicity*—be treated with as much respect as the Court accords to freedom from sexual orientation discrimination.

Thus the Court thoroughly shirked its opportunity (responsibility) to rec- ognize, *explicitly*, a doctrine of accommodation of competing rights. For it was obvious to all that the decisions of the national (i.e., British) authorities within their margin of appreciation had given no weight whatever to the idea of accom- modating Ladele's religious or conscience rights, but had proceeded instead, as the Equality Commission frankly acknowledged and the quotations in Section I above establish, on the basis that if the employers' anti-(sexual-orientation)- discrimination *aim* was legitimate, the whole policy itself (the means to the aim) was *automatically* legitimate; the need (in considering *means*) to avoid discrimi- nation on grounds of religion counted (in the eyes of the employers and the courts alike) for nothing. The scale of this missed opportunity can be under- stood better after a word about the remaining case, *McFarlane*.

McFarlane's incoherencies, and above all his *volens* entry into the position of sex counselor with *Relate*,[60] doubtless merited the dismissal of his case. But the ECtHR's disposition remains unsatisfactory. Like the English courts in *Ladele*,[61] it treats the legitimacy of the employer's anti-discrimination aim as decisive and sufficient to establish the legitimacy of the means (dismissal of McFarlane). To do this is to flout the idea of proportionality, an idea deployed pervasively in contemporary European (including British) decision-making: (i) the end/ aim must be legitimate and the means selected must be (ii) effective while (iii) impacting as little as possible on other rights or legitimate interests and (iv) on an overall balance fair.[62] The ECtHR in *McFarlane*, as in many another case, sim- ply omits step (iii):

While the Court does not consider that an individual's decision to enter into a contract of employment and to undertake responsibilities which he knows will have an impact on his freedom to manifest his religious belief is determinative of the question whether or not there been an interference with Article 9 rights, this is a matter to be weighed in the balance when assessing whether a fair balance was struck. . . . However, *for the Court the most important factor to be taken into account is that the employer's action was intended to secure the implementation of its policy of providing a service without discrimination.* The State authorities there-fore benefited from a wide margin of appreciation in deciding where to strike the balance between Mr McFarlane's right to manifest his reli-gious belief and *the employer's interest in securing the rights of others.* In all the circumstances, the Court does not consider that this margin of appreciation was exceeded in the present case.

In conclusion, the Court does not consider that the refusal by the domestic courts to uphold Mr McFarlane's complaints gave rise to a violation of Article 9, taken alone or in conjunction with Article 14.[63]

Now the doctrine of reasonable accommodation that Ladele sought in vain to persuade the Court to recognize is simply an implication, indeed a strict entail-ment of the third limb of the *standard* proportionality test. For the courts to duck and weave, as they do, rather than acknowledge their responsibility to insist upon reasonable accommodation of religious rights in face of more fash-ionable rights (such as those of self-proclaimed transgressors of sexual "hetero-normativity"), is for the judges to neglect their most basic duties of juridical craftsmanship and most basic responsibility of *applying the law (proportional-ity doctrine) that they themselves have created.* And, granting that their distaste for Christian sects (or for Christianity) and their anxieties (only occasionally expressed, but amply justified[64]) about what will soon enough be the largest religion in Europe, understandably incline them to deprioritize religious rights or interests, can there be excuse for their failure to attend to the distinction between being prevented from making a 24/7 public display of one's religious affiliations and being obliged to participate in activities that one's religious or non-religious conscience—one's best moral *judgment*—honestly holds to be morally wrongful?[65]

Bull v. Hall

Much of the UK Supreme Court's post-*Eweida/Ladele* decision in *Bull v. Hall*[66] focuses on a question we need not take up here: whether the private hoteliers' refusal to give the plaintiff homosexual civil partners a double bed *because they always refuse unmarried sexually involved couples such a bed*[67] amounts to *direct* dis-crimination on grounds of sexual orientation, or only to indirect discrimination.

The majority unpersuasively follow similar narrow majorities in England's higher courts in adopting a test of directness which misapprehends the primacy and shape of practical reasoning and intention; the dissenting minority, without challenging the error at its general root,[68] have clearly the better of the argument—but to no avail. As usual, this main part of the leading judgment of Lady Hale is entertainment primarily for lawyers,[69] since the judgment goes on to consider the appeal on the alternative assumption that the discrimination was only indirect, and hence unlawful only if not justifiable. Ringingly she declares it unjustifiable, and in this she speaks, unfortunately, for the other four Supreme Court Justices hearing the appeal, who simply concur without comment in this important, revealing part of her judgment. She and they thus disclose the new folk "sexual identity" wisdom now dominant[70] in our courts.

The judgment discusses justification twice: first, as to the defense of justification which the relevant enactments make available where discrimination is only indirect; second, as to the compatibility of those enactments (as interpreted by the courts) with the hoteliers' Article 9 ECHR religious and conscience rights. Here is the first discussion:

> [E]ven on the wording of the regulation itself, it is difficult to see how discriminating in this way against a same sex couple in a civil partnership could ever be justified. But it goes further than that. Parliament has created the institution of civil partnership in order that same sex partners can enjoy the same legal rights as partners of the opposite sex. They are also worthy of the same respect and esteem. The rights and obligations entailed in both marriage and civil partnership exist both to recognise and to encourage stable, committed, long-term relationships. It is very much in the public interest that intimate relationships be conducted in this way. Now that, *at long last,* same sex couples can enter into a mutual commitment which is the equivalent of marriage, the suppliers of goods, facilities and services should treat them in the same way.
>
> Added to these considerations are those which weighed with the judge. *To permit someone to discriminate on the ground that he did not believe that persons of homosexual orientation should be treated equally with persons of heterosexual orientation would be to create a class of people who were exempt from the discrimination legislation. We do not normally allow people to behave in a way which the law prohibits because they disagree with the law. But to allow discrimination against persons of homosexual orientation (or indeed of heterosexual orientation) because of a belief,* however sincerely held, and however based on the biblical text, *would be to do just that.*[71]

In reality, of course, the Bulls did not claim to be "persons who are exempt from the discrimination legislation." They claimed instead something very much narrower: to be exempt, by virtue of their conscientious/religious objection— an objection given effect in English law by Article 9 ECHR as adopted in the Human Rights Act 1998—from the obligation to *participate* in or directly facilitate *conduct* they judged intrinsically immoral. Lady Hale had earlier reported that this was the appellant-defendants' argument:

> Mr and Mrs Bull argue that they should not be compelled to run their business in a way which conflicts with their deeply held religious beliefs. They *should not be obliged to facilitate what they regard as sin* by allowing unmarried couples to share a bed. A fair balance should be struck [they contend] between their right to manifest their faith and the right of Mr Preddy and Mr Bull to obtain goods, facilities and services without discrimination on grounds of their sexual orientation.[72]

That reportage, however, is the last we hear from Lady Hale about the narrow scope of their claim, which—to evade the argument from fair balance—she converts into a claim to be exempt from the discrimination legislation as it bears on persons of homosexual orientation. This she does despite the established fact that the Bulls were entirely willing to provide, and did provide, all the other services and accommodations of their private hotel *to such persons* just like to anyone else, without a shadow of discriminatory action or expression.[73]

Here is Lady Hale's (and thus the Supreme Court's) second discussion of justification. It begins with a reasonable and helpful acknowledgment,[74] at long last, of "reasonable accommodation":

> The question, therefore, is whether it is "necessary in a democratic society," in other words whether there is a "reasonable relationship of proportionality between the means employed and the aim sought to be achieved" . . . [counsel for the Bulls] makes an eloquent plea for "reasonable accommodation" between the two competing interests. The mutual duty of reasonable accommodation unless this causes undue hardship originated in the United States and found its way into the Canadian Human Rights Act 1985. It can of course be found in our own disability discrimination law.
>
> I am more than ready to accept that the scope for reasonable accommodation is part of the proportionality assessment, at least in some cases. This is reinforced by the decision in *Eweida v United Kingdom* where the Strasbourg court abandoned its previous stance that there was no interference with an employee's right to manifest her religion if it could be avoided by changing jobs. Rather, that possibility was to

be taken into account in the overall proportionality assessment, *which must therefore consider the extent to which it is reasonable to expect the employer to accommodate the employee's right.*[75]

Here Lady Hale makes explicit what was at best implicit in the ECtHR judgment, which was so far from acknowledging this implication of its decision that in the *Ladele* and *McFarlane* phases of its *Eweida* judgment it ignored accommodation, both verbally and in substance. And in Lady Hale's judgment, too, the paragraph just quoted was the high-water mark of her acknowledgement of duty to accommodate. For what came next left that acknowledgement empty and verbal:

Nevertheless, Mr and Mrs Bull cannot get round the fact that United Kingdom law prohibits them from doing as they did . . . [and is] a proportionate means of achieving a legitimate aim. The legitimate aim was the protection of the rights and freedoms of Mr Preddy and Mr Hall. Whether that could have been done at less cost to the religious rights of Mr and Mrs Bull by offering them a twin bedded room simply does not arise in this case. But I would find it very hard to accept that it could.

Sexual orientation is a core component of a person's identity which requires fulfilment through relationships with others of the same orientation. As Justice Sachs of the South African Constitutional Court movingly put it in *National Coalition for Gay and Lesbian Equality v Minister of Justice*, 1999 (1) SA 6, para 117:

"While recognising the unique worth of each person, the Constitution does not presuppose that a holder of rights is an isolated, lonely and abstract figure possessing a disembodied and socially disconnected self. It acknowledges that people live in their bodies, their communities, their cultures, their places and their times. The expression of sexuality requires a partner, real or imagined."

Heterosexuals have known this about themselves and been able to fulfil themselves in this way throughout history. *Homosexuals* have also known this about themselves but *were long denied the possibility of fulfilling themselves through relationships with others. This was an affront to their dignity as human beings* which our law has now (some would say belatedly) recognised. Homosexuals can enjoy the same freedom and the same relationships as any others. But *we should not underestimate the continuing legacy of those centuries of discrimination, persecution even, which is still going on in many parts of the world.* It is no doubt for that reason that Strasbourg requires "very weighty reasons" to justify discrimination on grounds of sexual orientation. *It is for that reason* that we should be slow to accept that prohibiting hotel keepers from *discriminating against homosexuals* is a disproportionate limitation on their right to manifest their religion.[76]

"Slow to accept" meant, of course, "do not accept," and dismissal of the Bulls' appeal followed without further reason offered.

The half-truths and half-falsehoods of these paragraphs display the core of the now suddenly ruling ideology. At its base seems to be the hidden axiom that everyone is *entitled* to sexual fulfillment, an axiom that can seem rationally attractive only if the nature and conditions for such fulfillment are ignored. Lady Hale's inattention to the words "or imagined" which close her quotation from Justice Sachs, words which if taken seriously leave the rest of her argument devoid of foundation, is just one sign of the uncritical character of this unexpressed axiom. And even on its own expressed terms, her argumentation in the last paragraph simply tells those who conscientiously object to participating by complicity in homosexual sex acts that their Article 9 rights are completely overridden for this reason: that offence was given to [the dignity interests of] *past generations* of persons with (exclusively?) homosexual inclinations by prohibitory laws long repealed in England, though in force still in some faraway countries. A reason so weak and symbolic might conceivably have some weight against a religious concern to make a symbolic protest (somehow unprotected by the right to freedom of speech) against homosexual conduct or persons. But *that*—as I have been stressing, and as the paragraph's indiscriminate talk of "discriminating against homosexuals" quite overlooks—was not the Bulls' concern (or Ladele's or even McFarlane's). Lady Hale's appeal to past injustices is so loosely connected to the conclusion she needs that it is hard to distinguish from a raw cry of "payback time." "Get used to it," she seems to say—to being coerced either to *participate in* homosexual acts or celebrations, or to go out of business. No accommodation for conscience here.

Postscript

Stephen Law's Postscript is misdirected. My essay from beginning to end treats religious conscience on a par with non-religious conscience or a person's moral beliefs, of comparable depth, about what it is wrong for him to do (or not to do). The statement on p. 28 about the "specially important" status of "religious conscience" is a response, not to Law, but to the questions posed by the volume's organizers to the conference contributors. Moreover, it is a statement directed (as the works cited in note 37 make clear) to those who like Christopher Eisgruber and Lawrence Sager have argued in depth that neither conscience nor religious belief (or unbelief) is entitled to more legal weight than any deep passion and commitment that moves people (like, perhaps, Law's bigot with his quasi-aesthetic, pseudo-moral prejudice against race-mixing behavior).

2

Gay Rights versus Religious Rights

STEPHEN LAW

The United Kingdom has seen a revolution in its moral and legal attitudes over the last couple of centuries, particularly with regard to discrimination.

One of the earliest beneficiaries of changes to the law to protect minorities from unfair discrimination was the Roman Catholic community. The Catholic Relief Act in 1829 aimed to protect Roman Catholics from such discrimination. Legislation to protect Jews was soon to follow. Today, our freedom to hold and espouse, or reject and criticize, different religious beliefs, is protected by law.

Our moral attitudes toward women, black people, and gay people have also shifted dramatically, and this too has been reflected in the law. Gone are the days when women could be refused employment or the vote because they are women. Gone are the days when hotel owners could put up signs saying "No blacks." Gone, too, are the days when men having sex with men in private risked imprisonment.

Today, most of us subscribe to the principle that the state and the law ought to treat citizens equally. They should not discriminate between citizens or groups of citizens, granting privileges to, or penalizing, one group but not another, unless there is *some difference that justifies that difference in treatment.*

Of course it isn't always wrong for the state or the law to discriminate. We suppose it's right that the state should withhold from children rights and privileges that it extends to adults, and only progressively afford them those rights as they mature. But there is an obvious justification for that: younger children are not sufficiently mature to exercise those rights and privileges responsibly. It may also be legitimate for the state to make, say, breast cancer screening freely available to all women but not all men, on the grounds that the risk to men is significantly lower.

However, almost all of us accept that such discriminatory practices are proper only where there exists a difference between the two groups that actually justifies treating them differently.

So, for example, we suppose it is unacceptable for the state to withhold the right to vote from black people or from women. Racial and sexual differences may be relevant when it comes to whether people have a right to certain medical benefits, but it is irrelevant to whether they should have the vote.

The British public has largely come round to the view that state and the law should be neutral in this way. Most of us believe the state and law should treat citizens equally, irrespective of their sex, race, religion, or sexual orientation. Our legal framework largely reflects this view.

What role did religion play in this moral and legal revolution? In fact, as we survey the history of these developments, we find religious and non-religious arguments being used both to defend the old, discriminatory status quo, and also to justify new, anti-discriminatory laws.

For example, we find religious ideas and arguments being used to defend slavery, keeping the races separate, and withholding the vote from women. We find religious people arguing that God intended the races to stay apart and for women to take a subservient role.

Yet we also find religious people in the vanguard of those fighting for equal rights for women, black people, and indeed gay people. We find religious arguments and justifications given here too (such as that God made all of us "in his image").

Non-religious arguments also crop up on both sides of the fence. We find secular arguments given for giving women and black people equal rights. But we also find non-religious ideas and arguments used to justify withholding certain rights from such groups (such as that women and black people lack the native wit and intelligence required to vote responsibly, and that granting them such rights and freedoms will therefore undermine the social fabric).

For this volume, we have been asked to comment on the moral and legal frameworks that govern tensions between claims for equal treatment of gay people and for religious freedom. The point I am emphasizing here is that, as we survey the history of debates about equal rights in the United Kingdom, what we see in each case is *not*, as is often suggested, a clash between religious world views on one side and non-religious world views on the other. Rather, we find a variety of arguments and justifications—religious and non-religious—offered on both sides of each debate.

This diversity of religious and non-religious arguments and positions for and against claims to equal rights continues today. We find non-religious people arguing on non-religious grounds (e.g., consequentialist grounds) that same-sex marriages should not be permitted. Yet we also find religious people arguing on religious grounds that such marriages should be permitted.

I. The Current Situation

Since we have been asked to consider gay rights, let us pose the following question: What is the current public attitude toward gay people and gay sex in the

United Kingdom? The vast majority of British people see nothing morally wrong with same-sex relationships, per se. Indeed, they support legislation granting equal protection under the law to people who have sex with people of the same sex.

It seems that, even among Christians, such liberal attitudes are prevalent. A recent Ipsos MORI poll indicated that among those classifying themselves as Christian (52% of the population), those who disapprove of sexual relations between two adults of the same sex (29%) are greatly outnumbered by those who do not (46%). The same poll also found that six in ten Christian respondents (61%) agreed that homosexuals should have the same legal rights in all aspects of their lives as heterosexuals.[1]

True, the Catholic Church continues to disapprove of same-sex relationships. The official Catholic position on gay sex is usually justified in terms of "natural law," a justification that, as it is usually developed, also entails the sinfulness of masturbation and contraception. This is a justification even many Catholics find unconvincing. For example, a friend and colleague of mine—a Jesuit priest knowledgeable about natural law theory—tells me he sees nothing morally wrong with same-sex relationships.

The law that currently protects gay and bisexual people from discrimination in the workplace, in the provision of goods and services, and so on, is unlikely to be repealed in the foreseeable future. Still, there remain religious and non-religious people who believe that they are entitled to discriminate against people having gay sex. In particular, some Christians who disapprove of same-sex relationships have argued that they ought to be *exempt* from the equality legislation that applies to others. They maintain that such legislation restricts their own religious freedom to act in accordance with their religious conscience. It is on such claims of *exemption* to existing law that recent legal cases and media attention have tended to focus.

Recent examples involve a case in which the religious owners of a hotel refused, on religious grounds, to give a gay couple a shared bedroom,[2] and a case in which prospective foster parents who wanted to be able to teach children in their care their religious view on the wrongness of same-sex relationships claimed that their religious freedom would be unjustifiably curtailed were they not permitted to foster for that reason.[3]

In both cases, it was claimed that religious rights and freedoms were being trampled—that the rights of gay people were "trumping" the rights of the religious.

II. Conscientious Objection

Of course, we do, rightly, allow for some exemptions to the law, and to professional duties, on the basis of, for example, conscientious objection. We believe pacifists deeply committed to nonviolence should not be forced to take up arms. We do not require NHS doctors who have a deep moral objection to abortion to perform abortions. They are exempt from that duty.

Exactly when someone should be exempt on the basis of conscientious objection is, however, a hard question to answer. On the one hand, we can't allow that just any appeal to conscience provides grounds for exemption. If we did, the law would become unworkable. I could break any law I liked and claim immunity on the grounds that my conscience required me to do so. On the other hand, we don't want to say that in no case can a claim of conscientious objection constitute good grounds for exemption. So we need to develop criteria that determine when it's right to exempt someone on the basis of conscientious objection, and when it is not.

What sort of criteria ought we to apply? As I say, that is a hard and complex issue. Many factors should probably be taken into account, including the following: (i) Is the objection deeply held and can the objector give a coherent account of it? (ii) If we allow for the objection, or many such objections, will we infringe the rights of others, and/or is allowing the objection likely to have a serious negative impact on the quality of the lives of others?

While many factors probably need to be factored in when weighing up claims of conscientious objection, I am not persuaded that having a specifically *religious* objection should carry any additional weight.

Yes, I believe a Roman Catholic doctor who has a deep religious objection to abortion ought not to be required to perform an abortion. But that is because I believe no doctor who has a very deeply held moral conviction that abortion is wrong should be required to perform one.

Are we to say that a Roman Catholic doctor who morally objects to abortion should be exempt such duties, but not a doctor with an equally firm and considered objection to abortion who happens not to be religious? If these two doctors have an equal claim to be exempt, then it's not the former doctor's religiosity that's doing the justificatory work. On the other hand, if we exempt the Catholic doctor but not an atheist doctor, then what justifies us in treating them differently? Why should the conscientious objections of the religious carry more weight than those of the rest of us? Personally, I cannot see any justification for giving the religious conscience greater weight.

Are we are going to accept that hoteliers with deep-seated objections to same-sex relationships do not have the right to refuse gay couples a room, unless, that is, their objections are religious? And if the addition of a religious dimension to the objection is sufficient to exempt those hoteliers from the law, what about hoteliers with deep-seated religious objections to the mixing of the races? Do they, by virtue of the religious character of their objection, thereby earn the right to refuse mixed-race couples a room?

I cannot see that the addition of a specifically *religious* dimension to the conscientious objection of hoteliers who object to making rooms available to gay couples or mixed-race couples requires us to take their claim to be exempt from anti-discrimination laws any more seriously than if they objected on non-religious grounds.

A hotelier who refuses a mixed-race couple a room is a bigot. They will rightly fall foul of the law. It seems to me that, if a hotelier should turn out to be, not just a bigot, but a *religious* bigot—a member of the Dutch Reformed Church in South Africa, for example, whose views on racial mixing are underpinned by theology—that would not lend any further credence to the thought that the law should not apply to them. It seems to me that the same moral applies in the case of hoteliers who want to refuse gay couples a room.

Incidentally, during the April 2012 conference on which this volume is based,[4] it became clear that most of those who believed that hoteliers with specifically religious objections to giving a gay couple a shared bedroom ought, for that reason, to be exempt from legislation requiring them to do so were far less sympathetic to the view that hoteliers with specifically religious objections to giving a mixed-race couple a shared bedroom ought, for that reason, to be exempt from legislation requiring them to do so. Such individuals have some explaining to do. They need to explain (i) why the addition of a religious dimension to the former hoteliers' objections qualifies them for exemption, unlike those with *non*-religious objections. They also need to explain (ii) why these grounds for exemption do not then extend to the case of hoteliers objecting on religious grounds to giving a mixed-race couple a room.

It was suggested during the April 2012 conference that there is a difference between these two sets of hoteliers that explains why those refusing on religious grounds a same-sex couple a shared room should be exempt equal rights legislation, but not those refusing on religious grounds a mixed-race couple a shared room. The suggestion was that what the former hoteliers are objecting to is *behavior*. These hoteliers need not refuse individual gay people single rooms. They just refuse gay couples shared rooms because of the sexual activity that those couples might then engage in. It is that sexual activity that these hoteliers find morally repugnant.

However, we might ask: why, exactly, does the fact that religious hoteliers want to discriminate against individuals on the basis of their *behavior*, rather than some other characteristic, mean that we should be prepared to allow such discrimination to take place? Should we, then, allow Christian hoteliers to refuse Muslims bedrooms on the grounds that, while Muslims are fine in the lobby, they are likely to pray toward Mecca in the privacy of their bedrooms, and such non-Christian religious observance is not something the Christian hoteliers believe they should facilitate?

But in any case, even if we did permit such discrimination against behavior, it is precisely *behavior* that I am supposing the hoteliers refusing a mixed-race couple a room are objecting to. They don't turn away anyone on the basis of the color of their skin. Rather, these hoteliers will refuse a mixed-race couple a room because of the behavior they think that couple is likely to engage in while there. Sexual activity between people of different races might occur, and it is that *behavior* that the hoteliers find morally repugnant. So, again, why should we exempt the religious hoteliers wanting to turn away gay couples for fear of what they might do, but not these hoteliers wanting to turn away mixed-race couples for fear of what they might do?

III. Are Christians Being Victimized?

There is clearly a perception among *some* Christians that the laws that prohibit discrimination against gay couples are "anti-religious." Here is an illustration.

In *Johns*, the court case brought by the prospective foster parents wanting to be able to tell children in their care that homosexual relationships were morally wrong, their counsel, Mr. Diamond, opened his argument by saying, "This case raises profound issues on the question of religious freedom and whether Christians (or Jews and Muslims) can partake in the grant of 'benefits' by the State, or whether they have a *second class status*."[5]

Diamond identified the issue before the court as being "whether a Christian couple are '*fit and proper persons*' . . . to foster (and, by implication, to adopt) by reason of their faith" and "whether Christian (and Jewish and Muslim) views on sexual ethics are worthy of respect in a democratic society."[6] Diamond submitted his clients were in effect fighting "a blanket denial on all prospective Christian foster parents in the United Kingdom"—"indeed a blanket ban against all persons of faith"—and an "irrefutable presumption that no Christian (or faith adherent) can provide a suitable home to a child in need of a temporary placement."[7]

The judges, Lord Justice Munby and Justice Beatson, declared: "It is hard to know where to start with this travesty of the reality."[8] The judges continued:

> All we can do is to state, with all the power at our command, that the views that Mr Diamond seeks to impute to others have no part in the thinking of either the defendant or the court. . . . No one is asserting that Christians (or, for that matter, Jews or Muslims) are not "fit and proper" persons to foster or adopt. No one is contending for a blanket ban. No one is seeking to de-legitimise Christianity or any other faith

or belief. . . . No one is seeking to give Christians, Jews or Muslims or, indeed, peoples of any faith, a second class status. On the contrary, it is fundamental to our law, to our polity and to our way of life, that *everyone* is equal: equal before the law and equal as a human being endowed with reason and entitled to dignity and respect.[9]

Despite this statement, Christian Legal Centre (CLC) spokesperson Andrea Minichiello Williams claimed afterwards, on the basis of the judges' ruling, that "Britain is now leading Europe in intolerance to religious belief," and the CLC claimed that "the High Court has suggested that Christians with traditional views on sexual ethics are unsuitable as foster carers, and that homosexual 'rights' trump freedom of conscience in the UK."[10]

The Christian Simon Barrow, from the Christian think tank Ekklesia, commented on the *Johns* ruling:

It is wrong to call this judgment a "landmark ruling," since it does not lay down any new principle but upholds and affirms the law... However, it does further confirm what we at Ekklesia have been arguing for many years—which is that the era of Christendom, when Christian institutions and beliefs might be given special privilege, regard and exemption denied to others, is now over. For many—including Christians who wish to recover the levelling core of the Gospel message—that is good news, not a threat.[11]

The Christian Jonathan Bartley, also from Ekklesia, has said about this and similar legal cases:

People should be aware that behind many such cases there are groups whose interests are served by stirring up feelings of discrimination of marginalisation amongst Christians. What can appear to be a case of discrimination at first glance is often nothing of the sort. It is often more about Christians attempting to gain special privileges and exemptions.[12]

This last *Christian* opinion seems to me to be correct.

I do not want to suggest that there are no cases at all in which the freedom of religious speech has been unjustly restricted. An example involved the Christian Adrian Smith, an employee of Trafford Housing Trust, who reportedly expressed the view, in his own time, on a personal page of Facebook, that allowing gay weddings in churches was a "step too far." As a consequence, Smith was demoted to a much less senior and well-paid job.

Smith was undoubtedly treated unfairly. That is the view of Peter Tatchell, perhaps Britain's best-known gay rights activist, who said the following about the case:

> Adrian Smith made his comments in his own time on his own Facebook page, which is not viewed by the general public. He expressed an opinion. He did not personally discriminate against anyone. There is no evidence that he has treated any of his gay housing clients adversely. Smith voiced his opinion in a calm, non-abusive manner. He was not threatening or intimidating. His only possible misdemeanour is that he made his comments on a Facebook page where it mentions that he works for THT, which is allegedly contrary to THT regulations. This is hardly a major crime. It certainly does not warrant the disproportionate punishment inflicted upon him. . . . In a democratic society, Adrian Smith and others have a right to express their point of view, even if some people think it is misguided and wrong. Freedom of speech should only be penalised in extreme circumstances, such as when a person incites violence against others. Smith's words did not cross this threshold.[13]

Tatchell even offered to testify in court in Smith's defense.

So there are *some* cases (well, one at least) in which the rights of the religious to voice their religious opinions have been unfairly curtailed. However, other cases in which it appears that Christians have been unfairly gagged turn out, on close inspection, to be something else.

At the end of the April 2012 conference (at which I presented a shorter version of this paper), some of the speakers, myself included, were invited to discuss the issue of religious freedom in a Q&A session organized at the CLC. On arriving, all those attending were given a double-sided sheet of paper which listed a string of instances in which Christians had, it seemed, been treated unfairly— investigated, suspended, sacked, prevented from fostering, and so on—because they had dared to express their Christian views.

To get an impression of the reliability of these anecdotes, I picked one at random and looked it up online while the CLC's representative was still introducing the event. The CLC's handout said: "Peripatetic teacher Olive Jones—dismissed for offering prayer to family."

On the face of it, this sounds like a case in which a teacher has indeed been treated very unfairly. A teacher sacked merely for offering to pray for a family? Outrageous!

However, some quick research online suggested that this case was not quite what it appeared to be. The situation was this. A fourteen-year old girl with cancer, who could no longer attend school, was assigned a home mathematics teacher by a local council-run tuition service. The teacher, Olive Jones, spoke about miraculous healings and offered to pray both with and for the girl. The girl's mother said that Jones used every opportunity to talk about religion. She said her daughter was traumatized by Jones's comments and offers, and that she repeatedly asked Olive Jones to stop "preaching" to her daughter. The mother added that "the sessions with Mrs Jones became increasingly traumatic and we decided it was not appropriate for this woman to come to my home."[14]

As a result of the mother's complaint, Jones was suspended. Jones had been warned about her conduct three years before when another family complained about similar behavior.

Olive Jones immediately went to the CLC, which took up her case and issued a press release stating that Jones had been sacked the day after the complaint. As a result of this press release, the *Daily Mail* ran a front-page headline article in which it in turn repeated the claim that Jones had been sacked. In fact, the council insisted Jones had merely been suspended while they investigated. They also say they gave Jones several opportunities to come in and offer her side of the story. Instead, Jones went straight to the CLC. Jones is reported to have said about this case: "I am amazed that a country with such a strong Christian tradition has become a country where it is hard to speak about your faith."[15] The *Daily Mail* said in its editorial that this case was further evidence that "the fundamental problem, the slow takeover of this country by politically correct zealots, continues to grow."[16]

On closer examination, the Olive Jones case appears to be something rather different from what one might have guessed looking at the CLC's handout, press release, or the resulting *Daily Mail* editorial. What was complained about was *not* an innocent case of "offering prayer to family" but persistent preaching that caused both the daughter and her family considerable distress. Surely it was right that Jones's employer suspend her while they looked into this complaint, given both its serious nature, and also the fact that this was the second such complaint that had been made about Jones. Nevertheless, here was the CLC, two and a half years later, handing out leaflets stating that Jones had been immediately sacked for "offering a prayer to family." In the Q&A session immediately after the CLC representative had spoken, I asked if Jones had at least *eventually* been sacked. Someone more knowledgeable about the case was summoned who merely repeated the claim that Jones was sacked the day after the complaint was made.

This is just one case drawn from the CLC's long list of supposed injustices. If the first case I picked at random should turn out, on closer inspection, to involve no obvious injustice at all, and indeed if the CLC should, years later, still be providing information about the case that is not only highly misleading but in some respects false, that suggests to me that we ought not to place too much confidence in other alleged claims of injustice made by the CLC.

Is the freedom of British Christians to speak freely about their faith, and act in accordance with their religious conscience, being significantly and unjustly undermined? Media-hyped anecdotes such as that involving Olive Jones have succeeded in creating that impression in some circles, but many—including many Christians—remain skeptical.

Of course, not every case reported in the media is, however, as ludicrously insubstantial as that involving Olive Jones. I have already said that the Adrian Smith case involved a genuine injustice. Other cases do at least raise interesting and important issues—about conscientious objection, for example— when the facts are set out fully and accurately. Examples include the case of prospective foster parents who wanted to tell children in their care about the immorality of same-sex relationships (*Johns v. Derby City Council*),[17] a British Airways employee who wanted to wear a crucifix (*Eweida v. British Airways*),[18] and the hoteliers who wanted to be able to turn gay couples away (*Bull v. Hall*).[19] However, I am not persuaded that in any of these cases any injustice was done.

If the law, or other rules binding foster parents, say that foster parents should not teach children in their care that same-sex relationships are morally wrong (on the grounds that, e.g., gay children coming under the influence of such foster parents might be seriously harmed as a result), I do not see why prospective foster parents who want to teach such views to children in their care should be exempt *because their teaching is religious.*

If a British Airways dress code for its employees bans all jewelry, period, I do not see why the state should step in and guarantee an employee's right to wear certain jewelry *because it is religious* (certainly not in a case where there is no religious requirement that such items should be worn).

If hoteliers want to turn gay couples away, I do not see why they should be exempt from equal rights legislation that prohibits such discrimination *because their discrimination happens to be religiously based.*

In short, much of the evidence that there is widespread unjust treatment of Christians consists of (i) misleading anecdotes (as in the Olive Jones case) or (ii) cases (such as *Johns, Eweida,* and *Bull*) in which the alleged injustice has not, so far as I can see, been demonstrated.

The April 2012 conference began with an opening statement in which it was suggested that religious belief should be treated *equally* by the state and the law. Which indeed it should. It should not be accorded a lesser status than other forms of belief. But neither should it have a special, privileged status—not, that is, unless that special status can be justified.

What became clear during the course of the conference is that many of those who attended do not, in fact, want equal treatment. They want special treatment. They want religious symbols to be given special, privileged status not accorded other symbols. They want religious beliefs to get special, privileged protections, exemptions, or exclusions not accorded other forms of belief.

Special treatment can sometimes be justified, but the onus is on those demanding it to justify it, and as I say, that justification seems to me to be something that those demanding such treatment in this case have failed to provide.

IV. Other Religious Freedom and Equality Issues Ignored by the Conference

Finally, I want to set the above discussion within a wider context. The April 2012 conference was entitled "Religious Freedom and Equality: Emerging Conflicts in North America and Europe." However, the focus of the conference was narrow. We have been asked to focus exclusively on cases in which some religious people have fallen foul of equal rights legislation protecting gay people. Other controversial issues to do with religious freedom and equality have been entirely ignored. Here is just one example.

There are several state-funded schools close to where I live. However, despite my being a taxpayer who is paying toward all these schools, I am not free to send my child to all of them. Some discriminate against my children on religious grounds (e.g., Catholic schools that are oversubscribed—which they invariably are—prioritize Catholics). This kind of discrimination has serious repercussions for many families across the United Kingdom, quite a few of which will, for example, feign Catholic conviction and attend church regularly in order to get a priest to sign a piece of paper saying that they have demonstrated sufficient commitment for their child to qualify as a bona fide Catholic. One of the reasons such state-funded religious schools do well and are usually oversubscribed is that they tend to get better results by excluding children from poorer backgrounds.[20] Not surprisingly, then, parents are often desperate to get their child into the local state-funded religious school rather than the sink school alternative (there has, incidentally, been a huge increase in the number of state-funded religious schools across the United Kingdom).

There is growing conflict on this issue in the United Kingdom. The omission of this and similar issues in this discussion of "religious freedom and equality" in the United Kingdom—with this conference focusing exclusively on cases in which the *religious* are supposedly being discriminated against—inevitably creates a very lopsided impression of the overall political state of play.

V. Postscript

It was suggested prior to my writing this chapter that it would be helpful if conference participants John Finnis and Christopher McCrudden should have sight of it so they could respond in their essays, and that I should in turn have an opportunity to respond here. Finnis responds to my essay in his contribution to this volume (Chapter 1); McCrudden responds in an unpublished paper, "The Scope of the Right to Freedom from Religious Discrimination under the Human Rights Act 1998," which was originally prepared for the April 2012 conference.[21] What follows are my comments on Finnis's and McCrudden's response to the above.

My paper asks why the objections of a doctor to performing an abortion, or a hotelier to renting a gay couple a hotel room, or a registrar to performing a civil ceremony for a gay couple, should carry more weight than those who similarly object, but not on religious grounds. Why should the moral objections of a religious be given greater weight than those of the non-religious? I said that I could not, as yet, see any justification for privileging religious belief in this way.

Both Finnis and McCrudden attempt to answer this question. Before I look at their answers, a point of clarification.

It is uncontroversial that the conscientious objections of some religious people can rightly be deemed weightier than those of other non-religious people. Even the most hard-nosed secularist can agree that, for example, a Roman Catholic doctor's objection to performing abortion is rather more weighty than is the objection of a Manchester United fan to giving rival Manchester City fan a room in his hotel. We can acknowledge that the former objection is weightier without assuming that religiosity is what makes it so (for there are many other differences that might account for the difference in weightiness).

We can all also agree that moral objections are, as a rule, rather weightier than, say, mere aesthetic objections. Consider two doctors, both objecting to performing abortions, one on properly moral (if not religious) grounds, and the other on aesthetic grounds. The latter doctor merely finds certain surgical procedures, such as abortion, deeply "yucky." No doubt the moral objection should carry greater weight. Similarly, someone with a genuinely moral objection (if not religious) to performing a civil ceremony for a gay couple should be taken rather more seriously than someone who objects because, while not morally opposed to gay sex, finds the idea of both that sexual act, and those who engage in it, "yucky." In short, unless, for example, the objector's distaste is likely actually to impede the performance of a duty (conceivable in a medical case), *moral objections should be given greater weight than objections of a merely aesthetic sort*. We can all agree that moral objections are indeed much weightier than some other forms of objection—including mere aesthetic objections.

Now, religious objections often have a moral dimension. Where that is the case, then obviously, other things being equal, they should be given greater weight than, say, merely aesthetic objections. But of course this does *not* establish that religious objections should, by virtue of their being religious, be given more weight than non-religious objections.

My question was this: why, if, for example, two hoteliers have equally deeply considered and deeply held *moral* objections to renting a gay couple a room, should the fact that the objections of the former but not the latter are religiously grounded mean that the former's should be given greater weight? Similarly, if two doctors both have deeply held moral objections to abortion, why does the fact that only the former doctor's objections are religiously based justify us in giving the former's greater weight?

Why, other things being equal, should the specifically *religious* conscience carry greater weight? I have not, as yet, found a good answer to this question.

Response to John Finnis

In his brief response to my paper, John Finnis attempts to provide such an answer:

> The ground for treating religious conscience as specially important is that it is really of great importance that people should seek and form a responsible judgment about an issue of unsurpassed importance: the truth about the origin, significance, and destiny of the entire universe and of human beings as the only beings, within our experience, who are capable of engaging with reality on this uniquely profound way. Indeed, people have a moral duty to interest themselves in that issue, and to seriously seek the truth about it. A society which fails to acknowledge that duty, at least indirectly, is to that extent both frivolous and truncated, and in a deep, implicit way is undercutting its own claim to be taken seriously and defended (at the defenders' peril) against its enemies.[22]

Finnis then immediately concludes: "So: acknowledging the right to liberty of religious practice has nothing to do with giving religious people a privilege."[23]

I will comment on the longer quote first. Of course it is important that people reflect occasionally on the Big Questions about meaning, purpose, morality, and so on. A society made up of individuals who rarely if ever take a step back and ask themselves such searching questions is, I believe, a dangerous thing. But why does this require that we give the religious conscience greater weight?

I have spent most of my life pondering such issues. But I am not religious. Neither are very many other people who are nevertheless deeply engaged by such questions, who perhaps pursued philosophy at school, who buy works of popular philosophy, who attend public debates and discussion on such questions, and so on. They too "seriously seek the truth," as Finnis puts it. Indeed, they are often no less committed, and sometimes rather more committed, to that task than their religious counterparts.

So my question to Finnis is: why does the undeniable fact that it is important we think responsibly about such Big Questions entail that the conscientious objections of someone who reflects on such questions and embraces religion should carry more weight than the conscientious objections of someone who similarly reflects but is atheist or agnostic? Finnis supplies no answer, and so provides no justification for giving the religious conscience greater weight.

I turn to the shorter of Finnis's quotes: Finnis concludes that acknowledging the right to liberty of religious practice has nothing to do with giving religious privilege.

That acknowledging the right to liberty of religious practice has nothing to do with giving religious people a privilege is obviously true. Like Finnis, and indeed most of my fellow humanists, I believe in a right to liberty of religious practice. Religious and non-religious people have an equal right to express their views, raise their children as they see fit, conduct their meetings and services and so on, without interference. Finnis is correct—*that* freedom certainly has nothing to do with giving religious people a privilege.

However, the issue I actually raised is: why should the objections of the religious carry *more* weight than those of the non-religious? This, Finnis has failed to explain. And to suppose that the objections of the religious should carry greater weight *is* indeed to privilege them.

Finnis then adds:

> To treat a genuine religious objection (such as [Law] postulates) to mixing of races as of no more weight (as he holds) than a quasi-aesthetic prejudice against people of different color is, in my view, misguided.[24]

Finnis is here attacking a straw man. First of all, I did not compare a religious objection to the mixing of the races to a prejudice against people of a different color (I thought I made that clear, but it appears Finnis has misunderstood). The question I actually asked was: why should the conscience of someone with religious objections to mixing the races (or gay couples, etc.) carry more weight than someone who similarly objects but on non-religious grounds?

Secondly, and more importantly, I did not compare religious conscientious objections to objections made on merely "quasi-aesthetic" grounds. I never discussed "quasi-aesthetic" objections, whatever they are exactly. As we have already noted, given that a religious conscientious objection is often also a moral objection, it will then carry greater weight than a mere aesthetic objection (as I explained earlier). Finnis is certainly right about that. But of course *that* does not justify giving religious objections greater weight than their otherwise similar moral but non-religious counterparts.[25]

The question I raised is why, when two objectors make in all other respects similar *moral* objections to performing a certain legal or professional duty, should the fact that only one of the objections is religious mean that it should carry greater weight? Finnis has not come close to providing a satisfactory answer.[26]

Response to McCrudden

Christopher McCrudden sets up his piece with my remark that, when it comes to assessing claims of conscientious objection, I am "not persuaded that having a specifically religious objection should carry any additional weight." After an interesting discussion of European legal cases and in particular the idea of "reasonable accommodation," McCrudden finishes by suggesting that "the claim made by Ms Ladele addresses the issue raised by Stephen Law's chapter and proposes a way through."

The *Ladele* case involves Lillian Ladele, a registrar of births, marriages, and deaths employed by the London Borough of Islington who objected to performing civil partnerships.[27] Ladele objected to such partnerships on religious grounds. Her employer insisted she perform them and she resigned as a result. McCrudden argues that her employer should have at least considered whether a "reasonable accommodation" might be made in Ladele's case. "Alternative methods by which the local authority's aims could have been met without discriminating against the applicant were not considered." They should have been.

I take no view here on whether Ladele's employers should have accommodated Ladele's desire to continue to work but without her performing the civil ceremonies to which she objected, or whether they should at least have looked into the case for doing so. Perhaps it is right that, in these circumstances, the objections of an employee such as Ladele should be accommodated. As I said in my original paper, such cases of conscientious objection are complex, and many factors probably need to be taken into account. It may be that, in this case, they do tip the balance in favor of making an accommodation.

However, I do not see why the fact that Ladele has a specifically *religious* objection to performing such ceremonies means that there is a stronger case for her employers or the courts to look into making an accommodation than would be the case if Ladele's objection was non-religious (but no less moral). McCrudden seems to suggest that the addition of religiosity to a conscientious objection does indeed lend additional weight to the claim that an accommodation should then be made or at least considered. And, if I understand him correctly, the reason McCrudden thinks this extra weight is added is that religion, like ethnicity, constitutes a core aspect of an individual's identity.

"Identity" is an ambiguous term. What does the relevant (for want of a better expression) *identity-involving* character of a conscientious objection involve?

Are the moral judgments of the religious thereby more identity-involving than those of the non-religious? If not, then the identity-involving character of such judgments provides no basis for giving extra weight to the conscientious objections of the religious over the non-religious. If so, then we need some explanation of why this is so, and also of why a greater degree of identity-involvingness should lend greater weight to the religious conscience so far as reasonable accommodation is concerned. McCrudden's paper does not really explore these issues very much, if at all. But, if identity-relatedness is to constitute a sound basis for giving the religious conscience such privileged treatment, this all needs spelling out.

I know Anglicans whose religiosity is wishy-washy. I also know atheists whose commitment to atheism is deep and almost visceral. The suggestion that the formers' conscientious objections are more identity-involving strikes me as dubious.

Even if identity-involvingness can be shown to justify giving a conscientious objection greater weight (and this is a big "if," as we will see in a moment), and if we do then decide to discriminate between conscientious objections on the basis of their identity-involvingness, then we should just do that, rather than give the religious conscience blanket greater weight. Otherwise, we will inevitably end up unjustly giving greater weight to what will, in many cases, actually be the *less*, or at least *no more*, identity-involving commitment.

But in any case, why should we suppose that the identity-involving character of a conscientious objection lends it greater weight?

Consider those football fans who wear their team's colors, mark their bodies with signs of their devotion, attend weekly gatherings (football matches) at which there is singing and chanting, devote a period of each day to reading about the object of their devotion, and make regular pilgrimages abroad (Champions League). Their homes contain icons to the objects of their devotion. Their sense of community and belonging transcends national boundaries. Can we reasonably deny that a Manchester United fan's love of his or her team, and contempt for their Manchester City rivals, is not in very many cases deeply identity-involving?

Should we, then, give the conscientious objection of a Manchester United fan who refuses to have Manchester City supporters stay in his hotel greater weight than, say, a hotelier with an aversion to red hair who turns away "gingers" because the former is, after all, a *football fan*, and football allegiance is, as a rule, rather more identity-involving? No doubt we would reject the conscientious objections of both hoteliers to equal rights legislation, but should we neverthe-less give the former greater weight?

Or what of the Manchester United supporter who wants to wear a Manchester United pin on his British Airways uniform (analogizing to the case of *Eweida*)? Even if we reject the claim, should the fact that it is, after all, a *football supporter's* pin, and thus deeply identity-involving, give the claim greater weight?

(Incidentally, I can guess the indignation these examples will provoke in some religious folk. "You are suggesting that religious belief is no more impor-tant than football allegiance? How dare you?" But this is, of course, entirely to miss the point.)

What about humanist views, which are not religious, but are also often deeply identity-involving? Should the conscientious objections of humanists also be given greater weight? And what about political affiliations? Why is a liberal's commitment to liberal values and traditions, or a white supremacist's commit-ment to white supremacist values and traditions, any less identity-involving than the commitment of an Anglican to Anglican values and traditions? Does a racist suddenly deserve to have his claim to be exempt from human rights legislation at least taken rather more seriously (even if it is ultimately rejected) when we discover that he is also a Nazi white supremacist whose views on race are deeply entwined with his sense of self?

It is, to say the least, by no means clear that the identity-involving character of a conscientious objection lends it any greater weight, let alone significantly greater weight. But, to be fair to McCrudden, the thrust of his paper is legal, not philosophical or moral. He aims to show that, given certain *legal* judgments already made regarding identity and discrimination, a *legal* case might then be made for privileging religious belief in a certain way. Perhaps so. But whatever the legal merits of the case, to privilege religious in that way would, so far as I can see, be a philosophical and moral mistake.

When a religious person raises a serious moral conscientious objection, that objection deserves careful consideration. In weighing up whether or not to accommodate the objection, various factors should be taken into account, including, for example, the depth of the commitment, its moral nature, and so on. Having taken these factors into account, it might turn out that an accommo-dation is indeed justified. However, we still don't appear to have been given good reason why *religiosity per se* lends a moral objection any greater weight.

3

At the Door of the Temple

Religious Freedom and the New Orthodoxy

ARCHBISHOP PHILIP TARTAGLIA

When I was consecrated a bishop in 2005, I was not fretting about religious freedom in Scotland or in the United Kingdom. Yet just a few years later, I can say with a concerned and fearful realism that the loss of religious freedom is now arguably the most serious threat that the Catholic Church and all people of faith in this country are facing. The way this issue unfolds will determine how the Church will present itself to society for the foreseeable future. Will the Catholic Church—and other religious bodies and groups—have the space to adhere to, express, and teach their beliefs in the public square? Or will these basic elements of religious freedom be denied, driving the Church and other religious bodies to the margins of society, if not actually underground?

I. How Has the Question of Religious Freedom Arisen in the United Kingdom?

The question of religious freedom has arisen stealthily and rapidly.[1] In 2007, I warned the people of my diocese in a pastoral letter that religious liberty was under attack. The introduction of new regulations that aimed to outlaw discrimination on the grounds of sexual orientation in the provision of goods and services prompted my letter. These regulations were based on the Equality Act of 2006. It was evident that Catholic adoption agencies would be forced to go against the teaching of the Church by placing children with same-sex couples, or else run afoul of the law. Some agencies complied with this legislation and renounced their Catholic character. Others closed down. Only a few have done neither, skillfully arguing their case, continuing to operate as Catholic agencies facilitating adoption by suitable husbands and wives.

Subsequently, in two landmark cases, the courts in England ruled against the owners of a bed and breakfast facility who did not wish to accommodate homosexual couples under their roof,[2] and then disallowed a Christian couple from fostering children because they could not guarantee that they would treat homosexuality as a positive life choice for children in their care.[3] It was clear by then that, with the connivance of courts and the political establishment, religious freedom and freedom of conscience could be sacrificed on the altar of homosexual rights.

With this history, the Scottish bishops are in no doubt that if the government recognizes same-sex relationships as marriages, we will have to fight to preach and teach the true nature of marriage both from the pulpit and in Catholic schools, and we fear that Catholic men and women will be discriminated against in the workplace and in society. The danger is that the Catholic community will be forced into pariah status by aggressive secularism.

The issues at stake are at least two: the notion of religious freedom, and the notion of the state.

II. The Notion of Religious Freedom

In October 2011, I wrote to Scotland's former First Minister, Alex Salmond, about government policies that impinged on religious freedom. One of the issues I raised was the question of same-sex marriage. In a subsequent conversation, Mr. Salmond assured me that a law introducing same-sex marriage would not restrict the freedom of Catholics to practice their faith. I am not sure if he understood the difference between freedom of worship and freedom of religion, or if he understood it, but was perhaps being hopeful—or naïve—in not realizing that once legislation permitting same sex marriage was on the statute books, campaigners would call for sanctions against people who publicly expressed dissent from the new orthodoxy.

I was worried especially for Catholic teachers who had to deliver a religious education program in Catholic primary and secondary schools in which marriage is defined explicitly as a union between a man and a woman. If same-sex relationships are recognized as marriages, we will need to campaign for legislation to guarantee the religious freedom to dissent from the new orthodoxy in public and in private, in religious worship and preaching, in teaching, and in the upbringing of children. Given the way things are in the United Kingdom presently, I have no confidence that any such guarantees will be forthcoming.

In December 2011, David Cameron, the British Prime Minister, gave an address in Oxford commemorating the King James Bible.[4] He confirmed the place of Christianity in British history and life. I wrote to the PM to praise his

Oxford comments on the essential place of Christianity in British life and culture. In that letter, I said this:

> I was pleased to read news reports of a speech you gave recently in Oxford marking the 400th anniversary of the King James Bible in which you acknowledged the fundamental contribution of Christianity to British society, called for a revival of Christian values, and acknowledged the importance of the Christian faith and of other religious faiths to the majority of people in Britain today. I welcome your words at a time when many of us are concerned that freedom of religion, understood not simply as freedom to worship, but also as freedom to express and teach our faith, is in danger of being eroded in the United Kingdom by illiberal limitations being placed on what Christians can say and do. I hope that your wise words will be reflected in the decisions reached by Parliaments and Assemblies, by the courts and by regulatory bodies up and down the land.

I received no reply to my letter either from the Prime Minister or from any of his departments or aides. But my recent experience of dealing with government on both sides of the border tells me that, while freedom of worship may not be in question, freedom of religion in its full sense is something they are not prepared to explicitly underwrite.

III. The Notion of the State

In February 2012, then-Conservative Party Vice Chairman Baroness Warsi, as a follow-up to Pope Benedict XVI's 2010 visit to Britain, led a UK ministerial delegation to the Vatican for talks on matters of mutual concern. The Baroness, herself a Muslim, was quoted in the media expressing concerns that religion in Britain was being marginalized. One prominent response came from former Equality and Human Rights Commission Chief, Trevor Phillips, who said that religious beliefs end "at the door of the temple."[5]

This was a far cry from the Prime Minister's praise of the positive and essential role of Christianity in public life. But how can Christianity have a positive role in public life, one wonders, if it begins and ends at the door of the temple? And if religious freedom is limited to the interior of the temple, how different will Britain be from places like Saudi Arabia, where there is freedom of worship behind closed doors?

The modern theory of religious freedom forged in the Second Vatican Council advocates the compatibility of the Judeo-Christian tradition with democracy.

This doctrine, while asserting the supremacy of God, advocates rendering unto Caesar what is rightfully Caesar's, and has no ambition to replace the law of the land with a religious code that collapses the secular into the sacred. The secular autonomy of the state is safe with this Christian and Catholic view of the legitimate separation of church and state, in which the virtues generated by religious freedom will underpin and encourage democracy, while the democratic system will support and protect religious freedom.[6]

So the view expressed by Trevor Phillips that religious faith should not be allowed to enter the public square raises huge questions about the nature of the state. Phillips appears to endorse the notion of a state that fills all civic space and reaches out to control other institutions present within the state. It is a notion of the state with a rather limited understanding of subsidiarity. It is Big Government at its worst. It appears to have no respect for institutions, such as the family and the Church, which preexist the state, which straddle the private-public domain, and which have their own internal constitution. This is a state moving toward a kind of soft totalitarianism.

As Cardinal George Pell (formerly Archbishop of Sydney; now Prefect of the Secretariat for the Economy) observed in a lecture at Oxford in 2009, "modern liberalism has strong totalitarian tendencies." It tends to imply that institutions such as the family, the Church, and other agencies "exist only with the permission of the state and to exist lawfully, they must abide the dictates or norms of the state." This totalitarian liberalism is quite different from traditional liberalism, which "sees the individual and the family and the association as prior to the state," with the state existing only to fulfill functions that are beyond the capabilities of individuals and families.[7]

A state with a healthy understanding of subsidiarity will recognize and encourage free associations and institutions, especially the family, churches, and religious groups. These groups are goods in themselves, and encourage the development of the virtues that sustain a healthy democracy. A state that recognizes human associations that exist prior to the state, not just chronologically but in terms of the truths of the human condition, and recognizes the legitimate prerogatives of such associations within the civic space, recognizes the limits of its own competence and the boundaries of its authority. According to this proper understanding, the state would have no business changing the nature of marriage to accommodate same-sex relationships and no business imposing on the conscience of Catholic adoption agencies.

Pope-emeritus Benedict XVI expressed this fundamental understanding in speaking to a group of American bishops in January 2012:

> The Church's witness, then, is of its nature public: she seeks to convince
> by proposing rational arguments in the public square. The legitimate

separation of Church and State cannot be taken to mean that the Church must be silent on certain issues, nor that the State may choose not to engage, or be engaged by, the voices of committed believers in determining the values which will shape the future of the nation.[8]

How can this vision of church-state relations be accommodated or respected if the dominant ideology decrees that the Church's faith and principles must be left at the door of the temple? This looming question will not be resolved by the quintessentially saving British virtues of decency, fairness, and bumbling along. I sense that the Christian roots of these national "virtues" have been eradicated. The anti-religious agenda has a hard edge and is in no mood to compromise.

IV. Human Autonomy Rightly Understood

Religious freedom is more than freedom to worship; it is also the freedom to express and teach religious truth. It must include the freedom to evangelize, catechize, and serve the needy according to a religious community's own precepts. Religious freedom is thus intertwined with freedom of expression, thought, and conscience. Believers should not be treated by the government and the courts as a tolerated and divisive minority whose rights must always yield to the secular agenda.

As we have seen in the genesis of the threat to religious freedom in the United Kingdom, "the great question which exercises modern culture is the meaning of human autonomy and especially sexual freedom."[9] Cardinal Pell wisely remarks that "this struggle is fundamentally over a religious question" that "revolves around the reality of a transcendent order . . . One way of putting it is: 'Did God create us or did we create God?' The limited scope that secularism is prepared to concede to religious beliefs is based on the assumption that we created God. As long as the supremacy remains with man," then "faith is understood as a private therapeutic pursuit" that is merely permitted or tolerated. "But when people insist that faith is more than this and that the supremacy is not ours, [religion] is resisted; increasingly through the law."[10]

"The question of autonomy, freedom and supremacy plays itself out, among other places, in the contest between religious freedom and sexual freedom. Absolute sexual freedom lies at the heart of the modern autonomy project. It extends now well beyond preferences about sexual practices or forms of relationship to preferences about the method and manner of procreation, family formation, and the uses of human reproduction in medical research."[11] Cardinal Pell hit the nail on the head when he observed that "the message from the earliest days of the sexual revolution, always barely concealed behind the talk of 'free love,' 'live and let live,' and creating space for 'different forms of loving,' was that few limits on sexual autonomy will be tolerated. This is generating the pressures against religion in public life."[12]

It is difficult for Christians to know how to respond in this situation. We are in the midst of a cultural revolution that can be uncompromising and brutal. Christians have the more promising vision and more convincing arguments than secularists about the nature of human beings in their need of God, about the nature of the family, about the place of faith in public life, and about the relationship of faith to science and progress. However, the cultural mood is to dismiss these arguments and insights in summary fashion. Christians today are riding the tiger, and, if the present cultural trajectory were to go unchecked, I, and others like me, might reasonably fear being prosecuted in the courts in the coming years. But Christians need to be patient and steadfast and always ready to engage. Error may well have its time but eventually it consumes itself, and it will not have the last word. We may need to pick up the pieces of a shattered civilization, broken and exhausted by its extreme adventure with radical godlessness.

Whatever happens in the next few years, the Catholic Church has only one choice: to be herself by being true to Jesus Christ, whatever the cost. What kind of nation and what kind of democracy will we be? That is another question.

PART II

THE UNITED STATES

4

Wrongful Discrimination?

Religious Freedom, Pluralism, and Equality

RICHARD W. GARNETT

This volume addresses the tension between claims of equal rights and claims of religious freedom. More specifically, it treats the potential for, and the reality of, conflict between the enterprise of promoting equality through anti-discrimination laws and that of vindicating religious freedom by limiting the reach of such laws.

In the United States and in many other countries and communities, this tension is real. The controversy and acrimony that erupted in the spring of 2015 when the state of Indiana enacted, and then quickly revised, its Religious Freedom Restoration Act confirmed, and appears to have exacerbated, this fact. The "conflicts" that were characterized as "emerging" by prominent scholars in a prescient 2008 volume are now entirely present and unavoidable.[1] Indeed, the justices and the advocates acknowledged as much during the oral arguments in the Supreme Court's recent cases involving the legal definition of marriage.[2] As a general matter, in contemporary public and political discourse, the question is not so much whether anti-discrimination laws will be revised to prohibit discrimination on the basis of sexual orientation or whether legal recognition will be extended to marriages between people of the same sex but how, or if, traditionalist religious institutions, employers, and individuals will be accommodated.

This tension is not only real but also unavoidable and ineradicable because of here-to-stay and nontrivial disagreements among people of good will about the foundations and implications of human equality, dignity, and freedom, and also about the appropriate aims and reach of governments' power. True, it is sometimes declared that, in fact, there is no conflict between religious liberty and non-discrimination law. It is said that claims that there is such conflict presume or present a "false choice." However, such declarations usually involve an attempt to dissolve the conflict by assuming and imposing a contested definition of or boundary on "real" religious liberty. Certainly, if "religious liberty" does not and cannot include a right, in some cases, to discriminate then there is very little chance of conflict between religious liberty and anti-discrimination laws. However, religious liberty does sometimes include a right to discriminate in ways that would otherwise violate such laws.[3] The tension between religious liberty and (other) civil rights—between religious liberty and the aspirations of equality legislation and anti-discrimination laws—is sometimes real, but this fact is unremarkable and should be unsurprising. After all, the right to religious freedom is not the only civil right the exercise of which sometimes bumps up against the exercise of others.

It will be suggested in this chapter that this tension might be lessened, or at least better managed, if citizens and lawmakers thought more carefully about when and why "discrimination" is wrong and about the moral and constitutional limits on governments' efforts to prevent and remedy, in the name of equality, wrongful discrimination.[4] It will also be proposed that what Pope Emeritus Benedict XVI and others have called "healthy secularity" provides a way of thinking about these matters that is attractive, promising, and appropriately appreciative of pluralism.[5]

I.

Questions about the relationship, and the potential for conflict, between "liberty" and "equality" are, of course, among the oldest in political philosophy. These two ideals figured prominently in the rhetoric of the French Revolution but, as we all know, *liberté* and *égalité* fared better in revolutionary rhetoric than in revolutionary practice. Abraham Lincoln proclaimed that the United States was a nation "conceived in Liberty, and dedicated to the proposition that all men are created equal," but he knew perfectly well then, as we do today, that not everyone exercises and enjoys liberty consistent with that proposition.

The Constitution of the United States promises and requires "equal protection of the laws" and our commitment to "equal justice under law" is recorded in the stones of the Supreme Court itself. A wide range of federal, state, and local laws complement this promise by forbidding discrimination on various grounds and in various contexts, including housing, employment, and education. The proposition that it is not only true but—in the words of the Declaration of Independence—"self-evident[ly]" true that all human persons are "created equal" is foundational for us, as is the claim that we are "endowed by [our] Creator" with an "unalienable Right[]" to "Liberty." As Kenneth Karst put it, "[a] society devoted to the idea of equal citizenship will repudiate those inequalities that impose the stigma of caste and thus 'belie the principle that people are of equal ultimate worth.' "[6] The United States is such a society and aspires to act accordingly. At the same time, the idea of a "limited state in a free society"[7] is no less well-pedigreed in our tradition and is, according to Michael McConnell, among the "most fundamental features of liberal democratic order."[8] The commitments and aspirations to equality, in other words, are matched in our tradition by a resolution and determination to regulate and constrain the use of political authority or legal coercion in pursuing this goal.

Religious liberty, our "first freedom,"[9] was central to the founding generation's vision for the new American political community.[10] But the content of that liberty was contested, then as now, and so, as was noted earlier, this pride of place for religious liberty has not prevented conflict between it and some understandings of equality. Today, as before, a variety and growing number of incidents, debates, legal battles, and court decisions illustrate the tension between the desire and efforts of governments to combat invidious and irrational discrimination and the constitutional and other limits on these governments' power and ability to do so.

The recent and ongoing debates in a number of states—including Arizona, Indiana, Louisiana, and Georgia—over the enactment of general religious-exemption laws or accommodations relating specifically to those who object to participating in marriage ceremonies for people of the same sex are, perhaps, the most discussed and cited illustrations. In reality, however, religious-exemption cases involving florists, caterers, and photographers who object to same-sex marriage are far from representative of religious-accommodation cases generally. Critics of laws like the one enacted in Indiana engaged in hyperbole and misrepresentation when they charged, for example, that religious-freedom laws confer a "license to discriminate" and would return us to the days of segregated lunch counters.[11] Much of the rhetoric was inaccurate, even vicious, but the attacks were effective and continue to affect the reputations and economies of the relevant states.

Using a wider lens, or taking a longer view, reveals an array of other examples of the tension being considered. To mention just a few[12]: In April of 2015, a sex-trafficking bill that would have authorized the federal Runaway and Homeless Youth Program was held up and nearly derailed by an attempt to insert in the law a sweeping new non-discrimination provision that would have banned religious and other organizations receiving program funds from engaging in any discrimination on the basis of religion or sexual orientation, not simply in the treatment of young people but also in employment and in all other aspects of the organizations' work. During the same month, Archbishop Salvatore Cordileone of San Francisco riled parents, teachers, citizens, and activists—who hired an aggressive and expensive public-relations specialist to help make their case—by adding "morality clauses" to faculty and staff handbooks, language that stated

Catholic teaching on abortion, marriage, and sexual morality but that many pun-
dits and legislators joined in criticizing as "discriminatory" and "hateful."

Going further back, in 2006, Catholic Charities of Boston, which had been
placing children in homes for adoption for more than 100 years, ended its adoption work rather than comply with legal requirements that private adoption
agencies act in accord with the state law banning discrimination against gays and
lesbians.[13] The state legislature was unwilling to exempt Catholic Charities from
the requirement or otherwise accommodate what that agency saw as its competing obligation to act in accord with Church teaching on the matter. Similar
controversies have flared up across the country[14] and, indeed, in other countries
as well.[15]

Discrimination by religious entities that contract with the government to
provide social-welfare services is also a live question in the context of the activities of the Obama administration's "Office of Faith-Based and Neighborhood
Partnerships." The Office is the successor to President Bush's own "faith-based
initiative" and it works in a variety of ways with religious institutions and communities to "better serve individuals, families, and communities in need."[16] From
the outset, some have insisted that any public funds allocated to such institutions
for their work should come with an attached requirement that the institutions
not "discriminate" in hiring or in the provision of services, so that the government and the public can avoid funding or supporting such discrimination.

In the summer of 2011, at a "town hall meeting" in Maryland, President
Obama defended his "balanced" approach, which gives "more leeway" to faith-
based employers who receive federal money to hire in accord with their religious
mission, in the face of critics who insist that "tax dollars should not be used to
discriminate."[17] A few months later, an umbrella group of organizations called
the Coalition Against Religious Discrimination sent a letter to the president
reminding him that it has been "patiently waiting" for him to move to ban what
it calls "government-funded religious discrimination."[18] For now, however—and
notwithstanding renewed calls that it change the policy—the administration
has left in place an executive order that permits such agencies to hire in accord
with their religious character and mission.

II.

Many, many more examples could be identified and discussed, but the point
seems clear enough: there *is*, in the United States and elsewhere, a tension
between anti-discrimination efforts, which are efforts to pursue and protect
equality through and under law, and religious liberty.[19] This tension can be
seen not only in controversies about how and whether to exempt religious

institutions or individuals from otherwise applicable regulations but also in a wide variety of other contexts where governments can and do use the many "carrots and sticks" at their disposal—licensing requirements, accreditation standards, spending conditions, tax exemptions, and so on—to incentivize and deter. We should not expect this tension to resolve itself or disappear and, again, it cannot be defined away or dissolved. Perhaps, though, it can be mitigated if we reflect more closely on the foundations of religious freedom and on the premises of the anti-discrimination project.

Although some leading contemporary scholars are questioning whether religious liberty as such—that is, "special" treatment for religious practices, beliefs, and obligations—is needed or even justifiable,[20] I insist that religious freedom is and remains foundational and fundamental. Little that matters is secure if religious freedom is not.[21] It is not merely the result of governments' grace or concession but instead "has its foundation" in the "very dignity"—the *equal* dignity—"of the human person."[22] And, religious liberty is not only a matter of right; it also corresponds to what James Madison called, in his *Memorial and Remonstrance*, the "duty of every man to render to the Creator such homage and such only as he believes to be acceptable to him." "This duty," Madison continued, "is precedent, both in order of time and in degree of obligation, to the claims of Civil Society," and it is precisely this "preceden[ce]" that religious freedom expresses and vindicates.[23] To be sure, these characterizations and claims are contestable and, increasingly, contested. If religious freedom is justifiable, it can be and often is argued that it must be justified with reference to reasons that are themselves not "religious" but instead "secular," "public," "accessible," and so on. My view is that the strongest arguments for religious freedom as it has been understood and implemented in the American political and legal traditions are, like Madison's, "religious" and that scholars' and judges' increasing discomfort with such arguments does not bode well for the enterprise of protecting religious liberty through law.

In any event, to propose that religious freedom is crucially important and connected closely to bedrock truths about who and what we are is not to suggest that it cannot be abused or to imagine that it is absolute. It has long been the case—indeed, it has always been the case—that constitutional protections for religious freedom in America have been shaped by a recognition that religiously motivated conduct can disturb (as some early state constitutions put it) the "peace or safety of [the] state."[24] Americans like Madison were optimistic at the Founding that our religious-freedom commitment would add a "lustre to our country," but they did not think that this commitment would be costless nor did they breezily embrace license and chaos.

Modern and contemporary human-rights instruments similarly employ a balanced approach, not an absolutist one. For example, Article 9 of the European

Convention on Human Rights (ECHR) provides that the freedom to "manifest one's religion or beliefs" may be subject to "such limitations as are prescribed by law and are necessary in a democratic society in the interests of public safety, for the protection of public order, health or morals, or the protection of the rights and freedoms of others."[25] The 1982 Canadian Charter of Rights and Freedoms guarantees certain "fundamental freedoms" and "democratic rights" "subject only to such reasonable limits prescribed by law as can be demonstrably justified in a free and democratic society."[26] The Second Vatican Council's landmark *Declaration on Religious Freedom* acknowledged that this freedom is shaped and bounded by considerations of the "rights of others" and the "just demands of public order."[27] The right to religious freedom, the *Declaration* states, "is exercised in human society; hence its exercise is subject to certain regulatory norms" and, "[i]n the exercise of their rights, individual men and social groups are bound by the moral law to have respect both for the rights of others and for their own duties toward others and for the common welfare of all." The right is not denigrated by the *Declaration*'s recognition that "society has the right [and duty] to defend itself against possible abuses" in order to secure a "genuine public peace."[28]

So, there is no necessary, in-principle conflict between a deep commitment to the fundamental human right to religious liberty and an appreciation for the fact that political communities may and should use their regulatory and other powers to promote the common good and secure the public order. The challenge, of course, for such communities is to identify accurately the content of the common good and the demands of public order.

III.

It is widely believed that at least one of these "demands" is that human equality be respected and promoted and that discrimination be prohibited or discouraged. "Discrimination," we believe, is wrong. And, because "discrimination" is wrong, we believe that governments like ours in the United States—secular, liberal, constitutional governments—may and should take regulatory and other steps to prevent, discourage, and denounce it. We are right to believe these things and to believe that equality-vindicating anti-discrimination laws, if crafted and enforced well, "promote the common good, protect the rights of others, and secure the public order."

At the same time, it is not true that "discrimination" is always or necessarily wrong. Nor is it the case that governments always or necessarily should or may regulate or discourage it even when it is. "Discrimination," after all, is just another word for decision-making, that is, for choosing and acting in accord with or with reference to particular criteria. We "discriminate"—that is, we draw lines, identify limits, and make judgments—all the time. As Larry Alexander puts it, "All of us well-socialized Westerners know that discrimination against other human beings is wrong. Yet we also realize, if we think about it at all, that we discriminate against others routinely and inevitably."[29]

It is an obvious point, but still worth making: It is not "discrimination" that is wrong; instead, it is *wrongful* discrimination that is wrong. It is tempting and common, but also potentially misleading and distracting, to attach the rhetorically and morally powerful label of "discrimination" to decisions, practices, and views whose wrongfulness has not (yet) been established. After all, there is no reason to ban, regulate, or disapprove "discrimination" generally, as opposed to discrimination that has been shown, with reference to factors other than the mere use of decision-making criteria, to be wrong.

In addition, we do not believe that governments should or may prevent, correct, or even discourage every instance of *wrongful* discrimination. Some wrongs and bad conduct are beyond the authorized reach of government policy; some are too difficult or costly to identify, let alone regulate; others are, put simply, none of the government's business. What's more, it is not only that overenthusiastic or insufficiently deliberate campaigns against "discrimination," in the name of "equality," can conflict with or even undermine the fundamental and core idea of liberal, constitutional, and therefore limited government. There is also the need for an appropriate humility about our ability to identify with adequate confidence the content of our ideal of equality and to operationalize it through law and policy. One does not have to insist that the "idea of equality" is entirely "empty"[30] to admit that it is hotly and reasonably contested, and more easily admired than understood or implemented.[31]

Again: When we say that "discrimination" is wrong, what we actually mean is that wrongful discrimination is wrong, and when we affirm that governments should oppose it, we mean that governments should oppose it when it makes sense, all things considered, and when it is within their constitutionally and morally limited powers to do so. To label a decision or action "discrimination" is to note that one factor or another was or will be taken into account in the course of a decision; it is to invite, but not at all to answer, the questions whether that decision or action was or would be wrong and whether a public official or agency may or should forbid or discourage it. Answering these questions requires careful consideration of many factors and variables: Who is the decision-maker? Who are the affected parties? What is the criterion-for-decision? How will the decision and others like it affect our ability to respect and vindicate other goods? How costly would it be to regulate or try to prohibit such decisions? Does the decision in question "belie the principle that people are of equal ultimate worth"? And, is the decision one that a "limited state in a free society" has the authority to supervise? In other words, and as usual, context matters. It is not enough merely to report the occurrence of "discrimination," or to invoke the ideal of equality and assert its "primacy,"[32] or to declare—as the Supreme Court's decisions do and long have done[33]—particular decisions "invidious" or "odious," or certain criteria "suspect." These terms communicate something important and troubling about certain instances of "discrimination," but it is crucial to remember that they add something to what they modify.

It is not contrary to a commitment to religious freedom to say that governments may use their police and other powers to right and prevent wrongs and that "discrimination" can amount to such a wrong. Indeed, the important enterprise of respecting and protecting religious freedom in and through law is closely related to the also-important enterprise of deploying public power to identify, regulate, and discourage wrongful discrimination. We care about wrongful discrimination and so we care about wrongful discrimination by and against religious actors, for and against religious reasons, and along religious lines. Sometimes, a connection between discrimination and religion makes discrimination wrongful. At the same time, "discrimination" on religious or other grounds can also be a dimension of religious liberty that governments may or even must accommodate.[34] Sometimes, a government like ours may, will, and should regulate discrimination that targets religious status, or is motivated by religious belief, or is engaged in by religious actors. Sometimes, on the other hand, a government like ours may, will, and should protect, or at least leave alone, such discrimination. Sometimes, it is wrong—wrong in a way that implicates the concerns of a liberal, constitutional government—for religious communities and actors to "discriminate." Sometimes it isn't. In the former type of case, such a government will want to respond in some way and—so long as it is within its authority and is not too costly, all things considered, to do so—probably should; in the latter type, however, such a government should not intervene.

And so, as we engage and manage the tension between religious freedom and equality, we should be sensitive to the fact that the rhetorical, moral, and legal power of the anti-discrimination norm can sometimes distort or distract our thinking about how we do and should protect religious freedom through law. This is because the near-universal, if sometimes unreflective, conviction that "discrimination" is wrong means that assertions of religious freedom are sometimes heard as requests that the political authorities tolerate a wrong— i.e., "discrimination"—which they would otherwise prohibit, penalize, or discourage. Such requests then raise the question whether it is "worth it" for the authorities to do so, that is, whether doing so would complicate too much the government's own projects or conflict too glaringly with its values. According to this view, when accommodations are granted, they are regarded all around as concessions. Sometimes, to be sure, we do and probably should think about legal rights as protecting a liberty to do even the wrong thing (so long as the wrong thing is not too wrong). Our free-speech decisions and doctrines provide many examples, including the Supreme Court's recent rulings protecting depictions of animal cruelty,[35] hateful funeral protests,[36] and over-the-top-violent video games.[37] We should not forget, though, that a dimension of the freedom of religion is, sometimes, precisely the freedom to "discriminate" and that, sometimes, this freedom should be protected not because such discrimination is an all-things-considered tolerable wrong but because it is inextricably tied to a human right, is not wrong, and is beyond political authorities' legitimate reach.

IV.

This point can be developed and deepened by looking more closely at three well-known decisions of the Supreme Court: *Bob Jones University*,[38] *Christian Legal Society*,[39] and *Hosanna-Tabor*.[40] Each of these cases raises—as do many others—the question: "when and why is discrimination wrong?" And each involves, in similar but distinguishable ways, a government's response to discrimination by and because of religion.

Consider first the Court's well-known *Bob Jones University* decision. It was, until 1970, the policy of the Internal Revenue Service to grant tax-exempt status, under Section 501(c)(3) of the Internal Revenue Code, to private schools without regard to, or despite, those schools' racially discriminatory admissions policies. However, in 1976, after several episodes and rounds of lower-court litigation and administrative back-and-forths, the Service officially revoked the tax-exempt status of Bob Jones University—described by the Court as an "institution of learning . . . giving special emphasis to the Christian religion and the ethics revealed in the Holy Scriptures"[41]—after it determined that the University's disciplinary rule against "interracial dating" and its policy of denying admission to persons in interracial marriages violated a Revenue Ruling requiring that tax-exempt private schools have a "racially nondiscriminatory policy as to students."[42]

The University challenged the Service's decision and a federal trial court agreed with the University that the revocation of its tax-exempt status effectively, unjustifiably, and therefore unconstitutionally "penalized [it] for the exercise of its religious beliefs."[43] The relevant appeals court reversed, emphasizing the government's "compelling" interest in "eliminating all forms of racial discrimination in education," an interest that, when weighed against the severity of the burden imposed by the Service's decision on the University's religious practices, "tipped the balance" in favor of the Service.[44]

The Supreme Court affirmed, and much of its opinion was devoted to a discussion of fine points of charitable-trust law and the relevant Revenue Rulings and decisions by the Service. However, with respect to the University's insistence that the Service's policy "cannot constitutionally be applied to schools that engage in racial discrimination on the basis of sincerely held religious beliefs," Chief Justice Burger was unmoved.[45] Sometimes, he reminded readers, regulations that burden religiously motivated conduct are justified, and made constitutionally permissible, because they promote or protect a compelling state interest. This was such a case. Observing that "there can no longer be any doubt that racial discrimination in education violates deeply and widely accepted views of elementary justice,"[46] the Justices rejected the University's argument that the revocation of its tax-exempt status violated the First Amendment's religious-liberty guarantee. The "governmental interest at stake," the Justices insisted—that is, the "fundamental, overriding interest in eradicating racial discrimination in education"—"outweighs whatever burden [that] denial of tax benefits place[d] on [the University's] exercise of [its] religious beliefs."[47]

The *Bob Jones* case, then, involved a response by government to what almost everyone agrees is *wrongful* discrimination. The government did not only identify the discrimination as wrongful, it also set out to discourage it and make it more costly, thereby communicating the disapproval of both the political authority and the political community. The government determined that it made sense, all things considered, to deploy its various resources to fight this wrongful discrimination (remember, such deployment will not always make sense) and the Court did not have much trouble concluding that it was within the government's constitutionally limited powers to do so.

Fast-forward almost 30 years to the Court's 2010 decision in *Christian Legal Society*.[48] In this case, the Justices rejected by a 5-4 vote the Christian Legal Society's challenge to the Hastings College of the Law's rule that "registered student organizations" comply with the law school's Nondiscrimination Policy, which is now interpreted to require all such organizations to accept "all comers" as members.[49]

In 2004, after its application for official student group status was denied, the Christian Legal Society sought an exemption from the Nondiscrimination Policy, one that would accommodate its practice of requiring members and officers to sign a "Statement of Faith" and to live in accord with traditional Christian sexual morality. This request was also denied. The group was told that, to secure official status, a group "must open its membership to all students irrespective of their religious beliefs or sexual orientation."[50] The Society declined to change its own requirements and instead filed suit, complaining that the law school's denial of official student group status violated its free-speech, expressive-association, and free-exercise rights.

The trial court rejected these arguments, concluding that the law school's policy and decisions were viewpoint neutral, generally applicable, reasonable, and therefore constitutional.[51] The Court of Appeals for the Ninth Circuit cryptically, but efficiently, affirmed in a two-sentence-long unpublished memorandum.[52] In the Supreme Court, a great deal appears to have turned on the majority's decision to evaluate the law school's policy using public-forum doctrines rather than expressive-association precedents. As a result, the constitutionality of the policy depended not on whether it interfered with the Society's ability to express its preferred message, but instead on whether or not it was "viewpoint neutral" and, all things considered, "reasonable." And, after underscoring the importance of judicial deference to educational institutions' pedagogical decisions and discretion, the Court decided that it was.

Justice Ginsburg's discussion of the "reasonableness" of the all-comers policy reflects and is pervasively animated by the non-discrimination norm. It is reasonable, she said, for the law school to decide that the "educational experience is best promoted when all participants in the forum must provide equal access to all students" and that "no Hastings student [should be] forced to fund a group that would reject her as a member"; it is reasonable for it to conclude that an all-comers policy encourages "tolerance," "cooperation," and "readiness to find common ground"; and, it is reasonable to "convey[] the Law School's decision to decline to subsidize with public monies and benefits conduct of which the people of California disapprove[,]" namely, "discrimination."[53]

The implications of the *Christian Legal Society* case continue to unfold on other campuses and in other courts. Close investigation of, engagement with, and criticism of the decision by scholars have begun and, it is safe to say, will be exhaustive.[54] To connect the case to the discussion in this chapter, though, I suggest that although a majority of the Justices pronounced it reasonable for the law school to regard the discrimination at issue as being at odds with its mission and values, it is not as clear as it was in *Bob Jones* that the discrimination is really wrongful. True, the particular membership criteria that the Christian Legal Society sought to employ—that is, the Statement of Faith and compliance with traditional Christian standards of sexual morality—are controversial. Still, it probably does not strike most people as wrong for, say, a Republican club to exclude registered Green Party members. Nevertheless, the Hastings College of the Law, like the Internal Revenue Service with respect to Bob Jones University, decided that it was "worth it" to raise the cost of, though not to prohibit, discrimination by student groups, to express its opposition to such discrimination, and to attempt to convince others to oppose it, too. As in *Bob Jones*, the Court signed off on the law school's anti-discrimination efforts.

Finally, in January of 2012, the Supreme Court handed down one of its most important religious-freedom decisions of the last twenty years. Speaking for all nine Justices, Chief Justice John Roberts succinctly affirmed that the First Amendment protects the right of a religious group to "control . . . the selection of those who will personify its beliefs" and "to shape its own faith and mission through its appointments." The Constitution's free-exercise guarantee and no-establishment rule work together, he explained, and not, as is sometimes thought, at cross-purposes to protect religious groups' freedom by limiting the power of governments over the relationship between religious communities and their teachers, leaders, and ministers—in other words, by constraining the reach of regulatory authority over even wrongful acts of discrimination.

This was the Justices' first occasion to rule on the existence, rationale, and scope of the "ministerial exception." For about 40 years, federal courts have recognized that the First Amendment's Religion Clauses limit the application of employment-discrimination laws to decisions by religious institutions regarding clergy and other ministerial employees but, until this case, the Court had not squarely addressed this rule.[55] The case emerged from a dispute between a small school in suburban Detroit, operated by the Hosanna-Tabor Evangelical Lutheran Church, and a fourth-grade teacher (and commissioned minister) named Cheryl Perich. The school is pervasively religious and aims for an integrated "Christ-centered education," that is, for formation in the faith and not just training in skills. Perich was fired by the congregation and her "call" was rescinded after she threatened to bring legal action against the church under federal (and state) disability-discrimination laws. In a nutshell, she and the school's administrators disagreed over her readiness to return to teaching after a disability leave and she refused to resign or to resolve the disagreement through the church's own processes when she was told that her position had been filled by another teacher.

Now, in addition to teaching subjects such as math, science, gym, and art, Perich also taught religion classes, led the students in prayer and devotions, and was held out by the church congregation, to students and to the world, as having responded to God's call and embraced an essentially religious vocation. To the lawyers for the Equal Employment Opportunity Commission (EEOC), she was a victim of unlawful, wrongful retaliation who was punished unfairly for threatening to vindicate her legal rights. To those representing the church, however, her "insubordination and disruptive behavior" were harming both the religious and school communities and she was attempting to submit a question of religious discipline, teaching, and authority to the secular courts and undermining what James Madison called the "scrupulous policy of the Constitution in guarding against a political interference with religious affairs."[56]

A federal trial court dismissed her (and the EEOC's) lawsuit after considering her duties, function, and role—and also the fact that the church clearly considered her a minister—and concluding that Perich served at Hosanna-Tabor as a "ministerial employee."[57] The appeals court, though, disagreed.[58] Although the appeals court conceded the existence and constitutional foundations of a ministerial exception, it embraced a very different approach to the task of identifying "ministers," one that seemed to rely more on a timecard than on a qualitative and deferential assessment of her role in the school's religious mission. She spent, the court noted, "approximately six hours and fifteen minutes of her seven hour day teaching secular subjects, using secular textbooks, without incorporating religion into the secular material." Her "primary duties"—whatever her title and training—were characterized by the court as "secular" and so the ministerial exception, and the First Amendment, posed no barrier to her anti-discrimination lawsuit.

The court of appeals was certainly right to recognize that the ministerial exception's existence and importance do not supply the answers to every question about its application. It is one thing to say that the First Amendment does not allow government authorities to substitute the norms of anti-discrimination law for the judgments of religious communities about who will be their ministers; it is another to find the line separating these communities' "ministers" from their other employees.[59] Some cases are hard ones.

But not this one. Although they saw no need to "adopt a rigid formula for deciding when an employee qualifies as a minister," the Supreme Court Justices were, again, unanimous in their conclusions that, "given all the circumstances of her employment," Perich was a minister for purposes of the First Amendment and that "[b]oth Religion Clauses bar the government from interfering with the decision of a religious group to fire one of its ministers." Chief Justice Roberts noted that the question "is not one that can be resolved by a stopwatch." Instead, he and his colleagues emphasized the fact that her "job duties reflected a role in conveying the Church's message and carrying out its mission" and in "transmitting the Lutheran faith to the next generation." Two concurring opinions underscored the importance of restraining even well-meaning supervision by regulators and courts over decisions by religious institutions about ministerial employers. Justice Thomas emphasized that, because "the Religion Clauses guarantee religious organizations autonomy in matters of internal governance," civil courts should therefore "defer to a religious organization's good-faith understanding of who qualifies as a minister." In a similar way, Justice Alito, joined by Justice Kagan, insisted that "formal ordination and designation," although present in this case, cannot, given our country's religious pluralism, be a requirement. Rather, the exception must be tailored to its purpose, namely, to assure the freedom of religious groups to choose the personnel who are essential to the performance of "key religious activities," which include not only worship and ritual but also "the critical process of communicating the faith."

Hosanna-Tabor was correctly decided and crucially important.[60] True, even the Court's unanimous embrace of the exception and its rationale will not and should not end the debate about its merits and application. For the doctrine's defenders, it is a clear and important implication of religious freedom and church-state separation that secular governments not purport to second-guess or supervise decisions by religious communities about who should be their teachers, ministers, and leaders. To its critics, however, the doctrine is little more than an unwarranted "subsidy to religion that undermines core political values of equality and non-discrimination."[61] In their view, whatever burdens might be imposed on a religious community's religious liberty are outweighed by the "government's compelling interest in eradicating discrimination"[62] and also by rule-of-law values. At the end of the day, they insist, the ministerial exception rests on nothing more than the assertion that "religious groups are entitled to disobey the law."[63] Of course, the doctrine's defenders will respond that the claim actually is not that religious groups are entitled to disobey the law but instead that the Constitution does not, in some cases, permit the law to be applied.

Hosanna-Tabor interestingly complicates the scene set so far by the *Bob Jones University* and *Christian Legal Society* cases. Our political community has correctly determined that employment discrimination on the basis of disability is, generally speaking, wrongful; it is not as clear, though, that we have made or should make a similar judgment about "discrimination" by churches against commissioned ministers who refuse to follow religiously prescribed procedures for resolving certain disputes within the faith community. If *Bob Jones* suggests that the use of some criteria, such as race, for certain decisions is objectionable even by religious institutions and for religious reasons, *Hosanna-Tabor*, like *Christian Society*, at least raises the possibility that some criteria whose use is ordinarily objectionable, or objectionable when done by the government—such as willingness to affirm a Statement of Faith or to resolve employment disagreements within the church—might reasonably and unobjectionably be employed by such institutions and for such reasons. And, of course, *Hosanna-Tabor* complements the other two cases by highlighting the possibility that, sometimes, even discrimination that would otherwise be wrongful—or that *is* wrongful—is by virtue of our Constitution's text and structure outside the reach of the government's power to remedy. After all, the ministerial exception does not rest on an assumption that religious institutions and employers never behave badly. Certainly, they do and they should be criticized, by believers and nonbelievers alike, when they do. Whether they do or not, the ministerial exception is required by the Constitution.

These three cases confirm and expand upon, just as many others could have done, three observations that were offered earlier in this chapter. First, there is a close connection between the enterprise of respecting and protecting religious freedom through law and that of deploying public power to regulate, discourage, and condemn wrongful discrimination. Second, whether "discrimination" is, in fact, wrong depends not on the mere fact that the word has been used but instead on a number of factors, variables, and circumstances relating to the purpose and effect of the practice or conduct in question.[64] Third, that a particular instance or kind of discrimination is wrong does not necessarily mean that governments should regulate or oppose it, nor does it mean that governments—at least, constitutionally limited governments like ours—have the power to do so.

V.

"Why [is] discrimination . . . wrong when it is wrong[?]"[65] We believe that discrimination is wrong, when it is wrong, but we are not entirely sure what makes it wrong when it is. In any event, it is not likely that discrimination's wrongfulness comes down to the presence or absence of any one thing. For example, Prof. Hellman has argued that harm to a particular person subject to discrimination is neither necessary nor sufficient to establish that that discrimination is wrong,[66] and that the better question to ask is whether a distinction "demeans"—that is, denies the equal moral worth of—the person affected.[67] After all, as Robert Rodes has insisted, that "people are of equal ultimate worth" is and must be relevant to the legal enterprise.[68]

I believe that discrimination is wrong, when it is wrong, for pretty much the same reason that religious liberty is a fundamental human right: Every person is made in the image of and loved by God and as a consequence bears a dignity that should not be violated. This is as true for all of us as it is for some and it shapes and constrains both how we may and may not treat each other and how our governments ought and ought not to treat us. Discrimination is wrong when it denies or is intended to deny the equal dignity of every person. But, again: sometimes discrimination does this and sometimes it doesn't. Whether it does, or does not, depends.

Return, now, to the *Bob Jones* case. Even assuming that it was motivated by sincere religious belief, and notwithstanding the fact that it was engaged in by religious actors, the discrimination at issue there was wrong. Even if those doing the discrimination did not themselves intend to deny the "equal ultimate worth" of those affected, their actions did have that effect and did deny it. And although the question is a complicated one, given the relevant precedents and doctrines, we can accept for the sake of argument that it was both practicable and within the power of our constitutionally limited government to respond to that wrong by discouraging the discrimination in the way that the Internal Revenue Service did. To be clear: This is not because discrimination—even discrimination that employs criteria that are often suspect, such as race, ethnicity, sex, and religion—by schools and universities is always wrong or because all wrongful discrimination may be regulated or prohibited. Again, it depends.

Accordingly, whether the national government has the power to outlaw racial discrimination by religious institutions—putting aside questions about regulatory strings, public funds, tax exemptions, subsidization, and so on—is a different question. The Court in *Runyon v. McCrary* avoided the question of whether federal law could prohibit racial discrimination in religious schools.[69] Especially in light of the *Hosanna-Tabor* decision, it would seem that even wrongful discrimination in the selection of members for a religious community, activity, or enterprise—which many religiously affiliated schools are—will often be beyond the anti-discrimination norm's legal reach.

Unlike the discrimination at issue in *Bob Jones University*, the membership requirements employed by the Christian Legal Society and its "discrimination" against those who did not affirm the Society's Statement of Faith were not wrong, invidious, odious, or objectionable. It is understandable and unremarkable for a group that is devoted to a value, idea, or truth to limit its membership to those who are themselves so devoted. It does not necessarily demean a person, or call into the question a person's equal ultimate worth, to exclude her from an association if she does not embrace the association's aims or reason for being. It might, but it might not. It is a mistake to move too quickly from the observation that a person or group negatively evaluates an action to the conclusion that the group has demeaned or attacked the dignity of those who engage in that action. The Christian Legal Society's internal rules might reflect a mistaken understanding of moral reality, but it is not wrong, or even remarkable, for the Society to adopt policies for membership and leadership that reflect its understanding. And, because the "discrimination" practiced by the Christian Legal Society was not objectionable, there was no reason for the Hastings College of the Law to deny official status to the Society, to exclude it from the public forum created by its student-organizations policy, or even to express disapproval by withholding whatever small financial subsidy is involved in official recognition.

The Court confused apples and oranges, and it ignored critical distinctions, when it credited the law school's policy as a decision "to decline to subsidize with public monies and benefits conduct of which the people of California disapprove"[70] because it has not been established that the people of California disapprove the practice of limiting the membership of private associations to those who embrace those associations' mission and values. Perhaps they do disapprove, or will come to disapprove, but it would be a departure from common practice and understanding if or when they do. They do disapprove, and have chosen to regulate closely, discrimination by governments, commercial entities, and places of public accommodation when that discrimination involves the unwarranted use of certain suspect criteria. However, the Court assumed without argument or even discussion that the distinctions the Christian Legal Society wanted to draw, for its own purposes, should be treated the same as the superficially similar distinctions that, in many respects, California law regulates.

Hosanna-Tabor involved the government's regulatory, coercive response to discrimination that, at least in contexts other than religious institutions, is often seen as wrongful, invidious, and demeaning. I have already suggested that what might appear, at first glance, to be wrongful discrimination in the context of the relationship between a religious community and its ministers actually is not. The Catholic Church does not believe that it is authorized to ordain women to the ministerial priesthood and the Church's discrimination against women with respect to this particular ministerial office and this particular sacrament should not be seen as a wrong in a way that a secular, constitutionally limited government is authorized to remedy.

Sometimes, though, religious institutions and communities treat their ministerial employees badly; sometimes, they discriminate against ministers in a way that is wrong. What then? The Court's answer in *Hosanna-Tabor* is the right one. At some point, the power of a constitutionally limited government like ours to second-guess or prohibit even wrongful discrimination—even discrimination that is wrongful from the perspective of the religious community itself—runs out. As the Chief Justice emphasized, the "Religion Clauses bar the government from interfering with the decision of a religious group to fire one of its ministers." This is not the language of prudence, modesty, or abstention. It is true that there are lots of good, practical reasons for political decision-makers and civil courts to avoid making "religious" decisions. But this is not why the ministerial exception exists.[71] It exists not because decisions about selecting ministers are tricky but because religious communities have a First Amendment right to make them. This suggests, actually, that the term "ministerial exception" is imperfect, because it invokes a carve-out or a concession. It is true that our constitutional commitment to religious liberty means (among other things) that legislatures should sometimes stay their hands and forego applying regulations to conduct that would otherwise be within their jurisdiction. Such accommodations show respect for religious believers and often make life easier for regulators. But the real reason a secular court cannot tell, say, the First Baptist Church that it unlawfully failed to hire Mr. Smith to be its minister—the reason it cannot correct even wrongful discrimination by the church against Mr. Smith—is not because the government has conceded but because the government is constrained. It might look like the government is holding back, and generously granting an exception from its generally applicable and valid employment-discrimination laws, but in fact it is acknowledging a limit, imposed by the First Amendment, on the reach of its regulatory authority.

VI.

It was suggested at the outset of this chapter that what Pope Emeritus Benedict XVI and others have called "healthy secularity" provides an attractive, promising, and pluralism-respecting way of thinking about the tension between claims of equality and claims of religious liberty. During his 2008 visit to the United States, the Pope Emeritus praised America's "positive concept of secularism," in which government respects both the role of religious arguments and commitments in the public square *and* the important distinction between religious and political authorities.[72] "It is fundamental," the Pope observed similarly in France, "to insist upon the distinction between the political realm and that of religion in order to preserve both the religious freedom of citizens and the responsibility of the state toward them. On the other hand," he continued, "it is important to become more aware of the irreplaceable role of religion for the formation of consciences and the contribution which it can bring to . . . the creation of a basic ethical consensus within society."[73]

For the purposes of this chapter, what is most noteworthy about the "healthy secularity" model is that it is pluralistic and constitutionalist. It is pluralistic, first, in that it accepts as given the fact that reasonable people, associations, institutions, and communities disagree reasonably about things that matter.[74] Our governments and we do well to resign ourselves comfortably to the crooked timber of free society,[75] and courts, officials, and governments should acknowledge and accept their limited competence and prerogative to resolve authoritatively these disagreements.

The model is also "pluralistic" in another sense. Six decades ago, the great church-state scholar Mark DeWolfe Howe identified the "heart of the pluralistic thesis":

> The conviction that government must recognize that it is not the sole possessor of sovereignty, and that private groups within the community are entitled to lead their own free lives and exercise within the area of their competence an authority so effective as to justify labeling it a sovereign authority. To make this assertion is to suggest that private groups have liberties similar to those of individuals and that those liberties, as such, are to be secured by law from governmental infringement.[76]

Howe suggested that the Supreme Court's decision in *Kedroff v. St. Nicholas Cathedral*, in which the Court decided that it violated the Constitution for New York's legislature to transfer control over property owned by the Russian Orthodox Church from Russian to American control, was an example of the "pluralistic thesis" at work and he suggested that its influence might be seen elsewhere in constitutional law as well.[77]

Our evaluation of the practices and policies of intermediate associations and nonstate institutions should be informed by this pluralistic thesis. These institutions, I have argued elsewhere, transmit values and loyalties to us and mediate between persons and the state.[78] The First Amendment should be understood, consistent with the idea of "healthy secularity," to limit the government's right or power to standardize belief or impose orthodoxy by commandeering such expression or transmission. Diverse and different nonstate institutions can be seen as the hedgerows of civil society, as wrenches in the works of governments' excessive ambitions.[79]

"Healthy secularity" is also constitutionalist. Constitutionalism, among other things, is the project of protecting human freedom and promoting the common good by categorizing, separating, structuring, and limiting power in entrenched and enforceable ways. The American Constitution provides a first-rate illustration. As every law student learns (or should learn), those who designed and ratified the Constitution believed that political liberties are best served through competition and cooperation among plural authorities and jurisdictions, and through structures and mechanisms that check, diffuse, and divide power. The Constitution of the United States is more than a catalogue of rights; our constitutional law is, in the end, "the law governing the structure of, and the allocation of authority among, the various institutions of the national government."[80] The American constitutional experiment reflects, among other things, the belief that the structure of government matters for, and contributes to, the good of human persons.

These structural devices include familiar ones like separation of powers, judicial review, and federalism. They also include, however, the protections provided by the First Amendment to expressive associations and the distinction, or "separation," between religious and political authority. Mediating institutions like the Boy Scouts and the Christian Legal Society, like book clubs and bowling teams, like labor unions and Little Leagues, have a structural role in our democracy. They hold back the bulk of government and are, as Justice Brennan once put it, "critical buffers between the individual and the power of the State."[81] They are not only conduits for expression, they are also the scaffolding around which civil society is constructed, in which personal freedoms are exercised, in which loyalties are formed and transmitted, and in which individuals flourish. The ideal of equality should be pursued, the non-discrimination norm should be operationalized and enforced, and the values of liberal democracy should be expressed by the government in a way that respects the structural, constitutional role that nonstate associations—including, sometimes, associations whose internal practices include illiberal ones—play.

With respect to religious institutions, the point is arguably even stronger. As the Court appreciated in *Hosanna-Tabor*, the deference afforded to churches in the selection of ministers, teachers, teachings, and doctrines is not the result of a balancing of interests or of cost-benefit analysis. The ministerial exception, instead, is about history, first principles, jurisdiction, and power. As Justice Thomas wrote in his concurring opinion, "the Religion Clauses guarantee religious organizations autonomy in matters of internal governance[.]"[82] It is true that the line separating these matters from the many, many activities of churches covered by the government's police power is not clear or easy to locate, but this is no less true of the limits on the powers vested by the Constitution in the national government's three coequal branches.

Constitutionalism is, again, the enterprise of protecting and promoting human freedom through the use of structural devices that allocate, separate, facilitate, and limit political power. A "healthy," "positive" separation of church and state, correctly understood, is such a device. It is an arrangement in which the institutions of religion are distinct from, other than, and meaningfully independent of the institutions of government. It is a principle of pluralism, of multiple and overlapping authorities, of competing loyalties and demands. It is a rule that limits the state and thereby clears out and protects a social space within which persons are formed and educated and without which religious liberty is vulnerable.

At present, it seems that religious liberty *is* vulnerable, and for various reasons. That religious liberty is increasingly associated with certain "culture war" or "hot topic" issues and that it is regarded as or asserted to be merely a fig-leaf slogan for bigotry and prejudice is part of the explanation. That fewer people— in the United States and Europe, even if not in the world generally—identify as belonging to particular religious communities or traditions and therefore might not see themselves as having a personal stake in strong legal protections for religious objectors is another. When the challenge for a religious-liberty regime is to manage the possibility or reality of conflict or tension between religious minorities and, say, the regulation of hallucinogenic drugs or prisoners' beards, the challenge might seem relatively easy to meet. When, however, the clash in question pits or appears to pit traditional teachings and institutional authority against attractive, even if abstract, notions of identity, dignity, and equality, the challenge will be—and, at present, is—more formidable.

Civil Marriage for Same-Sex Couples, "Moral Disapproval," and Tensions between Religious Liberty and Equality

LINDA C. MCCLAIN

Introduction

Does access by gay men and lesbians to civil marriage—to use a common term, *marriage equality*—threaten religious liberty? Is marriage equality, along with its consequences for civil law, in direct tension with the religious freedom of persons who oppose it on religious grounds? If so, are exemptions from those civil laws appropriate? Does marriage equality pose a greater or lesser threat depending upon whether it results from successful constitutional litigation brought by same-sex couples or from a state law duly enacted by a democratically elected legislature and signed by an elected governor? Conversely, is it constitutionally problematic if "the people," through the ballot initiative or referendum process,

This chapter is an expanded and updated version of a paper originally prepared for the conference, "Religious Freedom and Equality: Emerging Conflicts in North America and Europe," held at Magdalen College, Oxford University, April 11–13, 2012. I am grateful to Georgetown University's Religious Freedom Project and to Kellogg College, Oxford University for including me in the conversation. Thanks also to Timothy Samuel Shah, Jack Friedman, and Melissa Proctor for editorial comments. I thank BU law librarian Stefanie Weigmann and BU law student Jessica Lees for help with research. I also thank the BU Department of Theology for affording me a chance to present this draft while I was a Faculty Fellow in the Religion Fellows Program. Because this chapter was substantially completed before the US Supreme Court's decision in *Obergefell v. Hodges* on June 26, 2105, I briefly indicate the relevance of my analysis to that decision and to religious liberty issues in the post-*Obergefell* landscape, but leave a full evaluation to later work.

take measures to prevent or, in some instances, override this marriage equality? Finally, what role does or should moral disapproval of homosexuality and of same-sex marriage play in public deliberation and decision-making about the quest for marriage equality?

This chapter situates these questions about marriage equality and religious liberty in the context of developments within the United States. I will offer three organizing frameworks for considering these questions. One framework is *congruence and conflict*, that is, the basic tension in the US constitutional order between two important ideas about the relationship between civil society and government: (1) families, religious institutions, and other voluntary associations of civil society are foundational sources or "seedbeds" of virtues and values that undergird—and are congruent with—constitutional democracy, and yet (2) these same nongovernmental entities are independent locations of power and authority that guard against governmental orthodoxy by generating their own distinctive virtues and values, which may conflict with public norms. I will explain how this framework helps to evaluate claims that marriage equality threatens religious liberty.

A second, related framework is the *distinction between civil and religious marriage* in US family law. Claims that marriage equality threatens religious liberty often blur—or reject—the distinction between civil and religious marriage and insist that the two must be congruent. Conversely, recognizing the distinction between civil and religious marriage helps make sense of the claim that marriage equality *is* compatible with religious liberty.

A third framework is the *role of moral argument* and, more precisely, moral disapproval, in justifying the law concerning civil marriage. This framework requires a grounding in the relevant United States constitutional jurisprudence concerning liberty and equality and its evolution in the last few decades, in the US Supreme Court's *Romer v. Evans* (1996) and *Lawrence v. Texas* (2003), toward a more critical examination of appeals to upholding traditional morality as a justification for legislative classifications that disadvantage persons based on their homosexuality. The precedents set in *Romer* and *Lawrence* rule out "animus" or a "bare desire to harm" as a rationale for such legislation. This jurisprudence is at the core of litigation over marriage equality in state and federal courts. Another crucial precedent in which the Court limited the role of "moral disapproval of homosexuality" as a justification for legislation is *United States v. Windsor* (2013), in which the Supreme Court (in a 5-4 opinion) struck down part of the Defense of Marriage Act (DOMA).[1] Although *Windsor* formally ruled only on the constitutionality of a *federal* ban on recognizing marriages valid under *state* law, numerous federal district and appellate courts found *Windsor*'s reasoning equally applicable and persuasive with respect to state bans on marriage by same-sex couples or on the recognition of such marriages, holding that such laws violate the Fourteenth Amendment; only one federal court of appeals—the Sixth Circuit—ruled to the contrary. On June 26, 2015, in *Obergefell v. Hodges*, the Supreme Court resolved this circuit split and reversed the Sixth Circuit's ruling. Observing that this case law in the federal appellate courts had "helped to explain and formulate the underlying principles" relevant to the Court's analysis, the Court (in a 5-4 opinion authored by Justice Kennedy) held that, under the Fourteenth Amendment, same-sex couples "may exercise the fundamental right to marry" in all states and that "there is no lawful basis for a State to refuse to recognize a lawful same-sex marriage performed in another State on the ground of its same-sex character."[2]

As requested by this volume's editors, I apply these three frameworks to particular legal, political, and policy controversies. I offer three examples—corresponding to the three branches of government: the legislative, executive, and judicial—where prominent religious leaders have identified threats to religious liberty.[3] The first example is the New York legislature's enactment of the Marriage Equality Act, which allows same-sex couples to marry. Religious leaders criticized the law both for its alleged departure from a true understanding of marriage and its purported failure to provide adequate religious exemptions (e.g., for public officials who refuse to take part in same-sex marriage). The second is the decision by the Department of Justice (DOJ) to stop defending DOMA in legal lawsuits challenging its constitutionality, including in the *Windsor* litigation. A prominent address on religious liberty stated that the DOJ had "attacked DOMA as act of 'bias and prejudice,' akin to racism, thereby implying that churches that teach that marriage is between a man and a woman are guilty of bigotry."[4] I look at arguments made by religious organizations in defense of DOMA and religious liberty in "friend of the court" briefs filed in the *Windsor* litigation. *Windsor* itself triggered new warnings about threats to religious liberty, fortified by charges in the strongly worded dissents that the majority had branded supporters for traditional marriage "bigots" and "superstitious fools" who had "hateful hearts" and "acted with malice."[5]

My third example is the ruling by the federal district court, in *Perry v. Schwarzenegger* (2010), that Proposition 8 (hereafter Prop 8), a ballot initiative that amended California's constitution after its high court ruled that same-sex couples must be allowed access to civil marriage, violated the US constitution because it lacked any legitimate purpose and instead rested on private moral or religious views.[6] Religious critics sharply criticized both the *Perry* opinion and the Ninth Circuit opinion affirming it. Because the Supreme Court, in *Hollingsworth v. Perry* (2013), declined to reach the merits and instead vacated the Ninth Circuit opinion (for technical reasons discussed later in this chapter), I focus primarily on the federal district court opinion.

All three examples helpfully raise the larger issues of religion in the public square and what religious liberty means in a pluralistic constitutional democracy. These issues are likely to remain at the forefront of public discourse and to arise in new legislative and judicial battles in the post-*Obergefell* landscape, in which all states must allow same-sex couples to marry and recognize those marriages. Even before the Court's ruling, in the wake of public criticism that "religious freedom restoration acts" passed in Indiana and elsewhere to protect religious business owners from "supporting" same-sex marriages instead protect discrimination and "bigotry,"[7] several prominent religious leaders issued a new statement about the need to "talk about religious liberty."[8] They argue that "civic harmony" is impossible "when basic moral convictions and historic religious wisdom rooted in experience are deemed 'discrimination.' "[9] The rhetoric in the *Obergefell* dissents that the majority's opinion threatens religious liberty and will be used "to vilify Americans who are unwilling to assent to the new orthodoxy" has already featured in recent statements about risks to religious freedom and calls for "constitutional resistance" to *Obergefell* and will likely feature in new controversies.[10] The three frameworks offered in this chapter may provide a helpful way to approach these conflicts.

I. Frameworks

A. Framework 1: Congruence and Conflict

Congruence and conflict refers to the tension I noted earlier between two ideas about the relationship between the institutions of civil society and the institutions of government. The first idea envisions a comfortable *congruence* between norms and values fostered by nongovernmental associations and those inculcated by government, or at least that the institutions of civil society are "mediating associations" that cultivate a "whole range of moral dispositions, presumably supportive of political order."[11] The second contemplates that the values and virtues generated by nongovernmental institutions may *conflict* with political values and virtues. How does this tension apply to the evident clash between religious liberty and marriage equality?

Some religious opponents of same-sex marriage assert that it will harm the institution of marriage and society if civil law redefines marriage so that it clashes with religious understandings of marriage. For example, on November 20, 2009, a group of prominent Christian clergy, religious leaders, and scholars released "The Manhattan Declaration: A Call of Christian Conscience."[12] Drafted by Professor Robert P. George (a prominent political and constitutional theorist at Princeton University), Professor Timothy George (Beeson Divinity School, Samford University), and the late Chuck Colson (Chuck Colson Center for Christian Worldview), it identifies three areas under supposed threat: life, marriage, and religious liberty.

The Declaration invokes congruence when it articulates the religious roots of the correct "objective" understanding of marriage. Citing biblical verses in Genesis (2:23–24) and Ephesians (5:32–33), it contends: "marriage . . . is the first institution of human society," the foundation of all other institutions.[13] The "impulse to redefine marriage" to recognize same-sex marriage, the Declaration states, "reflects a loss of understanding of the meaning of marriage as embodied in our civil and religious law and in the philosophical tradition that contributed to shaping the law" (5).

It is a mistake, the Declaration asserts, to believe that as a matter of "equality or civil rights," homosexual relationships should be recognized as marriage: "No one has a civil right to have a non-marital relationship treated as a marriage" (6). Those disposed toward homosexual sexual conduct are entitled to compassion and respect as human beings "possessing profound, inherent, and equal dignity" (5). However, they are not capable of marriage because of its "objective reality" as a "covenantal union of husband and wife" and its "sexual complementarity": the union of one man and one woman is "sealed, completed, and actualized by loving sexual intercourse in which the spouses become one flesh, not in some merely metaphorical sense, but by fulfilling together the behavioral conditions of procreation" (6). Thus, it is not "animus" or "prejudice" that leads the Declaration's signatories to "pledge to labor ceaselessly to preserve the legal definition of marriage," but "love" and "prudent concern for the common good" (7). This statement no doubt was aimed at some state court opinions (such as the Massachusetts high court, in *Goodridge v. Department of Human Resources* [2003]) rejecting traditional rationales for excluding same-sex couples from civil marriage as, in fact, manifestations of constitutionally impermissible prejudice or animus.[14] The Declaration contends that when new definitions of marriage in civil law disturb this congruence between religious and civil law, "genuine social harms follow," including threats to religious and parental liberty (6). The Manhattan Declaration, as I discuss below, filed a friend of the court brief in the Prop 8 and DOMA litigation.[15]

In *What Is Marriage? Man and Woman: A Defense*, Manhattan Declaration author Robert George, along with Sherif Girgis and Ryan Anderson, repeat the same definitional argument that same-sex couples are not capable of achieving the bodily union that is marriage's "objective reality," although without an explicit reference to religious beliefs.[16] The authors also filed a brief in the Prop 8 and DOMA litigation, to which I return in Section IV.[17]

B. Framework 2: Distinction between Civil
and Religious Marriage

The Manhattan Declaration rests upon an evident congruence between the "civil and religious law" of marriage. Civil and religious understandings of marriage, however, differ in many ways. Most fundamentally, while some religious opponents of same-sex marriage stress that God is not only the creator of the institution of marriage, but also the third party to every marriage, family law students in the United States routinely learn that *the state* creates the institution of civil marriage, sets the terms, and is a third party to every marriage—and divorce.[18] This state role is vividly clear in the famous Massachusetts same-sex marriage decision, *Goodridge*, when the Supreme Judicial Court explains:

> Simply put, the government creates civil marriage. In Massachusetts, civil marriage is, and since pre-Colonial days has been, precisely what its name implies: a wholly secular institution. No religious ceremony has ever been required to validate a Massachusetts marriage.
>
> In a real sense, there are three partners to every civil marriage: two willing spouses and an approving State. While only the parties can mutually assent to marriage, the terms of the marriage—who may marry and what obligations, benefits, and liabilities attach to civil marriage—are set by the Commonwealth. Conversely, while only the parties can agree to end the marriage (absent [one spouse's] death or a [void] marriage), the Commonwealth defines the exit terms.[19]

Other state high courts have made similar declarations about civil marriage and the state's role as a third party.[20] To recognize that civil marriage is a government-regulated institution is not to deny that, historically, Christian teachings about marriage, particularly the ecclesiastical law of England, have shaped family law in the United States (for example, the law of separation and certain grounds for annulment and fault-based grounds for divorce).[21] Thus, the phrase "wholly secular institution" might be misleading to the extent it suggests religious and secular understandings of marriage are wholly distinct.[22] As the late Lee Teitelbaum observed, "for most of American history . . . the law of marriage was consistent with and supported—if not created—by the views of dominant religious communities."[23] For example, "in the middle of the twentieth century," the Catholic Church's view "that artificial contraception is immoral" was "enforced or supported by law in some states."[24] Nonetheless, contemporary family law differs markedly from—indeed conflicts with—certain religious conceptions of marriage (including the conjugal model set forth in the Manhattan Declaration) that stress that marriage must be open to procreative acts, that men and women have complementary roles to play as spouses and parents, and that marriage—a permanent union—may not be dissolved.

Consider just three significant trends in family law: (1) the constitutionalization of family law, beginning with *Griswold v. Connecticut* (1965), which recognized the right of a married couples to use contraceptives; (2) family law's gender revolution (spurred by the Supreme Court's equal protection jurisprudence of the 1970s and 1980s), which eradicated state laws requiring different roles for husbands and wives, mothers and fathers, and shifted from a view of marriage as a hierarchical relation rooted in gender complementarity to a partnership of equals rooted in gender neutrality; and (3) the liberalization of divorce law, reflected in the so-called no-fault divorce revolution, which began in California in 1969, but quickly spread to the rest of the country (and, finally, to New York several years ago). All three of these trends are in tension with certain religious conceptions of marriage.

Many other trends in family law and society have shaped marriage law and social practice in directions that are at odds with many religious conceptions of marriage and family. For example, in marriage equality litigation, the US Conference of Catholic Bishops (USCCB) appealed to the "antiquity and near-universality" of marriage laws, attributing the one man–one woman definition to the state's interest in "channeling the [unique] sexual and reproductive faculties of men and women into the kind of sexual union where responsible childbearing will take place and children's interests will be protected."[25] This argument about the unique role of marriage in channeling heterosexual procreation and parental investment, however, is in tension with the evolution in the law of parentage in many states and in some federal laws, which: (1) recognize parental rights and impose parental responsibilities outside of marriage, both through new formal statuses, such as civil unions and domestic partnerships for same-sex (and sometimes opposite-sex) couples and through doctrines such as de facto parenthood; (2) permit adoption by unmarried individuals and couples (including, in some states, same-sex couples); and (3) allow the use of assisted reproductive technology to create children—and parental status—within and outside of marriage. States vary with respect to how far they have adopted or rejected these trends. However, all these ways of permitting and even supporting non-marital parenthood are pertinent to claims about the unique, channeling role of marriage.

My point here is that secular law already differs sharply in certain respects from religious understandings of marriage, a departure of which conservative religious critics of civil marriage law are keenly aware. One example is covenant marriage. Louisiana legislator Katherine Shaw Spaht felt called to propose "covenant marriage" to instantiate an ideal of marriage in keeping with Christian traditions of permanence and mutual sacrifice.[26] Even so, because her new model would still permit divorce (although on a more restricted basis), Spaht found that Louisiana's Catholic bishops could not support it.[27] A second example comes from marriage equality litigation. In their friend of the court brief submitted in support of Prop 8 and DOMA, George, Anderson, and Girgis contrast the "conjugal model" of marriage that these laws rationally advance with the "revisionist" model, acknowledging that "a revisionist view has informed certain marriage policy changes of the last several decades."[28] They contend that "[e]nacting same-sex marriage" would be "finishing what policies like no-fault divorce began"; this would "finally replace the conjugal view with the revisionist" and "multiply the marriage revolution's moral and cultural spoils, and make them harder than ever to recover."[29]

As state definitions of marriage change to permit same-sex couples to marry, the conflict between religious liberty and marriage equality arises in significant part due to underlying disagreement over the "nature" of marriage: as law and religion scholar Douglas Laycock explains, marriage simultaneously may be "a personal relationship, a legal relationship, and a religious relationship."[30] While "the secular side" sees marriage primarily as a "legal relationship" or "committed personal relationship between the spouses," "[c]ommitted religious believers see the religious relationship as primary."[31] Accordingly, such believers "see same-sex marriage legislation as the state interfering with the sacred, changing a religious institution," and, consequently, "[t]hey reject the change, and they reject the state's authority to make the change."[32] This rejection is evident, as discussed later in this chapter, in some religious objections to New York's Marriage Equality Law.

C. Framework 3: The Role of Moral Argument and Moral Disapproval

Political philosopher Michael Sandel famously criticizes liberalism for exalting choice without regard for the moral good for what is chosen. He contends that liberalism leads to a public square denuded of religious arguments and convictions. The issue of same-sex marriage, he contends, cannot be resolved within the bounds of public reason but requires "recourse to controversial conceptions of the purpose of marriage and the goods it honors."[33] While I disagree with Sandel's critique of liberalism, I agree with his valuable insight that arguments about purposes and goods are key to the marriage equality issue. However, as James Fleming and I explain elsewhere, arguments about individual rights *and* about the goods and purposes of marriage both play a role in judicial opinions recognizing marriage equality and are compatible with the constitutional liberalism we support.[34]

One alleged threat to religious liberty is that judges and the executive have ruled out moral disapproval as a legitimate reason to uphold laws excluding same-sex couples from civil marriage and have conflated moral disapproval with bias, prejudice, and animus. How, religious critics ask, can this possibly be correct? Isn't law, as the Supreme Court once put it,[35] constantly based on morality? Later in this chapter, I will discuss the role of moral disapproval in the federal constitutional challenges to DOMA and Prop 8.[36] In this section, I preview the relevant US Supreme Court jurisprudence. Religious critics have sharply criticized that jurisprudence from the outset, sometimes anticipating its possible future use to support same-sex marriage.

Romer v. Evans (1996) held that an amendment to the Colorado Constitution (Amendment 2), which had the effect of repealing several local laws that banned discrimination on the basis of sexual orientation and prohibited "any governmental entity from adopting similar, or more protective statutes, regulations, ordinances, or policies in the future unless the state constitution is first amended to permit such measures," violated the Equal Protection Clause of the US Constitution.[37] Justice Kennedy's opinion in *Romer* contains several key phrases that surface again and again in the constitutional challenges to Prop 8 and DOMA, as well as to restrictive state marriage laws. Justice Kennedy states that Amendment 2 "withdraws from homosexuals, but not others, specific legal protection from the injuries caused by discrimination, and it forbids reinstatement of these laws and policies"; that it imposes a "broad and undifferentiated disability on a single named group"; and that its "sheer breadth" is "so discontinuous with the reasons offered for it that the amendment seems inexplicable by anything but animus toward the class it affects" (631–633). In another often-quoted passage, he states: "Laws of the kind now before us raised the inevitable inference that the disadvantage imposed is born of animosity toward the class of persons affected" (634). Quoting an earlier Supreme Court case, *Department of Agriculture v. Moreno* (1973), he explains that equal protection means, at minimum, that "a bare . . . desire to harm a politically unpopular group cannot constitute a *legitimate* governmental interest" (634).[38] In a formulation that he draws from *Louisville Gas & Electric Co. v. Coleman* (1928) and repeats in *Windsor*, Kennedy states, "[d]iscriminations of an unusual character especially suggest careful consideration to determine whether they are obnoxious to the constitutional provision" (633).[39]

This formulation suggests a more searching form of rational basis review, even though *Romer* declined to find that homosexuality was a suspect classification, triggering intermediate or strict scrutiny. Even so, it stressed that the legislative classification must "bear a rational relationship to an independent and legitimate end" to "ensure that classifications are not drawn for the purpose of disadvantaging the group burdened by the law" (633). Amendment 2, Kennedy concludes, "confounds" this test—singling out a group of persons based on a single trait and then disqualifying them from protection "across the board" is "unprecedented in our jurisprudence" (633). The state of Colorado's primary rationale for Amendment 2 was "respect for other citizens' freedom of association, and in particular the liberties of landlords or employers who have personal or religious objections to homosexuality" (635); another rationale was "conserving resources to fight discrimination against other groups" (635). However, Kennedy concludes, the amendment's breath is too far divorced from these justifications to be credited. It "classifies homosexuals not to further a proper legislative end but to make them unequal to everyone else. This Colorado cannot do. A State cannot so deem a class of persons a stranger to its laws" (635).

In a memorable dissent, Justice Scalia accuses the majority of mistaking "a Kulturkampf for a fit of spite," countering that Amendment 2 is surely constitutional as a "modest attempt by seemingly tolerant Coloradans to preserve traditional sexual mores against the efforts of a politically powerful minority to revise those mores through use of the laws" (636). Colorado long ago had decriminalized sodomy. By contrast, Scalia points out that just ten years earlier in *Bowers v. Hardwick*—a case the majority nowhere mentions, let alone overrules—the Supreme Court *upheld* a state law imposing criminal punishment on homosexuals for sodomy. In Scalia's words: "If it is constitutionally permissible for a State to make homosexual conduct criminal, surely it is constitutionally permissible for a State to enact other laws merely *disfavoring* homosexual conduct" (641, emphasis in original). What's more: "Surely . . . the only sort of 'animus' at issue here [is] moral disapproval of homosexual conduct, the same sort of moral disapproval that produced the centuries-old criminal laws that we held constitutional in *Bowers*" (644). Amendment 2, he contends, is an example of how a society that eliminated criminal punishment can nonetheless continue to express "moral and social disapprobation" of homosexuality, and, in doing so at the state level, counter successfully the "disproportionate political power" of homosexuals who reside in "disproportionate" numbers in urban areas (645–647). Scalia paints a picture of Coloradan voters exposed to "homosexuals' quest for social endorsement," which is happening not just in places like New York, Los Angeles, and San Francisco but right there in the cities of Colorado. Finally, Scalia accuses the majority of taking sides in the culture wars with the Knights Templar (that is, with the views and values of the lawyer class) rather than with the "villeins" (evidently, the people of Colorado who passed Amendment 2 "to prevent piecemeal deterioration of the sexual morality favored by a majority of Coloradans" [652]).

Romer drew sharp criticism from conservative critics for usurping the political process, limiting the use of law to preserve traditional morality, and possibly opening the door to judicial imposition of same-sex marriage. In 1996, in a famous symposium in the journal *First Things*, Charles Colson, subsequent coauthor of the Manhattan Declaration, warned of "kingdoms in conflict" and that "the Court in *Romer v. Evans* effectively branded a bigot any citizen who considers homosexuality immoral."[40] He predicted that, under *Romer*, the Court would "easily find no compelling interest in confining marriage to a man and a woman."[41] He also, as in the Declaration, discussed the problem of what Christians should do when facing unjust laws.[42] In the same *First Things* symposium, Hadley Arkes, a key Congressional witness in support of DOMA, passed in 1996, warned that *Romer* opened the door to judges imposing gay marriage, which went contrary to the "natural teleology of the body."[43] Amendment 2 simply sought to ensure that "coercions of the law would not be used to punish those people who bore moral objections to homosexuality," which the Court now characterized as animus or blind prejudice.[44] *Romer*, Arkes argued, pronounced "the traditional moral teaching of Judaism and Christianity, as empty, irrational, unjustified."[45] This rhetoric about branding defenders of traditional marriage as bigots and prejudiced recurs, as I later discuss, in the dissenting opinions in *Windsor* and *Obergefell*.

In *Lawrence v. Texas* (2003), in another opinion by Justice Kennedy, the Court officially overruled *Bowers v. Hardwick* and held that Texas' law making same-sex sodomy a crime was unconstitutional. This ruling implicitly invalidated any remaining state anti-sodomy statutes. *Lawrence* is another critical component of the Court's jurisprudence concerning the weight of moral disapproval and features in Kennedy's subsequent opinions in *Windsor* and *Obergefell*. *Romer*'s invalidation of class-based legislation born of animus features in *Lawrence*, in which the Court emphasizes the "stigma" that the criminal statute imposes on homosexuals. It concludes that the state "cannot demean [homosexual persons'] existence or control their destiny by making their private sexual conduct a crime."[46] The Court acknowledges—as *Bowers* did—"that for centuries there have been powerful voices to condemn homosexual conduct as immoral" (571), shaped in part by religious beliefs and respect for the traditional family. Nonetheless, while "for many persons these are not trivial concerns but profound and deep convictions," Justice Kennedy (invoking *Planned Parenthood v. Casey*'s famous language) states: "The issue is whether the majority may use the power of the State to enforce these views on the whole society through operation of the criminal law. 'Our obligation is to define the liberty of all, not to mandate our own moral code'" (571). The Court said that it was not addressing whether homosexual intimate relationships warranted official recognition (impliedly, marriage).

Justice O'Connor, in her concurrence, is even more explicit about the import of *Romer* and about distinguishing the present case from a challenge to marriage laws. First, invoking *Romer*, she states: "Moral disapproval of a group cannot be a legitimate governmental interest under the Equal Protection Clause" (583).

To Texas' law she applies *Romer*'s conclusion about "rais[ing] the inevitable inference" of "disadvantage . . . born of animosity toward" (583) homosexual persons. By contrast to the statute upheld in *Bowers* (which she did not join in overruling), the Texas law—on its face—only criminalized sodomy by same-sex couples. Second, she distinguishes Texas' law, which brands "one class of persons as criminal based solely on the State's moral disapproval of that class" and conduct associated with it from a legitimate interest, "such as . . . preserving the traditional institution of marriage" (585). In a crucial passage, she says: "Unlike the moral disapproval of same-sex relations—the asserted state interest in this case—other reasons exist to promote the institution of marriage beyond mere moral disapproval of an excluded group" (585). Both proponents and opponents of DOMA cited frequently to Justice O'Connor's concurrence, albeit to argue different positions as to whether that law rested on more than "moral disapproval."[47]

Justice Scalia, in a fierce dissent, famously predicts the end of all morals legislation in the wake of overruling *Bowers*. The Court in *Bowers* had stated: "The law is constantly based on notions of morality, and if all laws representing essentially moral choices are to be invalidated under the Due Process clause, the courts will be very busy indeed."[48] He also warns readers not to believe the majority or O'Connor's disclaimers about the marriage issue: after, all, "'preserving the traditional institution of marriage' is just a kinder way of describing the State's moral disapproval of same-sex couples."[49] He asks: if "moral disapprobation of homosexual conduct" does not suffice as a "legitimate state interest," then on what basis could a state deny homosexuals the benefits of marriage? "Surely not the encouragement of procreation, since the sterile and the elderly are allowed to marry."[50] This last assertion has been cited *in support of marriage equality*, since encouraging "responsible procreation" features prominently as an asserted rationale for limiting marriage to opposite-sex couples, who (unlike same-sex couples) can procreate accidentally.

As with *Romer*, conservative critics of *Lawrence* debated whether the likelihood of a Supreme Court ruling favoring same-sex marriage "appeared to increase exponentially."[51] They pondered whether O'Connor or Scalia would prove to have the better argument with respect to whether the constitutionally legitimate interest in preserving the traditional institution of marriage would be viewed in later cases as something other than the constitutionally impermissible mere "moral disapproval of same-sex relations."[52]

Romer, in the context of Equal Protection, and *Lawrence*, in the context of Due Process, exemplify what constitutional commentators describe as a more careful or searching form of rational basis review, or, rational basis "plus" or "with bite." Such review, however, often does not expressly use the language of fundamental rights, suspect classifications, and strict scrutiny. *Romer* and *Lawrence*, as I discuss later, provide a template for Justice Kennedy's opinion in *Windsor*. In turn, *Lawrence* and *Windsor* are both building blocks for Justice Kennedy's majority opinion in *Obergefell*, which holds that same-sex couples have a fundamental right to marry in every state and that states must recognize their valid out-of-state marriages.

With these three frameworks in mind, I now turn to three examples of an evident conflict between religious liberty and marriage equality.

II. New York's Marriage Equality Act

My first illustration of an evident conflict between religious liberty and marriage equality is the New York legislature's voting, in June 2011, to allow same-sex couples to marry.[53] My first two frameworks are pertinent. Religious critics charge that the Marriage Equality Act (the Act) wrongfully departed from a religious conception of marriage and failed to afford adequate religious exemptions. By contrast, some legislators who supported the bill did so after wrestling with the relationship between religious and civil marriage and their obligations as lawmakers.

A. Analysis of Arguments

The New York legislature passed the Act without any judicial ruling that it must do so. Indeed, in *Hernandez v. Robles* (2006), the New York Court of Appeals ruled that the state's constitution did not require opening up civil marriage to same-sex couples because encouraging heterosexuals to procreate responsibly supplied a rational basis for providing the benefits and protections of civil marriage to opposite-sex, but not same-sex, couples. However, the legislature was free to do so if it chose.[54]

When the legislature approved the Act, the positive votes of Republican lawmakers who had opposed previous bills were critical. I will offer some illustrative examples of how these legislators articulated the relationship between civil and religious marriage.[55]

Republican Senator Stephen Saland characterized the Act as addressing the "dual issues of religious freedoms" and marriage equality.[56] He explained that he reasoned through the conflict between religious teachings about marriage and his conviction about the "right thing" to do. He emphasized his own "rather traditional background," including his marriage of 46 years, as well as "being raised by parents who preached to me the importance of tolerance, respect, and acceptance of others" and "always to do the right thing." His "intellectual and emotional journey" ended with him defining "the right thing as treating all persons with equality, [including] within the definition of marriage."[57] After the vote, he stressed that he appreciated that both "those for marriage equality and those who support the traditional view of marriage" have a "deep and passionate interest" in the issue. He explained that "as a traditionalist, I have long viewed marriage as a union between a man and a woman" and, as a believer in equal rights, he initially thought "civil unions for same-sex couples would be a satisfactory conclusion." However, he came to believe that equality required equal treatment as to marriage itself and that religious exemptions in the Act would protect religious freedom (as discussed later).[58]

A second example is Republican Senator Mark Grisanti. Initially, he simply opposed same-sex marriage, but felt obliged—as a lawmaker—to investigate: "As a Catholic I was raised to believe that marriage is between a man and a woman. I'm not here, however, as a Senator who is just Catholic. I'm also here with a background as an attorney, through which I look at things and I apply reason."[59] After much research and thought, he concluded: "I cannot legally come up with an argument against same-sex marriage." He made a rights-based argument: "Who am I to say that someone does not have the same rights that I have with my wife, who I love, or that have the 1,300-plus rights that I share with her? . . . I cannot deny a person, a human being, a taxpayer, a worker, or people in my district and across . . . the State of New York, and those people who make this the great state it is, the same rights that I have with my wife." Like Saland, he concluded that civil unions "do not work," but cause "chaos."[60] At the same time, the bill's religious protections for religious organizations were important to him, as a Catholic.

The distinction between civil and religious marriage also featured in some speeches by sponsors of the Act. Assembly-member Deborah Glick stated: "everybody is entitled to their religious belief. But they are not, according to our Constitution, entitled to impose those religious beliefs on others." She quipped: "when you take your oath of office, and declare, perhaps, by placing your hand on a Bible, that you will uphold the constitution, you don't place your hand on the Constitution of the State of New York and swear to uphold the Bible." Stressing the personal cost to her and her same-sex partner of being denied various benefits by the "civic institutions of this state," Glick described civil marriage as "the recognized and consistent shorthand that we all use to recognize and acknowledge committed, loving relationships and the families that exist within them."[61] This description helpfully identifies marriage's role in signaling that relationships deserve public recognition; that it is *civic* recognition stresses the distinction between civil and religious marriage.

In responding to the argument by opponents of the bill that "we shouldn't be changing the institution of marriage, 'which had existed for millennia,'" Assemblyman Richard Gottfried noted the continual evolution of the institution of marriage and the sharp distinctions between marriage practices that are part of "our own religious heritage" (such as polygamy) and contemporary civil marriage. Indeed, adhering to certain biblical commandments concerning marriage—such as taking a deceased brother's wife as one's second, third, or fourth wife—"would be a criminal act in this state and . . . in every state."[62]

By contrast, opponents of the Act warned that its new definition of marriage departed from—and lacked congruence with—religious understandings of marriage. Democratic Senator Ruben Diaz asserted: "[W]e are trying to redefine marriage . . . . I agree with Archbishop Timothy Dolan when he said that God, not Albany, has settled the definition of marriage a long time ago."[63] Diaz referred to the "great truth[]" that "marriage is and should remain the union of husband and wife" and asserted: "Same-sex marriage is a government takeover of an institution that government did not create and should not define."[64]

After passage of the Act, Archbishop Dolan, joined by his fellow bishops of New York, reiterated the Catholic Church's teaching that "we always treat our homosexual brothers and sisters with respect, dignity, and love," but "we just as strongly affirm that marriage is the joining of one man and one woman in a lifelong, loving union that is open to children, ordered for the good of children and the spouses themselves." He asserted that "this definition cannot change," expressing worry that "both marriage and the family will be undermined by this tragic presumption of government in passing this legislation that attempts to redefine these cornerstones of civilization." He urged a societal return to a "true understanding of the meaning and the place of marriage, as revealed by God, grounded in nature, and respected by America's foundational principles."[65] This stance assumes a necessary congruence between religious and civil definitions of marriage. Further, it illustrates Laycock's argument that religious opponents of "same-sex marriage legislation" view it as "interfering with the sacred" and "reject the state's authority to make the change."[66] Subsequent to the enactment of this law, for example, the USCCB released a statement that "[m]arriage is a fundamental good that must be protected in every circumstance. Exemptions of any kind never justify redefining marriage."[67]

It merits mention that religious clergy and institutions were active on both sides of the debate over the Act. Strong opposition by the Catholic Church contributed to the defeat of prior bills. Commentators who analyzed the factors contributing to the success, in 2011, of the Act found that one factor was the "concerted, sustained efforts by liberal Christian and Jewish clergy to advocate for [same-sex marriage] in the language of faith, to counter the language of morality voiced by foes."[68] The fact that there was religious support for the bill made it "'easier [for legislators] to counteract the claim of religious conservatives who say there is only one answer to this question.'"[69] Such supporters drew analogies to the critical role of religious support in passing the Civil Rights Act of 1964.[70]

B. The New York Act and the Religious Exemptions

The supporting statement for the Act provides a helpful clarification of the relationship between civil and religious marriage: "[T]his bill grants equal access to the government-created legal institution of civil marriage, while leaving the religious institution of marriage to its own separate, and fully autonomous, sphere."[71] The Act protects that sphere through expansive exemptions, including not only the "well-established constitutional and statutory principles that no member of the clergy may be compelled to perform any marriage ceremony,"[72] but also the freedom of religious institutions and benevolent organizations to "choose who may use their facilities and halls for marriage ceremonies and celebrations, to whom they rent their housing accommodations, or to whom they provide religious services, consistent with their religious principles."[73] They would enjoy exemptions from providing "accommodations, advantages, facilities or privileges related to the solemnization or celebration of a marriage."[74] These exemptions evidently were critical to passage of the Act, particularly for certain religious lawmakers supporting the bill.[75]

Whether or not religious exemptions are constitutionally required (beyond the obvious clerical exemption) or should be provided through state religious freedom restorations acts are matters of current controversy, as Robin Fretwell Wilson elaborates in Chapter 6 of this volume. In other writing, I have argued that exemptions may be justified as a prudential remedy, rooted in recognition of religious and moral objections to extending marriage to same-sex couples.[76] Such exemptions may prove to be a ladder to full, equal citizenship through acceptance of same-sex marriage, particularly given the generational divide concerning same-sex marriage.[77] Even otherwise conservative young people support same-sex marriage.[78] As Laycock observes: "Support for same-sex marriage is growing with extraordinary rapidity."[79] Tellingly, Laycock and Wilson, both of whom have teamed with other legal scholars to write a series of letters to urge the legislatures to include robust protection for religious liberty—"marriage conscience protection"—argue that now is the time to "lock in" exemptions because the next generation is likely to be willing to pass marriage equality laws without them.[80]

Even so, for those who insist on congruence between civil and religious definitions of marriage, lest government undermine marriage and the family, religious exemptions are unlikely to be an acceptable solution. For example, the 2012 "open letter" from religious leaders, "Marriage and Religious Freedom: Fundamental Goods That Stand or Fall Together," declares that, because of the "grave consequences" that follow from altering the definition of marriage, including threats to religious freedom, public officials should "support laws that uphold the time-honored definition of marriage."[81] An accompanying document prepared by the USCCB poses this question: "Let's say religious freedom could be fully or mostly protected by an exemption . . . would that then justify the redefinition of marriage?" The USCCB explains why the answer must be no:

> In practice, such exemptions either address genuine concerns but do so inadequately or address "red herring" concerns that are unlikely ever to arise. However, no religious exemption—no matter how broadly worded—can justify a supportive or neutral position on legislation to redefine legal marriage. Such "redefinition" is always fundamentally unjust, and indeed, religious exemptions may even facilitate the passage of such unjust laws.[82]

This approach strongly resists any change in civil law and does not view the route of religious exemption as wise or defensible. By contrast, some law and religion scholars—such as Wilson and Laycock—urge that the focus should not be on a "total win" by either supporters or opponents of same-sex marriage. Instead, religious conservatives should no longer seek to regulate other people's relationships, but instead secure protection of their own religious liberty. At the same time, advocates of marriage equality should deem it more important "to protect their own liberty than to restrict the liberty of religious conservatives" by insisting those with moral objections to their unions provide them goods and services.[83]

New York's law did not go as far as the robust "marriage conscience protection" proposed by Laycock and Wilson. For example, it did not relieve public servants of their duty to provide a license to applicants of the same sex who meet New York's eligibility requirements on the grounds that such marriages offend their religious beliefs.[84] Nonetheless, an elected town clerk's refusal to issue marriage licenses to same-sex couples because "God doesn't want me to do this"—and one couple's formal objection to this refusal—have featured in warnings of how redefining marriage threatens religious liberty (as in Bishop Lori's address).[85] In this volume and elsewhere, Wilson argues that such public servants should receive religious accommodation provided it does not impose a hardship on same-sex couples seeking licenses.[86] I do not believe a public servant has a "right" to a general exemption, although she might decide as a matter of conscience to resign rather than enforce what she views as an unjust law. However, I do not object to Wilson's idea of an office *voluntarily* organizing itself—if it has the staffing to do so—to accommodate such religious beliefs without persons seeking a license experiencing a direct refusal of service.[87]

As this volume goes to press, the issue of whether public officials may refuse to issue marriage licenses due to religious convictions is in the news afresh, as prominent opponents of marriage by same-sex couples are legally representing a Kentucky county clerk who was found in contempt of court—and briefly jailed—for steadfastly refusing to issue *any* marriage licenses at all or to permit her clerks to do so.[88] Illustrating the perspective that civil and religious definitions of marriage should be congruent, the clerk, Kim Davis, an Apostolic Christian, has asserted that, "To issue a marriage license which conflicts with God's definition of marriage, with my name affixed to the certificate, would violate my conscience. . . . [T]his is about marriage and God's word."[89] Clerks in other states similarly assert that "natural marriage cannot be redefined by government."[90] Moral disapproval of such marriages is also a theme in such appeals to conscience. Moreover, since *Obergefell*, some states have passed laws expressly permitting public officials to refuse to perform marriage ceremonies if they have "sincerely held religious objections."[91] Legal challenges brought to those laws will likely provide a further context in which to examine the issue of congruence and conflict.[92]

Returning to New York's Act, it also does not exempt for-profit businesses involved in providing goods and services (considered public accommodations) from serving same-sex couples if the owners believed doing so violated their religious or moral beliefs. This exemption survived challenge when the owners of a farm advertised as open to the public for wedding ceremonies and receptions declined a lesbian couple's request to hold their wedding there because the owners were Christian and "do not hold same-sex marriages . . . at the barn."[93] The couple brought a complaint under New York's Human Rights Law, alleging that the farm was a "public accommodation" that unfairly discriminated against them on the basis of sexual orientation. The owners countered that they were an exempt "private business." In 2014, an administrative law judge (ALJ) rejected that argument, pointing to the farm's "widespread marketing to the general public," encouraging members of the public to lease their facilities and use their services. The fact that the owners resided in part of the farm did not render the farm private, since the other areas were used "solely" for contracted events, like weddings and receptions. The ALJ (recently affirmed on appeal) concluded the owners were subject to the law and, had discriminated on the basis of sexual orientation, and awarded a fine of $10,000 and $1,500 to be paid to each individual woman.[94]

Some commentators view this outcome as too high a cost for religious persons engaged in commerce to pay; the farm owners subsequently stopped holding any weddings and receptions. Laycock, for example, argues that religious believers engaged in providing goods and services who have "deep moral objections" to same-sex marriage should not have to provide those goods and services so long as their refusal does not significantly burden a same-sex couple's ability to obtain such goods and services (for example, if there are no or few other providers of that service in the area).[95] In the New York case, the couple alleged the denial of service caused them "mental anguish," they stopped looking for a location for several months, and even then they were uncertain about looking in the same area lest they encounter similar reactions.[96] On the other hand, some commentators (in my view, correctly) argue that this type of ruling helps to ensure that businesses treat "all patrons with the dignity and respect they deserve" and that the "cost" of opening up one's business to the public is "that you can't discriminate."[97] This seems to be a strong sentiment in the firestorm of reactions to Indiana's recently proposed religious freedom restoration law, which included a "wave of boycotts and criticisms by business, sports and political leaders and other states."[98]

III. DOMA

My second example of an evident conflict between religious liberty and marriage equality concerns DOMA. Religious leaders criticized the decision by the Department of Justice of the Obama Administration to cease defending DOMA against constitutional challenges, stepping aside for Congress to do so, if it wished. For example, Bishop Lori described this change of position as an "attack" on DOMA that treated it "as an act of 'bias and prejudice,' akin to racism, thereby implying that churches, which teach that marriage is between a man and a woman, are guilty of bigotry."[99] Religious groups subsequently filed friend of the court (amicus curiae) briefs in support of DOMA in *United States v. Windsor*, in which the Supreme Court ruled in favor of Edith Windsor's challenge to DOMA. In this section, I recap the circumstances leading to the enactment of DOMA and the arguments made in support of it. I recount the Obama administration's stance of ceasing to defend it, using my third proposed framework—the Supreme Court's jurisprudence about the role of moral disapproval. I then highlight themes made in friend of the court briefs by religious organizations in support of DOMA. I briefly discuss the Supreme Court's decision in *Windsor*, both Justice Kennedy's majority opinion and the dissenting opinions.

A. The Enactment of DOMA

In 1996, Congress passed (and President Clinton signed) DOMA "to defend the institution of traditional heterosexual marriage" in response to a "very particular development in the State of Hawaii"—that "state courts in Hawaii appear[ed] to be on the verge of requiring that State to issue marriage licenses to same-sex couples." The purpose of Section 2 of DOMA was to "protect the right of the States to formulate their own public policy regarding the legal recognition of same-sex unions," and, thus, not be compelled to recognize any out-of-state marriage between same-sex couples. Section 3 defined "marriage" and "spouse" for purposes of *federal law* as referring "exclusively to relationships between persons of the opposite sex."[100]

At the time Congress enacted DOMA, no state in the United States allowed same-sex couples to marry. In 2004, Massachusetts became the first state to do so, after the Supreme Judicial Court of Massachusetts, in *Goodridge*, ruled in favor of a state constitutional challenge to Massachusetts's marriage law brought by several same-sex couples.[101] Issued just months after *Lawrence* overruled *Bowers*, the *Goodridge* opinion frequently drew on *Lawrence* in articulating how human dignity, respect, liberty, and equality are at stake in matters of sexual intimacy, marriage, and family.[102] Within several more years, several more states would allow same-sex marriage, as a result of either constitutional litigation or legislative enactment.[103] Yet more states (such as New York) indicated they would recognize such marriages, even if they did not (yet) allow them.[104] Because of DOMA, same-sex couples and states encountered practical problems when marriages, valid under state law, were not recognized for purposes of federal law. Spouses or surviving spouses were ineligible for the numerous federal benefits linked to marital status, such as, in *Windsor*, the exemption from estate tax a surviving spouse enjoys. Lawsuits filed by same-sex couples, surviving spouses, and the states themselves challenged Section 3 as unconstitutional.[105]

B. The DOJ's Changed Stance on DOMA's Constitutionality

The Department of Justice initially defended DOMA, even though (as did President Obama) it urged Congress to repeal it. On February 2011, the DOJ changed direction, a shift criticized by some religious leaders as a threat to religious liberty, because Attorney General Eric Holder attributed the motive for DOMA to "bias and prejudice."[106] By letter, Holder informed the Speaker of the House, Hon. John A. Boehner, that "after careful consideration, . . . the President of the United States has made the determination that Section 3 of [DOMA] . . . as applied to same-sex couples who are legally married under state law, violates the equal protection component of the Fifth Amendment," and accordingly, that the DOJ will not defend DOMA in the "new lawsuits" brought in the federal district courts of Connecticut and New York.[107] Holder and President Obama had concluded that "classifications based on sexual orientation warrant heightened scrutiny and that, as applied to same-sex couples legally married under state law, Section 3 of DOMA is unconstitutional" (2). If, however, the district courts in the Second Circuit concluded that rational basis should be the applicable standard for reviewing DOMA, the DOJ would "state that, consistent with the position it has taken in prior cases, a reasonable argument for Section 3's constitutionality may be proffered under that permissive standard" (6). However, it would leave it to Congress to make any such defense. Subsequently, Congress did so, through the Bipartisan Legal Advisory Group (BLAG) of the US House of Representatives.[108]

Why does Holder conclude that DOMA reflects "stereotype-based thinking and animus" of the sort that the Equal Protection Clause guards against, and suggests that it cannot survive the heightened scrutiny that is appropriate? Holder turns to prior Supreme Court precedents identifying four factors[109] that indicate whether a higher level of scrutiny than rational basis is appropriate for a classification. He finds that all four "counsel in favor of being suspicious of classifications based on sexual orientation," particularly "a significant history of purposeful discrimination against gay and lesbian people, by governmental as well as private entities, based on prejudice and stereotypes that continue to have ramifications today" (2). He refers to *Lawrence*, noting that "until very recently, states have 'demean[ed] the[] existence' of gays and lesbians 'by making their private sexual conduct a crime' " (2).[110] With respect to the fourth factor—"whether the characteristics distinguishing the group have little relation to legitimate policy objectives or to an individual's 'ability to perform or contribute to society' " (2)[111]—he observes that "recent evolutions in legislation" (such as the repeal of Don't Ask, Don't Tell), "community practices," "case law" (such as *Romer* and *Lawrence*), and social science "all make clear that sexual orientation is not a characteristic that generally bears on legitimate policy objectives" (3). Further, "there is a growing acknowledgment that sexual orientation 'bears no relation to ability to perform or contribute to society' " (3).[112] Although many circuit courts had concluded that only rational basis review is necessary for sexual orientation, he notes that many reasoned from analogy from *Bowers*, a line of argument no longer available since *Lawrence*.

Holder identifies "moral disapproval" as a primary purpose of DOMA, contending that "the legislative record underlying DOMA's passage . . . contains numerous expressions reflecting moral disapproval of gays and lesbians and their intimate and family relationships—precisely the kind of stereotype-based thinking and animus the Equal Protection Clause is designed to guard against" (4). The House of Representatives' Report accompanying DOMA (House Report) similarly emphasizes moral disapproval, for example, that DOMA properly reflects a moral conviction that traditional heterosexual marriage better comported with "traditional (especially Judeo-Christian) morality," while same-sex marriage "puts a stamp of approval . . . on a union that many people . . . think is immoral" (4, n. 7).

He noted that the DOJ—when it was defending DOMA—had already disavowed, in "numerous" legal filings, two rationales as "unreasonable": responsible procreation and child-rearing (3–4, n. 5).[113] With respect to the latter, "as the Department has explained . . . many leading medical, psychological, and social welfare organizations have concluded, based on numerous studies, that children raised by gay and lesbian parents are as likely to be well-adjusted as children raised by heterosexual parents" (3–4, n. 5).

In support of his conclusion that DOMA fails intermediate scrutiny because the Equal Protection Clause guards against the" stereotype-based thinking and animus" it reflects, Holder refers to *Romer* (where the Court, without explicitly using heightened scrutiny, rejected "the rationale that Amendment 2 was supported by the 'liberties of landlords or employers who have personal or religious objections to homosexuality')"; *Cleburne* (which ruled that "'mere negative attitudes, or fears' are not permissible bases for discriminatory treatment"); and *Palmore v. Sidoti* (which, in explaining why a court could not award custody based on racial bias, stated: "Private biases may be outside the reach of the law, but the law cannot, directly or indirectly, give them effect") (5).[114]

Many religious leaders have decried Holder's decision not to defend DOMA and his underlying analysis that DOMA's stated purposes—including "moral disapproval"—reflect animus and "stereotype-based thinking." I believe, however, that Holder's critical evaluation of these rationales is sound, especially given the evolution of the Court's Equal Protection jurisprudence and its overruling of *Bowers*, of the social science consensus about child outcomes and family forms, and developments in state law about evolving understandings of civil marriage. Holder's evaluation says nothing to *religious congregations* about having to perform or recognize such marriages. Instead, it is a conclusion that the *federal government* lacks a sufficient reason, under a heightened scrutiny standard, for not treating *civil marriages that are valid under state law* as valid marriages under federal law. The only threat to religious liberty that I perceive here is that religious opponents of extending civil marriage to same-sex couples may no longer carry the day in terms of having their convictions about marriage reflected in federal law.

C. *Windsor v. United States*: Proceedings in the Lower Federal Courts

In *Windsor v. United States*, Edith Windsor, the widow of Thea Spyer, successfully challenged Section 3 of DOMA in federal district court because, under it, she did not qualify for the unlimited marital deduction from federal estate tax and had to pay $363,053 when, "according to her last will and testament, Spyer's estate passed for Windsor's benefit."[115] Windsor and Spyer had been in a "committed relationship" since shortly after they met in 1963, and, as Spyer's health deteriorated, they married in Canada in 2007 (397).[116] Spyer died in 2009 and, after paying the estate taxes, Windsor sued in federal court, seeking a refund of the federal tax paid and a declaration that Section 3 "violates the Equal Protection Clause of the Fifth Amendment" (397). At the time they married, New York did not permit same-sex couples to marry, but by 2009, the relevant year for tax purposes, "all three statewide elected executive official[s]—the Governor, the Attorney General, and the comptroller—had endorsed the recognition" of marriages by New York same-sex couples (such as Spyer and Windsor) who validly married in other jurisdictions (398). As discussed earlier, in 2011 the New York legislature passed the Marriage Equality Act.

In 2012, the United States Court of Appeals for the Second Circuit affirmed the district court, becoming the second federal appellate court to strike down Section 3.[117] It did so applying intermediate scrutiny, the standard of review urged by the DOJ and Edith Windsor (if the court did not move all the way to strict scrutiny).[118] While the federal district court (following the First Circuit) read the Court's precedents, particularly *Romer*, to support a "more exacting rational basis review for DOMA," the Second Circuit observed that the Supreme Court "has not expressly sanctioned such modulation in the level of rational basis review," and that intermediate scrutiny was the more appropriate standard.[119]

D. Friend of the Court Briefs before the Supreme Court: Marriage, Moral Disapproval, and Religious Liberty

On December 7, 2012, the Supreme Court granted certiorari in *Windsor* and *Hollingsworth v. Perry* (the Prop 8 case). These intensely watched cases generated numerous amicus curiae briefs filed on both sides by states, members of Congress, medical and psychological organizations, bar associations, professors, individuals, and, most significantly for this chapter, religious organizations and leaders.[120] In other writing, I have analyzed these briefs.[121] In this chapter, I highlight themes in briefs filed by religious amici relevant to the relationship between civil and religious marriage and the evident conflict between marriage equality and religious liberty.

1. Arguments in Favor of DOMA and BLAG

(a) *Defending Traditional Marriage: Congruence of Civil and Religious Law*

Several amici who filed briefs in support of BLAG framed the litigation over Section 3 as improperly shifting from the democratic to the judicial arena a societal debate over what marriage is and should be. They further argued that the Constitution does not require one vision or the other and that is all the more reason "the people," not the judiciary, should decide. These arguments stress the congruence between civil and religious understandings of marriage and the importance of the polity getting marriage "right," that is, of having a truthful conception of marriage embodied in law.

Robert George, Sherif Girgis, and Ryan Anderson framed the debate over the definition of marriage as between the "*conjugal* view" of marriage as a "*comprehensive* union" of spouses "begun by commitment and sealed by sexual intercourse. . . . by which new life is made," and a "*revisionist* view," in which "marriage is essentially an emotional union, accompanied by any consensual activity" and seen "as valuable while the emotion lasts."[122] They contended that while the conjugal view "has long informed the law," the revisionist view "has informed certain marriage policy changes of the last several decades."[123] (As noted earlier in this chapter, this suggests recognition of a growing lack of congruence between civil and religious conceptions of marriage.) They warned that the consequences of striking down DOMA, which affirms the conjugal view, are serious. While prior legal developments in the direction of the revisionist view (such as liberalizing divorce law) have already undermined marriage as an institution, "[r]edefining civil marriage will obscure the true nature of marriage as a conjugal union," uniquely linked to procreation and childrearing, and, thus, undermine—rather than strengthen—marriage's "stabilizing norms," to the detriment of "spouses, children, and others."[124]

The amicus brief filed by the National Association of Evangelicals (NAE) and several other prominent religious denominations similarly framed the issue as a high-stakes debate over models of marriage.[125] They explained their interest in the litigation: "Faith communities have the deepest interest in the legal definition of marriage and in the stability and vitality of that time-honored institution" (1). The NAE brief elaborated two contrasting conceptions of marriage:

> The age-old, traditional understanding conceives of marriage as a union between a man and a woman that is inherently oriented toward procreation and childrearing and in which society has a profound stake. A more recent conception views marriage as primarily a vehicle for affirming and supporting intimate adult relationship choices, a vision that is not inherently oriented toward uniting the sexes for the bearing and rearing of children (2).

The brief further asserted that the newer conception is a "radical break from all human history," because "gender itself is irrelevant. What matters most is public endorsement of the adults' chosen relationship, obtaining official status for that relationship, and the official approval that comes with such endorsement and status" (11).

NAE further argued that Congress may act to protect a "valued moral norm" and that "many congressional enactments reflect unmistakable moral and value choices" (19). NAE also warned that "declaring DOMA void because it adheres to traditional moral and religious beliefs would fly in the face of this Court's teaching that the Constitution 'does not license government to treat religion and those who teach or practice it, simply by virtue of their status as such, as sub-versive of American ideals and therefore subject to unique disabilities' " (20).[126] NAE argued for a form of neutrality toward religion: "DOMA is entitled to be judged on its merits according to settled rules of law—not on a more demand-ing standard born of suspicion toward religion, religious believers, or their values" (21).

Amici often anchored their marriage-based arguments for DOMA to Justice O'Connor's statement, in *Lawrence*, that " 'other reasons exist to promote the institution of marriage beyond mere moral disapproval of the law.' "[127] For exam-ple, the Manhattan Declaration brief, after invoking Justice O'Connor's *Lawrence* concurrence, asserted that their position is not rooted in animus, but on "sin-cere belief and sound public policy considerations," since heterosexual mar-riage "encourages and supports responsible procreation and childrearing," and "redounds to the health and well-being of societies in general."[128] The Coalition for the Protection of Marriage similarly asserted that the "overwhelming inter-national consensus" that marriage should be reserved to "opposite-sex couples while supporting same-sex couples through other rights and legal mechanisms" was based "not on irrationality, ignorance, or animus toward gays and lesbians but on considered judgments about the unique nature and needs of same-sex couples and children."[129]

The insistence on congruence is evident in the briefs of some amici who appealed to religious and Biblical understandings of marriage in support of Section 3's preserving "traditional" marriage and warned of consequences if the civil law of marriage departs sharply from religious conceptions of marriage. Some amici resisted the very idea that civil and religious understandings of mar-riage could or should be distinct. For example, the Coalition for the Protection of Marriage asserted: "Although interacting with and influenced by other institu-tions such as law, property, and religion, marriage in our society is a distinct, uni-tary social institution and does not have two separate, independent existences, one 'civil' and one 'religious.' "[130] The Manhattan Declaration brief argued that the concept that societies give legal recognition to marriage to "encourage and support responsible procreation and childrearing" is "remarkably similar to the Christian belief that through marriage man and woman cooperate conjugally in the creative act of God Himself."[131]

Some amici also insisted that Congress could enact DOMA to defend tradi-tional notions of morality, including disapproval of homosexuality. For example, Westboro Baptist Church argued at length that homosexuality (along with adul-tery, abortion and the like) is such a serious sin that it will motivate God to pun-ish the United States by destroying it, similar to the Flood in Noah's time.[132] The Foundation for Moral Law asserted: "From Biblical law and other ancient law, through English and American common law and organic law, to recent times, homosexual conduct has been abhorred and opposed; the idea of a 'marriage' based on such conduct never even entered the legal mind until very recent times."[133] Thus, not only did "Congress's passage of the federal definition of marriage in DOMA [have] the force of that history behind it," but it also rested on "several present-day interests"—as "traditional marriage . . . began to come under attack through the courts in 1993"—such as "defending marriage and . . . traditional notions of morality."[134]

(b) *Protecting Religious Liberty and Avoiding a Clash of Rights*

Amici supporting DOMA warned that as civil laws changed their definitions of marriage, religious persons and groups adhering to traditional definitions would face threats to their religious liberty. New civil marriage laws would create a clash of rights. Thus, the Becket Fund for Religious Liberty argued that "because so many major religious groups center their teachings regarding sexual morality around opposite-sex marriage, changing the definition of marriage itself . . . trig-gers a distinct set of religious liberty concerns."[135] For example, "being forced to call a same-sex relationship a 'marriage' creates a conflict of conscience for many reli-gious organizations where 'civil union' or 'domestic partnership' would not" (29). DOMA, therefore, was a rational response to two religious liberty conflicts caused by marriage equality laws:

> *First*, objecting religious institutions and individuals will face an increased risk of lawsuits under federal, state, and local anti-discrimination laws, subjecting religious organizations to substantial civil liability if they choose to continue practicing their religious beliefs. *Second*, religious institutions and individuals will face a range of penalties from federal, state and local governments, such as denial of access to public facilities, loss of accreditation and licensing, and the targeted withdrawal of gov-ernment contracts and benefits (4).

The Becket Fund asserted that "DOMA and Prop 8 were rational responses to court decisions that gave legal recognition to same-sex marriage without addressing the significant church-state conflicts that would result" (2) from "burdens imposed by . . . supposedly neutral, generally applicable laws" (29).

This argument seems inapt as applied to *Windsor*, since New York enacted marriage equality through the legislative process and included religious exemptions.

The Christian Legal Society, joined by Catholic Answers and the Catholic Vote Education Fund, warned that classifying homosexuals as a suspect or quasi-suspect class would compromise religious liberties, and "necessarily diminish the ability of our nation's religious individuals and communities to live according to their faith."[136] If the Court created a "new suspect classification for sexual orientation," it would "take sides" in an already "broad and intense conflict between the gay rights movement and religious liberty regarding marriage, family, and sexual behavior" and "place millions of religious believers and organizations at a potentially irreversible disadvantage in their efforts to consistently live out their faith."[137]

The Chaplain Alliance for Religious Liberty asserted that repealing DOMA would impair "military religious liberty," since "it is very likely that service members who hold traditional religious beliefs on marriage and family will face, for the first time, military policies and duties that sharply [*sic*] hostile to their beliefs."[138] The brief predicted that chaplains and service members who belonged to "faith groups that support traditional marriage" would face a stark, forced choice between "their duty to obey God" and "their chosen vocation of serving their country" if laws "affirming marriage as the union of one man and one woman are invalidated as irrational and unconstitutional."[139]

Other amici warned that a civil regime recognizing same-sex marriage would create a new governmental orthodoxy at odds with religious liberty. For example, the Manhattan Declaration brief asserted that "redefining marriage imperils religious liberty and oftentimes requires that freedom of conscience be sacrificed to the newly regnant orthodoxy."[140] A new marriage regime that recognized same-sex marriage would "circumscribe[] the ability of the Christian faithful to put their beliefs into practice" (15). The brief included various examples, such as Christian adoption agencies shutting down because of their refusal to place children with same-sex couples, religious parents' inability to remove their children from public school classes advocating marriage equality, and Christian organizations having to end all medical insurance for employees' spouses because they do not want to cover same-sex spouses (15–19). The brief further contended that Christians would be limited in how they could educate their children (17).

Some religious amici contended that their religious objections to same-sex marriage were not animus and that for government to fail to give credence to those objections infringed upon their religious liberty. For example, the Liberty, Life and Law Foundation and North Carolina Values Coalition warned that marriage equality would infringe upon the "moral code of behavior" typical of religions, including the regulation of sexual conduct, with the result that "[a] state mandate to affirm same-sex marriage would have an explosive impact on religious persons who could easily treat all individuals with equal respect and dignity but cannot in good conscience endorse or facilitate same-sex marriage."[141] The Foundation further argued that "[a] person's religiously motivated refusal to recognize same-sex unions is not tantamount to unlawful discrimination, nor is it irrational animosity," and that, "[t]o hold otherwise would exhibit callous disregard for religion."[142] The evident logic of the Foundation's argument is that the Constitution protects religious beliefs and conduct, and, thus, morality based on religion provides a valid rationale for opposing same-sex marriage. The Foundation analogized to case law crediting conscientious religious beliefs in other contexts, concluding: "[t]he government must avoid showing hostility to religion by refusing to acknowledge religious motivation."[143]

2. Arguments for Windsor's Challenge to DOMA

Some religious amici filing in support of Windsor emphasized the distinction between civil and religious marriage and that redefining the former did not unconstitutionally burden the latter. They further pointed out that religious exemptions were a means of ensuring religious liberty. For example, the brief submitted by the Bishops of the Episcopal Church in California, New York, and several other states, the Jewish Theological Seminary, and numerous other religious groups noted a growing affirmation by religious faiths of the "dignity" of same-sex relationships and family life:

> The American religious panorama embraces a multitude of theological perspectives on lesbian and gay people and same-sex relationships. A vast range of religious perspectives affirms the inherent dignity of lesbian and gay people, their relationships, and their families. This affirmation reflects the deeply rooted belief, common to many faiths, in the essential worth of all individuals and, more particularly, the growing respect accorded within theological traditions to same-sex couples.[144]

The brief insists on the constitutional importance of the distinction between civil and religious marriage:

> Certain *amici* supporting reversal have argued that civil recognition for the marriages of same-sex couples would alter a longstanding "Christian" definition of "marriage." But this and other religiously based arguments for limiting civil recognition of marriage to different-sex couples cannot constitutionally be given weight by this Court.

Crediting such arguments would improperly both enshrine a particular religious belief in the law—itself prohibited under the Establishment Clause—and implicitly privilege religious viewpoints that oppose marriage equality over those that favor it (5).

The brief then argues that "[e]liminating discrimination in civil marriage will not impinge upon religious doctrine or practice," since "[a]ll religions would remain free—as they are today with nine states and the District of Columbia permitting same-sex couples to marry—to define *religious* marriage in any way they choose" (4). The brief first points out that "[t]he types of conflicts forecast by certain other *amici* already can and sometimes do arise under public accommodation laws whenever religiously affiliated organizations operate in the commercial or governmental spheres," and "[c]ourts know how to respond if enforcement of civil rights laws overreaches to infringe First Amendment rights" (4). "In any event," the brief concluded, "the issue largely is irrelevant here, because the couples affected by [DOMA] already are lawfully married under state law" (4).

Other amici stressed that, under the Establishment Clause, religious groups do not have "the right to have their religious views written into law so that others may be compelled to follow them."[145] Addressing claims by amici that "their 'religious liberty' . . . would be violated if this Court confirms a right to legal equality for gays and lesbians," because of "their Bible's condemnation of homosexuality," the American Humanist Association asserted that, "[b]ecause the First Amendment forbids, rather than requires, any law solely grounded in or codifying a religious 'moral' commandment, such objections can be accorded no weight."[146]

Other amici stressed the insufficiency of moral disapproval, even if rooted in religious belief. Thus, the Anti-Defamation League acknowledged the importance of religion in American life and that religious beliefs undoubtedly guided many lawmakers. It explained, however, that, "under a line of cases including this Court's decision in *Lawrence v. Texas*, a law must be rationally related to a legitimate government interest beyond the desire to disadvantage a group on the basis of moral disapproval."[147]

Some amici emphasized the civil nature of marriage law to assert that "the humanity of gay citizens can be reconciled with respect for religious freedom."[148] Utah Pride and many other statewide equality organizations contended: "the Constitution guarantees both the right of gay people to be treated as equals under civil law and the right of individuals and organizations to hold beliefs about homosexuality in accordance with their own consciences."[149] Appealing to the "secular context" and the "importance of neutrality," Utah Pride asserted that, "by affirming that all people—whether gay or straight—are entitled to equal treatment under the Constitution, this Court can unify the country around our shared values of liberty and justice for all."[150]

The American Jewish Committee (AJC) supported the state's authority to redefine civil marriage, but urged that broad protections of religious liberty were necessary if the state did so.[151] It voiced concerns similar to some amici *supporting* DOMA, "agree[ing] that significant religious liberty issues will follow in the wake of same-sex civil marriage" (10). It urged, however, that the issues could be remedied if "each claim to liberty in our system . . . [is] defined in a way that is consistent with the equal and sometimes conflicting liberty of others" (11). Thus, there would be "no burden on religious exercise when the state recognizes someone else's civil marriage," but there would be if "the state demands that religious organizations or believers recognize or facilitate a marriage in ways that violate their religious commitments" (3). The AJC saw parallels between the gay rights movement and its own assertion of the need for religious liberties:

> Both same-sex couples and religious dissenters also seek to live out their identities in ways that are public in the sense of being socially apparent and socially acknowledged . . . Religious believers . . . claim a right to follow their faith not just in worship services, but in charitable services provided through their religious organizations and in their daily lives (15).

As did some religious amici supporting BLAG, the AJC identified a variety of situations in which religious liberty might be compromised, including marriage counseling by clergy and housing in religious colleges (23–25). As one way to address these conflicts, the AJC also proposed that the Court reconsider its controversial (5-4) decision *Employment Division v. Smith* (1990), so that religious actors would be exempt from generally applicable laws that infringe on their freedoms unless application of the statute can survive heightened scrutiny (32–34). In my conclusion, I will return to this conflicting liberty framework, which views exemptions as a way to accommodate the liberty at stake on both sides.

E. *United States v. Windsor:* Justice Kennedy Completes a New Trio

On June 26, 2013, the Supreme Court announced its ruling in *United States v. Windsor.* In a 5-4 split, the majority, in an opinion authored by Justice Kennedy, held that Section 3 of DOMA was an unconstitutional deprivation of liberty of the person protected by the Fifth Amendment of the Constitution. The opinion was quickly hailed as a landmark by some and decried as judicial overreaching by others. Justice Kennedy said nothing explicit about the various religious liberty arguments made by amici, but he did discuss the role of moral disapproval. *Romer* and *Lawrence* provided a template for his opinion. *Windsor* joined those two cases to make a trio of landmark rulings by the Court, all authored by Justice Kennedy, about the status of gay men and lesbians. His majority opinion struck down Section 3 without moving to the intermediate scrutiny urged by the DOJ and the Second Circuit and instead confirmed—as the district court in *Windsor* and the First Circuit discerned—that *Romer* supports a more searching form of rational basis review when there are "discriminations of an unusual character."

In explaining the injury that Section 3 inflicts, Justice Kennedy contrasts New York's attempt to confer dignity and respect on a class by changing its marriage laws to allow same-sex couples to marry (and, prior to that, recognizing Edith Windsor's out-of-state marriage) with DOMA's denial of such dignity and respect. Indeed, Justice Kennedy concludes that "interference with the equal dignity of same-sex marriages, . . . conferred by the States in the exercise of their sovereign power" was DOMA's "essence."[152] In support of this conclusion, he cites the House Report, which appeals to defending "the institution of traditional heterosexual marriage" and states that "DOMA expresses 'both moral disapproval of homosexuality and a moral conviction that heterosexuality better comports with traditional (especially Judeo-Christian) morality'" (2693).[153] Citing *Romer* on the need for attentiveness to "discriminations of an unusual character," the majority states that DOMA's "unusual deviation from the usual tradition of recognizing and accepting state definitions of marriage" is "strong evidence of a law having the purpose and effect of disapproval of that class" (2693). Section 3's "avowed purpose and practical effect" are "to impose a disadvantage, a separate status, and so a stigma" on same-sex couples lawfully married under the "unquestioned authority of the States" (2693).

Justice Kennedy concludes that BLAG's arguments "are just as candid about the congressional purpose to influence or interfere with state sovereign choices about who may be married" (2693). Moreover, Section 3's constitutionally problematic purpose was to treat "as second-class marriages for purposes of federal law" any same-sex marriages that states decided to recognize (2693–2694). By contrast to the lower courts in *Windsor*, Justice Kennedy does not mention, let alone evaluate, rationales such as "caution," consistency and uniformity of benefits, and responsible procreation and optimal childrearing. He emphasizes a different aspect of uniformity that DOMA rejects: "the long-established precept that the incidents, benefits, and obligations of marriage are uniform for all married couples within each State, though they may vary, subject to constitutional guarantees, from one State to the next" (2692).

Evaluating DOMA's effect, Justice Kennedy stresses its sweep: it controls "over 1,000 statutes and numerous federal regulations" (2694). Given this broad scope of federal regulations bearing on marriage, "DOMA touches many aspects of married and family life, from the mundane to the profound" (2694). Articulating an aspect of marriage that I have elaborated elsewhere, the opinion explains that marriage entails rights *and responsibilities*, both of which "enhance the dignity and integrity of the person" (2694).[154] Yet DOMA deprives same-sex couples lawfully married under state law of such "rights and responsibilities" (2694). DOMA's creation of "two contradictory marriage regimes within the same State" diminishes "the stability and predictability of basic personal relations the State has found it proper to acknowledge and protect," and tells those same-sex couples that "their otherwise valid marriages are unworthy of federal recognition" (2694). Without explicitly addressing whether such couples have a federal constitutional right to marry, Justice Kennedy appeals to *Lawrence*: "the differentiation demeans the couple, whose moral and sexual choices the Constitution protects ... and whose relationship the State has sought to dignify" (2694).[155] Several times, Justice Kennedy repeats that DOMA "demeans" persons in "a lawful same-sex marriage" (2695). In a passage frequently quoted in post-*Windsor* federal challenges to state laws, he states that DOMA also "humiliates tens of thousands of children now being raised by same-sex couples" (2695). He concludes: "The federal statute is invalid, for no legitimate purpose overcomes the purpose and effect to disparage and to injure those whom the State by its marriage laws, sought to protect in personhood and dignity" (2696). In a sentence that receives much parsing in the dissents, he further adds: "This opinion and its holding are confined to those lawful marriages" (2696).

F. The *Windsor* Dissents: Taking Sides and Branding
Defenders of Traditional Marriage "Bigots"

The dissenting justices in *Windsor* did not explicitly address arguments made about the threat to religious liberty by striking down Section 3 of DOMA. They did, nonetheless, criticize the majority in language that has fueled further warning by religious leaders about threat to religious liberty if definitions of civil marriage change. In dissent, Justice Alito argued that Edith Windsor was asking the Court to "intervene" in a debate about the nature of marriage—namely, between the "conjugal" view and the "consent-based view." The Constitution, he insisted, said nothing about the matter, and so it should be left to "the people." While he did not cite to any specific amicus briefs for these models, he referred to George, Girgis, and Anderson's book, *What Is Marriage?* (mentioned earlier) for a "philosophical" account of the basis for the "conjugal" view (2718–2719). Justice Alito warned that analogizing the one man–one woman requirement for marriage to race or sex discrimination would "cast all those who cling to traditional beliefs about the nature of marriage in the role of bigots or superstitious fools" (2717–2718).

In dissent, Chief Justice Roberts asserted that "without some more convincing evidence that the Act's principal motive was to codify malice, and that it furthered no legitimate governmental interests, I would not tar the political branches with the brush of bigotry" (2696). Justice Scalia deployed the strongest language, arguing that, instead of letting "the People decide" the marriage debate, the Court had armed one side, and branded DOMA's supporters as "enemies of the human race," "enem[ies] of human decency," "members of a wild-eyed lynch mob," who had "hateful hearts," and "acted with *malice*" (2708–2710). He used racially inflected rhetoric, evident not only in the "lynch mob" reference, but also in suggesting the majority's inappropriate "condemnation" of Congress's motive in enacting DOMA was akin to the Courts' "scorn" directed at "the legislature of some once-Confederate Southern state" (2707).

Justice Scalia also reiterated his view stated in dissent in *Lawrence* that "the Constitution does not forbid the government to enforce traditional moral and sexual norms"; thus, moral disapproval was certainly a sufficient basis for DOMA, since the Constitution neither required nor forbade approval of same-sex marriage (2707). Finally, expressing disbelief at the majority's statement that the Court's opinion and holding were "confined to those lawful marriages," that is, marriages permitted or recognized under state law but denied federal recognition, Justice Scalia countered that the majority opinion, with a few simple alterations, provided a template that those challenging state marriage laws could easily use to assert that those state laws, like DOMA, were also motived by the "bare . . . desire to harm" (2709–2710).

As readers of this chapter may know, Scalia has proven to be correct on the frequent invocation of *Windsor*—including his dissent—by federal courts striking down state marriage laws, although not all courts have gone the route of animus or harm as a basis for such a ruling. Subsequent to *Windsor*, the focus is acute on characterizing the position of defending the one man–one woman definition of marriage and on whether and how motivation even matters. Some legal commentators, for example, charge the *Windsor* majority with engaging in a "jurisprudence of denigration" that attributes "malevolence" to Congress and—by implication—to the "millions of Americans" who support state laws defending traditional marriage and that "peremptorily dismisses and marginalizes" the losers in the controversy over marriage "with unsubstantiated (and in their own knowledge false) charges of hatefulnesses."[156]

The *Obergefell* dissents, as noted earlier, echo the *Windsor* dissents in using the rhetoric of bigotry to warn of threats to religious liberty. They do so even though Justice Kennedy seemingly avoided a "jurisprudence of denigration" by emphasizing that "[m]any who deem same-sex marriage to be wrong reach that

conclusion based on decent and honorable religious or philosophical premises, and neither they nor their beliefs are disparaged here."[157] Thus, dissenting Chief Justice Roberts charges that Justice Kennedy's majority opinion
portrays any who do not "share" the Court's evolved "understanding" that the
fundamental right to marry extends to same-sex couples as "bigoted" (2626).
Justice Scalia's dissent characterizes the majority as contending that the age-
old one man–one woman definition of marriage "cannot possibly be supported
by anything other than ignorance or bigotry" (2630). Justice Alito warns that,
despite the majority's "reassurances" about protecting conscience, those who
dissent publicly from the new "orthodoxy" will "risk being labeled as such and
treated as such by governments, employers, and schools" (2642–2643). It is
beyond the scope of this chapter to offer a full analysis of how the *Obergefell*
opinion and the several dissents address the evident clash between the fundamental right to marry and religious liberty. A critical point for this chapter is
simply that Justice Kennedy follows the above statement about the sincerity of
those who oppose marriage by same-sex couples with a caveat about translat-
ing those beliefs into civil laws that exclude such couples from the public institution of marriage. It is not the religious beliefs themselves but the unequal
treatment by the state based on such beliefs that offends the Constitution. As
Justice Kennedy explains:

> [W]hen that sincere, personal opposition becomes enacted law and
> public policy, the necessary consequence is to put the imprimatur of
> the State itself on an exclusion that soon demeans or stigmatizes those
> whose own liberty is then denied. Under the Constitution, same-sex
> couples seek in marriage the same legal treatment as opposite-sex cou-
> ples, and it would disparage their choices and diminish their person-
> hood to deny them this right (2602).[158]

In stressing the harm that comes from exclusion, Justice Kennedy emphasizes
marriage as a great *public* institution," a uniquely important "two-person union"
that the states and the federal government support by attaching to it "an expanding list of governmental rights, benefits, and responsibilities" (2601).

IV. The Fate of Prop 8 in *Perry v. Schwarzenegger*

My third example is the claim that *Perry v. Schwarzenegger*, a federal district court
ruling that Prop 8 (a ballot initiative that amended the California constitution
to enshrine the one man–one woman definition of marriage) violates the federal
constitution, threatens religious liberty, and precludes religious citizens from

bringing their beliefs into the public square. A procedural note will be help-ful: In *Perry v. Brown*, the Ninth Circuit affirmed the federal district court, draw-ing more criticism from religious leaders. The Supreme Court granted review of the Ninth Circuit's ruling, but ultimately, in the much-anticipated decision of *Hollingsworth v. Perry* (2013), declined to reach the merits of whether Prop 8 offended the federal constitution; instead, it concluded that Prop 8's proponents were private parties who lacked standing (under Article III) to appeal the federal district court opinion and vacated the Ninth Circuit opinion.[159] The impact of *Hollingsworth* was to leave the lower federal court ruling intact. Notably, Justice Kennedy (a Californian), in dissent, did not say how he would have resolved the case on the merits, but he strongly disagreed with the majority's ruling on standing, arguing that "the very object of the initiative system is to establish a law-making process that does not depend upon state officials."[160] Shortly after the Court issued its opinion, California state officials resumed issuing marriage licenses to same-sex couples.

All three of my frameworks inform my analysis of *Perry*.

A. The Enactment of Prop 8

What led to Prop 8 and the constitutional challenge to it? In 1999, California became the first state to enact a domestic partnership law. By referendum in a 2000 election, California voters adopted Prop 22, which provides that "[o]nly marriage between a man and a woman is valid or recognized in California."[161] The California legislature steadily expanded California's domestic partnership law, in the face of Prop 22, culminating in the Domestic Partner Rights and Responsibilities Act of 2003.[162] Beginning in 2005, when the Act took effect, domestic partners had nearly all the legal incidents of civil marriage, without the name.

In re Marriage Cases (2008) decided the question of whether, under California's constitution, the state must provide same-sex couples with access to civil *marriage*. In a lengthy opinion, the California Supreme Court concluded that (1) the fundamental right to marry protected by the state constitution's due process clause includes the right to marry a person of the same sex and (2) reserving the status of marriage for heterosexuals, while limiting gays and lesbians to the second-class domestic partnership status, constitutes unconstitu-tional discrimination on the basis of sexual orientation in violation of the state constitution's equal protection clause.[163] The court ruled that denying same-sex couples official recognition of their intimate, committed relationships as mar-riages denied them equal dignity and respect.[164]

Instead of resolving the matter, the high court's opinion was a catalyst for the campaign for Prop 8, a ballot initiative to amend California's constitution by defining marriage as the union of one man and one woman.[165] Money poured

into California from outside the state on both sides of the issue. Religious organizations mobilized to support the ballot initiative. An instructive example is the
Church of Jesus Christ of Latter-day Saints, where leaders called upon Mormons
to donate time and money to the campaign.[166] "During the 2008 election sea-
son," the First Presidency of the Church issued a statement "to be read by bishops over the pulpit in California wards,"[167] which explained:

> The Church will participate with this coalition in seeking [the initia-
> tive's] passage. Local Church leaders will provide information about
> how you may become involved in this important cause. We ask that you
> do all you can to support the proposed constitutional amendment by
> donating of your means and times to assure that marriage in California
> is legally defined as being between a man and a woman. Our best efforts
> are required to preserve the sacred institution of marriage.[168]

   This move by religious leaders, as Robert Putnam and David Campbell put
it, to "draw a clear connection between theology and politics, and then issue a
directive to congregant, was exceptional and almost wholly unexpected, according to many Mormons."[169] Nonetheless, given that "the preservation of the traditional family is a major focus of modern Mormonism," the surprise was not the
church's "stance" on Prop 8, but "how explicit and official that stance became."[170]
I offer this anecdote because it suggests the high stakes that religious groups perceived in Prop 8, and the quoted appeal reflects a view of a necessary congruence
between civil and religious marriage.

B. *Perry v. Schwarzenegger*: The Inadequacy of Private Moral Views as a Basis for Prop 8

When "super lawyer" team David Boies and Ted Olsen challenged Prop 8 in
federal district court on behalf of same-sex couples, they submitted extensive
expert testimony and documentary evidence during a lengthy trial. The State
of California declined to defend Prop 8 in court, and the Supreme Court of
California advised that the proponents of Prop 8 were allowed to defend it. They
put on only a few witnesses. Following the trial, Chief Judge Vaughn Walker
issued a lengthy opinion, concluding that Prop 8 violated the Due Process
Clause and the Equal Protection Clause of the US Constitution.[171] His opinion
contains many findings of fact, citing to specific evidence, in support of his conclusions of law (see 953–991, 993).
   Most pertinent to this chapter are (1) Judge Walker's findings about the role
of religious views about homosexuality in the campaign for Prop 8 and (2) his
legal conclusion that a "private moral view that same-sex couples are inferior

to opposite-sex couples" is "not a proper basis" (1002) for Prop 8's restricting same-sex couples from access to civil marriage. On the first point, Walker invoked testimony by expert witness Segura, who "identified religion as the chief obstacle to gay and lesbian political progress" (985) and noted the "sheer breadth" (955) of the coalition of religious groups forming the basis of Protect Marriage (the group seeking to pass Prop 8). The Prop 8 proponents' own expert witness Paul Nathanson, who was deposed but did not testify, stated that "religion lies at the heart of the hostility and violence directed at gays and lesbians" (945). Segura noted that Katherine Young, a second expert for the Prop 8 proponents who, again, was deposed but did not testify, "freely admits that religious hostility to homosexuals plays an important role in creating a social climate that's conducive to hateful acts, to opposition to their interest in the public sphere and to prejudice and discrimination" (986, paragraph 77[q]). In support of his findings that religious opposition to homosexuality fueled the Prop 8 campaign, Walker cited an advertisement, which asserted that "the 98% of Californians who are not gay should not have their religious freedoms and freedom of expression be compromised to afford special legal rights for the 2% of Californians who are gay."[172]

Turning to my second point, Walker found that the evidence shows conclusively that "Prop 8 enacts a moral view that there is something 'wrong' with same-sex couples."[173] The campaign, Walker found, appealed to the moral superiority of opposite-sex couples. By contrast, in litigation, the Prop 8 proponents reframed their arguments because, he infers, they recognized that Prop 8 "must advance a secular purpose to be constitutional" (931). Citing *Lawrence*, he stated that "the state does not have an interest in enforcing private moral or religious beliefs without an accompanying secular purpose" (930–931). In the litigation, proponents defended Prop 8 on these four grounds:

1. Maintains California's definition of marriage as excluding same-sex couples;
2. Affirms the will of California citizens to exclude same-sex couples from marriage;
3. Promotes stability in relationships between a man and a woman because they naturally (and at times unintentionally) produce children; and
4. Promotes "statistically optimal" child-rearing households; that is, households in which children are raised by a man and a woman married to each other (931).

The third argument is the responsible procreation argument, so central to other attempts to defend state marriage laws (including in *Obergefell*) as well as DOMA (as discussed earlier in this chapter).[174] The optimal childrearing argument also featured in the campaign.

In assessing these arguments, Walker asked "whether any evidence supports California's refusal to recognize marriage between two people because of their sex" and "whether any evidence shows California has an interest in differentiating between same-sex and opposite-sex unions."[175] To both of these questions, based on extensive testimony and documentary evidence, he answered no: same-sex and opposite-sex couples were similarly situated with respect to California's interest in encouraging stable households and optimal child-rearing. Thus, with those possible bases for Prop 8 ruled out, he framed the remaining legal question: "whether the evidence shows Proposition 8 enacted a private moral view without advancing a legitimate government interest" (932, 936, 973). His answer to and analysis of this final question generated intense criticism by religious leaders for its approach to the role of religion in public life and, in particular, in controversies over marriage.

What does Judge Walker mean by a "private moral view"? How does he distinguish between a private moral view and legitimate governmental interest? I will first focus on his evaluation of the irrelevance of gender to marriage and child well-being and then turn to his lengthy focus on the campaign for Prop 8.

First, Walker reasons that the conviction that marriage must be between one man and one woman turns on notions of gender complementarity rooted in religious views. Thus, "Prop 8 amends the California Constitution to codify distinct and unique roles for men and women in marriage" (975). Walker cites statements by Prop 8 supporters, contained in voter kits about God as the author of gender difference and gender complementarity (975, paragraph 61). Are such appeals as such out of bounds in the democratic process? The bigger problem, I believe, is that this message does not fit California's marriage law, which had "eliminated all legally-mandated gender roles except the requirement that marriage consist of one man and one woman" (998). The court bluntly states: "the evidence shows" that the gender restriction that Prop 8 now "enshrines in the California Constitution" is "nothing more than an artifact of a foregone notion that men and women fulfill different roles in civic life" (998).

Second, the irrelevance of gender to child well-being is central to Walker's conclusion that Prop 8 rests only on a private moral view. The court makes several affirmative findings about the factors contributing to child well-being, declaring that "the gender of a child's parent is not a factor in a child's adjustment," that "children do not need to be raised by a male parent and a female parent to be well-adjusted," and that "having both a male and a female parent does not increase the likelihood that a child will be well-adjusted" (980–981). He observes that California law supports parenthood by gay men and lesbians. His implicit argument is that while Prop 8 proponents assert, based on personal and religious beliefs, that children need a mother and father, with distinct gender roles, in order for children to flourish, neither social science literature nor California's law of parentage supports this belief. Therefore, it cannot be a legitimate interest for California to restrict marriage premised on a view about gender complementarity as a precondition for optimal child adjustment.

Third, he turns to the role of religion in the campaign and to the substance of the campaign messages themselves. Religious critics charge that Walker impugned the motives of California voters. Instead, Walker focuses on the role of religious beliefs about homosexuality in proposing and campaigning for Prop 8, that is, the public messages, not voters' private motives. First, he finds: "Religious beliefs that gay and lesbian relationships are sinful or inferior to heterosexual relationships harm gays and lesbians" (985). In support, he appeals both to deposition testimony by Prop 8 proponents' experts as to the history of religious prejudice against gay men and lesbians and its role in homophobia and prejudice, as well as to many doctrinal statements by religious traditions about homosexuality as a sin (e.g., that homosexual behavior is "a perversion of God's created order" and "a distortion of the image of God") (985–987, paragraph 77).

The court relates the historical role of "stereotypes and misinformation" about gays and lesbians in bringing about social and legal disadvantages. Walker cites expert testimony noting parallels between historical campaigns against gay rights and the campaign for Prop 8 (986–991). Experts for plaintiffs testified about the difficulty of making progress in the legislative process if a group is "envisioned as being somehow . . . morally inferior, a threat to children, a threat to freedom" (987, paragraph 78[h]). The Prop 8 campaign, the court repeats, "relied on stereotypes to show that same-sex relationships are inferior to opposite-sex relationships" (990, paragraph 80). He identifies messages about the lesser value of same-sex relationships, the lack of similarity between same-sex and opposite-sex couples, and that the former "do not deserve the full recognition of society." This, he says, is Prop 8's "social meaning." Prop 8 "places the force of law behind stigmas behind gays and lesbians" (973, paragraph 58) and "reserves the most socially valued form of relationship (marriage) for opposite-sex couples" (974, paragraph 60).

Prop 8 relied especially on "fears that children exposed to the concept of same-sex marriage may become gay or lesbian" (988, paragraph 79) and that public schools would instruct children about same-sex marriage, including the idea that it is okay to think about marrying someone of the same sex (988–991). Notably, some of the campaign rhetoric appealed to "tolerance" for the gay community, but drew the line at "acceptance"—allowing that community to redefine marriage for everyone else (988–989). Evidence showed that Prop 8 supporters decided that a potent campaign message would be on "how this

new 'fundamental right' would be inculcated in young children throughout
public schools" (988, paragraph 79[d]). As Richard Garnett makes clear in this
volume, determining what "tolerance" requires in a pluralistic polity is critical
in areas where rights may collide.[176] "Tolerance" as used in the Prop 8 campaign means not criminalizing private sexual conduct and perhaps even allowing domestic partnerships; it does not require official recognition of same-sex
relationships as marriages. The latter, in other words, is forced acceptance and
also a forced redefinition at odds with peoples' religious understandings of
marriage.

The court's extensive findings about the basic similarities between opposite-
sex and same-sex couples lead it to reject the Prop 8 proponents' argument that
the amendment advances a state's interest in treating same-sex couples and
opposite-sex couples differently by "using different names for different things."
The court reasons about the role of moral and religious views:

> [P]roponents assume a premise that the evidence thoroughly rebut-
> ted: rather than being different, same-sex and opposite-sex unions are,
> for all purposes relevant to California law, exactly the same . . . The evi-
> dence shows conclusively that moral and religious views form the only
> basis for a belief that same-sex couples are different from opposite-sex
> couples. . . . The evidence fatally undermines any purported state inter-
> est in treating couples differently; thus, these interests do not provide a
> rational basis supporting Proposition 8.[177]

The court then states an emphatic conclusion about the basic equality, and
perhaps Michael Sandel would say, equal moral worth, of same-sex couples:

> Many of the purported interests identified by proponents are nothing
> more than a fear or unarticulated dislike of same-sex couples . . . The
> evidence shows that, by every available metric, opposite-sex couples
> are not better than their same-sex counterparts; instead, as partners,
> parents, and citizens, opposite-sex couples and same-sex couples are
> equal . . . Proposition 8 violates the Equal Protection clause because it
> does not treat them equally (1002).

Note that this conclusion about sameness—equal worth—is rooted in an
evidentiary showing, an assessment of "metrics." This form of argument is that,
as we assess how these couples compare with respect to the purposes or goods
of marriage—intimate commitment, responsible parenting, and household
stability—we find that they are identical.

Finally, in his legal conclusions, Walker relies on *Romer* and *Lawrence* on the role of moral disapproval, stating: "a private moral view that same-sex couples are inferior to opposite-sex couples is not a proper basis for legislation." Again, he marshals evidence supporting the inference that "Proposition 8 was premised on the belief that same-sex couples simply are not as good as opposite-sex couples" (1002). He explains:

> Whether that belief [about comparative goodness] is based on moral disapproval of homosexuality, animus toward gay and lesbians or simply a belief that a relationship between a man and a woman is inherently better than a relationship between two men or two women, this belief is not a proper basis on which to legislate (1002).

In this passage, it bears emphasizing, Walker uses moral disapproval and animus *as alternative bases* for the problematic belief: they need not both be present; either is a constitutionally insufficient basis for Prop 8.

In support of his conclusion about animus, Walker cites *Romer*, where the Supreme Court said of Colorado's Amendment 2: "Laws of the kind now before us raise the inevitable inference that the disadvantage imposed is born of animosity toward the class of persons affected" (1003).[178] He also cites (as did Holder) to *Palmore*'s famous statement that, "The constitution cannot control [private biases] but neither can it tolerate them" (1003).[179]

On the moral disapproval point, Judge Walker analogizes to *Lawrence*, where, he notes, the Supreme Court asked "whether a majority of citizens could use the power of the state to enforce 'profound and deep convictions accepted as ethical and moral principles' through the criminal code." Here, Walker reasons, "the question is whether California voters can enforce those same principles through regulation of marriage licenses. They cannot." The court further appropriates *Lawrence:* "California's obligation is to treat its citizens equally, not to 'mandate its own moral code.'" Walker continues, citing Justice O'Connor's concurrence in *Lawrence:* "'Moral disapproval, without any other asserted state interest,' has never been a rational basis for legislation." Further invoking Supreme Court precedents, the court reiterates: "Tradition alone cannot support legislation" (1002).

In conclusion, the *Perry* court's rejection of private moral views is premised on an understanding of these moral views as, ultimately, based on animosity *or* moral disapproval without any other supporting reason. Far from offering such a reason, proponents of Prop 8 simply could not or did not counter the extensive evidence about the ways in which same-sex and opposite-sex couples are identical in the ways relevant to the state's regulation of marriage.

C. The Ninth Circuit's Affirmance: Mere
Disapproval Is Not Enough

Although the Supreme Court vacated the Ninth Circuit's affirmance due to a lack of standing by the Prop 8 proponents to appeal Judge Walker's ruling, it is useful to mention briefly the counterpart, in the Ninth Circuit opinion, to Judge Walker's discussion of the constitutional insufficiency of "private moral views" as the basis for Prop 8. This aspect of its opinion bears directly on the issue of religious freedom versus equality and the role of moral disapproval.

In evaluating possible rationales for Prop 8, the Ninth Circuit considers the desire to "restore[] the traditional definition of marriage as referring to a union between man and a woman."[180] This appeal to maintaining the traditional definition of marriage was made, for example, in the amicus brief filed by the USCCB and other religious groups. That brief argued that voters had many legitimate secular reasons for supporting the law and that even the religious reasons were not born of animus or hostility toward homosexuals, but of theological convictions about the nature and purpose of marriage. However, the Ninth Circuit cites *Romer* to dispose of the appeal to tradition: "tradition alone is not a justification for *taking away* a right that had already been granted, even though that grant was in derogation of tradition" (1092, emphasis in original). Amendment 2 "could not be justified on the basis that it simply repealed positive law and restored the 'traditional' state of affairs" (1092). The court also invokes *Lawrence* and *Loving v. Virginia*: "The fact that the government majority in a State has traditionally viewed a practice as immoral is not a sufficient reason for upholding a law prohibiting the practice; neither history nor tradition could save a law prohibiting miscegenation from constitutional attack" (1093).[181]

Religious opponents of same-sex marriage loathe this kind of invocation of *Loving*, arguing that it wrongly analogizes their stance to racial bigotry. However, the court's point is that history and tradition alone are not enough to justify stripping same-sex couples of the right to marry. In *Windsor*, Kennedy stated that "state laws defining and regulating marriage, of course, must respect the constitutional rights of persons," citing *Loving*. Numerous federal courts, ruling post-*Windsor* in favor of constitutional challenges to state marriage laws, have viewed Kennedy's invocation of *Loving* as a "disclaimer of enormous proportion." In such jurisprudence, *Loving* not only serves as a vital precedent for the fundamental right to marry, which includes the freedom to marry a person of one's choice, but also signals heightened scrutiny for evaluating restrictions on that right. [182]

The Ninth Circuit concluded that Prop 8 enacted "nothing more or less than a judgment about the worth and dignity of gays and lesbians as a class" (1094). It assessed the campaign for Prop 8 differently than did the USCCB brief, drawing on the district court's finding that stereotypes about the inferiority of same-sex relationships featured prominently in the campaign for Prop 8. For instance, the district court found that Prop 8 was motivated out of a "concern that people of faith and religious groups would somehow be harmed by the recognition of gay marriage" and "conveyed a message that gay people and relationships are inferior, that homosexuality is undesirable and that children need to be protected from exposure to gay people and their relationships" (1094).

In an analogue to Judge Walker's reference to a "private moral view," the Ninth Circuit concluded the Prop 8 violated the Equal Protection Clause because it "operates with no apparent purpose but to impose on gays and lesbians, through the public law, a majority's private disapproval of them and their relationships, by taking away from them the official designation of 'marriage,' with its societally recognized status. Prop 8 therefore violates the Equal Protection Clause" (1095). The district and appellate courts did not find persuasive the arguments that Prop 8's proponents and amici made that there *were* legitimate ends served by Prop 8. It is critical to appreciate that California had taken a step toward equality with respect to the family life of gay men and lesbians—according them, under domestic partnership law, the same benefits and obligations accorded spouses under civil marriage, rendering appeals to responsible procreation and optimal childrearing unpersuasive. In light of these developments in family law and the messages of the Prop 8 campaign, neither court found persuasive arguments for singling out this class and stripping away one right—to use the name "marriage"—for a relationship otherwise treated like marriage for nearly all purposes of state law.

Conclusion

In this chapter, I have offered three frameworks that may be helpful in evaluating claims that access by same-sex couples to civil marriage in the United States threatens religious liberty: congruence and conflict with respect to the relationship between civil society and government; the relationship between civil and religious marriage; and the role of moral disapproval as a basis for law. Although a way forward may be challenging, it is important to find a way to achieve a mutual adjustment of equal basic liberties. In this regard, it is notable that the Mormon Church, so prominent in the campaign against Prop 8, recently came out in support of anti-discrimination laws for lesbian, gay, bisexual, and transgender (LGBT) persons, so long as such laws protect the rights of religious groups.[183] Even so, recent controversies over efforts to pass state religious freedom restoration acts to protect business owners suggest that even religiously motivated refusals to serve customers seem uncomfortably like forms of discrimination rejected as part of an unjust past. On the one hand, defenders of religious liberty strenuously reject historical comparisons to objections to interracial marriage and to public accommodations laws that would bar racial discrimination in providing goods and services. They urge that robust accommodation of religious conscience and exemption from anti-discrimination laws are an appropriate concession to "surrender" by opponents of same-sex marriage.[184] On the other, when exemptions would reach beyond nonprofit religious institutions to for profit businesses owned by religious persons, some critics insist that such exemptions remind us uncomfortably of past forms of discrimination in the public sphere and that present-day civil rights law cannot allow such selective refusals.[185]

As this chapter goes to press, the most visible conflict over religious liberty, post-*Obergefell*, concerns what the scope of religious freedom and accommodation should be in the case of public officials whose duties include issuing marriage licenses or performing marriage ceremonies. For example, Ryan Anderson argues that "peaceful coexistence is possible" if states may protect public officials like Kim Davis, the Kentucky clerk mentioned earlier in this chapter, by enacting conscience-protection laws allowing them to "recuse themselves" from issuing licenses or performing marriages.[186] Already, the inevitable references to the civil rights era are proliferating, with supporters of Ms. Davis invoking the examples of civil disobedience by Dr. King and Rosa Parks and critics calling her a "bigot" and comparing her to Governor George Wallace and other recalcitrant public officials resisting court-ordered school desegregation.[187] For supporters of marriage equality (and here I include myself), it is disturbing to see religious opponents invoke civil disobedience that was aimed at ending discrimination and unequal treatment based on race in public institutions and public accommodations to justify present-day refusals by public officials to treat gay and lesbian citizens equally in access to—as *Obergefell* describes marriage—an "important public institution." Another disturbing use of historical analogy is that, invoking President Lincoln's statements about the infamous *Dred Scott* case, some prominent conservative religious critics of *Obergefell* have called upon "all federal and state officeholders" to refuse to accept *Obergefell* as binding precedent except for the plaintiffs immediately before the Supreme Court and "to recognize the authority of states to define marriage, and the right of federal and state officeholders to act in accordance with those definitions."[188] On the view of such conservatives, because of the "grave" consequences of *Obergefell*, including the vilification of believers in traditional marriage (as predicted by Justice Alito), public office holders should justifiably assist, legally and politically, "anyone who refuses to follow *Obergefell*. Another view of the matter is that—to quote Justice Scalia's earlier warning on the risk of an overly robust view of the free exercise of religion that would trump civil law—"to permit this would make the professed doctrines of religious belief superior to the law of the land and, in effect, to permit every citizen to become a law unto himself."[189]

The full implications of *Obergefell* for how to resolve constitutional commitments to the fundamental right to marry and to the free exercise of religion await further exploration. However, in closing, if one is mindful of the distinction between civil and religious marriage, then the words of one federal district judge upholding a challenge to Florida's marriage law may be apt:

> Liberty, tolerance, and respect are not zero-sum concepts. Those who entered opposite-sex marriages are harmed not at all when others, including these plaintiffs, are given the liberty to choose their own life partners and are shown the respect that comes with formal marriage. Tolerating views with which one disagrees is a hallmark of civilized society.[190]

6

The Politics of Accommodation

The American Experience with Same-Sex Marriage
and Religious Freedom

ROBIN FRETWELL WILSON*

Introduction

In war, litigation, and even the legislative process, parties go to battle when they fundamentally underestimate the other side's strength. Armed with a more realistic view of a rival's strengths, the same parties will sometimes come to the bargaining table, with a renewed appreciation for the advantages of negotiation and compromise.

---

* This chapter draws on two articles: Robin Fretwell Wilson, "A Marriage of Necessity: Same-Sex Marriage and Religious Liberty Protections," *Case Western Reserve Law Review* 64, no. 3 (2014): 1161–1268, http://papers.ssrn.com/sol3/papers.cfm?abstract_id=2448344 [hereinafter "Marriage of Necessity"] and Wilson, "The Calculus of Accommodation: Contraception, Abortion, Same-Sex Marriage, and Other Clashes between Religion and the State," *Boston College Law Review* 53, no. 4 (2012): 1417–1513, http://papers.ssrn.com/sol3/papers.cfm?abstract_id=2155867 [hereinafter "Calculus of Accommodation"].

It grows out of my work assisting the Utah Legislature to enact the Utah Compromise, as well as law reform work with two groups of scholars urging the inclusion of meaningful religious liberty protections in same-sex marriage laws.

This chapter takes into account same-sex marriage laws and judicial decisions as of November 11, 2014, but uses a snapshot of the sexual orientation non-discrimination protections and state constitutional amendments banning same-sex marriage as of October 22, 2013. Appendix 6.A was proposed explicitly to be included in voluntary same-sex marriage laws. Since that early proposal, more nuanced accommodations that bypass collisions entirely have developed and become part of balanced legislation, like the Utah Compromise. See Part I.A.

In many ways, those who oppose same-sex marriage and those who support it are both wrong about the strengths of the other side's position. Some same-sex marriage supporters push for rights surrounding marriage without qualification—even if it means forcing others to facilitate weddings by hosting the reception or providing other wedding-related services in violation of deeply held religious beliefs.[1] Some same-sex marriage opponents take an equally rigid approach. Even before the US Supreme Court's decision in *Obergefell v. Hodges*, these opponents resisted same-sex marriage on the grounds that it would destroy the moral foundation of society—whether or not the recognition came from a judicial decision or voluntary legislation that balances respect for gay couples with consideration for those who adhere to a traditional view of marriage.[2]

Until the recent juggernaut of federal judicial decisions mandating same-sex marriage that began with *United States v. Windsor*[3] and culminated in *Obergefell*,[4] a significant generator of marriage equality in the United States was the voluntary adoption of same-sex marriage laws by state legislatures and voters, as the timeline in Figure 6.1 shows. The voluntary embrace of marriage equality hinged on compromise. Same-sex marriage supporters traded meaningful, if imperfect, religious liberty protections for objectors for the right to marry.[5]

In June 2015, writing against the background of hundreds of thousands of same-sex marriages across the country,[6] the Court found a constitutional right to same-sex marriage in *Obergefell*, as many had expected.[7] Some naturally assume now that the Supreme Court has wiped away all remaining state constitutional bans on same-sex marriage, this victory erases all need to bargain. This supposition is short-sighted. Americans favor same-sex marriage but on the cusp of the Court's 2015 decision, were "evenly divided" on whether it "must be legal nationwide."[8] But more importantly, same-sex marriage is not the only legal protection in play. Throughout most of the country, the lesbian, gay, bisexual, and transgender ("LGBT") community lacks sorely needed statewide protections against discrimination in housing, hiring, and public accommodations.[9] Even after achieving the long sought-after goal of marriage equality, gay rights advocates almost certainly require the help of state legislators to enact LGBT non-discrimination protections—and that will be the moment when religious liberty protections for those who adhere to a traditional view of marriage will be balanced with LGBT rights.[10]

The public favors such live-and-let-live deals. Approximately half of the country says that "local officials and judges with religious objections ought to be exempt from any requirement that they issue marriage licenses to gay and lesbian couples," while 57% believes that "wedding-related businesses with religious objections should be allowed to refuse service to same-sex couples."[11]

History shows that compromise facilitates social progress. For proponents, legislative compromise delivered marriage equality years before it otherwise

Same-Sex Marriage Timeline

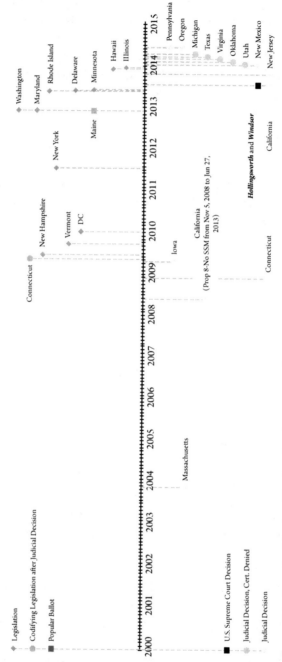

Figure 6.1. Same-Sex Marriage Timeline (until Oct. 6, 2014).

would have been adopted.[12] Over the last decade, efforts to enact same-sex marriage without qualification were self-defeating—bills that adopted a winner-takes-all, maximalist approach did not yield enduring legislative victories. Rather, only those bills that contained meaningful religious liberty accommodations garnered sufficient support to become, and remain, law.

For opponents, compromise delivered modest, but important, protections for religious organizations and individuals. Ironically, until 2012, there was no urgent need for opponents to trade recognition of same-sex marriage for meaningful religious liberty concessions. Until then, opponents had amassed 29 consecutive victories at the ballot box, resulting in constitutional amendments barring same-sex marriage in 29 states. However, as this chapter illustrates, long before federal courts began striking down state constitutional bans, the tide had shifted against opponents.[13] In 2012, the first constitutional amendment to ban same-sex marriage failed in Minnesota; same-sex marriage was adopted for the first time by popular vote in Maine[14]; and state laws recognizing same-sex marriage in Maryland and Washington both survived referendum challenges.

Even after *Obergefell* has enshrined a constitutional right to same-sex marriage, there are concrete gains to supporters and opponents alike from remaining at the bargaining table. For opponents of same-sex marriage, bargaining offers protections to religious objectors that are wholly absent from judicial decisions requiring the recognition of same-sex marriage. Further, the majority of now-struck state constitutional bans simply did not provide the bulwark against change that some assumed. Many constitutional amendments can be repealed almost as easily as enacting ordinary legislation. Further, given the steady shift toward wider public acceptance of same-sex relationships, opponents were running a race against time. That same public acceptance of same-sex marriage and LGBT rights more broadly means that opponents still face a closing window for securing religious liberty protections. With sufficient time, it will be possible, through legislation or ballot initiative, to enact non-discrimination protections *without* concomitant safeguards for faith communities. Not only is it right and just to provide basic protections against discrimination to the LGBT community, those basic protections are the key to securing the autonomy of faith communities to abide by their own beliefs about marriage.

For supporters, securing marriage equality was never the only pressing needs for the LGBT community. Until Utah's landmark legislation in 2015, only 21 states banned discrimination based on sexual orientation in housing, employment, or public accommodations in statewide law, as Part I.A documents.[15] Thus, the deep irony is that marriage equality has now come to parts of the country where the LGBT community lacks even the most basic protections. As Tim Gill of the Gill Foundation recently explained, many civil rights movements have "won something and then sat back and relaxed," leaving other pressing needs for another day[16]—a mistake that the LGBT rights community is committed not to repeat.

Even before *Obergefell*, bargaining over religious liberty had shifted from trading marriage equality for religious liberty protections like those found in voluntary same-sex marriage laws[17] to trading LGBT non-discrimination protections for religious accommodations. In March 2015, Utah passed "landmark" LGBT non-discrimination legislation that "balance[d] gay rights and religious freedoms."[18] Legislators elsewhere also introduced proposed legislation combining LGBT non-discrimination protections with religious liberty exemptions.[19]

In this climate of mutual need and gain, negotiating—although less gratifying for many—continues to serve both sides. Only compromise will yield significant protections for religious objectors *and* significant protections for the LGBT community against discrimination.

Legislators who have the power to craft such compromises are caught in the crossfire between warring sides. For some legislators, such compromises hold no appeal—they simply do not want to be seen as "selling out" their constituents, whether gay, religious, or otherwise.[20] But for other legislators in the middle, their resistance to doing more for gay couples or religious objectors involves an express set of reservations or "sticking points" about whether certain religious liberty exemptions are workable.[21] These concerns range from why legislators should ever accommodate religious objectors to whether accommodations should protect only those who directly perform a morally freighted service, like clergy who actually "tie the knot" for the same-sex couple. These concerns seem compelling at first blush. Yet, religious liberty accommodations that bypass collisions entirely, or that are qualified by hardship to same-sex couples—that is, accommodations that allow religious objectors to avoid facilitating a same-sex marriage *only* when a hardship will not result—transform what would otherwise be a zero-sum "I win, you lose" proposition into one in which marriage equality and religious freedom can *both* be affirmed.

This chapter makes two claims. First, quite simply, compromise is the optimal way forward for both sides—the constitutional entitlement to same-sex marriage in *Obergefell* leaves the LGBT community without much needed protections in other realms. Moreover, *Obergefell* itself provides "people of faith" with "no comfort."[22] This is not surprising: Legislatures had no opportunity to consciously balance the interests of religious believers with the equally important interests of the LGBT community. Second, this chapter contends that, nuanced legislation recognizing new civil rights while providing robust religious liberty accommodations allows legislators to advance *two compelling values*—LGBT rights and religious liberty. Part I begins with the political calculus impeding compromise. It shows that on the question of same-sex marriage and LGBT protections, the United States has become a classic constitutional and statutory "checkerboard"—with both sides racking up victories in state legislatures and at the ballot box. It then demonstrates empirically that in the same-sex marriage context, compromise led to legislative victories for marriage supporters, while a winner-takes-all approach failed. Although *Obergefell* now guarantees same-sex couples the right to marry, LGBT rights advocates can, through compromise, lock in other much-needed protections against discrimination which may not be forthcoming judicially as they recently did in Utah.[23]

On the other side, Part I acknowledges that opponents had won absolute victories at the ballot box in 29 consecutive ballot initiatives until 2012, when opponents experienced four stinging defeats.[24] Opponents now face the looming reality that future generations of voters increasingly—and in some states overwhelmingly—support not only same-sex marriage but LGBT rights more generally. Receding opposition means that same-sex marriage would have been possible politically across the country *without any protections for religious objectors* in a matter of years, just as LGBT non-discrimination protections are likely to be in the near term. Thus, the time to lock in common sense religious liberty protections is now. During this rapidly closing window, opponents should embrace compromise.

Now, some will assume that LGBT supporters, after winning on same-sex marriage, will simply pivot their momentum toward enacting sexual orientation non-discrimination bans. Yet, when same-sex marriage became a reality overnight in "red" states after the Supreme Court's 2014 refusal to accept a case for review (known as denial of certiorari),[25] collision points over same-sex marriage rapidly multiplied. Witness the steady drumbeat of headlines about lawsuits brought against bakers, florists, and bed-and-breakfast owners, together with the wave of resignations by magistrates and government employees who say they cannot, consistent with their faith, preside over or facilitate a same-sex marriage.[26] Pollsters are now asking Americans more nuanced questions about their "support" for same-sex marriage, revealing a live-and-let-live approach. People more readily support same-sex marriage if it comes packaged with religious liberty protections.[27] In a 2015 Associated Press-GfK poll, approximately half of the country said that, in states that allow same-sex marriage, "local officials and judges with religious objections ought to be exempt from any requirement that they issue marriage licenses to gay and lesbian couples," while 57% believed that "wedding-related businesses . . . should be allowed to refuse service to same-sex couples."[28] Importantly, every state that has voluntarily enacted LGBT non-discrimination protections to date has included religious liberty accommodations.[29] The polls and enacted laws suggest that going forward, limited opt-outs related to marriage solemnization will be part and parcel of legislative bargains.

Part II turns to substantive points of resistance to compromise. Part II.A first describes moral clashes over same-sex marriage that have unfolded in the past decade, clashes that religious liberty protections are designed to allay. Part II.A then turns to the first "sticking point" for legislators seeking to balance competing rights: that accommodations will be used to disguise bigotry. This part shows that courts have proven able to separate sincere from insincere objections in a range of contexts, from military conscientious objections to employment disputes.

Part II.B examines the notion that accommodations exempt people remotely associated with objectionable activity. In other contexts, exemptions have routinely encompassed not only those who directly perform a contested activity, but those who facilitate it, too. Part II.C grapples with the claim that same-sex marriage legislation establishes marriage equality but requires nothing in particular of the public and therefore no exemption is needed. This Part examines the scope of non-discrimination statutes enacted long before same-sex marriage. Without explicit protection, many objectors will face a cruel choice between their conscience and their livelihood.

Finally, Part II.D explores whether religious liberty accommodations will impose hardships on same-sex couples or undermine their dignity. This part argues that exemptions qualified by hardship to same-sex couples can avoid the real concern driving efforts to cabin the scope of accommodations—namely, avoiding hardship and embarrassment to same-sex couples. Creative approaches can make accommodations invisible to the public, avoiding dignitary harms to same-sex couples.

I. The Political Calculus of Compromise

In the same week in 2012 that President Obama became the first sitting president of the United States to endorse same-sex marriage—saying in an ABC News interview that same-sex couples should "be able to get married"[30]—North Carolina became the 29th state to enshrine in its Constitution a ban on such marriages.[31] In his endorsement, President Obama affirmed the value of being "respectful of religious liberty" when recognizing same-sex marriage, saying "it's important to recognize that folks who feel very strongly that marriage should be defined narrowly as between a man and a woman, many of them are not coming at it from a mean-spirited perspective. They're coming at it because they care about families . . . ."[32] Only weeks before, North Carolina's then–Speaker of the House, Thom Tillis, who voted to put the constitutional amendment on the ballot, was asked by a student at NC State to weigh in on the amendment. Far from confidently predicting victory, Tillis said that "If it passes, I think it will be repealed within 20 years."[33]

Although these two events could not stand in sharper contrast, they capture both the depth of the rift over same-sex marriage in America,[34] as well as the fluidity of views. As the remainder of this part illustrates, there is a premium on compromise for both sides in such a climate.

A. Checkerboard of Same-Sex Marriage Laws and Bans

The year 2014 stood as "the biggest year for gay-marriage legalization ever . . . bringing the total number of states that allow gay couples to wed to 35, plus the District of Columbia."[35] For the first time, the US map looked more "blue," shown in Figure 6.2 as light gray, than "red," which Figure 6.2 shows as dark gray.

This shift occurred in the wake of the Supreme Court's 2014 denial of certiorari, which put off the Court's ultimate decision in *Obergefell* until 2015 but green-lighted same-sex marriage for couples in Wyoming Utah, Oklahoma, Wisconsin, Indiana, Virginia, West Virginia, North Carolina, South Carolina, Colorado, and Kansas.[36]

Only days before, the country was overwhelmingly red, as Figure 6.3 shows in dark gray.

Judicial decisions wiping away democratically adopted constitutional and statutory bans remind us that droves of voters across the United States have endorsed bans. Indeed, the string of legislative victories by same-sex marriage supporters in statehouses across the country paled alongside the wins racked up by opponents, both at the ballot box and in statehouses. At the end of 2014, 12 states and the District of Columbia had voluntarily recognized same-sex marriage—one by popular ballot, the rest by legislation.[37] Yet, before federal courts began striking constitutional bans in earnest, states had banned same-sex marriage by constitutional amendment in 29 states[38] and by statute in 8 others.[39] By November 11, 2014, constitutional bans in only 16 states survived,[40] while every statutory ban had succumbed to the voluntary enactment of marriage equality (Delaware, Hawaii, Illinois, Maine, and Minnesota)[41] or been struck down (Indiana, Pennsylvania, West Virginia, and Wyoming).[42] Rounding out the pathway to same-sex marriage recognition, state courts in four states interpreted their own constitutions to require same-sex marriage.[43]

Even this snapshot masks deep flux. In spring 2012, Washington and Maryland became the 8th and 9th jurisdictions to recognize same-sex marriage.[44] The same day that Maryland's bill became law, opponents began efforts to overturn it by referendum in the fall 2012 election.[45] By summer 2012, opponents in both states had gathered enough signatures to put the two measures before voters in November.[46] Both ultimately survived challenge by exceedingly

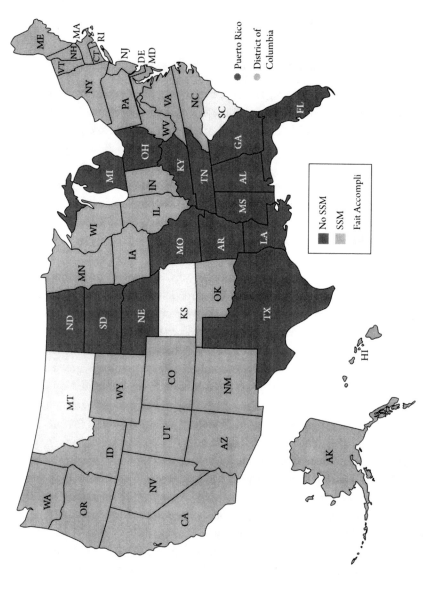

Figure 6.2. Same-Sex Marriage after Supreme Court's Certiorari Denial* (until Nov. 11, 2014). * See Wilson, "Human Costs," *supra* note 6.

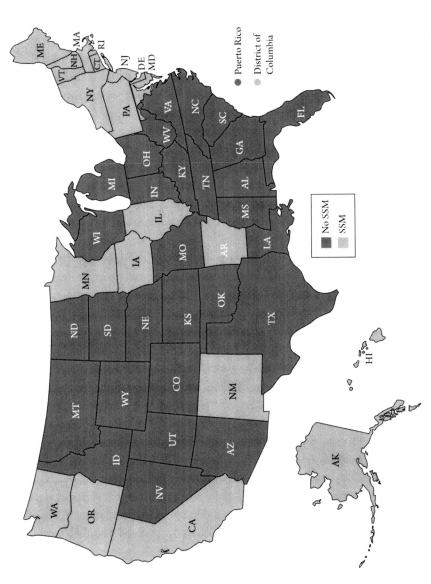

Figure 6.3. Same-Sex Marriage before the Supreme Court's Denial of Certiorari (until Nov. 11, 2014). * Arkansas temporarily allowed same-sex marriages in the window between a favorable state trial court ruling and the Arkansas Supreme Court's stay of that decision. Paresh Dave, "Arkansas Supreme Court Halts Same-Sex Marriages," *Los Angeles Times*, May 16, 2014, http://www.latimes.com/nation/nationnow/la-na-nn-arkansas-gay-marriage-stay-20140516-story.html.

narrow margins,[47] helped in significant measure by religious liberty protections embedded in the legislation. The incremental policymaking that took place in statehouses to balance religious liberty and marriage equality, described in Part I.B.1, permitted both sides to benefit from compromising.

Some naturally assume that the political calculus has shifted dramatically now that the Supreme Court has recognized a federal constitutional right to same-sex marriage. True, there is no incentive to trade religious liberty for marriage recognition after *Obergefell*. But the need to compromise—and benefits of compromise—have not abruptly disappeared. This is so because, until Utah's landmark legislation in 2015,[48] only 20 states and the District of Columbia barred discrimination based on sexual orientation in housing, employment, or public accommodations in state law, as Figure 6.4 shows.[49]

Only in the states shown in white in Figure 6.4 is there both a present right for same-sex couples to marry *and* state laws protecting LGBT individuals from discrimination. To be sure, Americans strongly support LGBT non-discrimination laws, seeing them as necessary to combat discrimination against LGBT individuals.[50] In 2014, 68% of Americans thought lesbians and gays faced "a lot of discrimination"—more perceived discrimination than that faced by every other minority group except Muslims.[51]

When asked, Americans overwhelmingly say lesbians and gays deserve protection from discrimination in public accommodations, housing, or employment.[52] In 2014, nearly 3 out of 4 Americans (72%) favored protections for LGBT individuals from employment discrimination.[53] Notwithstanding support for these protections, enacting non-discrimination laws is complex, involving more than just public support.[54]

Indeed, as same-sex marriage rapidly spread to formerly red states after the Court's denial of certiorari at the end of 2014, states witnessed the bargaining over religious liberty shift from trading marriage equality for religious liberty protection to trading non-discrimination protections for religious liberty protections like those found in the voluntary same-sex marriage laws.[55] Utah represents a striking bellwether of this shift. In January 2015, the Mormon Church called for legislation to "protect[ ] vital religious freedoms for individuals, families, churches and other faith groups while also protecting the rights of our LGBT citizens in . . . housing, employment and public accommodation."[56] Utah Senate Majority Leader Ralph Okerlund and others supported comprehensive measures to effect such a balance, believing "[i]t would polarize those two issues if we tried to move forward with one without the other."[57]

The Utah legislature successfully passed by overwhelming majorities a pair of bills that were signed into law by Governor Gary Herbert.[58] The first bill, SB 296, protects LGBT individuals from discrimination in employment or housing based on their gender identity or sexual orientation, but it exempts "[r]eligious

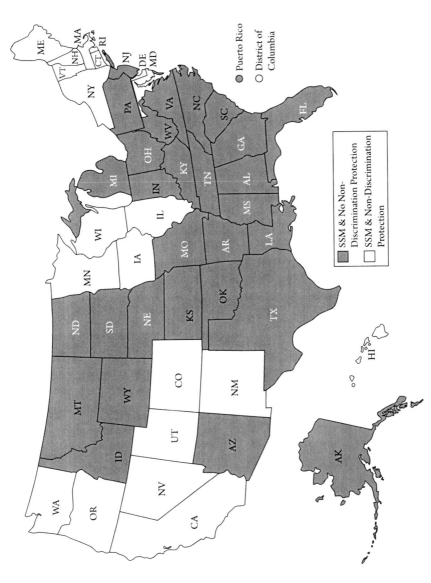

Figure 6.4. A Right to Marry without Basic Non-Discrimination Protections.

organizations and their affiliates . . . from the bill's requirements."[59] The second
bill, SB 297, permits faith groups to solemnize and host only those weddings
and receptions consistent with their faith and to limit religious counseling to
those in traditional marriages—without threat of civil suit or government penalty; it also requires county clerk offices to establish a process for solemnizing all
legal marriages—not required by Utah law before the Utah Compromise—but
the office may outsource the duty to any willing celebrant in the community,
avoiding the need to fire "[i]ndividual local officials who object to same-sex
marriage" or force them to quit their jobs.[60] In bypassing religious objectors
entirely, the Utah Compromise ensures the dignity of same-sex couples seeking
licenses, who receive access to marriage on exactly the same basis as straight
couples, and never even know whether someone in the office had a religious
objection.

The Utah Compromise contains other novel protections for religious liberty,
too. No one can be stripped of a professional license for speaking about marriage, family, or sexuality in a nonprofessional setting.[61] No covered employee
can be fired for political or religious expression outside the workplace, whether
giving to Proposition 8 or marching in a gay rights parade.[62] Political and religious speech receive equal treatment in the workplace, too, although employers
retain the latitude to bar all such talk.[63] Together, the measures marked "a major
step forward" because neither LGBT nor religious freedom advocates "allowed
the best to become the enemy of the good."[64]

As Yale University Professor William Eskridge notes, the "Utah statute . . .
never would have gotten anywhere if there had not been a lot of appreciation,
particularly by the Mormons and conservative Republicans, that LGBT people
are part of the community."[65] The Utah legislature responded to the tension over
forced recognition by the federal courts of same-sex marriage by "call[ing] a
truce in the culture war pitting gay rights against religious liberty."[66] Indeed, "the
Utah legislature . . . reminded politicians across the country that, in fact, half a
loaf is often better that no loaf at all."[67]

In 2015, other state legislatures signaled a willingness to bargain around
LGBT non-discrimination and religious freedom. For example, Michigan and
Wyoming made halting attempts to pass LGBT non-discrimination bills with
broad religious exemptions.[68] Nebraska legislators amended a LGBT non-
discrimination bill to "make it clear that religious corporations, associations
and societies are exempt from the non-discrimination requirements based on
religious belief."[69] And in Indiana, Senate Republicans introduced a bill to ban
discrimination statewide based on sexual orientation and gender identity in
housing, hiring, and public accommodations, "while carving out several exemptions for those with strong religious objections," a bill seen as the "opening salvo
of what is likely to be a long and arduous debate."[70]

As the next sub-part shows, the story of legislative recognition of same-sex marriage in the United States has been one of compromise—going forward, compromise is the key to securing much-needed protections for both sides.

B. The Political Realities on Each Side

1. *Supporters Need to Compromise*

When same-sex marriage advocates have negotiated, they have won legislative victories; conversely, when they have pursued a winner-takes-all approach without meaningful religious liberty accommodations that extend beyond the clergy and church sanctuary, they have lost. In the decade before *Obergefell*, legislators in nine states and the District of Columbia proposed same-sex marriage legislation shorn of protections for anyone other than the clergy and churches.[71] Those provisions offered faux "protection" because "[n]o one seriously believes that clergy will be forced, or even asked, to perform marriages that are anathema to them."[72] Such legislative proposals ultimately failed in every jurisdiction.[73]

In the single instance that a same-sex marriage bill with clergy-only protections managed to become law, it was later repealed by voters. In 2009, Maine legislators stubbornly refused to include robust religious liberty protections in Maine's same-sex marriage law. Instead, the legislature elected to provide only those protections already guaranteed by the Constitution[74]—and turned down more meaningful religious liberty protections like those advocated for in this chapter. Maine voters turned back the law in a "people's veto" by a relatively narrow margin: 52.9% to 47.1%. The inflexible, absolute character of the Maine statute naturally elicited the question raised by Professor Dale Carpenter after the loss: Would "includ[ing] broader protection for religious liberty in the legislature's [same-sex marriage] bill" have made a difference?[75] Arguably, it would have. After all, if a mere 3% of voters could have been swayed to change their votes by live-and-let-live religious liberty protections, Maine would likely have realized same-sex marriage in 2009.[76]

A scant three years later, in 2012, Maine voters enacted same-sex marriage by popular referendum. Voters responded "yes" to the question "Do you want to allow the State of Maine to issue marriage licenses to same-sex couples?" by a margin of 52.65% to 47.35%.[77] Notably, the ballot measure itself authorized specific legislation to "allow marriage licenses for same-sex couples and protect religious freedom," while exempting not only clergy but "any church, religious denomination or other religious institution."[78] These institutions may not be required to "host any marriage in violation of the religious beliefs of that member of the clergy, church, religious denomination or other religious institution."[79] Any refusal would not subject the group to "a lawsuit or liability and does not affect the tax-exempt status of the church, religious denomination or other religious institution."[80] One cannot, however, be completely confident that voters understood or gave weight to these religious protections in the run-up to the ballot question.[81] Certainly, ballot supporters emphasized it.[82] Yet Maine's rapid turn-about on same-sex marriage points to the value of compromise.

Like Maine's voter-driven enactment, every marriage equality bill that garnered sufficient support to become law—and endure—acknowledged the impact of same-sex marriage laws on believers who adhere to a traditional view of marriage.[83] Twelve jurisdictions voluntarily embraced same-sex marriage through the legislative process (Connecticut, Delaware, District of Columbia, Hawaii, Illinois, Maryland, Minnesota, New Hampshire, New York, Rhode Island, Vermont, and Washington).[84] Each law provided religious liberty protections to the clergy, but then reached beyond guarantees given by the First Amendment.[85]

A core of protections emerged for religious organizations[86] and individuals[87] who cannot celebrate or facilitate *any* marriage—including a same-sex marriage, interfaith marriage,[88] or second marriage—when doing so would violate their religious convictions.[89] Although each law describes the exempt activities in slightly different terms, generally they encompass the provision of "services, accommodations, advantages, facilities, goods, or privileges to an individual if . . . related to the solemnization of a marriage [or] the celebration of a marriage."[90] All but one jurisdiction insulates religious organizations from civil suits for refusing to celebrate marriages, while all but two explicitly protect such organizations from punishment at the hands of the government.[91]

Every state but Delaware extends the protection from lawsuits to religious nonprofits, like Catholic Charities or the Salvation Army.[92] Eight jurisdictions extend protections to benevolent religious organizations, like the Knights of Columbus, or to religious groups that sponsor marriage retreats or provide housing for married individuals.[93] Six states (Maryland, Minnesota, New Hampshire, New York, Rhode Island, and Washington) expressly exempt individual employees "managed, directed, or supervised by" a covered entity from celebrating same-sex marriages if doing so would violate their "religious beliefs and faith."[94] While it is not readily apparent how this protection adds to that for the individual's employer, one can imagine a lawsuit being filed against a church employee instead of the church. A single state, Delaware, permits justices of the peace and judges to solemnize only those marriages they choose to[95]—because this blanket protection permits objectors to "erect a roadblock to marriage," it should be conditioned on *not* creating hardship to same-sex couples.[96] In all, such robust religious liberty protections sweep far beyond the church sanctuary, providing accommodations that exceed what most scholars believe would be constitutionally demanded.[97]

As in Maine, legislation in Maryland and Washington faced referendum challenges. But unlike Maine's 2009 legislation protecting only the clergy, Maryland's and Washington's more robust laws survived challenge, albeit by narrow margins.[98] In each jurisdiction, the religious liberty protections in the law were featured on the face of the ballot.

Religious liberty protections are important not only to a law's success, but to its reality. Without such protections, religious groups and individuals that hew to their religious beliefs about marriage would be at risk of punishment by the government and would also be subject to lawsuits from private citizens. These risks are not speculative. The City of San Francisco withdrew $3.5 million in social services contracts from the Salvation Army when it refused, for religious reasons, to provide benefits to its employees' same-sex partners.[99] In New Jersey, the state's Division of Civil Rights found that a Methodist nonprofit association violated New Jersey's Law Against Discrimination when it denied the requests of two same-sex couples to use the group's boardwalk pavilion for their commitment ceremonies.[100] Separately, local tax authorities stripped the group of its exemption from ad valorem property taxes on the boardwalk pavilion, billing the group close to $20,000 in "rollback" taxes, although that loss was hastened by the group's own decision to tie its property tax exemption to a public lands program and the group ultimately paid less.[101] Some may see coercion by the government—through the denial of grants or other benefits extended to the public—as a perfectly appropriate way to make same-sex marriage opponents conform no matter what their faith asks of them. As this chapter shows, however, protecting equality need not come at the expense of religious liberty. But more fundamentally, it breaches the American social contract[102] to force religious objectors to heel just because the government has the power to do so.[103]

We have also seen clashes in the commercial arena where individuals have felt pressured to choose between their livelihoods and their religious convictions. In 2008, the New Mexico Human Rights Commission fined a small photography shop, Elane Photography, over $6,000 for refusing on religious grounds to photograph a same-sex commitment ceremony.[104] New Mexico did not recognize same-sex marriage until 2013.[105] The Supreme Court of New Mexico upheld the fine.[106] In Oregon, which bans LGBT discrimination, an administrative law judge ordered the owners of Sweet Cakes by Melissa in Portland to pay $135,000 to a same-sex couple after refusing to provide the couple a wedding cake.[107] In July 2015, an Oregon appeals court upheld the fine.[108]

Beginning with the first marriage equality decision, clashes have also erupted over the appropriate role of judges, magistrates, and marriage registrars. On the heels of Massachusetts' same-sex marriage decision,[109] state justices of the peace were told by counsel to then-Governor Mitt Romney that they must "follow the law, whether you agree with it or not."[110] Anyone who turned away same-sex couples could be held personally liable for up to $50,000.[111] Iowa and New York gave all government officials similar directives, which precipitated a host of resignations.[112] In one controversial case in New York, the town clerk instituted a new process to delegate the marriage license task to a deputy clerk who did not share the town clerk's religious objection to same-sex marriage—provoking charges that a "public official simply decide[d] to shirk the obligations of her office."[113]

In state after state, religious liberty accommodations helped same-sex marriage advocates secure long-sought legislative victories. In all but two states, proposed legislation offering "clergy-only protection" failed to garner enough support to become law only months before enactment of legislation with more meaningful protections, suggesting that robust exemptions made marriage equality laws politically feasible.[114]

For example, in 2007 and 2009, proposed legislation containing a clergy-only exemption passed the New York Assembly, only to die in the New York Senate.[115] Two years later, in 2011, Governor Andrew M. Cuomo proposed The Marriage Equality Act, a revised bill with more robust religious liberty protections described below. The New York Assembly approved the bill on June 15, 2011, by a vote of 80 to 63.[116] Although Governor Cuomo's bill improved on the non-protections in the 2007 and 2009 bills, it notably did *not* insulate religious objectors from government penalty.[117] The New York Senate then enlarged the protections and that measure passed on June 24, 2011, by a vote of 33 to 29.[118]

After Governor Andrew Cuomo signed New York's same-sex marriage law, the *New York Times* observed that the religious exemptions were

> just a few paragraphs, but they proved to be the most microscopically examined and debated—and the most pivotal—in the battle over same-sex marriage. . . . Language that Republican senators inserted into the bill legalizing same-sex marriage provided more expansive protections for religious organizations and helped pull the legislation over the finish line Friday night.[119]

Efforts to pass same-sex marriage legislation in Washington and Maryland followed similar trajectories.[120] In both states, religious liberty protections shifted the question for some legislators from *whether* to embrace marriage equality to *how* to balance that good with religious liberty.[121] As Speaker Michael Busch of the Maryland House of Delegates explained, more expansive religious liberty protections facilitated passage:

> We didn't want to inhibit any religious organization from practicing their beliefs. One of the issues was the adoption issue. We wanted to make sure

we didn't impede on the Catholic Church for adoption services. . . . I know for a fact that for two or three delegates [including religious liberty protections] was an important component in their decision to vote for it.[122]

Washington Governor Christine Gregoire explained how thicker protection for religious liberty figured in her own decision to back marriage equality legislation:

> I looked at what New York had done. I worked with our gay community. I told them that that was the only way I would introduce the bill. There were some people who wanted to compromise on [the religious liberty protections] in the future. But I said, "No," that this was in part a reflection of my evolution on the issue, and it wasn't compromisable.[123]

As noted above, Maryland's and Washington's laws both survived pitched and expensive referendum challenges. Together, these experiences suggest that exemptions took a powerful argument against same-sex marriage away from opponents.[124] Although counter-intuitive to some, as prominent gay rights leader Jonathan Rauch has pointed out, the smart move for LGBT rights supporters is to "bend toward accommodation," not away from it.[125]

With marriage equality now guaranteed, the temptation for many LGBT rights supporters may be to harden against compromise. This would be a mistake.

There is far more work to be done for the LGBT community even after securing marriage equality. Only 21 states and the District of Columbia ban discrimination based on sexual orientation in housing, employment, or public accommodations in state law,[126] leaving great swaths of the country where same-sex couples can marry but lack protection from discrimination in housing, hiring, and public accommodations. Only in the states shown in white in Figure 6.4 is there both the right for same-sex couples to marry *and* protection from discrimination based on sexual orientation.

Thus, although what would be traded necessarily changes now that the right to marry is assured, the motivation to bargain remains for LGBT rights supporters. The recent repeal of the Houston Equal Rights Ordinance or "HERO," which would have extended protections in housing, employment, and public accommodations to the LGBT community, is instructive. Going into the referendum, "[i]n 2015, in America's fourth-largest city and one of its most diverse, backing [HERO] might have seemed an obvious choice."[127] What should have been an easy electoral victory stalled for complex reasons, including the ordinance's "vagueness" and what many people of good will saw as scare mongering over public access to restroom facilities.[128] The *Christian Science Monitor* read HERO's repeal by a "resounding margin" as laying bare again "America's bitter and ongoing divisions over same-sex marriage and religious freedom."[129] Eskridge speculates that the Utah Compromise may have succeeded where HERO failed precisely because Utah Compromise "permitted those with religious objections to find a space to opt out."[130]

2. Opponents Need to Compromise

Before the judicial juggernaut shown in Figure 6.1, it was far easier to see why supporters of same-sex marriage should compromise than why opponents should. After all, opponents had amassed 29 consecutive victories at the ballot box before the stinging defeats delivered by the 2012 election.

Pre-*Obergefell*, legislative compromise over same-sex marriage averted an absolute defeat for opponents at the hands of a state or federal court.[131] Same-sex marriage by judicial decision alone was the real "nightmare for religious liberty" that opponents feared.[132] As Figure 6.5 and Appendix 6.B both underscore, judicial decisions leave religious objectors the most exposed. States shown in black in Figure 6.5 received no religious liberty protections tailored to marriage at the time same-sex marriage was recognized, because the right to marry arose by judicial decision.

The failure of the judiciary to protect religious objectors is hardly its fault. Courts lack the inherent ability of legislatures to balance competing goods in a plural society. Moreover, protecting religious objectors is not the issue before the court when it considers a constitutional entitlement, such as the right to same-sex marriage.

Even after *Obergefell's* mandate of same-sex marriage, compromising is still the path forward to religious liberty protections, protections that are likely to elude opponents later. Why?

If support for same-sex marriage is any indicator, support for LGBT rights will mushroom over time, making the denial of statewide non-discrimination protections for sexual orientation and gender identity increasingly untenable. Although most states lack these fundamental protections for the LGBT community, popular support for LGBT rights will likely hasten state legislation, without the need for judicial interference. But that shift can occur sooner, in a more positive way, if both parties compromise. Just consider how support for same-sex marriage grew over a decade into a force to be reckoned with. For several years running, a slim majority of Americans has believed that "marriages between same-sex couples should . . . be recognize[d] by the law."[133] In 2014, same-sex marriage support reached a "new high at 55%."[134] The public's embrace of same-sex marriage and LGBT rights more generally will only accelerate. For example, a string of polls reveal a deep generational fracture. In every state in the United States, opposition to same-sex marriage recedes with age, as Figure 6.6 illustrates.[135]

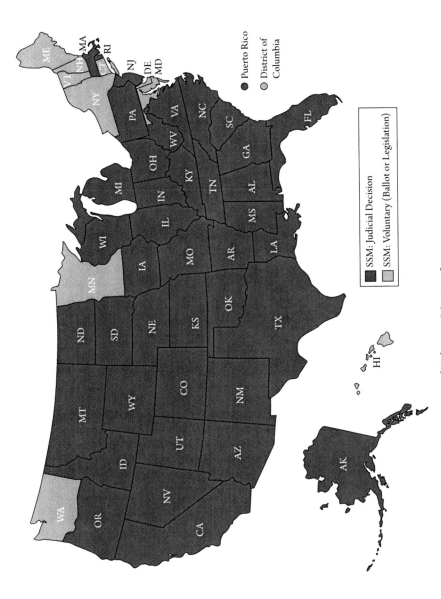

Figure 6.5. Degrees of Protection with Judicial Decisions and Voluntary Marriage Laws.

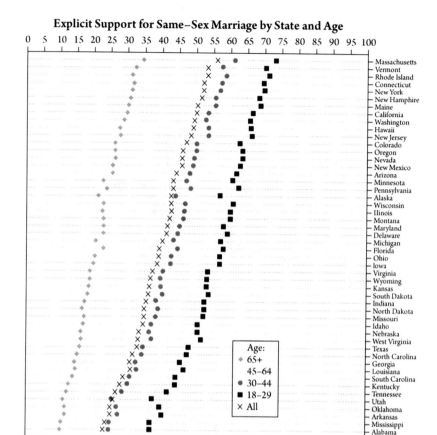

Explicit Support for Same–Sex Marriage by State and Age

Lax and Phillips (2009): data from 1994 to 2008, estimates weighted for 2008

Figure 6.6. Generational Support (and Opposition) to Same-Sex Marriage.ˑ
* Jeffrey R. Lax and Justin H. Phillips, "Gay Rights in the States: Public Opinion and Policy Responsiveness," American Political Science Review 103 (2009): 367–386, Fig. 8 (online appendix only), http://www.columbia.edu/~jrl2124/Lax_Phillips_Gay_Policy_Responsiveness_2009.pdf (reproduced with permission of authors).

More recent polls confirm that younger people support same-sex marriage at considerably higher rates than their older counterparts.[136] According to a 2014 poll by the Pew Research Center Forum on Religion and Public Life, 67% of Millennials—those born after 1981—"favor allowing gays and lesbians to marry legally," while a slim majority, 53%, of Generation X—those born between 1965 and 1980—support same-sex marriage.[137] Opposition to same-sex marriage largely concentrates in America's oldest generations, the Baby Boomers and the Silent Generation, those born between 1946 and 1964 and 1925 and 1945, respectively. Only 46% of Baby Boomers and 35% of the Silent Generation support same-sex marriage.[138] After the staunchest opponents pass from the scene, the landslide of support for same-sex marriage will only accelerate.[139] The contrast between America's oldest and youngest citizens portends a wellspring of support for gay marriage, which would have shown up at the ballot box even if *Obergefell* had not required states to recognize same-sex marriage. As Andrew Kohut, President of the Pew Research Center, astutely noted, "the electorate changes, and politics follow. . . ."[140]

This generational shift would have meant very little if existing state constitutional amendments banning same-sex marriage were unassailable. Ultimately, they did not prove immune from abrogation by the courts. But the bans would have crumbled in a matter of years without *Obergefell*.

One might think that amending state constitutions is as difficult as amending the federal Constitution, which requires "two-thirds of both houses of Congress and approval from three-fourths of the states."[141] In reality, however, "most state constitutions can be amended by majority vote on a ballot referendum. This ease of amendment led to 946 state constitutional amendments in the 1970s alone."[142]

A careful review of the process for amending the state constitution in the 29 states that until recently had constitutional amendments banning same-sex marriage[143] shows their vulnerability. Eight states (Georgia, Idaho, Kansas, Louisiana, North Carolina, South Carolina, Texas, and Utah) erected significant barriers to amendment, and therefore significant barriers to repeal.[144] Consider, for example, Utah, where the state's ban was struck by a lower court even before *Obergefell*.[145] Utah requires two-thirds of state legislators in both houses to amend the state constitution, after which a simple majority of the electorate must also approve the amendment.[146] Because this process is so onerous, once an amendment is adopted, it is highly unlikely to be repealed in the near future. Only a court's decision is likely to shatter it until a significant portion of the public believes it should fall.

But in the remaining states, constitutional bans enjoy only a mild or negligible lock-in effect. Eight states (Alabama, Alaska, Kentucky, Nevada, Oregon, Tennessee, Virginia, and Wisconsin) erected some barriers to repeal, but not ones as daunting as Utah's.[147] Generally, these states provide a legislative method for amendment, requiring only a majority of legislators and voters to amend the state's constitution. Some of these states also allow amendments by a periodic convention that either (a) requires approval by a simple majority of voters, but the convention may be called only after long periods of time (e.g., ten years), or (b) permits a convention to take place after two steps—approval by a majority of legislators and approval by majority of the electorate. Consider, for example, Virginia, which provides two paths to adoption or repeal: the legislative method—requiring approval by a simple majority of legislators in both houses and a simple majority of the electorate—and periodic constitutional conventions called by the legislature, where voters can approve amendments by a simple majority.[148] Because amendments can pass without supermajority support in the legislature, this process creates a milder lock-in effect.

Thirteen states (Arizona, Arkansas, Colorado, Florida, Michigan, Mississippi, Missouri, Montana, Nebraska, North Dakota, Ohio, Oklahoma, and South Dakota) fall in the final category, where constitutional bans can be adopted or repealed with relative ease.[149] A negligible lock-in state permits change with only a small fraction of voters petitioning for it, followed by a simple majority of voters voting for amendment. Typically, states require 10% of the electorate to initiate the process, but this percentage may range as low as 2% and as high as 15%.[150] Arizona is emblematic of this approach. It requires a petition to be signed by 15% of the total number of voters who cast votes for governor in the preceding election. At that point, the proposed amendment appears on the ballot to be decided by a majority of voters in a general election.[151]

In short, state constitutional amendments were surmountable in all 29 states to ban same-sex marriage in the state's constitution. In all but 8 states, constitutional bans could have been undone without "supermajority" votes by the legislature or the electorate, meaning that they were at risk long before *Obergefell* swept them away.

The speed at which opposition to same-sex marriage has receded in nearly all these states—including those states where the ban enjoyed a strong lock-in effect, a mild lock-in effect, or nearly none at all—is as important as the ease with which constitutional bans could be repealed. Figures 6.7 through 6.9 show actual support in 1994–1996, actual support at the time of the constitutional amendment, and projected support for 2012 and 2016.[152]

As Figure 6.7 shows, the eight strong lock-in states were not likely to enact same-sex marriage legislation of their own accord in the near future, based on either public support or the strength of the constitutional amendment.[153] But, by November 11, 2014, judicial decisions had wiped away bans in Idaho, Kansas, Utah, North Carolina, and South Carolina, and the remaining bans fell with *Obergefell*.[154]

Figure 6.8 highlights the flimsiness of state constitutional amendments. Of the eight mild lock-in states, a majority of the populations in three states (Nevada, Oregon, and Wisconsin) already supported same-sex marriage by 2012, putting those bans at risk without judicial challenges. By 2016, in five of the eight states a majority of the population was projected to support same-sex marriage (Alaska, Nevada, Oregon, Virginia, and Wisconsin).[155] Of course, bans in Virginia, Wisconsin, Oregon, Nevada, and Alaska had already been swept aside before *Obergefell*, permitting same-sex couples to marry in those states.[156]

Figure 6.9 tells an even starker story. Of the states with negligible lock-in effects, by 2012, a majority of the population in ten of the twelve supported same-sex marriage or were within striking distance of majority support (Arizona, Colorado, Florida, Missouri, Montana, Michigan, Nebraska, Ohio, North Dakota, and South Dakota).[157] By 2016, only four of the negligible lock-in effect states were not projected to have majority support for same-sex marriage (Arkansas, Mississippi, Missouri, and South Dakota).[158] Because the constitutions in these

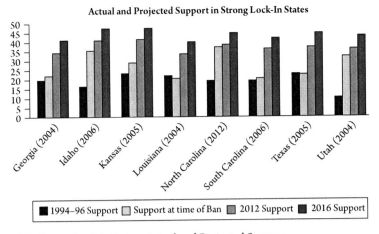

Figure 6.7. Strong Lock-in States: Actual and Projected Support.

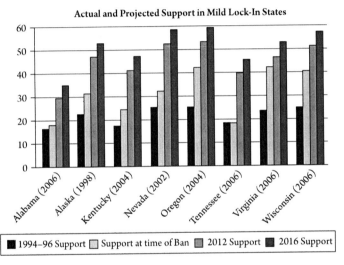

Figure 6.8. Mild Lock-in States: Actual and Projected Support.

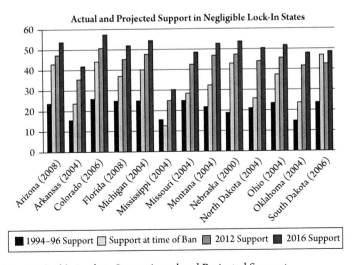

Figure 6.9. Negligible Lock-in States: Actual and Projected Support.

states are almost as easy to amend as enacting ordinary legislation, the need to bargain was at a zenith, however the Supreme Court decided *Obergefell*. The fact that, by November 11, 2014, bans in Oklahoma, Arizona, Colorado, Missouri, and Montana had already fallen, while decisions striking the bans in Florida and Arkansas were stayed, only underscored the necessity of bargaining.[159]

In short, if projected support approximates reality, legislation to recognize same-sex marriage would have been possible in the majority of the constitutional amendment states by the middle of the decade, whatever happened with *Obergefell*. And by 2020, putting aside the lock-in effect, virtually every state was likely to have sufficient support to voluntarily embrace same-sex marriage.[160] Only six states were projected to then show support below 50%, and all but two were projected to be within a few percentage points of majority support.[161]

Now that *Obergefell* dispositively decides the question of same-sex marriage, religious objectors who are bitterly disappointed may see no point in compromising now or no opportunity to do so.[162] Yet the same political flimsiness of constitutional amendments banning marriage reveals the folly of hardening in opposition to gay rights.

Gay rights advocates, eager to avoid the mistakes of past civil rights movements, have announced campaigns to capitalize on their momentum to wrest LGBT nondiscrimination protections from the political process, whether in state houses or by popular vote. Utah shows that in the legislative process, the interests of religious communities and individuals of faith mattered greatly and received unprecedented protections. If forced to pursue ballot measures, gay rights advocates surely will not build religious protections into the text of the ballot measure. Partnering with the LGBT community on compromise legislation offers another distinct advantage over gambling on an initiative: in some states, ballot measures may not be amended by the legislature except to "further the purposes of the ballot measure."[163] The spectre of losing all control over the extent of nondiscrimination protections and their impact on faith communities creates an urgency to reach reasonable compromises over gay rights now. But for compromise to succeed, proponents must be prepared to answer whether and how to balance competing interests in a single piece of legislation, a topic to which we now turn.

II. Overcoming Substantive Points of Resistance to Religious Liberty Protections

The LGBT community and religious traditionalists both benefit from compromise. Nonetheless, legislators and staffers charged with arriving at political consensus have expressed a number of substantive points of resistance to the religious liberty protections like the model provisions contained in Appendix 6.A.

A word about the proposals in Appendix 6.A is in order. Those protections were proposed in 2009 as part of any legislative package enacting marriage equality. I believe they can and should be part of a host of protections for faith communities in LGBT nondiscrimination legislation, as they were in the Utah Compromise. But I also believe that enacting them as stand-alone protections for religious objectors after *Obergefell*—even if qualified by hardship—extracts concessions for religious objectors while offering nothing for the gay community. Such one-sided deals are not only wrong, but have drawn the ire of the public and precipitated boycotts.[164]

If "hardship" exemptions protect the interests of both sides, as many believe they do,[165] why are the exemptions difficult for some legislators to embrace? Skepticism may stem from naked political assessments. But in my conversations with legislators, I have sensed a real struggle to vindicate two competing values—religious liberty and LGBT equality—with tensions along a number of specific lines. These substantive points of resistance range from whether accommodations disguise bigotry[166] to the idea that accommodations would impose hardships on a gay couple seeking services or undermine their dignity.[167] As shown below, religious liberty accommodations qualified by hardships—or that bypass collisions altogether—can transform a zero-sum proposition into one in which LGBT equality and religious freedom can both be affirmed.

A. Point of Resistance: "Exemptions Condone Bigotry in Disguise"

One point of resistance maintains that "exemptions condone bigotry in disguise." In other words, how can anyone tell the sincere from the feigned objection?

Whether a claimed belief is sincere or a convenient screen for ignoble acts is an issue common to many, but not all, religious freedom protections. Unlike freedom of speech, freedom of conscience does not protect the insincere.

True, some individuals may be motivated to make religious freedom arguments in order to receive better work hours, get away with using illegal drugs, or avoid criminal charges.[168] Many claims for protection, however, seek the ability to perform an act that is not only personally burdensome, but wholly meaningless apart from the religious faith that gives the act meaning. So, for example, claims to adhere to kosher dietary laws[169] or to go without medical care[170] burden the claimant significantly, but impose very little cost on others, making it very unlikely that someone would make an insincere claim.[171]

Even when an individual requests religious protection for an act that may impose a cost on others, that request may nonetheless carry significant personal costs for the individual. Consider nurses who allege that they have been coerced into assisting with abortions, despite federal and state statutes giving an

unqualified right to refuse.[172] Some have been threatened not only with termination, but also with losing their nursing licenses for "patient abandonment."[173]

Individuals who object on religious grounds to facilitating same-sex marriages have also incurred significant wrath in the marketplace, suggesting that an
objector would not lightly feign an objection. When a New Jersey bridal salon
refused to assist a woman with a bridal gown for her same-sex marriage, the story
went "viral," soon gracing not just the pages of a local newspaper, but national
media outlets as well, like the *Los Angeles Times*.[174]

As others have noted:

> If an exemption, say from participating in the sale of morning after pills,
> confers no ordinary advantage on the person who claims that participa-
> tion would violate his conscience, and if the seeking of an exemption is
> likely to cause irritation of superiors or colleagues that could down the
> road hurt one's chances for a promotion or informal benefits, a person
> has no incentive to make an insincere claim.[175]

Even though many individuals will not be motivated to feign a religious
objection, sincerity questions can and do arise in some cases—from military
conscientious objectors to prisoners requesting religious liberty accommodations. In each context, courts have generally proven competent to separate
the sincere from the insincere plaintiff. In the prison context, the Religious
Land Use and Institutionalized Persons Act ("RLUIPA") directs prison officials not to "impose a substantial burden on the religious exercise of a person
residing in or confined to an institution. . . ."[176] Some prisoners bring lawsuits
based on religious claims to harass prison administrators or to gain perks they
cannot otherwise secure. For instance, in 2010, an Orange County, California
inmate claimed to follow the Seinfeld holiday religion, Festivus, to get double portions of food.[177] There, prison officials determined that the inmate's
religious claim was not sincere. Obviously, prisoners also bring claims with
merit.[178]

Because both sincere and insincere claims can arise, in *Cutter v. Wilkinson*, the
Supreme Court gave prison officials considerable leeway to test the sincerity of a
prisoner's stated need for accommodation before a prisoner plaintiff could take
advantage of RLUIPA's accommodations for religion:

> [P]rison officials may appropriately question whether a prisoner's reli-
> giosity, asserted as the basis for a requested accommodation, is authen-
> tic. Although RLUIPA bars inquiry into whether a particular belief or
> practice is central to a prisoner's religion, the Act does not preclude
> inquiry into the sincerity of a prisoner's professed religiosity. The truth

of a belief is not open to question; rather, the question is whether the objector's beliefs are truly held.[179]

The Court reaffirmed this approach in *Burwell v. Hobby Lobby Stores, Inc.*[180] Interpreting the federal Religious Freedom Restoration Act ("RFRA")[181] to prohibit the government from forcing closely held, family-owned corporations to cover drugs and devices they religiously oppose, so long as less restrictive means were available,[182] the Court necessarily grappled with whether mandated coverage substantially burdened the plaintiffs' religious beliefs. Writing for the Court, Justice Alito explained that "it is not for us to say that [plaintiffs'] religious beliefs are mistaken or insubstantial. Instead, our 'narrow function . . . in this context is to determine' whether the line drawn reflects 'an honest conviction.'"[183]

The military has long had a detailed system in place for evaluating the sincerity of conscientious objections to military service.[184] Sincerity tests parallel the examination of "pretext," which is common to most employment discrimination litigation in federal court. Under the framework developed by the Supreme Court in *McDonnell Douglas Corp. v. Green*,[185] courts must evaluate whether an employer's proffered non-discriminatory reason for an adverse employment action is a pretext for invidious discrimination.

Although these contexts differ in important ways, together they demonstrate that courts have the institutional competence to decide whether a claimed religious objection to same-sex marriage is sincere or merely pretext for animus.

This is not to say that deciding the sincerity of a religious belief is an easy task. Sincerity must be determined "without a view as to [the] truth or falsity" of the religious belief being claimed, a point that the Supreme Court established in *United States v. Ballard*.[186] There, the government indicted leaders of a religion called "I Am" for mail fraud after they solicited donations from individuals they promised to cure of diseases. The Court held that the jury could properly decide whether the leaders sincerely believed that they had the ability to heal but could not evaluate the religious belief itself. Further, as Professor Chemerinsky points out, "[t]here is no measure for sincerity,"[187] although a number of commentators have suggested guides for evaluating it. For example, Professor Greenawalt notes that when someone "loses her job or is demoted because she actually refuses to perform an act," this helps to "demonstrate a true claim of conscience."[188] But he observes that "those whose claim for an exemption is granted usually are not put to such a test, . . . opening an exemption . . . to those with lukewarm reservations."[189]

While it is true that legislative protections proposed in Appendix 6.A as part of a legislative package enacting marriage equality would have shielded most religious objectors from lawsuits, this does not mean that objecting is cost-free. As noted above, many refusals are met with social opprobrium or stigma from one's employer, coworkers, or community, even when there are existing protections.[190]

Neither does it mean that religious objectors get a free pass. Lawsuits may follow, and, if an exemption is structured like that in Appendix 6.A,[191] objectors who are sued may find that their beliefs are, in fact, subjected to a searching examination for sincerity. In the end, the difficulty of assessing sincerity remains "one reason for the law to avoid exemptions," but that reason "must be measured against the positive reasons to grant such exemptions."[192]

B. Point of Resistance: "Objectors Are Protected from Doing the Deed (Solemnizing a Relationship), and That Is Sufficient"—or "Society Should Protect the Clergy, and Only Them"

Every draft same-sex marriage bill has unambiguously protected the refusal to solemnize a marriage,[193] a wholly unnecessary protection given the shared intuition that churches and clergy cannot be forced to solemnize marriages in violation of their religious tenets.[194] But legislators responsible for the text of marriage equality bills have been much more skeptical when it comes to crafting a "compromise that permits continued discrimination outside of solemnizing a marriage in a church sanctuary."[195] Professor John Corvino captures nicely the tension over protecting more than solemnization when he observes that the fight about religious liberty protections is not about the clergy, but about "the not-strictly-religious things that religious organizations often do: renting out banquet space, for example. And it's about religious individuals who for reasons of conscience wish to discriminate in secular settings."[196]

Although unstated, Corvino's comments encompass three related claims: first, that facilitating a ceremony is not a religious act in the way that performing the ceremony itself is; second, that an objector's claim weakens when it extends to services routinely provided by commercial entities, such as renting a banquet hall; and finally, that a religious objector may legally or morally object when asked directly to "do the deed"—to solemnize a relationship—but that an objector's moral or legal claim weakens when less direct actions are at stake.[197]

Let's begin with whether facilitating a same-sex marriage should be entitled to protection. Religious objectors, from wedding planners to caterers, all may seek to step aside from providing certain services because they "feel that they are being asked to promote or facilitate sin in a way that makes them personally responsible for the sin that ensues."[198] Professor Douglas Laycock believes there is a tendency "to dismiss these feelings of moral responsibility" because "the person providing services to a same-sex couple is not participating in the . . .

conduct she considers immoral and cannot reasonably think of herself as responsible for it."[199] Yet, he contends, this is a mistake: "[m]any religious traditions have a long history of theological teaching attempting to identify the point at which one who cooperates with another's wrongdoing, or even one who fails to sufficiently resist, becomes personally responsible for that wrongdoing."[200] Certainly, with other actions, ideas of complicity and vicarious moral responsibility have not seemed so far-fetched—they underpinned, for example, boycotts of companies doing business in South Africa during apartheid.[201]

The religious liberty exemptions folded into existing same-sex marriage laws, described in Appendix 6.B, have treated claims of facilitation as worthy of respect: all exempted religious institutions from facilitating or celebrating a marriage through such actions as providing the space for a reception.[202] And six states exempted individual employees of religious organizations from the duty to "celebrate or promote" same-sex marriage if doing so would violate their "religious beliefs and faith."[203]

But those same laws offer no protection to businesses or individuals in the marketplace who provide catering, flowers, reception halls, or gowns.[204] This brings us to the question of whether the law should distinguish between religious organizations and for-profit commercial vendors, even when they provide identical services.

In other contexts, the law has not drawn the line for an exemption along a nonprofit versus for-profit divide. For example, with respect to abortion, many conscience clauses exempt nonprofit and for-profit providers alike. Thus, the Church Amendment provides that the receipt of certain federal funds cannot be used by courts or public officials to force any entity to "make its facilities available for the performance of any sterilization procedure or abortion if [it] is prohibited by the entity on the basis of religious beliefs or moral convictions" or to "provide any personnel for [such services]."[205] This protection is not limited to nonprofit organizations or denominational hospitals. Clearly, abortion services are provided in the commercial marketplace by non-objecting institutions.[206] So, at least in the abortion context, it is what objectors are being asked to do, not what kind of corporate form they take, that merits conscience protection.

Of course, it was precisely the refusal of the *Hobby Lobby* Court to draw the line for protection at religious nonprofits, and no further, that has so many up in arms now.[207] The deep and sustained blowback over *Hobby Lobby* is likely to make any compromise that encompasses for-profit entities harder to arrive at, whether that protection comes from new generalized protections like RFRA or from narrowly drawn, well-constructed specific exemptions.

Just as conscience protections have not historically been limited to nonprofit organizations, neither have they extended protection only for direct participation. Again, abortion conscience clauses are illustrative. Many insulate not just the physician who performs the abortion, but any person being asked to assist in its performance. This is true of both state-level exemptions[208] and federal conscience protections.[209] Some reach services outside those that most would view as "core"—the abortion procedure itself—to encompass more peripheral activities, like training and referrals for abortion.[210] Some healthcare conscience clauses are so broad that they exempt objectors from performing any service they find objectionable if the facility receives certain program funding from the federal government.[211]

The accommodation of an employee's religious beliefs in the employment context follows this pattern as well. Title VII of the Civil Rights Act of 1964 ("Title VII") requires employers to provide reasonable accommodations for an employee's religious practice or belief unless the employer will experience an undue hardship.[212] As thinned-out as Title VII's protections now are,[213] Title VII imposes this duty even when the objector does not directly facilitate an activity to which she objects. Thus, Title VII's protections have extended to nurses who do not want to assist with an abortion,[214] post office clerks processing clerks who processing draft registration forms[215] and IRS agents who process applications for tax exemptions.[216] Although employers may consider hardships to themselves and other employees in granting or refusing an accommodation, nothing suggests that only those directly involved in a challenged activity can or should be exempted. The expansive protections in the employment and healthcare contexts reflect the reality that many activities implicate one's conscience.

It is, however, possible that a claim for exemption may be so remote that it is beyond cognizance and society's willingness to protect it. For instance, an Iowa Attorney General Opinion concluded that the state's abortion conscience clause would not extend to a pharmacist making up the saline solution used in abortions.[217]

By their very terms, the exemptions in Appendix 6.A assume a pre-existing duty to serve or law against sexual orientation discrimination, to which there would be a limited step-off for "provid[ing] goods or services that assist or promote the solemnization or celebration of any marriage."[218] Some, like Professor Kent Greenawalt, have asked if this would cover the clerk signing the paperwork, the one who hands it to the customer, and the cashier, too. All these services arguably facilitate the same-sex marriage because they involve the license. It is difficult to pinpoint the precise degree of involvement warranting an exemption. But clearly, an exemption should not cover the security officer who unlocks the clerk's office in the morning because unlocking the building is not particular to facilitating same-sex marriages—the office must be unlocked to facilitate all of the office's other business throughout the day. Put another way, because the office must be open to the public for a number of services, there is no meaningful sense in which the guard's service "celebrates" or "assists" the "solemnization" of any particular couple's marriage. Neither is there any reason for the security guard to know the occasion for any particular couple's visit to the clerk's office, which suggests that any refusal has nothing to do with sincere religious objections to the marriage. Importantly, society can afford to take a more expansive, not crabbed view of "assisting" with the promotion or celebration of same-sex marriage if the exemption is qualified by hardship to the same-sex couple[219]—hardship introduces a significant limiting principle, as does the sincerity test. Thus, at a time when the public remains deeply divided about same-sex marriage, legislators can soften the blow for people who cannot, consistent with their faith, facilitate same-sex marriages. Ideally, legislators will craft creative solutions to bypass objectors entirely, while guaranteeing seamless access to marriage for all couples as the Utah Compromise did. Barring that, legislators should allow religious objectors to step aside when doing so would not impose costs on same-sex couples, as Part II.D explains.

C. Point of Resistance: "No One Is Being Asked to Do Anything So No One Needs Protection"

Legislators have expressed ambivalence and genuine confusion about how same-sex marriage can trigger a threat to religious liberty, asking for, in the words of D.C. Councilmember Jim Graham, "concrete examples .... Otherwise [people will worry that legislators are just] thinking in [a] kind of 'airy fairy way' about possible problems."[220] This chapter has outlined numerous concrete examples of individuals and organizations being asked to perform acts that they cannot, for reasons of faith, perform—judges being asked to solemnize marriages; religious organizations being approached to provide space for weddings or receptions; town clerks being asked to process the paperwork for marriages when other non-objecting personnel are immediately available to provide the needed service. This sub-part will focus on just one concrete example.

The idea that no government official or employee will be asked to do anything that would burden them overlooks a stream of threats to government employees and officials that they must serve everyone who walks through the door, even if another willing person can perform the needed service. For instance, Massachusetts justices of the peace,[221] Iowa country recorders, magistrates, and judges, and New York town clerks[222] have all been told that refusing to serve all couples will result in criminal misdemeanor prosecutions or other sanctions.[223]

Many government employees and officials believe they are at risk, prompting them to resign in advance of collisions.[224] Because every state to voluntarily embrace same-sex marriage had a preexisting statute banning discrimination based on sexual orientation, government employees had little recourse if they could not do the service.[225] The clashes sketched above are all premised on violations of these non-discrimination statutes, with claims framed as sexual orientation or marital status discrimination.[226] The penalties for violating non-discrimination laws are sobering. For instance, in Massachusetts, violators may be fined more than $50,000 and spend up to a year in jail.[227] In Connecticut, violators can spend 30 days in jail.[228]

Because non-discrimination statutes have provided a vehicle for challenges, some contend that objections to same-sex marriage are like other forms of discrimination against lesbians and gays.[229]

This is simply not true. Laws prohibiting discrimination on the basis of classifications such as race date back to the 1960s and 1970s, long before anyone envisioned same-sex marriage.[230] These laws address commercial services, like hailing taxis, serving burgers, and leasing apartments, where it is hard to imagine that a refusal to serve another individual can reflect anything other than animus toward that individual.

Refusals to assist with a same-sex marriage, however, are different—they can stem from something other than anti-gay animus.[231] For many people, marriage is a religious institution and wedding ceremonies are a religious sacrament.[232] For these individuals, assisting with marriage ceremonies has a religious significance that ordering burgers and driving taxis simply do not. Many have no objection generally to providing services to lesbians and gays, but they would object to directly facilitating a marriage—just as some religious believers would object to facilitating an interfaith or second marriage.

Without explicit protection in the non-discrimination or same-sex marriage law, many will be faced with a cruel choice: your conscience or your livelihood.

More to the point, if no one will seriously be asked to do anything, it costs nothing to allay the fears of people who are simply asking for a way to both honor their convictions *and* live together with same-sex couples in peace.

D. Point of Resistance: "Same-Sex Couples Should Not Have to Bear the Cost of Another's Religious Objection"

Like the religious liberty protections in the Utah Compromise, the package of exemptions in Appendix 6.A was proposed as part of legislation effecting marriage equality. Both strive to balance the interests of same-sex couples with the religious concerns of others. Anytime one asks advocates on either side to balance interests, the natural response is "why should we do that?" Ask legislators, and they want to know not only *why* one should balance interests, but precisely *how.* To answer either question, it is necessary to explain how a given religious liberty accommodation would work.

In a limited set of instances, collisions between religious objectors and same-sex couples can be bypassed entirely, as the Utah Compromise did with marriage solemnization. Where religious objections cannot be creatively bypassed, legislators face the daunting task of attempting to reconcile competing interests in two very different settings: government offices and the commercial marketplace. Because they raise distinct concerns, different restrictions must be placed on the ability of religious objectors to step aside. However structured, exemptions for religious believers will be better received when packaged with meaningful protections for the LGBT community.

1. Bypassing Religious Objectors

In the best of circumstances, accommodations for government workers strike many fair-minded Americans as wrong—they believe government employees should not be able to pick and choose what duties to perform, notwithstanding the norm established in Title VII that we should accommodate religious belief or practice when feasible.[233] Accommodations for magistrates and marriage registrars pose an additional challenge: once couples have the right to marry, the state cannot enact unqualified religious objections that could operate to bar access to marriage.[234] To shut down access to marriage is to deny the right just granted in *Obergefell.* Just as people of good will were appalled when Orval Faubus stood on the front steps of Arkansas's Central High School to block black children from entering, we should not tolerate government actors erecting a choke point on the path to marriage.[235]

Utah, the second most religious state in America, faced the very real possibility of widespread religious objections by government officials who otherwise may have been tasked with solemnizing marriages.[236] For the first time in Utah law, the Utah Compromise guaranteed access to marriage solemnization for all couples requesting it. But even as it placed this duty on state clerk's offices, it also permitted them to outsource that function to willing celebrants in the community.[237] In Utah, judges, religious authorities, and other elected officials may solemnize a marriage. Some thinly staffed state offices outsourced the new function for simple reasons of efficiency; others did so to respect the religious beliefs of co-workers.[238] By specifying that the duty to provide access to marriage may be fulfilled only with willing celebrants, Utah avoided the need to fire employees—*without* asking gay couples to bear the cost of another's religious objection. By instituting the same process for gay couples and straight couples alike, Utah ensured the dignity of gay couples. Utah also avoided the kind of ugliness and refusals by state employees that same-sex couples have experienced after *Obergefell*[239] —a horrible experience for anyone during what should be one of the happiest times of their life.

2. *Conditioning the Right to Object on Causing No Hardship to Others*

Bypassing collisions is not always possible, however, necessitating more conscious attempts to reconcile competing interests. When balancing competing interests, great care must be given to how religious liberty protections are structured. The package of same-sex marriage exemptions in Appendix 6.A would have given state employees and officials—judges, justices of the peace, and marriage license clerks—as well as individuals in ordinary commerce—like bakers, photographers, caterers, and musicians—the ability to step aside from facilitating *any* marriage for religious reasons, but only when no hardship would result to same-sex couples. In the case of government employees, an employee could step aside only if another willing employee is promptly available to do the service without delay or inconvenience.

Under the exemptions in Appendix 6.A, commercial vendors could have stepped, too, when it would not substantially burden same-sex couples—in which case, religious liberty must yield.

To be clear, under both constructions, in a straight-up contest between religious liberty and marriage equality, religious liberty yields. Of course, as with any rule that seeks to balance two competing interests, hardship exemptions will involve some line drawing—specifically, what would count as "promptly" or as "inconvenience" or "delay." Such line drawing should be accomplished through the legislative process, permitting states to make choices that reflect the facts on the ground in that state—for instance, how urban or rural the state is, the number of willing providers of a needed service in locales across the state, etc.[240] It is natural for states to make different policy decisions; as Jonathan Rauch has observed, "[t]here's no reason that Massachusetts and Texas need to do the same thing[;] [n]ot everyone should agree on everything and not every state should look alike."[241]

Many religious believers ask why their rights simply do not trump since, in the words of Chief Justice John Roberts, their "freedom to exercise religion is . . . actually spelled out in the Constitution."[242] Neutral and generally applicable laws do not violate Free Exercise guarantees, no matter how much they burden an individual's or organization's exercise of religion.[243] And restricting the ability to object to situations when no hardship for same-sex couples would result is principled: unqualified religious objections cannot operate to bar access to marriage now that the Court has spoken dispositively.[244] Further, a qualified exemption has value for religious objectors; in the vast majority of cases involving government employees, the objector can be staffed around.[245]

On the other side of the ledger, some will ask why same-sex couples should ever have to experience any dislocation, however slight or remote. The case for a qualified exemption rests, in part, on two predictive judgments. First, public attitudes toward same-sex relationships are likely to become more divided, not less, in the absence of accommodations—this inflexibility will create lots of religious martyrs. And that will ensure that the issue "remains alive, bitter, and deeply divisive."[246]

Second, it is unnecessary to use the coercive power of the law to force religious objectors to "go along" *if* the market provides an adequate corrective, as it has in some parts of the country. For example, in August 2011, a New Jersey bridal salon allegedly refused to assist a lesbian woman with her gown because the woman "came from a nice Jewish family, and it was a shame that [she] was gay."[247] Although the owner denied the charges, outraged members of the public plastered the store's Facebook profile with comments, and Yelp, the business review mobile application, reported it, too.[248] Presumably, the salon owner lost all the business of gay couples in her community—in itself a sufficient penalty to limit refusals to those who feel quite strongly about it.[249] The salon owner may also have lost business from friends of those gay couples and others who heard about her stance. This example illustrates that, often, objectors will pay a cost in the market for objecting. Although whether the market will offer a sufficient corrective is a difficult question and likely to be answered differently by legislators across the country, it matters to whether and how to grant religious liberty protections.

As the next subparts explain, the contexts for government employee and commercial exemptions differ in important ways, warranting different protection.

3. Government Employees

As noted above, government employees' objections implicate access to the status of marriage, potentially allowing objectors to act as a choke point on the path to marriage. Because the state has a monopoly on marriage—no one may statutorily marry without the necessary license from the state—the state should not undercut the right to marry by enacting broad, unqualified conscience protections.

How could an exemption cause this kind of dislocation? Imagine that a same-sex couple resides in Nowhere, New York, and that there is only one town clerk that can help the couple complete their application for a marriage license. By refusing to assist the same-sex couple, that clerk could effectively bar them from the institution of marriage. Under the package of proposals in Appendix 6.A, the objector's religious liberty would have had to yield to the same-sex couple's right to marry "promptly."

Of course, outside this rare case of a hardship, where there are other clerks who would gladly serve the couple promptly and no one would otherwise lose by honoring the religious convictions of the objector, objectors' convictions should be honored.

The notion of "promptness" is not infinitely malleable. It would not be prompt to ask same-sex couples to wait any significant amount of time for a license that heterosexual couples would receive immediately. Neither should same-sex couples be asked to wait in a separate line. Instead, any staffing around of religious objectors should happen before the public presents for a service, which can be accomplished by asking objectors to recuse themselves *ex ante* in writing. Once staffed around, the objector never needs to come into contact with the public when seeking the objected-to service. How would this work?

Imagine a couple, Steve and Adam, arrive at the marriage office, which has three officials, Faith, Hope, and Charity. Only Faith has a religious objection. If all the clerks randomly greet individuals and couples who present, disaster looms. Faith easily could pop up to assist Steve, only to find him later joined by his same-sex partner. If Faith then refuses to assist the couple, the couple surely will notice and be offended. Instead, Faith should be required to file a written objection and step aside from assisting with all marriages. Hope or Charity can then greet the public and farm out work, leaving Faith to perform other official duties, such as issuing subpoenas and taking affidavits.

Note what does *not* happen when so structured: Faith never encounters Steve and Adam but neither does she receive a pass; she performs other office functions. Steve and Adam never wait longer or step into another line. They never know any individual magistrate's views, including Faith's. By proactively addressing Faith's objection, Steve and Adam suffer no embarrassment. Dignitary harms evaporate when accommodations are invisible.

Far from overlooking dignitary harms, the risk of dignitary harm should guide policymakers in fashioning solutions that minimize the net harm of permitting religious objection.

A common refrain from accommodation skeptics is that religious objectors in government service should do every service available at the office or resign.[250] This stance conflates the work of the office with the work of any given employee. That is, a citizen's right to obtain a marriage license is against the state, not any particular employee. Moreover, as the discussion of Title VII above demonstrates, it is appropriate, and sometimes legally required, to allow employees to step aside from part of their jobs when they can reasonably be accommodated and there would be no undue hardship.[251] Although the US Court of Appeals for the Seventh Circuit has taken a very narrow view of such accommodations when sought by police officers and firefighters,[252] other circuits do not take such a narrow view—especially when sought by employees doing routine, predictable, and easily staffed-around work.[253]

Quite simply, magistrates and licensure clerks are not firefighters, and any objection is unlikely to cause great dislocation to staff around.

More fundamentally, this stance vilifies people who could not have known when they took their jobs that they would be asked to facilitate a same-sex marriage. Many government employees began working for the government long before the advent of same-sex marriage, and a large portion of them are already eligible to retire.

Dismissal or resignation would likely be very costly to these employees. A job in the state licensure office pays well and provides generous benefits; and many long-time employees have built up retirements that would be wiped out or significantly curtailed if they exit rather than violate a religious conviction.[254] Just as important as these very human costs is the fact that collisions will gradually become less and less significant. We know that resistance to recognition of same-sex relationships largely follows generational lines.[255] This suggests conflicts over same-sex marriage will recede over time until objection "gradually fade[s] away, and nearly all the rest [of those who oppose same-sex marriage] will go silent, succumbing to the live-and-let-live traditions of the American people."[256]

4. Commercial Vendors

The package of proposals in Appendix 6.A would have delivered marriage equality while giving more room for religious objectors in the stream of commerce to object unless the couple could not get the service without a substantial hardship. Now that marriage equality is recognized, that deal likely is not feasible, even with significant qualification, unless the state can proffer sexual orientation non-discrimination protections now absent in statewide law. Even then, balancing the rights of LGBT individuals and religious traditionalists will be a tough sell for reasons explained below.

Why might one build in greater leeway for small mom-and-pop wedding vendors to step aside from providing a service than for government employees? First, the service denied is not nearly as important as blocking a person's access to a legal status and there are likely to be fewer hardships (the phone book of virtually every city or county contains dozens of photographers, for example). Second, a qualified exemption "lowers the stakes" in the debate about same-sex marriage and LGBT rights more generally, about which public opinion continues to be split. Houston's 2015 repeal of the HERO ordinance provides an important caution that in winner-takes-all contests, gay rights sometimes lose out—to the detriment of important social progress. Third, qualified religious liberty protections preserve as much religious freedom as possible in a liberal society without significantly encroaching on others, which we should generally strive for, especially where the costs to the public are cabined. Finally, a qualified exemption provides "elbow room" for citizens with widely divergent views to live together in a pluralistic society.

Weighed against all these positives is the insult from being denied a service. As Professor Laycock has pointed out, "the American commitment to freedom of speech ensures that same-sex couples will be reminded . . . from time to time" about how others feel, especially while opinion remains deeply divided.[257]

The government should be concerned about whether same-sex couples are subjected to insult. Indeed, the costs to gay couples today in being excluded from public accommodations are poignant. When a Tennessee hardware store can, without repercussion, openly post a sign that says "no gays allowed," gay people are treated as "less than."[258] All people of good faith—gay or straight—lose from that coarsening. True, the public often polices such discrimination, but it will not always do so.

Sometimes, the law can create a buffer zone between religious traditionalists and the rest of the world that satisfies the needs of both. The Utah Compromise broadened existing exemptions for religious groups and small businesses in its civil rights laws governing housing and hiring to give religious communities and individuals the autonomy to operate schools, offer counseling, and support marriage (through, say, married student housing) as they had before same-sex marriage was recognized and LGBT non-discrimination protections were enacted; to speak about marriage, family, and sexuality as they had before; and to remain in taxpayer-paid jobs without sacrificing access to a state service. For such consessions, the gay community cemented employment and housing protections in the nation's most politically conservative state that exceed those provided in New York.[259] Carefully drawn exemptions allow people deeply divided over the common good to coexist in peace.

But to date, no public accommodations law at the federal or state level has combined religious exemptions with a right to be served. In Tennessee and much of the rest of the country, religious traditionalists can exclude gay people for religious reasons or no reason at all—when it comes to hardware stores and ordinary services without religious meaning, that should be wholly unacceptable. The failure of public accommodation laws to share the public square means that in states that do ban sexual-orientation discrimination, gay couples can demand access, whatever the consequences for small mom-and-pop wedding vendors. Some bakers, photographers, and bed-and-breakfast owners who adhere to a traditional view of marriage may be forced to a painful choice: serve everyone or be fined or hounded out of business.[260] As Part I noted, many see forcing the closure of someone's business as harsh and pointless if other comparable services are readily available elsewhere.

After *Obergefell* common sense protections that permit religious traditionalists and gay couples to coexist may be possible *if the interests of both communities are advanced*, as the Utah Compromise shows. But in the public accommodations context, such protections will require a wholly new approach that deliberately seeks to share the public square.

One way to divide the public square is to enact protections qualified by hardship to same-sex couples. In this scheme, small wedding vendors with less than five employees would be permitted to decline to facilitate any wedding when doing so would violate her religious convictions *so long as* the couple can secure the service without a substantial hardship. This approach has a lot of intuitive appeal. Wedding vendors cannot legally block access to the legal status of marriage, as objecting marriage registrars and clerks could do. The plethora of photographers and bakers in most locales suggests there are likely to be few hardships. In much of the country, there likely will be lots of businesses who want to serve same-sex couples and will actively seek them as clients.[261] As Professor Laycock explains, "same-sex couples will generally be far happier working with a provider who contentedly desires to serve them than with one who believes them to be engaged in mortal sin."[262]

States that have existing non-discrimination bans pose the hardest challenge. Enacting stand-alone protections for religious objectors—even ones qualified by hardship—will be seen as a rollback of existing civil rights protections.[263] Such measures also extract concessions for religious objectors while offering up nothing for the gay community. Perhaps marriage-related protections can be offered alongside express protections for gender identity or tied to protections in spheres where LGBT individuals are not now protected, like access to credit or higher education.[264]

At the very least, any concessions for religious business owners should preserve the dignity of our gay neighbors. To do that would require the kind of seamless treatment the Utah Compromise arrived at when it outsourced the marriage function to willing celebrants in the community, bypassing any religious objectors. How religious wedding vendors can be permitted to step aside while preserving the dignity of gay couples is the thorny question facing legislatures across the country today.[265]

Conclusion

Ultimately, religious objectors must make convincing claims for legislative accommodations because they are not shielded from generally applicable laws as a matter of constitutional right. In the end, no matter how thoughtful an exemption or claim for accommodation may be, individuals realistically seeking religious liberty protections must thoughtfully engage the points of resistance to giving such accommodations. The rapidly changing political calculus surrounding same-sex marriage and LGBT rights shows that, for now, both sides advance values important to them by shaping laws that affirm both LGBT rights *and* religious liberty.

Appendix 6.A

PROPOSED SAME-SEX MARRIAGE PROTECTIONS

The Marriage Conscience Protection that I and others proposed, prior to *Obergefell* as a part of compromise marriage equality legislation would have read[266]:

Section ____

(a) Religious organizations protected

Notwithstanding any other provision of law, no religious or denominational organization, no organization operated for charitable or educational purposes which is supervised or controlled by or in connection with a religious organization, and no individual employed by any of the foregoing organizations, while acting in the scope of that employment, shall be required to

(1) provide services, accommodations, advantages, facilities, goods, or privileges for a purpose related to the solemnization or celebration of any marriage; or

(2) solemnize any marriage; or

(3) treat as valid any marriage

if such providing, solemnizing, or treating as valid would cause such organizations or individuals to violate their sincerely held religious beliefs. This section shall not permit a religious organization engaged in the provision of healthcare, or its individual employees, to refuse to treat a state-recognized marriage as valid for purposes of a spouse's rights to visitation or to surrogate healthcare decision making.

(b) Individuals and small businesses protected

(1) Except as provided in paragraph (b)(2), no individual, sole proprietor, or small business shall be required to

(A) provide goods or services that assist or promote the solemnization or celebration of any marriage, or provide counseling or other services that directly facilitate the perpetuation of any marriage; or

(B) provide benefits to any spouse of an employee; or

(C) provide housing to any married couple

if providing such goods, services, benefits, or housing would cause such individuals or sole proprietors, or owners of such small businesses, to violate their sincerely held religious beliefs.

(2) Paragraph (b)(1) shall not apply if
   (A) a party to the marriage is unable to obtain any similar good or services, employment benefits, or housing elsewhere without substantial hardship; or
   (B) in the case of an individual who is a government employee or official, if another government employee or official is not promptly available and willing to provide the requested government service without inconvenience or delay; *provided that* no judicial officer authorized to solemnize marriages shall be required to solemnize any marriage if to do so would violate the judicial officer's sincerely held religious beliefs.
(3) A "small business" within the meaning of paragraph (b)(1) is a legal entity other than a natural person
   (A) that provides services which are primarily performed by an owner of the business; or
   (B) that has five or fewer employees; or
   (C) in the case of a legal entity that offers housing for rent, that owns five or fewer units of housing.

(c) No civil cause of action or other penalties

No refusal to provide services, accommodations, advantages, facilities, goods, or privileges protected by this section shall

(1) result in a civil claim or cause of action challenging such refusal; or
(2) result in any action by the State or any of its subdivisions to penalize or withhold benefits from any protected entity or individual, under any laws of this State or its subdivisions, including but not limited to laws regarding employment discrimination, housing, public accommodations, educational institutions, licensing, government contracts or grants, or tax-exempt status.[267]

Appendix 6.B

CORE LEGISLATIVE RELIGIOUS LIBERTY PROTECTIONS

State	Expressly exempt clergy from duty to solemnize any marriage[a]	Expressly exempts a religious organization (including nonprofits) from duty to "provide services, accommodations, advantages, facilities, goods, or privileges" (or similar) for solemnization[b]	Expressly protects covered objectors from private suit and/or government "penalty"[d]	Expressly exempts "religious programs, counseling, courses, or retreats" (A)[e]; housing for married individuals (B)[f]; or insurance coverage by fraternal organizations (C)[g]	Expressly allows a religiously affiliated adoption or foster care agency to maintain its manner of services (e.g., place children only with opposite-sex couples)[h]	Expressly exempts non-clergy authorized celebrants (e.g., judges and justices of the peace) from duty to solemnize[i]
Same-Sex Marriage by Legislation						
Conn.[j]	✓	✓	✓		✓[k]	
Del.	✓	✓	✓[l]			✓
D.C.	✓	✓	✓	(A)		
Haw.	✓	✓	✓			
Ill.	✓	✓[m]	✓			
Md.	✓	✓	✓	(A), (C)	✓[n]	

Minn.	✓	✓	(B)	✓[o]
N.H.	✓	✓	(A), (B), (C)	
N.Y.	✓	✓	(B)	
R.I.	✓	✓	(A), (C)	✓[p]
Vt.	✓	✓[q]	(C)	
Wash.	✓	✓	(A)	
Same-Sex Marriage by Ballot Initiative				
Me.	✓	✓[r]		
Same-Sex Marriage by Judicial Decision				
Calif.	✓	✓[s]		
Iowa				
Mass.				
N.J.	[t]			
N.M.				
Okla.				
Utah				

(Continued)

Continued

[a] See Conn. Gen. Stat. § 46b-22b (West 2009); Del. Code Ann. tit. 13, § 106 (2013), http://delcode.delaware.gov/title13/c001/sc01/index.shtml; D.C. Code § 46-406(c) (LexisNexis 2012); S.B. No. 1 H.D.1 § 572-D, 27th Leg, 2nd Spec. Sess. (Haw. 2013); S.B. 10(a-5), 98th Gen. Assemb. Reg. Sess. (Ill. 2013); Md. Code Ann., Fam. Law §§ 2-201, 2-202, (LexisNexis 2012); Minn. Stat. Ann. § 517.09 (West Supp. 2013); N.H. Rev. Stat. Ann. § 457:37(II) (Supp. 2013); N.Y. Dom. Rel. Law § 11(1) (McKinney Supp. 2014); Vt. Stat. Ann. tit. 18, § 5144(b) (2012); R.I. Gen. Laws Ann. § 15-3-6.1(b) (LexisNexis 2013); Wash. Rev. Code § 26.04.010(4) (LexisNexis 2013). See also Me. Rev. Stat. Ann. tit. 19-A, § 655 (Supp. 2013); Cal. Fam. Code § 400 (West Supp. 2013).

[b] See Conn. Gen. Stat. § 46b-150d (2013); D.C. Code § 46-406(e) (2013); Md. Code Ann., Fam. Law §§ 2-201, 2-202 (West 2013); 2012 Md. Laws §§ 2-3; Minn. Stat. Ann. § 363A.26 (West 2013); N.H. Rev. Stat. Ann. § 457:37(III) (2013); N.Y. Dom. Rel. Law § 10-b(1) (McKinney 2013); R.I. Gen. Laws Ann. § 15-3-6.1 (West 2013); Vt. Stat. Ann. tit. 18, § 5144(b) (2013); Wash. Rev. Code Ann. § 26.04.010(5) (West 2013); S. 1, 27th Leg, 2nd Special Sess. 2 (Haw. 2013); S. 10 § 209(a-10), 98th Gen. Assemb, Reg. Sess. (Ill. 2013); see also Me. Rev. Stat. tit. 19-A, § 655 (2013).

[c] See Conn. Gen. Stat. § 46b-150d; D.C. Code § 46-406(e); Md. Code Ann., Fam. Law §§ 2-201, 2-202; 2012 Md. Laws §§ 2-3; Minn. Stat. Ann. § 517.09 (West 2013); N.H. Rev. Stat. Ann. § 457:37(III); N.Y. Dom. Rel. Law § 10-b(1); R.I. Gen. Laws Ann. § 15-3-6.1; Vt. Stat. Ann., tit. 18, § 5144(b); Wash. Rev. Code Ann. § 26.04.010(6); S. 1, 27th Leg, 2nd Special Sess. 2 (Haw. 2013); S. 10 § 209(a-10), 98th Gen. Assemb, Reg. Sess. (Ill. 2013); see also Me. Rev. Stat. tit. 19-A, § 655.

[d] See Conn. Gen. Stat. § 46b-150d; Del. Code Ann. tit. 13 § 106 (West 2013); D.C. Code § 46-406(e)(2); Md. Code Ann., Fam. Law §§ 2-201, 2-202; 2012 Md. Laws §§ 2-3; Minn. Stat. Ann. § 517.09; N.H. Rev. Stat. Ann. § 457:37(III); N.Y. Dom. Rel. Law § 10-b(1); R.I. Gen. Laws Ann. § 15-3-6.1; Wash. Rev. Code Ann. § 26.04.010(4); S.B. 10 § 209(a-10), 98th Gen. Assemb, Reg. Sess. (Ill. 2013); S. 1, 27th Leg, 2nd Special Sess. 6 (Haw. 2013); see also Me. Rev. Stat. tit. 19-A, § 655.

[e] See D.C. Code § 46-406(e); Md. Code Ann., Fam. Law §§ 2-201, 2-202; 2012 Md. Laws §§ 2-3 (provided so long as the program receives no government funding); N.H. Rev. Stat. Ann. § 457:37(III) (exempting "the promotion of marriage through religious counseling, programs, courses, retreats, or housing designated for married individuals"); R.I. Gen. Laws Ann. § 15-3-6.1 (exempting the "promotion of marriage through any social or religious programs or services"; Wash. Rev. Code Ann. § 26.04.010(7)(a)(ii). New York may also protect this. See N.Y. Dom. Rel. Law § 10-b(2) ("[N]othing in this article shall limit or diminish the right . . . of any religious or denominational institution or organization . . . from taking such action as is calculated by such organization to promote the religious principles for which it is established or maintained.").

[f] See Minn. Stat. Ann. § 363A.26 (providing that religious organization are not prohibited from "in matters relating to sexual orientation, taking any action with respect to . . . housing and real property"); N.H. Rev. Stat. Ann. § 457:37(III); N.Y. Dom. Rel. Law § 10-b (2) ("[N]othing in this article shall limit or diminish the right . . . of any religious or denominational institution or organization . . . to limit employment or sales or rental of housing accommodations or admission to or give preference to persons of the same religion or denomination . . .").

[g] See Md. Code Ann., Fam. Law §§ 2-201, 2-202; N.H. Rev. Stat. Ann. § 457:37(IV); R.I. Gen. Laws Ann. § 15-3-6.1(e) (West 2013); Vt. Stat. Ann. tit. 8 § 4501(b) (2013); see also Md. Code Ann., Ins. § 8-402 (2013) (defining "fraternal organization"); 2012 Md. Laws §§ 2-3.

[h] See 2009 Conn. Legis. Serv. § 19 (West); see also Md. Code Ann., Fam. Law §§ 2-201, 2-202; Minn. Stat. § 517.201; R.I. Gen. Laws Ann. § 15-3-6.1(e) (West 2013).

i Del. Code Ann. tit. 13, § 106 ("[N]othing in this section shall be construed to require any person (including any clergyperson or minister of any religion) authorized to solemnize a marriage to solemnize any marriage, and no such authorized person who fails or refuses for any reason to solemnize a marriage shall be subject to any fine or other penalty for such failure or refusal.").

j Connecticut passed legislation on the heels of a judicial decision requiring same-sex marriage. See Appendix 6.B.

k Conn. Gen. Stat. § 46b-35b (2013) (providing that the "manner" of services will be unaffected by the recognition of same-sex marriage, unless program publicly funded).

l Del. Code Ann. tit. 13 § 106 (providing that refusal shall not subject any person to "any fine or other penalty for such failure or refusal").

m S. 10 § 209(a-10), 98th Gen. Assemb., Reg. Sess. (Ill. 2013) (covering only the "facility" and extending only to organizations with "principal purpose" to advance religion).

n Md. Code Ann., Fam. Law § 2-202 (West 2013) (requiring no "promotion of marriage" through services unless program publicly funded).

o Minn. Stat. Ann. § 517.09 (West 2013).

p R.I. Gen. Laws Ann. § 15-3-6.1(e) (West 2013) (requiring no "promotion of marriage" through "any social or religious programs or services").

q Vt. Stat. Ann. tit. 9 § 4502(l) (West 2013) (insulating against only a "civil claim or cause of action" and not against government penalty).

r Me. Rev. Stat. tit. 19-A, § 655 (2013) (providing that no "church, religious denomination or other religious institution" must "host" any marriage when doing so would violate its "religious beliefs").

s Cal. Fam. Code § 400(a) (West 2013) (providing that "[a]ny refusal to solemnize a marriage under this subdivision, either by an individual or by a religious denomination, shall not affect the tax-exempt status of any entity").

t Griego v. Oliver, 316 P.3d. 865, 871 (N.M. 2013) ("Our holding will not interfere with the religious freedom of religious organizations or clergy because (1) no religious organization will have to change its policies to accommodate same gender couples, and (2) no religious clergy will be required to solemnize a marriage in contravention of his or her religious beliefs.").

Appendix 6.C

STATES RECOGNIZING SAME-SEX MARRIAGE AND METHOD OF RECOGNITION (THROUGH NOVEMBER 11, 2014)

Same-Sex Marriage Legal	
State	*Legislation/Decision*
Alaska	*Hamby v. Parnell*, No. 3:14-CV-00089-TMB, 2014 WL 5089399 (D. Alaska Oct. 12, 2014).
Arizona	*Connolly v. Jeanes*, No. 2:14-CV-00024 JWS, 2014 WL 5320642 (D. Ariz. Oct. 17, 2014).
California	*Perry v. Schwarzenegger*, 704 F. Supp. 2d 921 (2010), *aff'd sub nom. Perry v. Brown*, 671 F. 3d 1052 (2012), *aff'd sub nom. Hollingsworth v. Perry*, 133 S. Ct. 2652 (2013).
Colorado	*Burns v. Hickenlooper*, No. 14-CV-01817-RM-KLM, 2014 WL 3634834 (D. Colo. July 23, 2014).
Connecticut	*Kerrigan v. Comm'r of Pub. Health*, 289 Conn. 135 (2008), recognized same-sex marriage. The legislature then enacted same-sex marriage through legislation. Conn. Gen. Stat. § 46b-20 (2009).
Delaware	Del. Code Ann. tit. 13 § 101 (2013).
Hawaii	Haw. Rev. Stat. § 572-1 (West 2013).
Idaho	*Latta v. Otter*, No. 1:13-CV-00482-CWD, 2014 WL 1909999 (D. Idaho May 13, 2014), *aff'd*, 771 F.3d 456 (9th Cir. 2014).
Illinois	750 Ill. Comp. Stat. 5/201 (2014).
Indiana	*Baskin v. Bogan*, No. 1:14-CV-00355-RLY, 2014 WL 2884868 (S.D. Ind. June 25, 2014), *aff'd*, 766 F.3d 648 (7th Cir.), *cert. denied*, 135 S. Ct. 316, *cert. denied sub nom. Walker v. Wolf*, 135 S. Ct. 316 (2014).
Iowa	*Varnum v. Brien*, 763 N.W.2d 862 (2009).
Maine	In 2009, the Maine legislature passed a same-sex marriage bill, Me. Rev. Stat. Ann. tit. 19-A, § 650-A (2013), that voters later repealed by referendum. Maine voters enacted same-sex marriage by ballot initiative in 2012.
Maryland	Md. Code Ann. Fam. Law §§ 2-201 (LexisNexis 2012).
Massachusetts	*Goodridge v. Dep't of Pub. Health*, 440 Mass. 309 (2003).

State	Legislation/Decision
Minnesota	Minn. Stat. Ann. § 517.01 (West 2013).
Missouri (STL)	*Missouri v. Florida*, No. 1422-CC09027 (Mo. Cir. Ct. Nov. 5, 2014).
Nevada	*Latta v. Otter*, 771 F.3d 456 (9th Cir. 2014).
New Hampshire	N.H. Rev. Stat. § 457:1A (2010).
New Jersey	*Garden State Equal. v. Dow*, 82 A.2d 336 (N.J. Super. Ct. Law Div. 2013). Months before this decision, Governor Christie vetoed a 2012 same-sex marriage bill that contained modest religious liberty protection for organizations. See Kate Zernike, "Christie Keeps His Promise to Veto Gay Marriage Bill," *New York Times*, February 18, 2012, at A19.
New Mexico	*Griego v. Oliver*, 316 P.3d 865 (2013).
New York	N.Y. Dom. Rel. Law § 10-a (McKinney Supp. 2014).
North Carolina	*Fisher-Borne v. Smith*, No. 1:12CV589, 2014 WL 5138914 (M.D.N.C. Oct. 14, 2014); *Gen. Synod of the United Church of Christ v. Resinger*, No. 3:14-CV-00213-MOC, 2014 WL 5092288 (W.D.N.C. Oct. 10, 2014).
Oklahoma	*Bishop v. United States ex rel. Holder*, No. 04-CV-848-TCK-TLW, 2014 WL 116013 (N.D. Okla. Jan. 14, 2014), *aff'd sub nom. Bishop v. Smith*, 760 F.3d 1070 (10th Cir.), *cert. denied*, 135 S. Ct. 271 (2014).
Oregon	*Geiger v. Kitzhaber*, 994 F. Supp. 2d 1128 (D. Or. 2014).
Pennsylvania	*Whitewood v. Wolf*, 992 F. Supp. 2d 410 (M.D. Pa. 2014).
Rhode Island	R.I. Gen. Laws § 15-1-1 (2013).
District of Columbia	D.C. Code § 46-401 (LexisNexis 2012).
Utah	*Kitchen v. Herbert*, No. 2:13-cv-217, 2013 WL 6697874 (D. Utah Dec. 20, 2013), *aff'd*, 755 F.3d 1193 (10th Cir.), *cert. denied*, 135 S. Ct. 265 (2014)..
Vermont	Vt. Stat. Ann. Tit. 15, § 8 (2009).
Virginia	*Bostic v. Rainey*, 970 F. Supp. 2d 456, 461 (E.D. Va.), *aff'd sub nom. Bostic v. Schaefer*, 760 F.3d 352 (4th Cir.), *cert. denied sub nom. Rainey v. Bostic*, 135 S. Ct. 286, *cert. denied*, 135 S. Ct. 308, *cert. denied sub nom. McQuigg v. Bostic*, 135 S. Ct. 314 (2014).

(*Continued*)

State	Legislation/Decision
Washington	In 2012, the Washington legislature passed a same-sex marriage bill. Wash. Rev. Code § 26.04.010(1) (West 2012). The bill was put to a state vote as Referendum 74; the referendum passed, thereby legalizing same-sex marriage. 2012 Wash. Sess. Laws S.S.B. 6239 (Referendum).
West Virginia	Almost a month after West Virginia stopped defending the State's same-sex marriage ban, *McGee v. Cole*, No. CIV.A. 3:13-24068, 2014 WL 5802665 (S.D.W. Va. Nov. 7, 2014), held that the State must allow same-sex marriage.
Wisconsin	*Wolf v. Walker*, 986 F. Supp. 2d 982 (W.D. Wis.), *aff'd sub nom. Baskin v. Bogan*, 766 F.3d 648 (7th Cir.), *cert. denied*, 135 S. Ct. 316, *cert. denied sub nom. Walker v. Wolf*, 135 S. Ct. 316 (2014).
Wyoming	*Guzzo v. Mead*, No. 14-CV-200-SWS, 2014 WL 5317797 (D. Wyo. Oct. 17, 2014).

Favorable Same-Sex Marriage Decision Stayed	
State	**Decision**
Arkansas	*Jernigan v. Crane*, No. 4:13-CV-00410 KGB, 2014 WL 6685391 (E.D. Ark. Nov. 25, 2014); *Wright v. State*, 2014 WL 1908815 (Ark. Cir. 2014).
Florida	*Brenner v. Scott*, 999 F. Supp. 2d 1278 (N.D. Fla. 2014). Many state judges have also held that same-sex couples must be allowed to marry. See, e.g., *Huntsman v. Heavilin; Pareto v. Ruvin; Brassner v. Lade.*
Missouri	*Lawson v. Kelly*, No. 14-0622-CV-W-ODS, 2014 WL 5810215 (W.D. Mo. Nov. 7, 2014).
Texas	*De Leon v. Perry*, 975 F. Supp. 2d 632 (W.D. Tex. 2014).

Circuit Court Rulings That Made Same-Sex Marriage Inevitable	
State	**Decision**
Kansas	*Kitchen v. Herbert*, 755 F.3d 1193 (10th Cir.), *cert. denied*, 135 S. Ct. 265 (2014).
Montana	*Latta v. Otter*, 771 F.3d 456 (9th Cir. 2014).
South Carolina	*Bostic v. Schaefer*, 760 F.3d 352 (4th Cir.), *cert. denied sub nom. Rainey v. Bostic*, 135 S. Ct. 286, *cert. denied*, 135 S. Ct. 308, *cert. denied sub nom. McQuigg v. Bostic*, 135 S. Ct. 314 (2014).

Die and Let Live? The Asymmetry
of Accommodation

STEVEN D. SMITH*

The increasingly apt term "culture wars" refers to a polarizing tendency in which Americans are coming to coalesce around opposing political agendas that themselves murkily reflect divergent conceptions and evaluations of individualism, community, equality, authority, tradition, sexuality, Christianity, and the meaning and mission (if any) of America.[1] At the moment, the controversy over same-sex marriage is the most fiercely contested political and cultural battle,[2] but the intensity of that particular battle is likely due in part to the fact that same-sex marriage is only one particularly salient issue within a larger struggle.

Indeed, even the current debate over same-sex marriage immediately and explicitly implicates more than the issue of how marriage will be defined. Thus, religious conservatives typically oppose same-sex marriage on the merits, but in addition they worry about the effects of legal recognition of same-sex marriage on religious freedom.[3] On the other side, proponents of what they like to call "marriage equality"[4] sometimes dismiss this concern as unwarranted; in the alternative, they may acknowledge the conflict and explicitly argue that equality (as they understand it) should take priority over the traditional commitment to freedom of religion.[5] In between these parties is a group that I will call the moderators; among legal scholars this group includes people like Tom Berg,[6] Alan

* I thank Larry Alexander, Rick Garnett, Andy Koppelman, Michael Perry, Maimon Schwarzschild, Nomi Stolzenberg, George Wright, and participants in the conference on Religious Accommodation in the Age of Civil Rights, held at Harvard Law School on April 3–5, 2014, for helpful comments on an earlier draft. Since the conference was held, the conflict discussed here has developed; in particular, the Supreme Court's decision in *Obergefell v. Hodges*, 576 US __, (2015), appears to have settled the issue of the legalization of same-sex marriage, at least for the time being. A brief postscript to this article notes some of the conspicuous changes. A similar version of this chapter was published in the Southern California Law Review. I have received permission to reprint this.

Brownstein,[7] Douglas Laycock,[8] and Robin Wilson.[9] The moderators, while supportive of same-sex marriage, regard the danger to religion and religious exercise as serious, but they think it should be possible to satisfactorily accommodate both sides. They typically present their own favored position as a "live-and-let-live" approach.[10]

Thus, in a series of important articles,[11] Laycock argues that support for religious freedom and for same-sex marriage (and sexual equality generally) have much in common: in each case, he thinks, the goal is to respect individual identity and autonomy and to protect minorities who have historically been oppressed.[12] But even if Christian conservatives cannot make common cause with secular egalitarians, or vice versa, the parties ought to be able to embrace a mutually acceptable *modus vivendi*.

More specifically, the law should recognize same-sex marriage while providing generous exemptions so that religious believers and institutions that oppose the practice are not required to recognize or facilitate such marriages. This compromise would largely or fully accommodate the legitimate interests of each side, Laycock suggests, so the only reason why the compromise is not realized is that the contending parties are intransigent. "Each side," he says, "wants a total win."[13] Thus, proponents of sexual equality insist on enforcing anti-discrimination laws against religiously scrupulous counselors, photographers, pharmacists and others, even though these professionals' services or products are readily available elsewhere, and even when no sensible same-sex couple would actually want the assistance of, say, a counselor or photographer who is religiously opposed to their union. In such litigation, Laycock observes, the goal is not to gain a needed remedy but rather to punish opponents, and to drive them out of business.[14] Conversely, Christian conservatives oppose measures such as same-sex marriage even when these measures would leave the religious believers themselves free to marry according to their own beliefs and commitments. "The religious side," Laycock asserts, "persists in trying to regulate other people's sex lives so long as it thinks it has any chance of success."[15]

The force of Laycock's and other moderators' diagnosis and critique, and the rhetorical power of their attempt to claim the reasonable "middle ground," derive in important part from an implicit claim of symmetry. This claim informs both the prescriptive and the critical aspects of the moderators' arguments. There is a prescriptive appeal to symmetry in the effort to cast the moderators' favored outcomes—such as the legalization of same-sex marriage together with accommodations for the religiously scrupulous—as balanced and equally respectful of each side's legitimate interests. This is the claimed symmetry of "live and let live." And there is a critical symmetry in the effort to cast people on each side who hesitate to embrace the proffered compromise[16]—mainly, the Christian

conservatives and the secular egalitarians[17]—as similarly and equally intransigent, equally insistent on "a total win," equally eager to "oppress the other"[18] or
(as the saying goes) to "impose their values" on everybody.

Although I believe Laycock's diagnosis of our situation contains a good deal
of truth and insight, I also think its implicit claim to symmetry, both in its prescription and in its criticisms, is unwarranted. As a consequence, its overall diagnosis of our situation seems to me at the same time unfairly critical and unduly
complacent. In this essay I will try to explain these demurrals.

Before attempting that explanation, though, I ought to make two "full dis-
closure" acknowledgments and one caveat. First, I do not offer this essay as
an impartial "view from nowhere." Although I am no appointed spokesperson
for "Christian conservatives" (and indeed, as a Mormon, I would not even be
accepted as a Christian at all by many of them), I do find myself meandering
along their side of the cultural battleground; so that is the perspective I will be
speaking from in this essay. Given that Christian conservatives hardly appear to
be overrepresented in the academy, I trust it will not be an undue imposition
on academics—who typically profess a strong commitment to diversity (which
in theory might include intellectual diversity)—to hear from someone sympathetic to that perspective.

Second, while I disagree with Laycock, Wilson, Berg, Brownstein, and company in important respects, I also admire them[19] and applaud their efforts to find
or construct common ground. I even wish those efforts could succeed. More
specifically, although I myself do not support same-sex marriage, at this point in
our history, if I thought that Laycock's compromise position could hold and if
I had the power to enact it, I would. But in fact Laycock himself is not sanguine
about the possibility of accommodation, and I am even less optimistic, for reasons I will try to present in this essay.

Here is the caveat: in talking about the "culture wars" we tend to lump people on each side together and to treat the opposing "sides" to some extent as
monoliths. Such simplifying descriptions are obviously artificial. Each "side"
is composed of millions of people who differ in their exact goals and commitments. Some people are leaders and spokespersons while others are complacent and perhaps not very attentive followers. Some are more aggressive and
extreme than others in their objectives and their rhetoric. And each side, like
any large-scale social phenomenon, will have a few "crazies" (as Laycock aptly
puts it[20])—think of the Westboro Baptists—who are an embarrassment to
their own ascriptive allies and who have no realistic chance of dictating any
larger agenda, but who nonetheless are capable of grabbing attention and causing mischief. These complications should not preclude us from talking about
social movements, I think, or about "culture wars"; still, it is prudent to keep
these qualifications in mind.

I. To Accommodate, or to Be (Maybe) Accommodated? That Is the Question

Let us start with the issue of the day. Suppose a state—or *all* states—were to legalize same-sex marriage while also building ample religious exemptions into the law.[21] Would that arrangement be symmetrical, in the sense of being equally respectful toward and accommodating of those who favor and those who religiously oppose same-sex marriage?

We might restate the question in the indignant or accusatory tone in which it is usually pressed. Many favor extending marriage, but no one proposes restricting it, to same-sex couples. Thus, laws and judicial decisions authorizing men to marry men and women to marry women still permit men to marry women (and vice versa). So anyone with a traditional view of marriage is still perfectly free to marry an opposite-sex spouse if she or he so chooses. And at least if religious exemptions are built into such a law, then churches and clergy would not be compelled to marry same-sex couples in contravention of a church's religious beliefs—or to recognize such unions as "marriages" at all. So then, what legitimate interest of the religious traditionalist would be impaired? How can the traditionalists be viewed as anything other than busybodies attempting to "impose their values" on—or as Martha Nussbaum puts it, "lord it over"[22]—others with different views and values?

Before answering, we might turn the question around. In its decision legalizing same-sex marriage that led to the passage of Proposition 8, the California Supreme Court observed that California law already recognized a status of domestic partnership that was available to same-sex couples and that was virtually identical in its legal features to marriage.[23] And of course it was always possible for such couples to regard themselves as married, to present themselves to others as married, and even to have their unions solemnized in a church that would declare the union to be a "marriage." Why then was it so imperative for *the law* to offer such couples the possibility of a legal status officially *labeled* "marriage"?

The answer, it seems, lies in part in what is sometimes called the expressive function of the law. Even (or perhaps *especially*, as the California Supreme Court suggested) if "domestic partnership" is identical in its legal features to "marriage," the law's calculated omission to extend the term "marriage" to such partnerships effectively sends a message that these unions are not of equal dignity with the opposite-sex unions that *are* described by the law as "marriages." Even if the law didn't explicitly *say* this, many discerned such a message.[24] And indeed the message was likely intended: why else would supporters of "civil unions" or "domestic partnerships" have insisted on different labels for the different kinds of relationships? It is understandable that same-sex couples might resent this symbolic denial of equivalence.

But then of course the reverse is also true: if the law applies the label of "marriage" without distinction to both opposite-sex and same-sex couples, the law sends the contrary message—namely, that such unions are of equivalent status, and that both are equally "marriages." People or churches are free, of course, to believe for themselves that these unions are not really marriages, whatever the law may say—just as they were free before the court's decision to believe for themselves that such unions *were* marriages. But after the state court's decision, equivalency became the official position endorsed by the law in California, as it has now become in all fifty states as a result of the Supreme Court's ruling in *Obergefell v. Hodges*. And that official message contradicts the religious beliefs of traditionalists: it is thus a message effectively implying that traditional religious beliefs on the subject are officially disfavored or rejected.[25] Just as it is understandable that same-sex couples might resent an official message implying that their unions are not equivalent to opposite-sex marriages, it is understandable that religious citizens might resent a message indicating by clear implication that their religious beliefs on this subject are mistaken.[26]

Even more importantly, adherents to both positions understand that governmental expressions on such matters are not *merely* and innocuously expressive: such messages have practical and sometimes coercive consequences. For example, whatever may or may not be legally *mandated*, the ideas and commitments so expressed will likely come to be reflected in the public school curriculum.[27] Thus, traditionally Christian parents understand that in recognizing same-sex marriage, the state has not only sent a message implying that their own religious beliefs are to that extent wrong; they understand that if their children attend public schools, they will likely be the recipients of instruction tacitly or explicitly contradicting what the children are taught at home or at church, and indicating by clear implication if not explicitly that these religious teachings are backward and hurtful.

In addition, expressions of official governmental positions may be expected to affect public policies and judicial decisions. Anti-discrimination laws will likely have different implications and a different scope once the law's official position is to treat same-sex marriages as legal and equivalent to opposite-sex unions.[28] Conflicts between such anti-discrimination provisions and, say, rights to freedom of religion, association, or speech are often resolved through what is euphemistically called "balancing." And although there has never been any workable metric or methodology for performing such "balancing,"[29] official declarations of policy can affect how much metaphorical "weight" courts assign to the competing interests.[30]

While moderators make appeals for "live and let live" accommodation, therefore, the contending parties themselves understand that the struggle is over who will be doing the accommodating to whom. Proponents of same-sex marriage perceive, correctly, that domestic partnership is not likely to have *all* of the same legal features and advantages as marriage; and even if it does, in such an arrangement heterosexual marriage is the "normal" position and it is the same-sex couples who are being accommodated. By the same token, citizens with more traditional beliefs perceive that a law recognizing same-sex marriage, even if it comes with religious freedom "exceptions" or "exemptions," reverses these positions: now *they* are the ones who are the outliers hoping to be accommodated.

But for both psychological and practical reasons, many people understandably prefer to be in the position of deciding whether and what to accommodate than to be in the position of hoping and pleading to *be accommodated*. They would rather be the *tolerators*, so to speak, than the *toleratees*. Beyond the sense of alienation or exclusion that may attend being an "accommodated" or "tolerated" outsider,[31] there is the real danger that accommodation may be withheld or seriously restricted—if not immediately, then after the dominant party has consolidated its position. These are real and legitimate concerns, and even if you think they are in some contexts exaggerated (by one side or the other), it is a misdescription to depict each side as merely and gratuitously attempting to "oppress" or "impose its values" on others.

The discussion thus far partly supports but mostly contradicts the moderators' implicit claims of prescriptive and critical symmetry. Thus, whatever its pragmatic merits, the moderators' prescription—namely, for legal recognition of same-sex marriage together with exemptions for religious objectors—cannot accurately claim to be symmetrical in the sense that it is equally respectful of both of the contending positions and their legitimate interests. On the contrary, the prescription privileges the party supporting same-sex marriage by accepting their view as the official governmental position while casting religious objectors as the outsiders to be "accommodated" through the adoption of "exceptions" or "exemptions." The moderators' critical suggestion of a sort of equivalency-in-intransigence between proponents and opponents of same-sex marriage who decline to embrace the proffered compromise also seems misguided. In fact, neither side is being *merely* intransigent, or is acting purely gratuitously to "impose its values" on its opponents. Rather, both sides are acting on legitimate interests in resisting being placed in the demeaning and vulnerable position of (hopefully) accommodated or tolerated outsiders.

Admittedly, insofar as both sides are acting on legitimate interests and concerns, there *is* a sort of symmetry in their stances. This is a thin symmetry, however. To be sure, each side understandably fears that if it is placed in the position of needing accommodation, that accommodation may be withheld or withdrawn, if not immediately then in the future. But it does not follow that the risk of not being accommodated is equal for each side.

So a relevant and even urgent question, it seems, is this: on the supposition that it may find itself in a politically subordinate position, and thus in need of accommodation, for which side in the cultural struggle is the risk of being denied accommodation more serious? Which side—the religious conservatives or the secular proponents of sexual liberty and equality—has more to lose if the other side establishes itself as politically dominant?

II. The Comparative Risks of Non-accommodation: A Short-Term Reckoning

We might begin by considering that question within a relatively short timeframe—five or ten or twenty years, say. Imagine that within the near future, one side or the other is largely successful in realizing its currently articulated goals or agenda. Which side, if thus rendered subordinate, would find itself in a more untenable situation? Although my purpose here is to criticize Laycock's and the moderators' implicit claim of symmetry, as someone who stays relatively detached from politics, current events, and even lower court litigation, I emphatically do not want my criticism to rest on any pretension to superior knowledge of political trends and agendas. So I will take my assessment of the different sides' ambitions largely from Laycock's own discussions.

So, to begin with, what does the party of sexual freedom and secular equality have to fear from the Christian conservatives? I have already quoted Laycock's assertion that "[t]he religious side persists in trying to regulate other people's sex lives so long as it thinks it has any chance of success."[32] That sounds ominous. But here I think Laycock settles for a long-standing but misleading stereotype—albeit one that few in his academic audience may be inclined to challenge. In fact, Laycock's own more detailed analysis persuasively contradicts this particular accusation.

With respect to contraception, for example, Laycock explains (correctly, I think) that "[n]early all Americans think they are entitled to use contraception and that it is no one else's business." These "nearly all Americans" include the religious conservatives. Consequently, "[i]t is unimaginable that any American state would now attempt to ban contraception"; indeed, "the bishops gave up that battle long ago."[33] And a page or two before his accusation that I quoted above, Laycock reports that although religious conservatives continue to oppose abortion and same-sex marriage, "[e]very other form of non-commercial sexual

behavior has been deregulated, either de facto or de jure, and religious conservatives have mostly acquiesced."[34]

> There is no significant lobbying to enforce or re-enact fornication laws,
> adultery laws, sodomy laws, or laws against gay and lesbian sex. No-
> fault divorce is much lamented, but there is no significant effort to roll
> it back. Even the effort to restrict pornography has largely collapsed,
> with its energies redirected to child pornography. On all these issues,
> churches teach what people morally *should* do, but they no longer seek
> to control by law what people *may* do.[35]

So it seems that by and large, religious conservatives are *not* trying to "regulate other people's sex lives." Indeed, that description seems subtly askew even
in the area of abortion. As Laycock knows, and reports, Christian conservatives
oppose abortion because they believe the practice takes the lives of innocent
human beings.[36] These conservatives are acting, as they suppose, to protect those
lives. It is true, to be sure, that restrictions on or prohibitions of abortion would
have constraining effects on some people's sexual activity and decisions. Even
so, it is misleading to declare that the conservatives are "trying to regulate other
people's sex lives," as if this were the *purpose* or objective of their antiabortion
efforts. (Just as it would be a distortion to say that environmentalists are "trying to destroy jobs and force Americans into unemployment": although some
restrictions favored by environmentalists could foreseeably have such effects,
that is presumably not the goal or purpose of such restrictions.)

All of this is not to say that secular egalitarians would have nothing to worry
about if conservative Christians were to achieve political dominance. More specifically, if Christian conservatives achieved more political power than they currently have (including within the judiciary), such that they were able to enact
their stated agenda, then in the area of sexual equality it seems likely that three
unfortunate developments would result—unfortunate from the perspective of
the egalitarians. First, abortion would likely be severely restricted or even prohibited. Second, same-sex marriage would not be legalized; laws or judicial decisions already recognizing the institution in states like Massachusetts, California,
and a growing number of states would presumably be repealed or overruled.
Third, although the right to purchase and use contraceptives would not itself
be threatened, the Health and Human Services' "contraception mandate" would
probably be rescinded; even employers without any religious objection would
probably not be legally required to provide health insurance that covers contraceptives. To be sure, many employers would likely provide such coverage anyway
for policy or economic reasons; even so, women would be unable to count on
their employers, or the government, to supply or subsidize such contraceptives.

Conversely, if the secular egalitarian party or coalition were to achieve dominance and to enact its program, we can again summarize the burdensome consequences for religious traditionalists under three main heads. First, legal protections for freedom of conscience would likely be repealed or severely restricted, at least in matters affecting sexuality and sexual conduct. Thus, doctors who have scruples against performing abortions, pharmacists who object to dispensing contraceptives or abortifacients, and employers who object to providing insurance coverage for contraceptives or abortifacients would find little or no relief in the law; they would thus likely be forced to choose between either violating their consciences or withdrawing from their professions or businesses.[37]

Second, anti-discrimination laws would be applied to prevent discrimination on grounds of sex or sexual orientation. Perhaps a narrow "ministerial exception" would be retained permitting the Catholic Church, say, to continue to maintain a male-only priesthood; even so, many religious employers and church-affiliated institutions such as charitable organizations and religious universities would likely have to modify their practices or else, once again, close up shop. (This of course is not so much a prediction as a description of what is already happening.)[38]

Finally, it is likely that religious institutions with teachings or practices that offend prevailing egalitarian principles would be treated less favorably in other burdensome though less directly and formally coercive ways. Citing the well-known *Bob Jones* case,[39] some proponents of egalitarian views already call for the denial of tax-exempt status to religions whose doctrines are deemed contrary to egalitarian policies.[40] The fate of the Christian Legal Society in the *Hastings* case[41] is another instance: Christian clubs might thus be—indeed often already are[42]—denied official certification in university settings and thus excluded from the benefits that accompany such status, especially including the ability to participate with other student associations in sign-up and promotional activities. These kinds of unfavorable treatment do not flatly prohibit religious associations from existing or living in accordance with their officially disfavored beliefs. But associations that do so are placed at a considerable disadvantage relative to other kinds of associations.

In the relatively short term, therefore, Christian conservatives and secular egalitarians face different sets of potential burdens if they find themselves in a politically subordinate position and hence in need of accommodation. There is no obvious or uncontroversial way to measure and compare those different sets of potential burdens. For one thing, each side in the culture wars, because it does not share the convictions or commitments of its culture war opponents, will naturally see the burdens faced by those opponents as relatively trivial: the risk, it will seem, is only that of being legally induced to do what they plainly ought to do anyway.[43] So, for example, if you see a moral objection to contraception as hopelessly anachronistic and almost unintelligible, it will be easy to view the burden of a contraception mandate on objecting institutions as negligible.[44] But if you regard the use of contraceptives as a grave moral evil and the provision of contraception coverage as a form of cooperation with that evil, the burden becomes much more formidable: basically, your choice is between committing a serious moral transgression and abandoning your career, or perhaps shutting down a business that you may have spent a lifetime building.

In addition, the extent of the burden would depend on other contingencies. For example, if the legalization of same-sex marriage were denied and rolled back but an approximately equivalent status of "domestic partnership" were recognized, as in California before the judicial intervention, the burden on same-sex couples would be largely limited to the expressive harm discussed earlier. Similarly, if the contraception mandate is withdrawn but contraceptives are readily available in other ways—through organizations such as Planned Parenthood, for example—the actual burden on women would be real but relatively slight. Similarly, the extent of the burden entailed by restrictions on abortion would depend on whether exceptions—such as exceptions for rape and incest—were included.

Although there is no uncontroversial metric for assessing relative burdens, however, it seems clear that the risks faced by the opposing sides are different, and asymmetrical. Speaking in general terms, we can say that the risk to the secular egalitarian side lies in the possibility of limited but direct restrictions on their freedom in matters of sexuality. Probably the clearest risk of this kind is still the possibility of significant restrictions on abortion.

The major risk faced by religious conservatives, by contrast, is that of being put to the choice of violating their convictions or commitments—of being unfaithful to their God, as they perceive the matter—or instead of being increasingly relegated to the margins of society. A determination to maintain fidelity to their convictions might well mean that they could not own and operate a large business or university, or work as a physician, pharmacist, wedding photographer, or landlord. Indeed, as Laycock explains, much anti-discrimination activity in this context seems calculated to drive religious conservatives out of these professions.[45] In addition, although religion no doubt transcends economics, insofar as it is practiced by and through human beings it is not immune to economic influences.[46] Thus, forgoing tax-exempt status or university certification may place a religion at a serious competitive disadvantage in the marketplace of causes and associations—a disadvantage that may portend marginal status and long-term decline.

Suppose we move beyond issues directly affecting sexual morality to another area of dispute in the culture wars—namely, the issue of "religion in the public square." Once again, each side's agenda promotes measures that will understandably be seen as unwelcome or oppressive by the other side. But also once again, the potential impositions are not symmetrical.

Thus, religious conservatives often seek to maintain—and secular egalitarians struggle to remove—official religious expressions or symbols, such as legislative prayer, the words "under God" in the Pledge of Allegiance, or crosses on public property.[47] The persistence of such expressions is resented by at least some secular citizens who, as Justice Sandra Day O'Connor argued, may be made to feel like political "outsiders."[48] Conversely, removal of such expressions may be viewed by some religious citizens as a rejection of their own beliefs; indeed, insofar as their beliefs call for public acknowledgment of God, removal plainly *is* a rejection of those beliefs.[49] Even so, the rejection is arguably not as overt or "in your face" as would be publicly sponsored expressions or symbols, say, explicitly endorsing atheism. In this respect, even if there is no fully "neutral" stance for government to take, the imposition on secular citizens from religious symbols may seem more severe than the imposition on religious citizens would be from their removal.

In an arguably more important context, however, the relative imposition runs very much the other way. Thus, secular theorists and activists often argue that political decision-making should be limited to secular grounds and considerations; religious beliefs and commitments should be excluded from consideration in political decisions.[50] This view was officially and decisively reflected in what turned out to be the dispositive judicial decision in the Proposition 8 case: in deciding whether that measure was rationally supported by any legitimate interest, Judge Vaughn Walker ruled that reasons based on religion (and also "private moral beliefs," whatever that might mean) could not count.[51] Given that according to evidence in the case an overwhelming majority of churchgoers favored Proposition 8 while an equally overwhelming majority of non-churchgoers opposed it,[52] this exclusion of religious reasons heavily handicapped one side relative to the other. Not surprisingly, the exclusion of what Judge Walker viewed as religious reasons[53] secured the invalidation of the measure.

As the Proposition 8 case illustrates, exclusion of religious convictions from political decision-making would powerfully disadvantage highly religious constituencies, or even effectively disenfranchise them. To be sure, religious citizens would still be permitted to vote or run for public office—but only on the condition that they leave their most central beliefs and commitments at home. But in that case it is not really the devout citizen himself or herself who is voting or running for office, but rather an artificial construction—the devout citizen attempting to impersonate someone else, someone who is not devout.[54] This restriction is strongly asymmetrical: possibly with some minor qualifications, the secular citizen is permitted to act on all of his beliefs and convictions, but the religious citizen is commanded to bracket her most essential beliefs and convictions.[55] And as in the area of anti-discrimination efforts, the effect is to marginalize devout citizens. Just as anti-discrimination efforts may push object-ing religious believers out of economic marketplaces, exclusion of religion from public decision-making pushes religious believers, at least *qua* believers, out of the political domain.

The secular agenda thus arguably reflects a strategy, not necessarily toward "religion" but toward conservative or traditional forms of religion, much like the position candidate Lincoln adopted with respect to slavery—not to prohibit or abolish it, but rather to confine and disadvantage it and thereby to place it "in the course of ultimate extinction."[56] But this observation already points us beyond the relatively short time frame indicated by the competing sides' currently articulated goals and agendas and prompts a more long-term question. Suppose that one party or the other achieves and solidifies a position of political domi-nance: what are the prospects that this now-dominant party will be inclined to an overall position of tolerance or accommodation?

III. The Asymmetrical Prospects of Accommodation

That question is inherently conjectural, and it also prompts a reminder of my introductory caveat: the various supporters of each party surely differ in their inclination to tolerate or accommodate opposing views and practices. Even so, the question is an important one. So, if we step back from the spe-cific controversies of the day and extend our time frame to, say, the remain-der of the twenty-first century or even beyond, then from which party in the culture wars—the religious conservatives or the secular egalitarians—can we more confidently expect to see an overall attitude or policy of toleration and accommodation if that party happens to flourish and to achieve political dominance?

To a typical academic audience, that question may sound rhetorical, maybe even facetious. It is well known (at least among some constituencies) that Christians, from the time of Constantine through the Middle Ages and per-sisting up to the most visible and vocal self-identifying members of that faith today, are constitutionally inclined to intolerance and persecution. Conversely, today's secular egalitarians are (or at least deem themselves to be) heirs of the Enlightenment—the proud great-great-grandchildren of Voltaire and Jefferson. And from that period to the present a broad-minded, humane toleration (in close conjunction with a commitment to "reason" and, by easy implication, to "rea-sonableness") has been a defining characteristic of the movement—at least in its own estimation.[57] Although there are no doubt happy exceptions, Christians are by nature intolerant. Secular egalitarians are the opposite.

So goes a familiar opinion. It is an opinion I do not share: although the issue is complicated, the opposite conclusion, though necessarily speculative, seems to me more plausible. *At least at this point in our history*, I believe, we have less reason to expect toleration from secular egalitarians in a position of political dominance than from Christians. In this section I will try to explain that view.

A. Toleration as an Achievement

It is important to begin, I think, by noticing one common but mistaken assumption that might skew our expectations on this issue. Today, in some cultural contexts, it is often assumed that toleration is in a sense the rational and reasonable and natural posture—the posture that humans would naturally assume if their thoughts or passions were not somehow distorted or misdirected. Thomas Jefferson's oft-quoted comment can illustrate the point. "It does me no injury," Jefferson remarked cheerily, "for my neighbor to say there are twenty gods, or no god. It neither picks my pocket nor breaks my leg."[58] On a certain set of assumptions, Jefferson's remark can have the character of a self-evident truth. For example, if you take it for granted (a) that your legitimate concerns extend only to your own personal "interests," understood mainly as including your financial and physical flourishing, and (b) that theological issues are mostly matters of abstract speculation that have little impact on more practical matters,[59] then it will seem obvious that your neighbors' religious beliefs are no concern of yours.[60] A position of toleration in such matters will consequently seem natural and reasonable. Why *should* anyone go to the trouble and expense of interfering in a neighbor's religion any more than they should waste time and effort meddling in his choice of "high heat" or "low heat" settings on his patio grill?

On this view, the propensity of some people or some officials to take an interest in other people's concerns (religion, marriage, sexual practices, and so forth) will appear to be a departure from this reasonable, natural position—a departure that looks to reflect a kind of pathology. Intolerance seems to call for explanation in terms of some sort of unfortunate, dysfunctional psychological urge (based on insecurity, perhaps, or maybe aggression, or a need to dominate[61]) to interfere where one has no legitimate concern and nothing to gain except the perverse satisfaction of bossing other people around.

If we start with this assumption, we might easily project that, given the chance, secular egalitarians will be tolerant. After all, why shouldn't they be? Being secular, they are presumably not afflicted with the sort of pathological zeal or dogmatic faith that might lead them to want to "impose their values" on other people. Christians, conversely, are defined precisely by that sort of zeal and faith, so it is to be expected that they will want to "lord it over others," as Nussbaum says.

As against this assumption that toleration is natural and intolerance an aberration, Oliver Wendell Holmes famously expressed the opposite view. "Persecution for the expression of opinions seems to me perfectly logical. If you have no doubt of your premises or your power and want a certain result with all your heart you naturally express your wishes in law and sweep away all opposition."[62] Holmes of course went on to attempt a rationale for resisting that logic of persecution. Whether or not his "marketplace of ideas" rationale was successful,[63] however, Holmes at least understood that toleration is not just a sort of natural, effortless default position, but rather something that has to be argued for, or worked at. Toleration is an achievement, not a sort of easy natural inheritance.[64]

Holmes's assessment seems supported by a vast amount of historical experience. Historians tell us that until the last few centuries or so, toleration was usually not viewed as a virtue at all, but rather as a sign of weakness, subversiveness, or at least lack of commitment to the truth.[65] And indeed, this perception was not obviously mistaken. Is it a coincidence that most (though not all[66]) of the most celebrated early modern advocates of toleration within what was then a largely Christian culture—Montaigne, Bayle, Locke, Voltaire, Jefferson, Mill—were also openly or quietly skeptical of the prevailing orthodoxy? If we look farther back to the pre-Christian past, our conclusion should not change. Although historians in the Enlightenment tradition have often liked to depict classical paganism as naturally and benignly tolerant,[67] this assessment tends to confound indifference and toleration. For the most part, Roman authorities did not care about the religious opinions and practices of the various communities and cultures within the conquered territories. But when Roman officials perceived a religion as potentially threatening to the civil order or the culture of *Romanitas*, they could be as unhesitatingly and ruthlessly repressive as any medieval inquisitor.[68]

We need not try to decide, however, whether persecution of difference is irrationally pathological or instead "perfectly logical," as Holmes asserted. The important point for our purposes is simply that if we consider the matter from a historical and empirical perspective, then it seems evident that human beings often are inclined to attempt to prevent their neighbors from believing or saying things deemed to be false, and from engaging in practices deemed to be wrong or immoral. Even today, in the midst of a culture that purports to esteem toleration, openness, diversity, and multiculturalism, we admire someone who is tolerant with respect to things we regard as good or at least harmless—religious opinions, perhaps, if we are of a Jeffersonian mindset. But with respect to things we deem false or pernicious—racism, for example, or sexism—"toleration" hardly seems the appropriate stance.

Thus, people and institutions proudly announce that they have a "zero tolerance" policy toward one or another evil practice—cheating, or drugs, or bullying, or harassment, or consorting among faculty and students, or . . . intolerance. And proposals to introduce into the public school curriculum a view such as intelligent design—even in the gentlest way or on an "equal time" basis with competing views—do not evoke paeans to Holmes's open "marketplace of ideas." Instead, as is often the case with views opposed by the scientific and judicial establishments, they bring to mind something closer to the old Catholic slogan: "Error has no rights."[69]

The modest moral of these observations is simply that toleration is not preordained to be the "natural" attitude or position; it is an achievement (of contestable value, to be sure). If we had to generalize, it would probably be more accurate to say that *intolerance* is the natural or normal human tendency.[70] As a result, toleration is something that has to be worked for, cultivated, and justified. A movement's capacity for tolerance may depend on whether there are resources or rationales supporting tolerance within the movement's beliefs; it may depend as well on historical conditions that encourage the movement to develop and articulate these rationales and to put them into practice.

This observation leads to a slight reformulation of the question this section began with. Which party in the cultural struggle, we can ask—the conservative Christian party or the secular egalitarian party—is better endowed with the rationales and the experience that would support a stance of accommodation or toleration if the party has the good fortune to become a politically dominant power? That is a complex and speculative question, obviously; here I can do more than venture some general observations.

B. Christian Toleration

In the case of Christians, we have a body of developed doctrine and almost two millennia of experience from which to make our projections. This evidence is complex, and mixed. Over the centuries, the Christian religion has been the source both of massive intolerance—we can incorporate by reference here the usual litany of Christian offenses: the Inquisition, the Crusades, the burning of witches, and so forth—and of a principled commitment to and practice of religious and other forms of toleration.

A common view holds that the pagans of late antiquity were broadly humane and tolerant, and that the new Christian rulers who came to power with Constantine and his successors instituted a reign of intolerance. As I have argued at length elsewhere,[71] the truth is considerably more complicated. Very briefly: pre-Christian Roman rulers tended to be pragmatic and external in their approach to religion. As noted, the Romans cared little about the internal beliefs and attitudes of their subjects; so long as these subjects performed their civic responsibilities and did not stir up division or rebellion, the Romans were content to let those subjects worship how and whom they chose. But if a religion came to be viewed as subversive, it would be savagely repressed.[72]

Christianity, by contrast, cared deeply about the internal condition of people, about what people believed; and this concern could support both a more intrusive intolerance and a more principled commitment to toleration or religious freedom. Both propensities have been manifest throughout the ensuing centuries, but there has also been a discernible trajectory. As a rough generalization, we might say that over time the commitments to freedom and toleration have become more prominent and accepted, at least in the West, while the bases for intolerance have receded in Christians' understanding of what their Gospel prescribes.

So if we ask about the likelihood of Christians today demonstrating tolerance, there are reasons to predict a fair measure of toleration. First, Christian beliefs contain the *intellectual resources or justifications* to support policies of toleration of non-Christian beliefs and practices. Two justifications in particular should be noticed. One is the rationale of the *imago dei*—the idea, taken from Hebrew scripture, that *all* human beings, of every race and creed, are created by and in the image of God.[73] This belief provides a foundation for commitments to human dignity and to the equal worth of persons; indeed, some have argued that no secular justification to date has been able to do the work of that biblical justification.[74] And of course the commitments to human dignity and equal human worth have animated the modern project of defining and protecting human rights.

Another distinctive Christian rationale derives from the belief that only a free and voluntary faith is acceptable to God. Locke explained the basic idea: "All the life and power of religion consist in the inward and full persuasion of the mind; and faith is not faith without believing."[75] Consequently, compelled but insincere professions of faith, "far from being any furtherance, are indeed great obstacles to our salvation, . . . add[ing] unto the number of our other sins those also of hypocrisy, and contempt of his Divine Majesty."[76] This belief can be, and historically has been, extended beyond religion to cover other kinds of belief, expression, and even action, thereby animating the development of legal commitments to freedom of religion and freedom of speech and, more broadly, to personal autonomy.

Of course, if I may indulge in understatement, these rationales for toleration have not always been manifest in Christian practice: once again, the litany of egregious offenses is familiar. But that observation points to another reason to expect Christians *today* to be inclined toward toleration of those who disagree with them. Although the rationales for toleration were present (and were prominently articulated) from the outset,[77] in the centuries following the political ascendency of Christianity in the late Roman Empire, and in response to the ongoing threat of conquest by outside so-called "barbarians," and later under the canopy of Christendom, it was easy for rulers and others to downplay these more lenient themes in favor of Christian beliefs more supportive of political and cultural uniformity, and thus of intolerance. But in the centuries since the Protestant Reformation and the wars of religion, Christendom has irretrievably collapsed, and Christians have been led, or perhaps forced, to come to terms with pluralism. In this situation, the rationales for freedom have been articulated and recited over and over again, until they are woven inextricably into the typical contemporary Christian's understanding of the Gospel.

The fact is that by now Christians in Europe and North America have had the experience of centuries of living with pluralism, democracy, and a significant scope of freedom for diverse opinions and lifestyles; indeed, all of these things evolved within a broadly Christian cultural and political framework. And Christians have by and large accepted and internalized the theological rationales supportive of such arrangements. There are exceptions, to be sure—the so-called Christian Reconstructionists, for example, or the Westboro Baptists. And yet almost all American Christians, conservative or liberal, find these extremists a deplorable embarrassment.

To be sure, their Christian beliefs and values may lead more mainstream traditionalists to take positions on issues such as abortion or same-sex marriage that secular egalitarians find objectionable and oppressive. Christian citizens today may also resent being compelled by law to support or subsidize practices—such as, for some Christians, contraception or abortion—that conflict with their religious convictions.[78] On particular political and legal questions, in short, traditional Christians reach conclusions at odds with those that would be reached by secular egalitarians. It is possible to characterize those unwelcome conclusions as "intolerant"—possible, but not perspicuous. Different faiths, ideologies, and political movements will inevitably reach different specific conclusions regarding what law should prohibit, permit, and encourage: to characterize such differences under the castigating label of "intolerance" risks depriving the term of useful meaning.

If instead we ask whether even conservative Christians today in the West are inclined to impose "Christianity" on their fellow citizens, or to place disparate legal burdens on non-Christians, I submit that the answer is quite clearly no. The major wars of religion in the West ended three-and-a-half centuries ago, and there is in this country neither any appreciable movement toward nor any possibility of returning to the "confessional state," or to the conditions of

Christendom. By contrast to notable predecessors such as Charlemagne or Alfred the Great, Christians today would scarcely imagine the possibility of forcing anyone to be baptized as a Christian, or of punishing anyone for not accepting Christian beliefs, rituals, and practices. Indeed, as Laycock notes,[79] there is no impetus today or any realistic chance to return even to the 1950s, when the law reflected Christian sexual morality in a more thoroughgoing way by prohibiting (at least officially, though rarely in practice) fornication, adultery, and homosexual conduct.[80]

C. Are Secular Egalitarians Reliably Tolerant?

Whether a similar policy of accommodation or toleration can be expected of potentially triumphant secular egalitarians is less certain, in part because secular egalitarianism does not have the same long history or developed body of doctrine that Christianity has.[81] The idea of equality has deep and venerable roots in the American experience, of course: we associate it with the Jeffersonian assertion in the Declaration of Independence that "all men are created equal" and with Tocqueville's classic study of *Democracy in America*, with its sober, guarded celebration of what Tocqueville viewed as the new and transforming movement to equality. But any claims of contemporary egalitarians to a direct genealogical connection to luminaries such as Jefferson and Tocqueville are contestable at best.[82]

As Peter Westen and others have famously demonstrated,[83] the basic normative commitment to "equality," or to the idea that likes should be treated alike, is an empty vessel to which no one does or could really object—we are all egalitarians in the broad sense, and could hardly be otherwise—but whose substantive content must come from other sources. For Jefferson, that content was supplied by a providential worldview largely inherited from Christianity.[84] Tocqueville's study was similarly pervaded by invocations of providence.[85] Contemporary egalitarians, by contrast, typically make a point of disavowing reliance on theological inputs, which are viewed as "sectarian." It is arguable, consequently, that contemporary secular egalitarianism is a novel historical phenomenon,[86] with little more than a verbal tie to the more venerable American practices and commitments associated with the theme of "equality." Whatever the sources of the substantive content of contemporary egalitarianism may be, they do not come from traditional Christian or Judeo-Christian beliefs—not consciously at least.

Though secular, however, contemporary egalitarianism gives away nothing to traditional religion in the area of zeal, or fervor. Writing presciently a third of a century ago, the sociologist and political theorist Robert Nisbet observed the potential power of what he called "the New Equality."[87] Nisbet argued that "[e]quality has a built-in revolutionary force lacking in such ideas as justice or liberty. . . . Equality feeds on itself as no other single social value does. It is not long before it becomes more than a value. It takes on . . . all the overtones of redemptiveness and becomes a religious rather than a secular idea.[88] And Nisbet commented that

> it would be hard to exaggerate the potential spiritual dynamic that lies in the idea of equality at the present time. One would have to go back to certain other ages, such as imperial Rome, in which Christianity was generated as a major historical force, or Western Europe of the Reformation, to find a theme endowed with as much unifying, mobilizing power, especially among intellectuals, as the idea of equality carries now.[89]

If Nisbet's observations were broadly accurate in 1975, they seem even more apt today. It remains uncertain whether contemporary egalitarianism also contains within itself rationales for self-restraint or toleration comparable to the *imago dei* and "voluntary faith" rationales associated with Christianity. Maybe such rationales do exist, or could be developed, or imported. Conversely, it is possible that whatever propensities to tolerance the new secular egalitarians currently exhibit (like, arguably, their commitment to equality itself) are a residual carry-over from the struggles of the Christian past, and that over time the egalitarians will be even less inclined to accommodate what they will view as backward and oppressive views and ways of life.[90]

But let us suppose for purposes of argument that contemporary egalitarianism does contain incipient justifications for toleration, or could import them. Even so, it has had little time and opportunity for such restraints to develop. Following Nisbet, we might thus compare contemporary egalitarianism to Christianity in the fourth century. Christianity contained justifications for tolerance or religious liberty, and these justifications were cogently articulated by Christians such as Constantine's advisor Lactantius; nonetheless, in the intoxicating exuberance of newly achieved political dominance, Christian rulers felt little inclination to act on these rationales. Consequently, centuries passed before these rationales came to prevail in Christian thought and practice. Triumphant secular egalitarians would be like the early, newly empowered Christians, and unlike the paganism of late antiquity, in that they care intensely about what is in people's minds and hearts—about even "unconscious" prejudices[91]—and they are also like the fourth-century Christians in that they have thus far had little opportunity to develop and act on whatever resources for self-restraint their movement may contain. Indeed, we might extend the analogy: contemporary secular egalitarians are like fourth-century Christians in that they evince an acute sense of resentment over perceived historical and present oppression from their political and cultural opponents, and such resentment is hardly conducive to attitudes of respect for or accommodation of those opponents.[92] This observation is consistent at least with the efforts of secular egalitarians, noted by Laycock, to use anti-discrimination laws to punish recalcitrant photographers, bakers, and counselors and drive them out of business even when gays and lesbians do not actually want their services.

Two qualifications to this assessment should be noted. First, once again there is the caveat: egalitarians are not all of a piece. Just as is the case with Christians, or with people of any other large-scale movement or persuasion, some are likely inclined to be accommodating of difference while others are not. The problem, however, from the Christian perspective, is that the courts together with anti-discrimination laws are available to the tolerant and the intolerant alike. Thus, it could well be the case that many same-sex couples and many other Americans who support the secular egalitarian movement would be happy enough to "live and let live," as the saying goes, and so would not be motivated to drive out of business the occasional photographer or baker or fire the occasional CEO who has scruples against same-sex marriage. But so long as some individuals *are* so motivated, and so long as at least some judges are happy to oblige, the scrupulous photographer or baker remain at risk.[93]

Second, prediction is always hazardous, and assessments of a relatively new and amorphous movement are inherently speculative. To the cultural opponents of the new egalitarianism, this is precisely the concern. We can speculate that if secular egalitarians achieve political domination, they *might* turn out to be admirably tolerant—more so than some of their current actions might suggest. That possibility can't be ruled out. But would you want to trust your fortunes, and your future, to that sort of conjectural possibility?

Conclusion: French Lessons

Professor Laycock thinks we can learn lessons relevant to our current culture wars from history, and in particular from French history. More specifically, he thinks the crabbed protection given to religious freedom in France today can be traced back to the Catholic Church's opposition to the French Revolution,[94] and he writes ominously of what might happen if Christians today position themselves on the wrong side of the Sexual Revolution that began in the 1960s. "If you stand in the way of a Revolution and lose, there will be consequences," Laycock warns ominously. "The consequence of fighting the Sexual Revolution so hard and so long may be to turn much of the country against religious liberty—or at least to turn public opinion towards a very narrow, more French-like understanding of religious liberty."[95]

Laycock may be right, although I confess to having doubts both about the lesson he draws from the French Revolution[96] and about its contemporary implications. Suppose the Catholic Church, say, or the LDS Church were to accept the legalization of same-sex marriage while continuing themselves to condemn such unions as morally wrong: would this be enough to rescue them from being on "the wrong side of the Revolution"? Or is Laycock basically (though perhaps inadvertently) calling for complete capitulation and conformity on this and other issues of sexual morality?

Be that as it may, I do agree that it is helpful to draw historical comparisons here, including comparisons to happenings in France. I would go farther back, however, (as Laycock has also done[97]) and suggest that the culture wars we are witnessing today can perspicuously be viewed as a contemporary (although, thankfully, less violent) version of the wars of religion that occurred in France, among other places, in the aftermath of the Protestant Reformation. That comparison may yield insights about the proper diagnosis of our own conflicts, and about the limited prospects for resolving those conflicts through accommodation.

Thus, half a millennium ago, an encompassing Christendom was rent into major warring factions. The division began with what might have seemed relatively minor and remediable disagreements—mainly over the efficacy and appropriateness of indulgences—but it soon became apparent that these issues opened into much larger disagreements over the character of God, the nature of human freedom or agency, and the structures of authority in society. Contrary to the hopes and expectations of many at the outset, both within the established order and among the reformers, these differences proved intractable, and open conflict resulted.

Between the more extreme parties, there were always moderators who thought that a sensible *modus vivendi* should be achievable. In France,[98] the royal family, effectively ruled by the Queen mother Catherine de Medici, strove in the conflict's early years for compromise and accommodation of both the Catholics and Protestants, or Huguenots. In addition, there was a loose party of more pragmatic politicians and thinkers, including people such as the theorist of sovereignty Jean Bodin, who were known as "politiques," and who consistently urged what they regarded as a "live and let live" position in which civil peace was elevated over sectarian commitments.[99]

Despite these voices of compromise and moderation, the French fought a series of bloody civil wars from the 1560s up until 1592, with the Edict of Nantes. And even that decree did not really bring an end to the violence: indeed, its author, Henry IV (he of the apocryphal "Paris is worth a mass"), was assassinated twelve years later by a zealous partisan of the Catholic cause. Even under the Edict, Protestants were increasingly restricted, and in 1685 the Edict was officially revoked, resulting in the widespread flight of Protestants from the country.

From the standpoint of the moderators, or "politiques," all of this strife, bloodshed, and persecution must have seemed tragically unnecessary. Why should it be so difficult for Catholics and Protestants to live peacefully together? Some cities were effectively designated as Protestant havens while the rest of the county was Catholic: why was this arrangement so unacceptable to each side? Indeed, Paris was even then a big place: so what could have been so objection-able about having a Protestant church or two in one part of town and Catholic churches in other neighborhoods?

From our own standpoint, the politiques' frustration and also their prescrip-tion may seem vindicated by history. Any decent-sized American city today will have some Catholic parishes (of different liturgical and homiletical styles, to suit the aesthetic and theological proclivities of different parishioners), a variety of Protestant churches, as well as a host of other churches or temples or mosques or religious communions, not to mention a chapter of the American Humanist Association (and also, of course, a number of athletic fields and sports bars, catering to a different sort of religiosity). This pluralism seems perfectly natural; nobody feels the need to bully or fight with people as they travel to or stay away from the various places of worship or communion. So, why was such a situation so difficult for the French of the sixteenth century to embrace?

And yet I would suggest that this understandable and partly warranted impa-tience of the complacent moderates, then and now, was and is also short-sighted on two levels. First, it fails fully to acknowledge that in any situation of conflict or negotiation, even if a tolerable *modus vivendi* is one's goal, a cheerful readi-ness to compromise is not necessarily the most efficacious strategy for achieving that goal.

The French Protestants had this lesson impressed on them in brutal fashion. Flocking to Paris in 1572 to celebrate the scheduled wedding of their champion, Henry of Navarre (the future Henry IV), to the Catholic princess Margaret in what looked to be a conciliating arrangement, they instead ended up being slaughtered by the tens of thousands in the St. Bartholomew's Day Massacres. The Edict of Nantes, limited as its policy of toleration was, was achieved not by prompt, good-hearted giving-in, but only by decades of struggle among parties fully committed to their respective causes. Moving to the present: if Laycock's description of the Christian conservatives is accurate, egalitarians are understandably reluctant to strike a truce with them; and if Laycock's portrayal of the egalitarians is even by-and-large correct, then conservative Christians would be foolish to expect them nicely to enter into any sort of respectful and enduring compromise. Some sort of tolerable *modus vivendi* may eventually be worked out—I for one hope so—but it will not be the product of quick and easy acquiescence.

But, second, moderating proposals evaluate the proffered compromises, and pronounce them satisfactory and "reasonable," in accordance with the moderators' own, typically moderate or muted (or, less charitably, mushy) values and commitments. Thus, we today (mushy moderates all, or almost all, at least by contrast to our aggressively pious sixteenth-century predecessors[100]) may look out on today's sprawling buffet of faiths, quasi-faiths, healing therapies, and soothing spiritualities and find the prodigious menu delightful. A little something for every taste and grade of devotion. And if the result is that religion today is typically complacent and "wishy-washy," to quote Stephen Macedo, that is all to the good: it is precisely "wishy-washy" or "watered-down" religion that liberal pluralists like Macedo seek to cultivate,[101] in the interest of civil peace in this world (which is after all the only world we can observe or have much confidence in, and thus for practical purposes the one that matters).

But of course the contending faithful of the sixteenth century would probably have given a different assessment. They might rather be appalled by our current situation, and might lament that the genuine faith they fought for has long since expired. In this vein, the historian Brad Gregory observes that "[i]nstitutionally and intellectually, our world is one the committed early modern Christians could scarcely imagine. I am certain they would not have wanted to live in it."[102]

I of course express no view here about whether our militantly pious predecessors were right or we are right. And in fact I'm really not sure how we would go about resolving that issue, or from what sort of standpoint we could impartially judge: by *our* (much moderated) values, *we're* right—but then what would you expect? So my modest purpose here is merely to suggest that the symmetrical "live and let live" proposition of today's moderators may misassess what is at stake. And we should accordingly not be surprised if partisans on either side of the culture wars do not rush to embrace that oh-so-sensible proposition.

Postscript

The conference for which this paper was prepared was held at Harvard in April 2014; the draft of the paper was actually written in late 2013. Since then, the political and legal scene has been changing rapidly with respect to these issues. Most obviously, the Supreme Court's decision in *Obergefell v. Hodges*,[103] decided June 26, 2015, has arguably rendered moot the moderators' proposed compromise, as well as the part of this essay specifically commenting on that compromise. Now that the Court has construed the Constitution to require legal recognition of same-sex marriage (while remaining mostly silent or noncommittal on matters of religious freedom[104]), religious conservatives no longer have the option of trading acceptance of same-sex marriage for the adoption of religious freedom protections. The "window of opportunity"[105] that Robin Wilson urged conservatives to take—or, depending on your perspective, to leap out of—is closing quickly, for better or worse.

But the "window" has not closed completely. Much attention has been given to the so-called "Utah Compromise" in which the State of Utah, supported by the (Mormon) Church of Jesus Christ of Latter-day Saints, enacted a statute prohibiting discrimination based on sexual orientation in various sectors while also adopting religious freedom protections. Same-sex marriage in Utah had already been judicially imposed; so the Utah Compromise shows that compromises involving religious freedom need not involve recognition of same-sex marriage. The measure has been both praised—hailed as the path to cultural reconciliation—and condemned[106]; it is too early at this point to assess just how the measure will work out.

Whatever compromises may or may not be adopted, however, *Obergefell* means that the propensity of progressives or secular egalitarians to demonstrate tolerance will now be conspicuously tested. And events since the draft of this paper was written do not, I think, provide much material for hopefulness. Consider, for example, the much-publicized Brendan Eich affair: a founder and CEO of a major high-tech corporation was forced to resign when it was discovered that he had donated to support California's Proposition 8.[107] Or consider the massive reaction—by egalitarian advocates but also by politicians, major corporations, media, athletic associations, and others—when Indiana adopted a statute almost identical to the federal Religious Freedom Restoration Act, enacted almost unanimously by Congress and with the effusive support of President Bill Clinton, just over two decades earlier. The eagerness of opponents to resort to distortion, exaggeration, and sometimes outright mendacity[108] in their successful campaign against the statute does not reflect or portend significant progressive tolerance for viewpoints at odds with the progressive agenda.[109] On the contrary, as the egalitarian juggernaut overwhelms courts, legislatures, and political campaigns, the leading progressive politicians and scholars at the moment exude a "take no prisoners" attitude.

Earlier, this essay mentioned the possibility that the progressive or egalitarian side would discover or develop rationales for tolerance comparable to the classic rationales derived from Christian premises. That is still a possibility, no doubt, but there is little discernible movement in that direction at the moment. If anything, the movement is going in the other direction. Thus, leading scholars on the egalitarian side have been working to develop a constitutional rationale[110]— sometimes called the "third-party harms" argument—that would render unconstitutional many of the most consequential forms of religious accommodation. Other egalitarian scholars advance the argument that legal accommodation of religious scruples based on complicity—such as those in the much discussed *Hobby Lobby* case[111]—unconstitutionally demean the dignity of those whose conduct the religious objectors find immoral or sinful.[112] Considered purely as legal arguments, both the "third-party harms" proposal and the "anti-complicity" argument are, in my own judgment, extraordinarily weak[113]; but my judgment is no basis for predicting that the arguments will not be accepted by courts. (It may provide some basis for predicting the opposite.) In any case, the relevant point for present purposes is that the development of such proposals is not indicative of any progressive movement to develop rationales for toleration. On the contrary.

Despite these gloomy observations, the caveats noted in the essay are still cogent. Progressives and egalitarians are not a monolith any more than Christians are: some will be more inclined to be tolerant than others.[114] And the future is still impossible to predict with any confidence. At the moment, it seems that the political and legal momentum is mostly in the egalitarian direction. But the pendulum might swing the other way. Or there could be a political backlash. This seems unlikely at the moment, but it *could* happen. If it does, we may have a chance to see how tolerant religious conservatives will be.

PART III

CONTINENTAL EUROPE

Claims for Homosexual Equality and Religious Freedom in Tension

Moral and Conceptual Frameworks

ROCCO BUTTIGLIONE

I. What Are the Moral and Conceptual Frameworks That Govern the Tensions between Claims for Homosexual Equality and Religious Freedom?

A Metacritique of the Question

It is an old philosophical habit dating to the times of Socrates and Plato to ask the question *ti esti*, "what is this?" When we ask this question, we often find that we are not so sure about the general presuppositions of our reasoning. In order to determine whether our ideas and beliefs possess the firm foundations that they seem, at first glance, to have, a German philosopher might say that we need an exercise of metacritique.[1] A French philosopher might invite us to deconstruct the same concepts.[2]

Thus, in an effort to understand the tension between claims for homosexual equality and religious freedom, let us first interrogate the concepts that frame the issue: "homosexuality," "discrimination," and "toleration."

A. On Homosexuality: Nature, Culture, or Both?

What do we mean when we make use of the word "homosexual?" Let us approach this question from an oblique direction, keeping in mind its relevance to the question of gay marriage. In gay rights language, sexual orientation is often presented and understood by analogy to race. People are homosexual, we are told, in the same way that people are black: they are simply born that way; it is who they *are*. People are "black" because genes in their DNA encode for a dark pigmentation of the skin. They are black because they are born as such; they inherit this trait from their parents. But is this also the case with homosexuals?

There have been attempts to find a chromosome that could explain the difference between heterosexuals and homosexuals in the same way the differences between men and women, or between whites and blacks, are explained. Some years ago a discovery of this chromosome was announced and widely publicized in the media.[3] Subsequent research, however, has not confirmed this claim, although this fact has not been as widely publicized as was the initial alleged discovery.[4]

It is only fair to say that we do not know the answer; homosexual preferences (as most human characteristics) are not clear-cut. They are the result of a complicated interaction of causes.[5] Some of them are biological, some of them are cultural, and some must be tracked back to the life stories of the individuals.

A look at history seems to confirm this conclusion. For instance, it is well known that pederastic relations—sexual relations between an adult male and an adolescent male—were common in ancient Greek society. Were the ancient Greeks therefore homosexuals? No—but they were not heterosexuals either. Nor can we say they were bisexual in the modern sense of this word. In the ancient Greek world, homosexuality was generally regarded as acceptable in certain periods of life, but unacceptable in others. For example, it was acceptable for a prepubescent boy to be courted by an adult male, but not for an adult male to court another adult male of roughly the same age.

But even the ancient Greeks who condoned and practiced homosexual relationships did not consider the possibility of gay marriage. In their worldview, homosexual relationships between men and boys were an educative experience that one should go through, but eventually grow out of.[6] Moreover, these relationships were considered a supplement, not a replacement, to marriage. The ancient Greeks expected that all men would marry a woman in order to have children to take care of them in old age, and to continue the family line and the life of the city. Although Plato recognized that this may be more difficult for those who have stronger homosexual leanings, he does not make an exception for them. He only comments that getting married and begetting children is an act of obedience to the law.[7] Did Plato and the Greeks therefore express an attitude of contempt and discrimination against gay people? As we will see later, perhaps they simply grasped the societal function of marriage.

In the Roman world, the situation was more complicated. On the one hand, part of the ruling class, like the ancient Greeks, found educational value in pederasty (the well-known story of Hadrian and Antinous bears witness to this). On the other hand, another part of the ruling class and most of the common folk, at least in the years of the Republic, adhered to a different code of sexual conduct.

Active homosexuality was accepted; passive homosexuality was despised.[8] The "lord" did not find it inconvenient to have intercourse with another man as long as he played the part of active male. But to be effeminate was a grievous offense. In any case, what we see is that in these societies, homosexual preferences were not attributable to a clear cultural or biological cause. Yet we also find that these preferences were not a substitute for the institution of (heterosexual) marriage, and did not give rise to any recognized forms of homosexual marriage.

Considerations from the psychological sciences bear on the question of homosexuality's nature as well. We are not born with a ready-made sexual identity. Though we have a biological identity in the form of DNA, the acquisition of a particular sex role is the outcome of an education—the result of a social process. We internalize the meaning of the fact that we have a penis or a vagina, and assume the corresponding sex roles. Typically, this internalization takes places in the context of a loving relationship with our parents, who are our first and fundamental role models. The meaning of sexuality that results from this process of internalization stands at the core of individual personal identity and the collective culture of a civilization.[9]

As background to the foregoing considerations, we can ask the question: is homosexuality a biological condition, or the result of a cultural and moral choice? In other words, is homosexuality a matter of natural fact or a lifestyle? I contend that it is a cultural phenomenon—a lifestyle—but one that is set against a biological background. It is important here to make a clarification: to say that homosexuality is a lifestyle does not contradict the fact that the issue of homosexuality is something given, independent of the will of the individual, and not a result of his or her free choice. When the process of constructing a sexual identity is completed, it is very difficult to reverse it. In that sense, people do not choose to be attracted to people of the same sex. But they do choose to *act* on that attraction. In some cultural contexts, that choice is accepted or encouraged, whereas in others it is discouraged or forbidden. Nevertheless the decision to engage in homosexual behavior is a question of lifestyle. While there may be biological reasons for experiencing homosexual attractions, they are situated against cultural reasons for voluntarily taking up a *lifestyle* of homosexuality.

Understood as a lifestyle, we can see the difference between the principle of non-discrimination applied to African-Americans, on the one hand, and homosexuals, on the other. In the case of African-Americans, to be African-American is not the result of a choice. It is just a natural fact. I cannot approve or disapprove of a natural fact. If I do, I deny the inherent human dignity of the human being in question. I can, however, approve or disapprove of a human choice or a human lifestyle. In doing so, I do not deny the inherent equality of all men who are equally endowed with intelligence and free will, and who therefore possess the same fundamental dignity. I simply disagree with the use that an individual or some individuals have made of their freedom and power of choice.

I do not want to expand on the reasons why some of us find the homosexual choice or the homosexual lifestyle to be objectionable.[10] It is enough here to explain why the issue of homosexuality is a legitimate object of moral, cultural, and political discussion.

Because homosexuality involves a biological dimension in which the element of individual choice is absent, the Church should be very careful in speaking of individual moral responsibility. I may think that homosexuality per se is wrong and nevertheless recognize that the individual homosexual is entangled in what some theologians would call a "situation of sin," without personal responsibility or only with a limited personal responsibility.[11] A negative moral judgment against homosexuality does not imply an attitude of discrimination toward homosexuals, who retain all their human rights.

On the other hand, this very recognition of the power of culture—that it may coalesce into a second nature—makes it necessary to discuss the prevalence that we should give homosexual lifestyles in the public square. If the acquisition of traditional male and female roles constitutes a positive cultural acquisition, shall we try to preserve it in the educational system? Shall we cooperate with families in the transmission of the set of values linked with these roles to the following generation? *This is the crucial issue.* If homosexuality were a mere biological fact, we could do nothing to influence the prevalence of heterosexual or homosexual attitudes in the world of tomorrow. If it is a cultural lifestyle, by contrast, it is a matter of common concern whether it will predominate in the future. Do we want our children exposed on an equal basis to heterosexual and homosexual models in the moment in which their sexual identity is being formed? And who has the authority to decide? The parents? State authorities? Show business?

I have the impression that not all those who participate in this discussion appreciate what is at stake. The entirety of our cultural system (and our moral and legal systems) is based on the idea of the free and responsible individual. Kant captured this idea in his concept of the transcendental ego.[12] The free and responsible individual can resist the impulses of uncontrolled passion to do what is good. He is not dominated by the passion of the moment but pursues rational ends through his/her actions. His/her ends are rational in the sense that they are consistent in time—they do not change too often and do not contradict each other—and they obey the moral imperative of considering in the definition of one's good the legitimate demands of the good of others.[13] The exercise of one's liberty allows for an equal exercise of the liberty of others and considers the person in oneself, always as an end and never only as a means.[14] In Kant, this idea of the free individual arises, in a certain sense, out of itself.

The so-called Frankfurt School has applied the sociological and psychological presuppositions of this structure of individual liberty and rationality to the family. Through the unconditional love of the mother we learn that we are unique human beings, with the right of having and pursuing our own ends. And through the discipline imposed by the father, we learn that we have duties as well, and that we have to confirm our will in self-control, our liberty in law. This implies cooperative roles between man and wife in forming individuals. The institution of the family may change in time, but we should be very careful in considering what values are at stake, and what we run the risk of losing with each proposed change.[15]

Ultimately, the fact that homosexuality is a lifestyle does not imply at all that it is not a legitimate lifestyle. It only means that as a lifestyle it is a legitimate topic of discussion, and not all those who disapprove of this lifestyle ought to be considered homophobes.

B. On Discrimination

To make further progress in our inquiry, we must now investigate the meaning of the word "discrimination." The word comes from Greek and means to make distinctions, to differentiate, but it can also mean to accommodate according to a scale of preference. Today, however, "discrimination" has effectively become synonymous with "*unjust*" or "*unjustified*" discrimination. This conflation of terms obscures the important fact that no order—especially no moral order—can be established without making distinctions, and thus strictly speaking, discriminating. As Richard Garnett persuasively argues in his contribution to this volume, it is vital that we distinguish between discrimination as "justified distinction," on the one hand, and discrimination as "unjustified prejudice," on the other.

The notion of unjustified discrimination derives from the principle of equality. In the Aristotelian formulation, the principle of equality demands that equal cases be treated equally, and that different cases be treated differently.[16] Accordingly, treating different cases in the same way would be equally unjust as treating similar cases in a different way. Now, if we apply this framework to the differential treatment of a particular group or class of persons, the relevant question is whether that differential treatment is supported by a corresponding relevant difference in the cases under consideration. For example, whether it is justified to treat homosexuals differently than heterosexuals on the issue of marriage depends on whether, in relation to marriage, the case of homosexuality is equal to that of heterosexuality. If it they are not equal in all relevant respects, a difference in treatment does not constitute unjustified discrimination. When it comes to marriage, are we dealing with like cases? Let us explore further.

It is a matter of fact, I would argue, that all men are born equal in dignity. But they differ from one another in many other aspects, such as race, ethnicity, sex, language, skill, intelligence, economic class, education, health, age, and physical make-up, to name a few. Some of these differences allow for, or even demand, differential treatment under certain circumstances; others do not. For instance, if I sit on a college admissions board, I cannot justifiably deny admission to applicants shorter than five feet tall. This is because physical height is not a relevant or justifiable difference in the context of access to education. But if I am a professional basketball coach selecting my team, I may justifiably discriminate by selecting only those players taller than five feet. Here, unlike in the first example, excluding those shorter than five feet does not violate their equal rights, much less their equal dignity. It simply reflects that the fact that sports are driven by performance, and that players under five feet are unable to perform at the requisite level. Consider another example. I may happen to be musically untalented. While I have the right not to be discriminated against in certain contexts for my lack of musical talent, I cannot consider myself the victim of unjust or unlawful discrimination if the Vienna Philharmonic Orchestra denies me access to the job of first violin.

Some differences that were once deemed to be natural and requiring unequal treatment we now know to be socially produced and not reconcilable with unequal treatment. Sometimes discrimination produces inequality and this inequality itself is used to justify discrimination. In continental Europe, we have become more attentive to this issue since the Second World War. In many continental European states, and especially in Italy,[17] the constitutions crafted after the war paid particular attention to "second-generation rights," or social rights.[18] For example, a person may not be intelligent enough to be eligible for university, not because they lack natural potential, but because their skills and native intelligence have not been properly developed through adequate education. States that recognize second-generation rights assume responsibility for this student's plight; they endeavor to remove the obstacles that prevent the full development of each citizen's potential.

We must, however, point out two qualifications, or challenges, to this duty that second-generation rights demand of the state. The first is that even when fully developed, the potential of each citizen will still greatly vary. The full development of each citizen's potential will not give us a society in which all are equal in all respects, and in which vast differences in skills and attitudes do not exist. Even the best policies devised to cultivate each citizen's full potential cannot overcome the vast differences in natural endowment across a population.[19]

The second qualification is that it is not easy to provide equal opportunities for all citizens. As always in human affairs, nature and culture are deeply intertwined; it is impossible to completely disentangle them. For instance, the son of a loving couple is likely to preserve an emotional advantage over the son of a couple whose relationship is tormented. In the former case, the love of his parents will make him bolder and more at ease facing the challenges of life. Likewise, the son of a family of professors raised among books is more likely to acquire a familiarity with intellectual matters at an early age than an equally naturally endowed person who lacks such precocious training.

The modern state attempts to overcome the social and natural disadvantages that thwart the full development of its citizens' potential. But what shall we do after all that we can do has already been done? What shall we do with the differences that remain? At least three different answers can be given. The first says that the remaining differences should be accepted and allowed to play their role in social life. According to this view, for example, it is in the general interest of society to admit into universities those students who are best prepared, because they will make the best lawyers or physicians or professionals. In this way, the public welfare is better served. This first answer corresponds to the achievement principle, which considers social or economic inequalities legitimate if they are the result of individual performance in competition.

A second answer proposes that we act as if the remaining differences did not exist. This is the answer that the so-called policy of "affirmative action" presupposes. Certain individuals, it holds, should be given preference in admission to universities or in the allotment of resources because of their origin, not because of their merit. This reverses Aristotle's equality principle. Here we are asked to treat situations that are not equal as if they were equal. Is that appropriate? Is it legitimate? Here we should be very careful.[20] I do not want to deny that a quota system like affirmative action may sometimes be effective in easing tensions among different ethnic groups, thus helping to preserve the civil peace. In the United States, affirmative action has helped to strengthen the African-American middle class, which has been positive for American democracy, even if the same effect could have been pursued through better financing higher education for the poor. A system of quotas may also help to more rapidly increase the number of women on the governing boards of social, political, and economic institutions, although it could be objected that it would have been more effective to remove the obstacles that make it more difficult for women to reach those assignments in the first place.

The question becomes even more delicate when we enter the realm of criminal law. Should we guarantee heightened legal protection to social groups that are understood to be the targets of social hatred? This is the case of so-called hate crimes. Should we accept that a behavior constitutes a felony if it is directed against a person who belongs to one ethnic or social group, but constitutes only a misdemeanor or no offense at all if it is directed against a member of another social group? We should keep in mind that hate-crime measures are exceptions to the general principle of the equality of all citizens before the law. However, the danger that every social group will try to claim for itself similar privileges looms large. In the end, the very principle of equality of all citizens before the law would be shaken. Even if we accept affirmative action or other quota systems for a limited number of designated groups, such as women and racial minorities, a question still remains: should we extend these privileges to lifestyles?

A third answer to the problem of lingering social differences supposes that the state has a duty to remove all the obstacles that do not allow me to attain the ends I pursue. Those who subscribe to this view are often individuals or groups that feel discriminated against for some perceived difference, and demand to be put on an equal footing with other individuals or groups. This produces a kind of social game in which everybody is asked to act, out of respect for those who cannot stand being different, as if the individual or group claiming discrimination possesses a unique quality or difference to be protected. There is a clear difference between this formulation, which I shall call the principle of radical equality, and the rationale for second-generation rights. The idea of second-generation rights is premised on the duty of the state to remove the obstacles that thwart the full development of its citizens' *potential*. According to the principle of radical equality, however, the state has an unconditional duty to support the attainment of all ends, even ones that may not be possible. This is problematic, needless to say, because it is quite possible that I set for myself an end that does not fall within the realm of my potential. In response, a defendant of second-generation rights might argue that the state in fact has no duty of conferring on me a social status or a social role I lack the capability to exercise.

The principle of radical equality is also at odds with the achievement principle. Whereas the achievement principle recognizes legitimacy in competition, the principle of radical equality shies away from it. This contrast arises between the two principles due to their differing responses to the experience of being inferior or different. At any given moment, we are all inferior to others in countless different ways, contexts, and fields. Awareness of one's inferiority can be vexing. The real question is how one attempts to overcome this unpleasant feeling. On the one hand, the achievement principle suggests that one attempts to better oneself—to make oneself less inferior—by entering into loyal competition with others. This requires the exertion of the will and hard labor, but also the capacity to concentrate one's efforts in those areas in which one is better endowed. Nobody can excel in all possible domains, and success in a certain art or business often requires that one doesn't venture into others.

On the other hand, the principle of radical inequality attempts to overcome the uneasiness of being aware of one's own inferiority by refusing to engage in competition altogether, by demanding that all distinction be abolished. Here, the quest for equality transforms into an aggressive demand against society that all its members act as if I possessed all the qualities I desire to possess. If somebody objects to this demand and refuses to comply with my pretension, the principle of radical equality would authorize me to indict him for discrimination. If we accept this way of reasoning, the meaning of the word "discrimination" undergoes a tremendous change. It expands from a limited to a much more general theory of unjustified discrimination. Here, there is no longer any room for legitimate distinction. All discrimination is unacceptable. Everything and everybody is equivalent to everything and everybody else. Not only does this efface the Aristotelian idea of equality, but it negates the Aristotelian principle of noncontradiction. It also obscures the distinction between desire and reality, pretending that society must comply with all our pretensions of possessing the qualities we wish to possess—of being what, as a matter of fact, we are not.

C. On Toleration

Another concept needing clarification is "toleration." If one accepts the enlarged vision of discrimination embedded in the principle of radical equality, one disavows the principle of toleration in two different but converging senses. The principle of toleration demands, first, that I recognize the right of others, even and especially those I disagree with, to express their ideas and to exercise their rights. As Voltaire is supposed to have said, "I disapprove of what you say, but I will defend to the death your right to say it."[21] But then toleration must also imply, second, that I have an equal right to express my own disagreement, or even my moral condemnation of, the ideas and actions of others.[22] The principle of radical equality accepts toleration in the first sense, but denies it in the second. It shields social differences from criticism, refusing to tolerate any disagreement or disapproval aimed those differences.

The idea of toleration, moreover, implies that there is one truth and multiple intellects arguing about this truth. Nobody can pretend to possess truth in its entirety, and this is the reason why we disagree. We respect each other because each one of us recognizes in our opponent the dignity of being capable of truth. We also agree that truth demands the homage of the unconstrained and free will and intellect of the human person. If we compel a person to proclaim something true out of bribery or fear or compulsion, this will not be a valid assent to truth. Instead, this would be an offense to truth, deprived, in this way, of the possibility of entering into a dialogue with this person.

If you substitute the word God for the word truth you find yourself in the center of one of the main tenets of Christian faith.[23] The philosophical argument in favor of toleration, without losing its pure philosophical value, has a theological soul. Intolerance is not only an affront to human freedom, but also a sin against God. In this sense there is a direct contradiction between toleration and relativism. As I explained in the preceding paragraph, toleration presupposes the existence of truth, but recognizes the impossibility of grasping the whole truth.[24] If there were no truth, we could not disagree on what is true; a dialogue could not begin. By the same token, if truth were easy to reach, we would likely not disagree on it; truth would present itself (almost) incontrovertibly.

On the subject of truth, the idea of toleration goes hand in hand with the original, more limited idea of non-discrimination: that one has the right not to be discriminated against for their ideas even if those ideas happen to be wrong (or untrue). The enlarged idea of non-discrimination implicit in the principle of radical equality, by contrast, does not want to know the difference between true and false, between right and wrong. It simply asserts that there is no truth—each truth or proposition is equally valuable (or equally void of value). It is forbidden to forbid and this is the only prohibition that remains. It is forbidden to think in terms of higher or lower values and it is forbidden to consider one lifestyle better than another.

Here, toleration is precluded by removing the possibility of legitimate disagreement. According to this line of thought, those who express a judgmental attitude—that is, those who insist in thinking in terms of good and bad—should not be tolerated. In this scenario, nobody possesses Voltaire's courage to offer one's life in order to preserve the rights of those who judge to pass their judgments.

This movement from a limited to an enlarged concept of discrimination mirrors the transition from a restricted to an enlarged concept of relativism. The restricted concept of relativism points out the fact that truth is too large to be possessed in its entirety by a single person. I can be certain of the truth I have grasped, but I must always keep in mind that other human beings have a grasp on truth. I must try to reach a broader, more inclusive formulation of truth in which the experience of others is also adequately considered. In this way we grow together toward the ultimate truth, which lies beyond the reach of mortal beings.

The absolute notion of relativism, by contrast, pretends that no truth exists. This has two notable implications. First, it implies that the argument of an opponent need not be seriously taken into account. If there is no ultimate truth, then everybody is equally right (and wrong), and thus there is no justifiable basis to disagree. Second, the affirmation of a right once depended upon an understanding of human nature and of the nature of right being considered. This was the starting point for the idea of natural rights—which emerged out of the Glorious Revolution of 1689[25] and the French Revolution—and later, human rights.[26] But absolute relativism rejects the idea of "natures," since a nature implies a truth. This makes it extremely difficult, if not impossible, to discuss and justify rights. In the place of sound arguments for rights, absolute relativism has established a new criterion: rights are justified according to the intensity with which I feel that I should have what I want. This intensity is thought to be sufficient legitimation to insist upon compliance with my demands. I have a right to what I am ready to struggle for. The result is the sophistic principle against which Plato spoke in the *Republic*[27]: that everybody has as much rights as he has power.

At the end of this methodological discussion I wish to make one last point: We should never forget that "homosexual" and "heterosexual" are just words. What is real is the human being who may happen to be homosexual or heterosexual, or homosexual in a certain period of his life and heterosexual in another. We do not have rights because we are homosexual or heterosexual; we have rights because we are human beings. It is possible to respect and love a human being whose sexual behavior we consider to be wrong. In real life, we share the world with other human beings who may have important disagreements with us on many issues. We are husbands and wives, parents and children, brothers and sisters. It may happen, and often happens, that we disagree on crucial matters with people we love. We must learn to disagree without losing reciprocal respect. Love and disagreement are not incompatible. I should not force on others the truth I have recognized, but if I truly love another human being it will be impossible for me not to express what I see as true.

This invites us to start from the experience of each individual, from the common social and historical experience that we all have as humans. In order to do that, we have to shed our prejudices and pre-constructed suppositions, which do not allow us to enter into an authentic cognitive contact with reality.[28] We have to listen to things in themselves, to the experiences of the other, and to our own life experiences.[29] Ideologies proceed in a deductive way. Given a certain set of first principles, necessary consequences are drawn to match any possible occurrence of life. People who do not agree on first principles are supposed, as a consequence, to be unable to lead a real dialogue. However, if we start with life experience, if we are willing to be challenged by the experiences of others, and if we try to incorporate our own experience and the experience of others in a broader framework, then perhaps a mutual understanding is possible.[30]

II. How Are the Tensions between Claims of Homosexual Equality and Religious Freedom Illustrated in Particular Legal, Political, and Policy Controversies?

Right to Same-Sex Marriage

Today, a growing number of people demand that the state recognize a right to marriage between homosexuals.[31] I argue that whether this demand is justified or not depends on the essence of marriage—the meaning of the word "marriage." In turn, I argue that the essence of marriage lies in its social function: procreation.

According to the Italian Constitution (but I strongly suspect that the situation in other legal orders is not very different), "family is a natural society founded on marriage."[32] Family, in other words, is not possible without the procreative power intrinsic and unique to heterosexual marriage. Children stand at the center of the family, which is to say that children stand at the center of marriage. Some claim that marriage is based on intimacy and love between partners. But falling in love is an emotional state that often happens more than once in a lifetime, in relationships that do not result in marriage. Marriage, on the other hand, is unique in that it involves a powerful bond and a shared destiny, one that is called into being by the presence of children, or at least by the recognition of the fact that the sexual relationship is ordered to the generation of children.[33]

Children need to have one father and one mother. Their emotional growth, flourishing, and development of a mature personality depend on a polarity between parents who are the primary source of education and influence in their lives. As a general rule, the mother is the love-giver who makes the child sure that whatever they do, they will remain the object of her unconditional love.[34] The father, by contrast, is the lawgiver who teaches the child that they have duties as well as rights and will be held responsible and eventually punished if they do not comply with the law. In each family this arrangement is subject to variations.[35] But shall we say that it has no biological basis?

Fatherhood and motherhood are essentially different from one another. The father may leave after intercourse, perhaps never knowing that he has become a father. For nine months of pregnancy and for some months thereafter, the child will scarcely take notice of even the most loving and caring father. The baby, to the contrary, is immersed in the biological and emotional world of the mother.[36] The baby hears the beating of her heart and listens to her voice even before being born. In most cases, the baby will suckle the milk of the mother. The mother is the world of the child, whereas the father is a foreigner who is introduced step-by-step by the mother into the emotional world of the child. It seems apparent, therefore, that men and women are not equally suited for the two polar roles that shape the personality of the child. Whatever the individual variations that take place in each couple, it seems that the woman has a natural predisposition to the role of the unconditional love-giver and that the father is better suited for the role of the lawgiver.[37]

The institution of marriage channels the energies of the parents toward work for their children. Through marriage, parents are able to instill in their children the personality traits necessary to live happy and productive lives. Through marriage, parents teach their children how to be self-confident and responsible for others, how to be creative and law-abiding, individualistic, and communitarian. Much of what we consider to constitute the core of the western civilization has this specific form of marriage at its basis.

That the heterosexual form of marriage has prevailed across human history and cultures is no accident; the institution of marriage stands at the very roots of civilization for a reason. Marriage has a unique capacity to harness human sexuality in a meaningful and productive way. Sex is one of humans' two main instincts (the other being the instinct of self-preservation). Marriage provides an outlet and a restraint for this sexual instinct by creating a framework through which we are able to discover the profound value of another, committing ourselves to this person in a loving and lasting relationship with him or her. In turn, by establishing a set of moral prohibitions around sexuality, this framework gives necessary form to otherwise amorphous human relationships. For example, rape may not be contrary to a primal sexual instinct to procreate. But marriage, recognizing that rape runs counter to the loving and personal nature of human sexuality, forbids it.

Marriage is not only responsible for producing children; for raising and educating them, guaranteeing their proper development; and for harnessing humans' sexual instinct. Marriage also creates a bond across generations. This function is extremely relevant for the common good and for the public sphere. For without children, without sustaining a bond across generations, a nation perishes. Parents take care of children when they are young; and children take care of parents when they are old. This is an alliance between generations. In contemporary societies this truth runs the risk of being forgotten, since we are used to thinking that in our old age we will survive on pensions and state welfare.

It is apparent, however, that there would not be any state, nor any welfare, if there were not a generation of young people to keep our states and our nations alive. In the past, each individual took care of their parents in their old age. Today, one generation collectively takes care of the previous; but the nature of this relation does not change. This is why the family has a social function that other affective or sexual relations do not possess, and thus why the family possesses a unique legitimate demand to be supported by the state.

Some people think that the denial of marriage to homosexuals implies a kind of disdain for the love experience of the gay couple as if it meant that gay love couldn't be authentic. This attitude is reasonable if marriage is understood simply as a kind of official recognition of a psychological state of affairs, but wholly unreasonable if marriage is seen as a social institution that has the function of begetting and educating children. Children can, of course, be born outside of family and wedlock, yet the family still provides the best environment to raise and educate children. But it is evident that children *cannot* be born of a same-sex couple, as same-sex couples are incapable of procreation. Consequently, same-sex couples cannot exercise the social function of marriage. The relationship between two homosexuals therefore should not be equated with that of two heterosexuals. Whereas the latter are capable of entering into what we call "marriage," the former are by definition precluded from doing so.

Now the question at hand becomes clear: does a union of two homosexuals fit the pattern of marriage? It appears that it does not. The English word for marriage can give us a clue as to why. It is the word matrimony, which comes from the Latin *matrimonium*. Matrimonium derives from *munus matris*, which comprises two meanings: the task of the mother and the protection of the mother. In other words: the protection given to the mother in order to help her to perform her task. No mother (or more generally no parenthood) means no matrimony. If no children are conceived through a couple's sexual activity, as is the case with a homosexual couple, why should this couple receive protections devised for parents?

As we have seen, the legitimate reason and purpose for marriage is to bear children, to rear them and to educate them. This reason for marriage is not created by the state. Rather, the state recognizes a state of affairs created through a free act of will of the spouses. An act of will that has an object different from the proper object of marriage cannot produce a marriage. Accordingly, the state cannot justifiably proclaim as marriage something that is not a marriage according to its essence. Nor can the state attach to it the rights and duties that are proper to marriage. I know that some of us may not feel at ease with concepts like "the essence of marriage." So I shall translate for them the same concept in other words. Marriage has a social function: the begetting and rearing of children. The state cannot proclaim as marriage something that does not perform that social function.

There are several objections that can be leveled against this argument. The first says that if marriage is centered on the child, infertile heterosexual couples should not be allowed to marry. The answer to this objection is that the law takes into account what generally takes place.[38] It may happen that in one specific case the general rule is violated. If a man and a woman get married but do not have children, their intention is not fulfilled. But it was nevertheless correct and constituted a valid marriage because all the needed presuppositions of a valid marriage were in place, but the children did not come. And if we know in advance that the children will not result from a marriage, as with an infertile heterosexual couple? Man and wife entered into life with a legitimate expectation that they would become father and mother, and we cannot thwart their legitimate expectations when they discover that they will not be able to beget children. They have entered into a process of constituting a female or male identity oriented toward marriage and it seems improper to deny them the possibility of getting married, even if in their case the consummation of marriage through the production of offspring will not take place.

For those who do not consider this explanation wholly satisfying, I must confess that perhaps here I am influenced by a Catholic bias in favor of the indissolubility of marriage. As a matter of fact, in most non-Catholic environments, and even for a large part of the Middle Ages, an unfruitful marriage was considered as invalid or dissolvable because it contradicted the social finality of marriage.

Let us consider a second objection. Some say that homosexuals can fulfill the social function of marriage by adopting children. Here, two questions arise. The first is: do we want children to be reared without the polarity of the two different sexes participating in their education? It seems to me that children need a father and a mother for a healthy growth. One learns to become a man or a woman by looking at the way in which one's father and mother move and act in the world, and especially through the way in which he or she looks to his or her spouse. Through heterosexual marriage, children learn the sexual difference that makes life so exciting. Do we want to exclude this difference from the world? The result would be a way of life much poorer and much more boring. I shall not consider here the educational value of the polarity between the love-giving mother and the lawgiving father, because I have already dealt with it at some length. It remains true, however, that the idea of adoption is not very satisfactory. Do not forget that homosexuality is a lifestyle. If it should grow to encompass a greater number of people, it would easily outgrow the limited number of children who are in need of an adoption and that argument would rule itself out.

Third, some point out that if we exclude from marriage the function of procreation—that is, of begetting and conceiving offspring (and we Italians seem to have excluded it at least in some of our legislation)—then there is no longer any ground to distinguish between marriage and homosexual partnership. On this view, the refusal to give homosexual partnerships the name "marriage" can only be regarded as the expression of hidden contempt for homosexuals. Moreover, this point of view recommends that we blur any functional distinction between parental roles, and that we consider man and wife to be not only morally equal but functionally identical (and this also seems to be the case in some of our marriage legislation). This argument concludes, therefore, that there are no criteria to adjudicate a difference between homosexual and heterosexual marriages.

This objection is well grounded and introduces us to the real issue. The real issue is not whether homosexuals should be allowed to get married, but what marriage is. Whether homosexuals may perform the act of will constituting their union as marriage is wholly dependent upon what marriage is. If marriage is just a ceremony through which we solemnize a sexual relationship, then there is no good reason to refuse this ceremony to homosexuals. If, on the other hand, marriage is a community of destiny created in order to beget, rear, and educate children, then it is apparent that gay people cannot get "married." To refuse them the ceremony of marriage and the status of marriage therefore does not constitute an act of arbitrary discrimination.

To conclude, let us briefly observe how the conception of marriage presented in this chapter fares against recent jurisprudence in the European Court of Human Rights (ECtHR). According to ECtHR precedent, the definition of marriage—whether or not it should be extended to encompass homosexual partnerships—is left entirely to the member states. Thus, we have some states that allow gay marriage, and others, such as Italy, that do not. In the case of *X. v. Austria*, decided February 19, 2013,[39] the ECtHR upheld the authority of member states to define marriage. Specifically, it ruled that Austria is free to accept or refuse gay marriage, and to concede or deny to gay couples the right of adoption. The Court specified, however, that if Austria extends to heterosexual unmarried couples the right to adopt children, then on the basis of the principle of equal treatment, it cannot refuse the same right to homosexual couples.

On the one hand, *X. v. Austria* indicates that the Court recognizes that marriage is (or may be if the member state so chooses) a social institution centered on the procreation and education of children and therefore not accessible to gay couples. On the other hand, by demanding that joint adoption rights be extended to homosexual couples (in instances in which this right is available to heterosexual couples), the Court suggests that homosexual couples are equal to heterosexual ones. However, this does not seem to do justice to the importance of the polarity of the sexes within the couple that rears and educates children. Ultimately, it remains to be seen whether, in future cases, the ECtHR leans toward a traditional conception of marriage oriented around children, or whether it pivots toward a broader conception of marriage that includes same-sex partnerships.

Same-Sex Partnership and Religious Exemptions in Italy

Constitutional Textualism versus European Consensus

ANDREA PIN

Introduction

According to its Constitutional Court, the Italian legal system does not allow same-sex marriage, but only the legal recognition of same-sex partnerships, while giving broad protection to conscientious objection. In this respect, the sacrifice of same-sex marriage seems to have spared Italy the growing difficulties in squaring same-sex marriage rights with religious freedom.

But in Italy as well as in other jurisdictions, the circumstances are quite fluid, affected as they are by multilayered human rights protections in Europe and rather incomplete constitutional interpretations, which fail to provide reasonable explanations for their judgments. Therefore, the human rights agenda in this field is unpredictable and needs to be tackled more seriously than it is at the moment.

This chapter will analyze how Italian law at the present stage addresses issues concerning same-sex couples, as well as consider the impact that the multilevel European human rights protection scheme has on it. It will deal with the role that religion and religious freedom play and are likely to play in this field in the coming years, as well as the importance of sound constitutional interpretation regarding institutions like marriage and principles like equality.

In order to address this topic, I first will sketch the European attitude toward same-sex couples' rights (Part I); then I will summarize the Italian legal attitudes toward the legal protection of same-sex couples and explore this protection's background and implication (Part II). Afterward, I will analyze the place of religious freedom in the area of same-sex couples' rights and its legal protection in Italy (Part III). In the conclusion, I will briefly maintain that the Italian legal culture's techniques of interpreting the Constitution and balancing rights and interests should be reconsidered to also include arguments that religious communities normally utilize. Religions and other moral traditions should have not just the right to be accommodated *once* rights for same-sex partners are introduced, but also the right to discuss these rights *before* they are introduced. This is not just in the interest of religions, but also for the sake of adjudicating rights properly.

I. The European Framework on Same-Sex Marriage

There is a great European struggle concerning the official recognition of same-sex couples. European states' laws on this topic vary considerably.[1] Some countries have accorded full marriage rights to same-sex couples, endowing them with the right to marry; recently and notably, this is the case in France and Great Britain. Others have endowed same-sex couples with comparable rights, but without classifying them as marriages. Still others have introduced more limited rights provisions for same-sex couples.

The series of second-degree legal partnerships found in Europe oftentimes applies to heterosexual couples as well as to homosexual couples. But the debate focuses on giving legal recognition to same-sex couples, rather than on the existence of such legal partnerships in and of themselves. And there is good reason to focus on the situation of same-sex couples. In fact, the urgency of protecting same-sex relationships is greater than the need to accord legal recognition to unmarried heterosexual couples.[2] Same-sex couples lack the possibility of achieving legal protection that heterosexual couples already receive through the institution of marriage. Heterosexual unmarried couples who decline to marry can be said to refuse the legal protection that is already available—whereas this is impossible for same-sex couples.

Although European models vary, a shared line of thought can be found throughout the Continent: same-sex relationships are seen as a social reality that expresses and fulfills individual lives.[3]

This is true first and foremost with regard to the European Convention on Human Rights (hereafter, the Convention) and the institutions that oversee the Convention's enforcement. The European Court of Human Rights, with its *Schalk and Kopf v. Austria* (2010) decision,[4] changed its previous attitude and brought same-sex partnership under the scope of Art. nos. 8 and 12 of the Convention, which protect the right to privacy and family life, and the right to marriage and found a family, respectively. Asked to determine whether same-sex couples should be endowed with full marriage rights, the Court affirmed that marriage is but one of many available solutions for vesting same-sex relationships with rights, and that states have broad room in deciding if and when to introduce any kind of same-sex partnership. But it clearly stated that such regimes fit within the Convention's protection of family life,[5] an affirmation that has already had a sizable influence over European states' attitudes, such as that of Italy.

The Convention's protection of same-sex partnerships was later reinforced in the *Vallianatos and Others v. Greece* (2013) judgment,[6] where the European Court of Human Rights Grand Chamber found Greece in violation of Art. 14 of the Convention, which forbids discrimination against Convention rights, in conjunction with Art. 8's protection of family life. That country had excluded same-sex couples from its registered partnership regime, which was alternative to marriage but still made available only to different-sex partners. The Court found that this choice discriminated against homosexual couples. Finally, and very recently, the European Court of Human Rights came back to the issue of same-sex partnerships in the context of *Oliari and Others v. Italy*,[7] a case that will be considered in greater depth below, since it connects directly to the Italian legal order.

The European Union legal system is not absent from this scenario. The EU Charter of Fundamental Rights frames the right to marry in an apparently lofty and state-deferential way by stating, "The right to marry and the right to found a family shall be guaranteed in accordance with the national laws governing the exercise of these rights" (Art. 9). But a more recent March 13, 2012 European Parliament Resolution, "Equality Between Women and Men in the European Union—2011," evidences the EU institution's positive inclination to recognize same-sex partnerships. This resolution is important for two reasons. First, it "regrets the implementation by some Member States of restrictive definitions of 'family' in order to deny legal protection to same-sex couples and their children."[8] Second, it calls "on the Commission and the Member States to elaborate proposals for the mutual recognition of civil unions and of same-sex families across Europe between those countries which already have the relevant legislation in place."[9] The first affirmation tells us that the European Parliament believes that same-sex couples should be legally protected. The second affirmation suggests that states that already have legislated on same-sex partnership accord a mutual recognition of such partnerships, so that same-sex couples can have their rights recognized in any state that has such legislation.[10] In so doing, the European Parliament states that the recognition of legal effects for same-sex partnerships is becoming part of European Union law, to the extent that a mutual recognition of civil unions and same-sex families is needed.[11] Nonetheless, the Resolution also avoids talking about a right to same-sex marriage, preferring more general terms such as "civil unions" and "families."

The European Court of Human Rights is aware of this EU trend and rein-forced its legal reasoning in *Schalk and Kopf*,[12] noting that, "Certain provisions of European Union law also reflect a growing tendency to include same-sex couples in the notion of 'family.' "[13]

Therefore, in Continental Europe the belief that same-sex couples are a vital, positive social institution is quite common,[14] although legal systems disagree in ranking them: some place same-sex partnerships at the level of traditional marriage, while others place them at an inferior level. This is the context in which the Italian legal system recently addressed the issue of same-sex marriage.

II. The Italian Constitution and Same-Sex Partnerships

When the Italian Constitutional Court, which renders judgments on the constitutional legitimacy of domestic laws, delivered its seminal decision in 2010 (judgment no. 138)[15] on same-sex marriage, it did not deal with a broad interpretation of social phenomena or the concept of "marriage," as derived from the overwhelmingly Catholic Italian tradition. The pre-Constitution civil code provisions[16] that prescribed or understood marriage as between a man and a woman had been challenged under Art. 3 of the Italian Constitution, which commands the principle of equality, and Art. 29, which opens by stating: "The Republic recognises the rights of the family as a natural society founded on marriage." The Constitutional Court used the Constitution as a shield against same-sex marriage claims without delving deeply into the philosophical or cultural realms: it did not take any position in favor of or against any moral traditions, but rather affirmed an *originalist* interpretation of the Constitution.[17] It adhered to the text and declared that the wording of the Constitution *does not allow* grouping homosexual and heterosexual relationships under the same constitutional umbrella: the institution of marriage.

The Court drew from the fact that, even though the constitutional text does not explicitly mandate that marriages be celebrated between a woman and a man, this understanding can implicitly be derived from Art. 29, para. 2, which states that "Marriage entails moral and legal equality of the spouses within legally defined limits to protect the unity of the family."[18] If the Constitution states that the two spouses are legally equal, the argument went, then the Constitution implicitly indicates that they are biologically different: a woman and a man. After all, the Constitutional Court reasoned, the Italian Constituent Assembly that operated between 1946 and 1948 and drafted the 1948 Republican Constitution was aware of homosexual relationships' existence. Therefore, it deliberately refused to include them under the constitutional marriage protection. And from this Constituent Assembly's noninclusion of same-sex marriage stems the prohibition of its introduction through Parliamentary legislation. Same-sex marriage is not simply unmentioned in the Constitution; it is even implicitly prohibited by it.

Tradition, as an argument, played only a minor role in the judgment. Admittedly, the Constitutional Court highlighted that heterosexual marriage draws from a "multimillennial tradition," but this tradition was mentioned only because the civil code provisions that still govern marriage predated the constitutional text: the Court needed to highlight the continuity between pre-Constitution Italian law and the Constitution in order to affirm that the framers clearly wanted to keep that longstanding tradition according to which marriage is between a man and a woman.

The only reference to the nature of marriage is found in the very short specification that "the (potential) creative purpose of marriage [. . .] distinguishes it from homosexual unions." This minor affirmation, which took for granted that homosexual unions cannot have a creative purpose, eroded, however, when the Constitutional Court later allowed heterologous fertilization—fertilization through using donor gametes—in 2014 (judgment no. 162). By admitting this practice, the Court potentially expanded the potentially "creative" capacity of marriage to encompass biologically sterile couples. Since the Court never elaborated the concept of "creative *purpose*"—for instance, to draw distinctions between heterosexual marriage and other types of unions that with the help of technology could still give birth to children—that small affirmation lost much of its meaning after the decision on heterologous fertilization.

After this strong endorsement of the constitutional text's original meaning, the Court contrasted it with social evolution and the increasing movement in favor of the recognition of same-sex relationships, denying[19] that the text is flexible enough to lose its original meaning or to align it with social and cultural changes.[20] The Court, however, took advantage of *Schalk and Kopf* to maintain that no pressure came from supranational human rights protection bodies to enforce same-sex marriage, since that judgment had recognized the broad spectrum of possibilities that the Convention's provision on the right to family life left to the states.

Although the Court endorsed the originalist interpretation of the Constitution, it also said something new. It affirmed that the Parliament can and should pass legislation regulating same-sex relationships, since such partnerships represent a legitimate social group, which finds protection under the Italian Constitution on a more general basis. According to the Court, same-sex partnerships express the personality of those who compose them. Thus, they must be protected under Art. 2 of the Constitution, which states that "The Republic recognises and guarantees the inviolable rights of the person, as an individual and in the social groups within which human personality is developed." There is, therefore, not just room for recognition, but even a constitutional indication that same sex partnerships have the right to be recognized officially, provided that they are not made equal to marriage; it is the Parliament's duty to regulate such partnerships. In so doing, the Constitutional Court clarified that there is a clear gap between same-sex and heterosexual partnerships according to the Italian Constitution. But far from being mere social relationships that are irrelevant to the law, same-sex partnerships express human personality and therefore deserve some constitutional protection.

The Court's decision did not use any rational, traditional, moral, or religious justifications to exclude gay couples from marriage. And I think that this approach is partially understandable, but partially evasive, as I will show below.

The decision of the Constitutional Court, however, did not close the door to debate or really prompt the Parliament to intervene to regulate the status of same-sex partnerships. Notwithstanding the Court's continued solicitations, the Parliament has not yet passed any legislation on this issue.[21]

Shortly after the Constitutional Court delivered its judgment, the Court of Cassation was involved in the same-sex marriage issue.[22] The Court of Cassation serves as the Supreme Court and court of last resort in Italy for cases, ensuring that the law is interpreted consistently. Even though the Italian legal system is not a common law system, and the Court of Cassation does not address constitutional issues, its decisions are extremely relevant and normally influence the whole jurisdictional system.

The case at stake regarded a same-sex Italian couple who married in the Netherlands under Dutch legislation and sought official recognition in Italy. Recognition of marriages that are performed abroad is normally achieved through their transcription in the public registry of the couple's place of residency, and the local mayor is in charge of processing this act.[23] The Italian legal system, however, forbids the implementation of acts that are "contrary to the public order," a sweeping term that certainly includes constitutional values. And this was precisely the case in which the "public order" limitation had to come into play, since the Italian Constitutional Court had just declared that same-sex marriage is incompatible with the Italian Constitution.

The Court of Cassation was fully aware of the conflict between the Italian Constitution and the possibility of same-sex marriage recognition. There was no such fundamental right to marry for same-sex couples, and the Dutch same-sex marriage could not be transcribed in the Italian registry.

The Court of Cassation prompted an impressive shift in the Italian jurisprudence, however. It gave much weight to the social and legal changes in Europe and elsewhere, with same-sex couples being involved in stable relationships, and endowed them with some legal significance. This approach was strikingly contrary to the Constitutional Court's reasoning that this kind of relationship was already known when the Constitution was framed, and was intentionally left out of the constitutional protection to marriage. The Constitutional Court had said that the framers were aware of this phenomenon, but the Court of Cassation said that the Constitution was outdated.

The Court of Cassation drew from the Constitutional Court's decision its concern for protecting same-sex relationships under specific circumstances. This protection could also amount to equating their status to that of married couples, but not on a general basis. It backed this affirmation with the justification that the European Court of Human Rights, in its *Schalk and Kopf* decision, and the European Union Charter of Fundamental Rights' broad protection of the family, included same-sex couples under the umbrella of marriage rights. These arguments previously had been avoided by the Constitutional Court, which conversely had highlighted the states' high degree of discretion in addressing same-sex couples' claims.

In doing so, the Court of Cassation explicitly integrated Italian family law with European Union law and the European Court of Human Rights' jurisprudence. This multilayered approach is much more evolutionary than the Constitutional Court's. In the Court of Cassation's view, the changes in EU law and the European Court of Human Rights' jurisprudence could not affect the heterosexual nature of marriage, but they could nonetheless push for changes in Italian law in more limited but concrete ways, such as same-sex couples' right to a house, family pensions and benefits, and the like. With the exception of heterosexual marriage, Italian law was more structurally exposed to changes by supranational legal systems: since EU law and the European Court of Human Rights' jurisprudence now are integrated with the Italian constitutional right to have a family, domestic courts can interpret Italian law in a new way and provide same-sex couples with new concrete rights and measures, without having them wait for a legislative change of the Italian law.

The Court of Cassation's decision is therefore extremely relevant in several respects. On one hand, it paves the way for a more progressive legal interpretation, which would be driven mainly by supranational human rights protection. On the other hand, it envisions situations in which judges can provide same-sex couples with concrete measures without having to wait for the legislature's intervention. Such an approach increases the possibility that same-sex relationships gain piecemeal protection, but also that specific arrangements create unpredictable collisions with the religious freedom of individuals and groups. After all, the Court of Cassation's reasoning, in comparison with the Constitutional Court's, (a) takes the regulation of same-sex couples out of the hands of the legislature and gives it to the judiciary; (b) explicitly confirms that domestic judges can equate married and same-sex couples under specific circumstances; and

(c) legitimizes legal interpretations that, under the pressure of the supranational human rights regimes, could expand the number of circumstances in which this leveling takes place.

A more recent decision of the Italian Constitutional Court confirms the trend of disconnecting the concept of family from the heterosexual paradigm. With judgment no. 170 (2014) the Constitutional Court dealt with a situation in which a spouse underwent a process of gender reassignment.[24] According to Italian law, when a member of a married couple changes gender and has it transcribed in the official registry, the marriage is dissolved.[25] Evidently, the Italian legislation took gender difference as an essential requisite for marriage: absent that requisite, the marriage was terminated.

In this case, the Constitutional Court continued to follow its 2010 jurisprudence on the impermissibility of same-sex marriage and the constitutional relevance of same-sex partnerships, which still lack legislative protection. But it highlighted the specific situation in which the law deprived a couple the possibility of a stable relationship after years of shared, constitutionally protected life, singling out the couple's status from any other kind of homosexual union. The couple had a shared history in which it had enjoyed reciprocal rights and duties; it could not reasonably pass from the high level of protection provided by marriage status to no protection at all. Explicitly drawing from German jurisprudence, the Court said that this shift from total protection to no protection was not a *proportionate* measure.

The Court underlined that the needs of that couple could not be ignored by a lack of any legal protection for their relationship. But such protection did not necessarily coincide with the one provided by marriage status; the extremely diverse European environment, with multiple, diverging state policies addressing same-sex relationships, confirmed that several models of protection were available. The Court therefore struck down the piece of legislation that failed to allow a married couple, one of whose members had changed his or her gender, to transform their marriage status into another protected status, if they both wished.

It must be noted that the Court framed the constitutional issue as a conflict between a public and a private interest: the preservation of the heterosexual model of marriage as a state interest, on one side, and the interest of the couple affected by the gender reassignment process on the other.[26] This classification seems to be quite important to measure the implications for the protection of religious freedom, as we will see later.

A. The Decisions and the Backgrounds

In its seminal 2010 decision, the Italian Constitutional Court basically froze the interpretation of the constitutional provision about marriage to its *original* meaning, and made it particularly resistant to most, but not all, legal changes.

According to the Constitutional Court's doctrine, the European Court of Human Rights provides the conclusive interpretation of its Convention and integrates national constitutional law with it. Consequently, Parliamentary legislation must comply not just with Italian constitutional law, but also with the European Court of Human Rights' jurisprudence. In other words, if the European Court finds that European consensus has built new rights or broadened existing ones, these findings will affect Italian legislation. But this happens with the *caveat* that the Convention, as interpreted by its own Court, cannot conflict with Italian constitutional provisions.

Now we can understand why the Constitutional Court firmly established that the concept of heterosexual marriage as enshrined in the Italian Constitution is not susceptible to Parliamentary changes. This affirmation implies that, even if the European Court determines that by consensus the Convention's scope now covers the right to same-sex marriage, this will not modify the heterosexual feature of marriage in Italy, since it is constitutionally imposed.

Conflicts between Italian constitutional law and the European Court of Human Rights' case law on same-sex marriage are not merely theoretical. The European Court of Human Rights anticipated and made room for emerging consensus when it affirmed that the field of rights concerning same sex-couples had to "*still* be regarded as one of evolving rights with no established consensus."[27] The European Court clearly foresaw changes, since it allowed States time to make them. In its words, "States must also enjoy a margin of appreciation in the *timing* of the introduction of legislative changes."[28]

The 2010 Constitutional Court's judgment implicitly tried to resist such changes. Precisely by saying that the Constitution lacks space for same-sex marriage, the Court affirmed that the Italian legal system runs against the creation of such a consensus-based right to same-sex marriage. In other words, the Italian Court said to the European Court, in a rather direct way, that Italian law is not simply silent on this subject, but even contrary to same-sex marriage, and therefore counterbalances the possible expansion of consensus. Interestingly, the Constitutional Court's 2014 judgment no. 170, which focused on the implication of gender reassignment on marriage status, also did not rely on the European Court of Human Rights' jurisprudence. It used such jurisprudence mainly to emphasize that the European Court gives states room to shape such situations.

Rather different has been the approach of Italy's Court of Cassation, which instead highlighted that the umbrella of Art. 12 of the Convention was broadening to encompass progressively more types of relationships. The Court of Cassation's approach made significant use of the Charter of Fundamental Rights of the European Union as well. This reference is exceptionally relevant. According to the long-established doctrine of the Constitutional Court, European Union law prevails even over constitutional provisions, with the exception of supreme constitutional principles and values, which trump the enforcement of EU law at the domestic level. Therefore, the Court of Cassation's utilization of European Union law alters the framework significantly: if the Court of Cassation's approach prevails, although the constitutional text is read as not permitting same-sex marriage, it could still be enforced in Italy as part of EU law. If the Constitutional Court wants to preserve the heterosexual model of marriage in the face of EU law's endorsement of same-sex marriage, then it should qualify it as a supreme constitutional value. This designation would still preserve the heterosexual character of marriage.

The Constitutional Court has given little, if any, information on the reasons that back its reading of heterosexual marriage as unchangeable. However, had it done so, it would have probably clarified also whether heterosexual marriage is a supreme constitutional principle. This would have given insight into how the Constitutional Court would react to the hypothetical incorporation of same-sex marriage in the context of EU law. In short, the Constitutional Court probably could have done a better job by providing its readers with some hints that support its interpretation of the Italian Constitution.

Justifications have a prominent role, in the long run. The European Court of Human Rights' *Oliari and Others v. Italy* (2015)[29] decision testifies to this. Here, the Court utilized the Italian Constitutional Court and the Court of Cassation's judgments on same-sex partnerships to rule that Italy's lack of legal recognition for same-sex couples is a violation of Art. 8 of the Convention. It built the necessity of providing same-sex couples with a certain set of rights upon the Italian case law, and narrowed down the space for state discretion that *Schalk and Kopf* had given to them. The Italian Constitutional Court had largely ignored—and even opposed—the European Court; but the European Court drew from the Constitutional Court's own affirmations to condemn Italy.

The European Court condemned the Italian government for not having accorded same-sex couples a registered partnership regime that would provide them with "moral and material support, maintenance obligations, and inheritance rights."[30] The Court construed its argument upon two fundamental pillars. The first is the "movement towards legal recognition of same-sex couples which has continued to develop rapidly in Europe," which the European Court has noted since *Schalk*.[31] The second pillar, which is the crucial justification for the decision, is that the Italian legislature failed to follow up the Constitutional Court and the Court of Cassation's judgments by putting in place some protection for same-sex partnerships. In the European Court's words, "the Italian legislature seems not to have attached particular importance to the indications set out by the national community, including [. . .] the highest judicial authorities in Italy."[32] In other words, the European Court found a contradiction between the Italian (lack of) domestic legislation, on one hand, and the Italian judiciary, on the other hand, and concluded that this contradiction amounted to a violation of the Convention.

B. The Missing Arguments

Theoretically, one can find several rationales for extending the institution of marriage to same-sex couples. Some of the reasons that are most commonly affirmed are as follows: (a) the principle of equality[33]; (b) the principle of equal dignity, which would allow gay couples the same social ranking that heterosexual couples can achieve; (c) the right to self-determination (or privacy) of *couples* or, alternatively, of *individuals*,[34] which would be hampered if some couples or individuals were excluded from the institution of marriage. All three of these justifications can be found in the European context. We can consider them briefly.

The justification from the principle of equality maintains that, were marriage allowed only for heterosexual couples, this limitation would violate equality, since the determinations of homosexual and heterosexual people to get married would be treated differently. Some decisions would be valued more than others. And, the argument goes, there is no reason to exclude homosexual couples from the right to marriage: such extension of marriage does not violate the rights of those who do not want to take advantage of it or the rights of the heterosexual couples who already enjoy it.

Under the "equal dignity" justification, it is quite common to acknowledge that marriage has a specific social dignity, which parallels, as well as grounds, its special legal status. To deny it to gay couples, then, would amount to a disqualification of their relationships' dignity.[35]

Self-determination—which in Italy and other legal systems takes the place of American *privacy*—lies at the center of legal reasoning: the main issue that must be addressed in order to introduce a new right is whether there is a claimant for that right. This explains why self-determination has been considered as a fundamental right and principle and has led to the creation of a long list of other rights: abortion, in vitro fertilization, death, and same-sex marriage. It is interesting to notice that the concept of self-determination is absent in the Italian Constitution and many other European states' constitutions. In Italy, for instance, courts[36] and legal scholars seldom utilized it until recently. It was precisely with the latest wave of rights that self-determination became more important and influential in protecting new interests. It is not by chance, then, that self-determination has reinforced the principle of equality in supporting the extension of marriage to same-sex couples in Italy, where it was used in the trial that prompted the 2010 Constitutional Court's decision on same-sex marriage.

It is quite understandable that equality, dignity, and self-determination emerge as dominant arguments in courts and parliaments. On one hand, such arguments are easier to handle than balancing competing claims. They usually do not need to be integrated with other interests. This happens because equality and self-determination tend to shift the burden of proof onto those who do not want to introduce a new right. If a case is addressed from the standpoints of equality and self-determination, then the new right presumptively should be introduced. It is those who oppose the right who have to demonstrate why it shouldn't be accorded.[37]

The 2010 Italian Constitutional Court took a position that avoided both balancing rights and giving precedence to equality, dignity, and self-determination. It preferred to limit itself to the constitutional text, gave it an originalist reading, and shied away from providing more explanations for not allowing same-sex marriage.

Societal transformations can explain the sweeping influence of equality, dignity, and self-determination principles; and these principles' influence, in turn, can show why the Constitutional Court asserted itself to the point of stating that marriage as envisioned by the framers is not susceptible to accommodations for homosexual couples.

Few alternatives were easily available for the Court. The balance between competing claims has become increasingly difficult with the growing pluralism of national societies. The diversity of claims and interests derives from the coexistence of different cultural and religious identities. It is not just a matter of economic, social, or cultural gaps that can be filled through policies or different political views.[38] Different political opinions can be balanced, weighed, and synthesized in rather unified political ideals and visions. Different standpoints can overlap and agree on certain compromises when addressing the distribution of resources, opportunities, and welfare. State constitutions were drafted largely for this purpose: it was necessary to provide the means to temper class conflicts and to find shared solutions. Political and cultural debates were supposed to focus on taxation, welfare, and public expenditures. On the contrary, cultural, ideological, and religious views cannot be easily synthesized. They tend to be disparate; they cannot be balanced. Compromises are not easy solutions when strongly rooted ideals or opinions are at stake.

This is true for a large number of equality claims today. The principle of equality has constantly prompted the implementation of rights. But, until the 1990s, fights for equality aimed to include people and social classes that had been at least partially excluded from full participation in political and social life, for several reasons. Racial and religious minorities and noncitizens requested full rights to *participate in a shared, common life*—and they largely succeeded. By advocating for equality, they obtained the same rights that had been acknowledged for others. The goal was to allow everyone to enjoy the rights that only some had enjoyed until that point; the principle of equality made this possible.

But new rights hardly work only in this way. Contemporary plural societies[39] are characterized by disagreements[40] about ideals of life, truth, and the good. People have different goals, not merely different opinions on how the same goals should be achieved. For instance, the protection of the fetus as a living being is an alternative concern to the protection of a woman's will to terminate a pregnancy.

Various cultural and religious groups may diverge on public goals as well as on private life, society, and law. But they do not necessarily conflict on how they would shape their countries—they also can simply request to be left alone to pursue their own collective and individual goals. In the context of competing visions of a common life, there can be a never-ending struggle because every group exchanges opinions about public life and looks for broad consensus. But, if cultural and religious traditions do not aspire to a common life, then there is no need for consensus: all that is needed is freedom to live in accordance with one's ideals.

Religiously and culturally diverse groups tend to view disagreement on moral grounds.[41] And if the parties fail to reach a moral consensus about certain legislation, or if they are unwilling to look for such a consensus, their disagreement will probably lead the dissatisfied parties to seek insulation from other parties' ways of living.

The pluralism of contemporary societies explains why courts and legislators rarely go beyond principles of equality, dignity, and self-determination to search for other justifications that could play a role in addressing the difficult extension of marriage to same-sex couples. The principles of equality, dignity, and self-determination allow courts and parliaments to decide this issue without investigating the *justifications of marriage*. Any debate about the justification of marriage may lend itself to moral arguments.

This is also true, of course, for decisions *against* the extension of marriage to same-sex couples, as the Italian Constitutional Court's judgments make clear. They focused on constitutional text without reflecting on the justifications that undergird the special position that the Constitution accords to marriage. The Court merely decided that the text does not encompass same-sex couples—but did not go so far as to explain why the framers decided that marriage must have such a specific shape that could not be influenced by the passing of time.

And when the Court reflected on the creation of a specific legal protection for same-sex couples, it made the same mistake. It asserted that such relationships help individuals fulfill their personality, but did not say how they did so. It also failed to delineate the relationship between marriage and these partnerships.

Therefore, both the protection of same-sex couples—or the denial of such protection—and the protection of heterosexual marriage lack justification outside of the vague references to the meaning of "marriage" that the framers enshrined in the Constitution; to the (potential) "creative purpose" of marriage that is fading after the Constitutional Court made heterologous fertilisation lawful; and to human rights protection under Art. 2 of the Italian Constitution. Same-sex marriages, according to the Constitutional Court, are inconsistent with the constitutional text, but same-sex partnerships are normal forms of human relationships. And the justifications for both affirmations are quite elusive.

C. The Role of Justification in the Same-Sex Marriage Debate

The two standard ways of addressing the same-sex marriage issue are both largely disappointing: textual interpretations can prevent the extension of marriage to same-sex couples and curb the debate itself, but invoking dignity, equality, and self-determination can contribute to avoiding the debate as well.

Other reasons should be considered seriously before extending or refusing to extend marriage to same-sex couples, and the Italian Constitutional Court may need to address them in the future. In fact, textualism is not necessarily decisive. According to the Italian Constitutional Court's case law, if EU law comes to incorporate same-sex marriage among its fields of competence, then the Italian Constitutional Court will need to reconsider its judgments that denied it. Only if *heterosexual* marriage is considered a supreme constitutional principle, will it resist EU law; otherwise, EU provisions will prevail. In the long run, the Italian Constitutional Court will need to make up its mind and decide if the Constitution is fundamentally grounded on the principle that marriage is only between a woman and a man.

At this point, the Court is presented with three options: (a) the Court can strictly adhere to the constitutional text again, and accord its implicit assumption that heterosexual marriage is a supreme constitutional value; (b) drawing from the erosion of the "creative purpose" that would distinguish marriage from same-sex partnerships, it can reread the constitutional text to align with new rights claims in the name of equality and self-determination, and distill the substance of marriage from its heterosexual tradition, placing same-sex couples under the umbrella of marriage; or (c) it can both reinterpret the constitutional text and explore all the justifications that can be advanced, including "tradition," "morality," "natural law theory," and so on.

If the Constitutional Court investigates the nature of marriage more deeply in order to consider its justifications and benefits, it will need to grapple with multiple issues, rather than quickly dismissing them. Any concept of marriage will unavoidably demarcate the relationships that have access to marriage from those who do not enjoy such right.[42] Therefore, the reasons for leaving some relationships without the protection of marriage need to be openly expressed.

Traditionally, marriage embeds moral values: sexual and affective fidelity; the presupposition that there is a link between affection, sex, and childbirths; and complementarity of genders.[43] Society and law can disavow all of these moral aspects, but they should address these values when dealing with the identity of marriage because they affect its role and understanding. Aspects such as public morality, natural law, and tradition, which have been shaped and interpreted by religious traditions throughout human history, will come into play alongside the concepts of equality, non-discrimination, dignity, and self-determination. For example, the longstanding western—both religious and secular—tradition of marriage does play a role in other contexts, such as in debates on polygamy. In fact, it is widely recognized that monogamy is one of the western legal tradition's major achievements, an aspect of civilizational progress to be proud of. In this respect, tradition does work—among other justifications—as a quasi-normative argument and a shield against the introduction of polygamy; it depicts monogamy as an irreversible achievement of western family law. Thus it is inconsistent to use it in the polygamy debate, while dismissing it in the debate about same-sex marriage.[44] We can expect that when it comes time to decide if marriage must be heterosexual in Italian constitutional law, religious and secular traditions will contribute to such reflections.

Here religion can play a role. The fact that the values synthesized in marriage are sometimes expressed in religious words does not confine such values to the religious realm. Historically, religious groups have vigorously backed the moral, social, and political roles of marriage, as the western world has known it for millennia.

We are now experiencing a process of shifting away[45] from the longstanding opinion that marriage is heterosexual.[46] The European Parliament Resolution of March 13, 2012, "Equality Between Women and Men in the European Union—2011," maintains this approach. It mentions the "implementation" of "restrictive definitions of 'family'" that would have been recently introduced by some European states "in order to deny legal protection to same-sex couples" and then criticizes them.[47] Actually, marriage has been conceived as an institution between a woman and a man for millennia by several religious and secular traditions. Until recently, this view of marriage was not understood in terms of imposing a limitation on the right to marriage. With this in mind, recent examples of laws limiting marriage to heterosexual couples are better understood as *reactions* to the implementation of same-sex marriage. It is unreasonable to frame that which came first only as a limitation of a right—it is rather the crucible from which the right itself was formed, whether we believe that this right should be extended to encompass same-sex couples or not.

It is probably not by chance that tradition has not yet been adequately explored when it comes to the issue of heterosexual marriage. Tradition itself probably needs to elaborate the issue of heterogamy more openly. Marriage's heterosexual character is part of such a longstanding tradition that the need for justifying it probably did not appear before the current proposals to change some of its most classic features: as Charles Taylor pointed out, people can believe something strongly and reasonably, even if they are unable to explain why.[48] Nevertheless, an explanation is most needed today, as technology and laws have made childbirth available outside of heterosexual relationships,[49] and as parliaments and courts have expanded the same concept of "family" to include unmarried couples.

The Italian Constitutional Court itself has missed the opportunity of addressing the relationship between marriage and parenthood. In its judgment no. 162 (2014) it extended the availability of heterologous fertilization techniques[50] to fertilization for sterile or infertile heterosexual married couples. It established the existence of an absolute right to have children, stemming from the couple's right to self-determination, and made such techniques legally available to all married couples. The Court located this right to self-determination and parenting children within the constitutional right to have a family (Art. 29); but it failed to explain how the right to have a family produces the right to have children using DNA of individuals from outside the marriage.

Moreover, an understanding of marriage's justifications is necessary in order to protect its value, whatever change is made to it. In fact, the need for a deeper understanding of marriage lies beneath the arguments in favor of same-sex marriage. Advocates of same-sex marriage maintain that marriage has an intrinsic dignity that same-sex couples could never achieve through second-class partnerships. This explains why outlawing the institution of marriage so that every couple—regardless of its gender combination—can make the same civil partnership agreement is quite rarely endorsed. If marriage were outlawed, all couples would be treated on an equal basis. But society then would lose one of its historical pillars.

Ultimately, both same-sex marriages and second-class partnerships for same-sex couples leave us unsatisfied because they lack very strong justifications; and the merely textual justifications of heterosexual marriage fail to do a better job describing marriage's foundations. On the contrary, they make the necessity of a justification for *marriage in itself* more evident. And here too religious traditions can play a great role in elaborating reasons for marriage.

On the contrary, the need to preserve the social value and dignity of marriage probably suggests a prudent use of some common concepts such as *privacy*—or self-determination—especially in contexts, such as the Italian one, which use it to shield individuals from other members of society, rather than from the state. Those who debate the expansion of marriage to same-sex couples clearly believe that marriage has a shared social value and an intrinsic public dignity. In this context, the privacy argument is misleading; it separates the choice of partners—which would be deferred to the realm of privacy—from the public recognition of their partnership. It seems incoherent to claim that the gender of the two spouses is just a matter of privacy, while maintaining that the consequences of such partnership have a social value and a public dignity.[51]

III. The Place for Religious Freedom

The framework in which religious freedom claims would operate in the presence of a hypothetical regime for same-sex couples in Italy differs widely from a framework that would allow religions to contribute to the debate about the introduction of same-sex partnerships. Religious liberty does not fully protect religious communities against the effects of the introduction of same-sex marriage or other kinds of same-sex partnerships.

Religious freedom is often used to protect individuals or groups from performing an act that under normal circumstances they would be expected to perform,[52] such as military service or working on Saturdays—examples of what are usually called conscientious objections. Or, it can protect religions from being required to perform acts that are contrary to their own creed, including the celebration of same-sex marriages.

In practice, such objections do not prevent same-sex marriage from being introduced. If religious freedom is used as a religious excuse, it can be effective in insulating religious peoples and groups from the introduction of same-sex marriage. It nevertheless works *after* the enforcement of same-sex marriage, but not *before* and during the debates on it. In this respect, religious thinking and religious freedom play two different roles: the former comes into play during the debate about the introduction of such new rights, while the latter typically operates only after a right has been introduced, at which point religious freedom has already lost its political leverage.[53]

Moreover, this insulation is incomplete and can vary with circumstances. If the conflict between the protection of those who disagree with the new right and the protection of those who enjoy it is unavoidable, those who disagree will probably lose. In fact, when the protection of the conscientious objection cannot be accommodated with the protection of same-sex partnerships—say, if officers object to registering such partnerships—then the right to same-sex partnership will usually prevail: those who object will be forced to perform the act they oppose. Once a new right enters into force, shared, common life comes to include it, and therefore those who oppose it yield to it in cases where no accommodation is available.

Accommodating Rights of Same-Sex Couples and Religious Freedom in Italy

Since the Italian Constitutional Court has denied the expansion of marriage to include same-sex partnership, the most likely situation concerns religious freedom claims in the context of same-sex partnership rights, such as official transcriptions or welfare provisions of any kind. The Court of Cassation's affirmation that domestic jurisdictions will be able to accommodate same-sex partnerships on a concrete basis, even in absence of a general applicable law on this matter, makes the situation hard to predict. It is mere speculation to hypothesize where the conflict between same-sex couples' rights and religious freedom might take place. This uncertainty poses a challenge for striking a balance between the two competing claims, as the acts that people may be requested to perform can have very different levels of connection with the religious belief.[54]

In this regard, the European Court of Human Rights defers the role of accommodating such claims to each state, believing that they have "a certain margin of appreciation whether and to what extent" religious freedom should be accommodated.[55] In fact, it found no violation of religious freedom in the United Kingdom's refusal to accommodate an employee's request not to register same-sex partnerships because of her religious beliefs.[56]

The Italian constitutional framework, however, has quite a strong protection of religious objections. Constitutionally protected religious freedom is understood as encompassing freedom of conscience, and conscientious objections fall within the perimeter of the latter. Therefore, conscientious objections have a strong constitutional framework, which is attentively scrutinized by the Italian Constitutional Court. Sincerely held religious or moral beliefs surely are covered by such protection; [57]and there is little doubt that such beliefs are sincerely held and therefore worthy of protection. The aforementioned arguments that relate to natural law or morality and that oftentimes are used against the recognition of same-sex partnerships testify that such claims are not preposterous.

The refusal to allow exemptions for religious reasons would probably be seen as a disproportionate burden on religious freedom. In recent years, the Italian Constitutional Court has consistently utilized proportionality scrutiny, which in comparative constitutionalism is increasingly becoming the preferred tool to weigh competing claims without entirely sacrificing any of them.

As portrayed by the Constitutional Court in one of its seminal judgments on the use of this kind of scrutiny, "The proportionality test, which has been adopted by this Court as well as by many European constitutional jurisdictions [...] commands the piece of legislation under review be scrutinized [...] be necessary and able to achieve the legitimate aim, because, amongst a set of appropriate measures, it is least restrictive of competing rights and establishes not disproportionate burdens in pursuing of such aims."[58] Striking a balance between same-sex couples' rights and religious freedom claims would therefore consist in implementing same-sex couples' demands in a way that is least restrictive of religious freedom; if it happens to restrict religious freedom, it should do so only proportionally.

The most delicate part has to do with the protection of same-sex couples through a special regime that is supposedly different from marriage but can occasionally overlap with it. Since the regime is not equated with marriage, the Constitutional Court could even find that it does not interfere with religious belief in heterosexual marriage, and refuse to accord religious exemptions.

The Court could also take a different approach, building upon its observations that same-sex couples, albeit unable to consummate a marriage per se, have the right to enjoy the same degree of marriage protection *under specific circumstances*. If the legislation that is implemented reflects this approach and endows same-sex couples with the very same kind of protection that is accorded to married couples on certain topics, then the Court could consider that, concretely, same-sex couples and married couples are evenly protected and therefore religious exemptions must be accorded as they would be for same-sex marriage.

The 2014 Constitutional Court judgment on the preservation of marriage after a spouse's gender reassignment sheds light on the likely Italian legal preference for broad religious freedom accommodations. The Court there struck a balance between what it calls the "state interest" of the preservation of marriage as it is—and that which makes it unchangeable—and the "couple's interest" in having their relationship preserved after gender reassignment. This qualification is not without consequences. The public "state interest" sides with the traditional understanding of marriage as heterosexual, while the couple has a constitutional, yet only private, interest. Consequently, religious believers who do not want to perform an act contrary to their consciences are not confronted with same-sex couples' "state interest," but with their mere "private" interest. The conscientious objection protection is therefore destined to be quite significant.

A sound debate on same-sex partnership, same-sex marriage, and marriage is also needed to determine whether religious freedom claims operate always in the same way—although the role of religious thinking in the debate about same-sex partnership is surely different from the role that religious freedom plays as an objection to performing acts that are related to same-sex partnerships. In other words, the reasons that back the introduction of a legal regime for same-sex couples are also important in order to contrast them with religious freedom claims as well. Finally, such debates are further needed to highlight the level of sincerity and cogency of religious opinions on these types of partnerships: preposterous religious freedom claims cannot be equated to sincerely held beliefs about marriage and same-sex partnerships. This will help identify the degree of religious freedom protection that is needed under the variety of different circumstances.

Conclusion

After briefly sketching the status of same-sex couples' rights in Italy, this chapter has suggested we reconsider the place of religion, of religious freedom, and the justifications for implementing or denying a set of rights for same-sex partnerships.

A merely textualist reading of the Italian Constitution fails to fully show *why* it endows marriage with a special protection, and *why* this protection also would cover its heterosexual character. Far from being a merely theoretical question, this understanding can shed light if and when a conflict between EU law and constitutional law emerges: if marriage's heterosexual nature is deemed an essential feature of the Constitution, then it will resist the implementation of EU law; otherwise, it will give way to EU-demanded same-sex marriage.

Understanding the reasons that undergird support for and opposition to same-sex marriage and same-sex partnerships, including those channeled through religious traditions, is crucial to strike a balance between same-sex couples' rights claims and conscientious objectors' claims. According to Italian constitutional doctrine, objections must be rooted in the beliefs of conscience; comprehending these reasons will enable Italian institutions to decide if and to what extent they can accommodate both claims.

This is particularly true if the Parliament passes a law enforcing a same-sex partnership regime that is different from the marriage regime. In this scenario, courts and legislators will need to explore if the inner conflict of objectors is as deep as if same-sex marriage were to be introduced.

All things considered, it is particularly important that the reasons that ground the religious conscientious objections to same-sex marriage are discussed and utilized within the debate about the enforcement of the new right as well. Religious freedom allows religions to address this issue openly, to bring arguments about it, and to witness to their commitment to their marriage ideal. Perspectives on gender complementarity,[59] the ability to have children naturally, and the relationship between anthropology and biotechnologies should be addressed in such debates, rather than treating them as arguments that merely back religious groups in seeking exceptions for those who disagree with its introduction. They should be considered as arguments *about* a right—and thus evaluated *before* a right enters into existence—instead of merely as an expression of the right to religious freedom.

Considering religious freedom before or after the enforcement of a new right makes a significant difference. The use of religious freedom *just* as a shield *against* a new right tends to insulate an individual or a community against the society. It is submissive and fails to truly contribute to a social and shared judgment on the new claim.[60] And finally, it gives the impression that religious liberty is intrinsically conservative—whereas a religion may simply be expressing longstanding fundamental values in traditional language.

The narrow use of religious freedom as a shield against new rights parallels the contemporary use of equality as an instrument of social insulation and disintegration. Contemporary ideological, religious, and cultural disagreements need debate more than isolationist rights in order to preserve the social meaning of institutions such as marriage.

The conflict regarding same sex-marriage does not necessarily derive from supposed conflicts between the religiosity of the people and the secularism of courts, or between the dictatorial majorities that do not want same-sex marriage and the claims of supposedly hyper-protected minorities. The opposition between society and courts about marriage may stem from the difference between a *thick* debate about marriage, which society needs, and a *thin* reading of marriage, which courts and parliaments often rely on. Ultimately, it is not just the topic that is divisive; it is also the way in which such debates are addressed.

A Scandinavian Perspective on Homosexuality, Equal Rights, and Freedom of Religion

MAARIT JÄNTERÄ-JAREBORG

I. Introductory Remarks

A. Equal Rights for Homosexuals in Relation to Freedom of Religion

In recent decades, the *legislative course of action* in the Scandinavian states has been systematically focused in one specific direction, namely, toward increased protection and social inclusion of homosexuals as a particularly vulnerable group in society. Family law reforms have constituted a central instrument for achieving these goals. The aim has been to remove legal differences of treatment, in full or in part, with respect to what applies to heterosexual persons. In their revised form, most regulations of family law apply irrespective of a person's sexual orientation, thus enabling marriage between persons of the same sex and joint parental rights. Legislation has also ensured state assistance for homosexual persons to become parents according to the same legal conditions as heterosexual persons, for example, regarding the right to assisted fertilization treatments or adoption of children.

This chosen course of action raises concerns of freedom of religion, considering that "homosexual behavior" remains highly controversial (or forbidden) within most religions and that the contemporary Scandinavian states are multi-faith societies with, at least, large Muslim minorities. Can state law simply overrule faith communities' and believers' understanding of homosexuality, marriage, and parenthood and force another outlook upon them?

To begin, it needs to be pointed out that the notion of freedom of religion can be understood in many different ways. In the *Scandinavian legal context*, we are dealing with a very limited notion. The core content of the constitutionally protected freedom of religion comprises freedom of worship (alone or together with others), freedom from legal persecution, and protection against discrimination on the basis of a person's faith. It also comprises a person's freedom not to have any religion. The legal sources do not provide criteria or detailed recommendations regarding the borderline for the protection. From a Scandinavian *legal* perspective, nevertheless, its scope remains very narrow. No civil servant can, for example, refuse to follow the laws of the state by reference to his or her religiously motivated opinions or conscience regarding homosexuality, without risking dismissal from office. As a public agent covered by labor law, a *civil servant* has the obligation to perform all the tasks that are included in the office. Enactments concerning this issue have been approved by a political majority in the Scandinavian national parliaments, which have not considered religiously motivated arguments to be sufficient to prevent their adoption.

A more nuanced position applies with respect of faith communities and their ministers. In their case, due to concerns of religious freedom, the state-granted right to solemnize legally valid marriages includes no *legal obligation* to solemnize marriages or a specific marriage. It is up to each faith community to decide who does or does not qualify for marriage within the faith community. The clergy's right to refuse to marry, for example, same-sex couples resembles the so-called conscience clause, which was of vital importance when the Scandinavian Evangelical Lutheran Churches opened their priesthood for women, starting from the late 1950s. Its aim was to enable those ministers who were opposed to the reform and who were not willing to conduct services together with female priests to stay within the church. The legal status and continued validity of the conscience clause are, however, disputed. In contrast, an explicit provision of law was enacted in connection with the same-sex marriage reform stating that no duty applies to ministers of a faith community to solemnize a marriage.

It has been argued that the Scandinavian states are "blind toward religion" by not recognizing the presence and impact of religion in people's lives. In Scandinavian societies, religion belongs to the private sphere of life, to the individual and the family. Many people perceive it as embarrassing when this privacy is violated in public or semi-public spaces.[1] Yet, there exists a special Scandinavian tradition of dialogue between the state and, in particular, the national (Evangelical Lutheran) Folks' Church (see Section II.B), whenever planned legal reform might be of a special concern to the latter. In order to engage society at large, the most important minority churches, in addition to other bodies, are also consulted by the state when relevant law reforms arise.

B. The Scandinavian Developments in a Nutshell

A major legal event within family law was the creation of the institution of registered partnership by a law enactment of Denmark in 1989, which enabled same-sex couples to formalize their relationship and to acquire the rights enjoyed by married (heterosexual) spouses. The other Scandinavian states followed suit and introduced similar legislation between the years 1992 and 2002. In all of them, the new institution was restricted to same-sex couples.[2] Partnership registration was designed to be a pure civil ceremony, not least due to religious freedom concerns of faith communities, which initially objected to its introduction. Later on, the Scandinavian Evangelical Lutheran Folks' Churches adopted special rituals to bless a registered partnership or, in the case of Finland, a special prayer.

Twenty-five years later, it is evident that from a Scandinavian perspective, the institution of registered partnership for same-sex couples will remain in legal parentheses, that is, as a highly interim solution. Four Scandinavian states— Norway (2008), Sweden (2009), Iceland (2010), and Denmark (2012)—have extended the legislative notion of marriage to cover couples of the same sex and repealed legislation on registered partnership. In November 2014, the Finnish parliament decided to follow suit; new legislation is expected to be adopted in 2015.[3] The marriage liturgies of the Church of Sweden, the Church of Iceland, and the Church of Denmark have been revised in order to embrace same-sex marriages, whereas the Church of Norway has abstained. It is too early to speculate how the Church of Finland will respond, once the new legislation has been adopted in Finland. In all of these states, legislation grants same-sex couples access to joint parental rights.

C. The Focus of This Contribution

This contribution aims to describe Scandinavian legal developments toward equal rights for same-sex couples *both* as legally recognized couples *and* as parents of children. The aim is to demonstrate *another model* of approaching these issues. A "religious dimension" will be included by reporting on how Scandinavian legislative courses of action have been received by the faith communities active in these countries, and how their concerns have been met in the legislative procedure. Importantly, different interpretations of the Bible have been considered possible by these states' national Folks' Churches, which demonstrates religion's adaptability to surrounding society and, above all, shows that equal rights to same-sex couples can be regarded as in line with the message of the New Testament. It should be noted that, although this topic can be approached from many different angles, this contribution remains limited to law.

The geographical term "Scandinavia" is used here in a broad sense as including Denmark, Finland, Iceland, Norway, and Sweden.[4] Due to the complexity of the issues within these different nations, the more detailed accounts herein focus on Sweden, which has the largest population and whose legal system I am most acquainted with. I will briefly comment on the *Pastor Green Case*,[5] which made international headlines in November 2005 when it was finally decided by the Swedish Supreme Court. I will also briefly remark on the case of *Vejdeland and Others v. Sweden*,[6] on which the European Court on Human Rights ruled in February 2012. Both of these cases concerned (1) alleged agitation against homosexuals, which is a criminalized offence under Swedish law; and (2) drawing the line between the constitutionally protected right of free expression and (in the *Pastor Green Case*) freedom of religion. Finally, I will briefly touch upon the case of *Hämäläinen v. Finland*,[7] decided by the Grand Chamber of the European Court as late as in July 2014. This case concerned the state's (Finland) public interest in keeping the institution of marriage restricted to opposite-sex couples, even when the marriage had been contracted *before* the applicant's change of her gender from male to female, and the applicant's right to private life and family life under the European Convention on Human Rights (ECHR).

II. Relevant Legal and Religious Features of Scandinavian States

A. The Priority of Legal Sources

The *legal systems* of the five Scandinavian states are commonly considered to form a group of their own within continental European civil law family. These states share, to varying degrees, a common historical, cultural, and legal heritage. A special tradition of institutionalized Scandinavian legal cooperation exists, which, for example, in the field of family law, has resulted in very similar enactments.[8] The Scandinavian enactments on registered partnership were nevertheless adopted without any formalized legal cooperation, each state acting on its own but following the model set by Denmark in 1989. All the successive enactments have also been adopted independently by each state, even if they reflect the same values and outlook.

In Scandinavia, statutory law, adopted by the national parliaments, is the primary source of law. The states' constitutions rank highest among statutory law. In Sweden, for example, a court or a public body may not apply any provision of law that it considers to be in contradiction with the constitution. According to legal tradition, whenever the wording of a statutory provision is not sufficiently clear, the court should seek guidance from the statements made by the national government in its bill to parliament, which preceded the enactment in question. The court should also take into account the reasoning in law commission reports that precede a governmental bill, and in the legal literature. Case law is not regarded as binding, but normally Supreme Court precedents are carefully taken into account by the lower courts (and by the Supreme Court itself). The Supreme Courts of the Scandinavian states do not have the status of constitutional courts.

Scandinavian states are parties to the ECHR and have implemented it into their national legal systems as directly applicable law and, in the case of Sweden and Norway, equal to constitutional provisions. As contracting states they have the obligation to safeguard, within their territories, the full exercise of the Convention rights, and to take notice of the European Court of Human Rights' rulings concerning the Convention's interpretation. If this interpretation cannot be combined with the wording of the state's national law, the latter should be amended. Essentially, however, the European Court's rulings are taken into account within a positive law framework, that is, *within* the application of national statutory law. These rulings may result in a more restrictive or more extensive interpretation of the latter than originally intended by the national legislature, according to the statements in the relevant governmental bill. The Swedish courts' rulings in the *Pastor Green Case* (below Section V.C.1) must be understood as the outcome of such reasoning.

B. The Organization of Religious Life

With regard to religious life and its organization, there are several crucial similarities among Scandinavian states. Of relevance, *first*, is that each of them has a national "Folks' Church"—Evangelical Lutheran—which is or has been closely linked with the state since the days of the Reformation in the 1500s and which dominates the country's religious life.[9] The great majority of the population in each of the states are members to the national church. Yet church attendance rates are very low. This is why Scandinavians are said "to belong without believing"[10] (one reason, among others, for this peculiarity is a desire among Scandinavians to maintain solidarity with the state's Evangelical Lutheran heritage). *Second*, these states have only recently become multi-faith societies, as a result of large-scale (often refugee-based) immigration from Muslim countries. Even if the other faith communities in the Scandinavian states have gradually gained a more equal footing to the national Folks' Churches, the latter continue to enjoy special privileges by state law.

Third, for centuries, the national Folks' Churches were extremely influential in society, exercising a total hegemony on the moral values of the population, including matters of family life and sexuality. A reaction to this came in the early 1900s when the Nordic states, acting in cooperation with each other, took measures to introduce a modern, secular Scandinavian family law, guided by the ideas of Enlightenment. Traditional (religiously and morally supported) family law values were weakened, for example, by introducing the principle of irretrievable breakdown of marriage as grounds for divorce decades before other European jurisdictions. From the national churches' point of view, this was a severe loss, symbolizing their diminishing social influence. At the same time, Lutheran theology has contributed to institutional secularization.[11]

C. The Culmination of a Legislative Policy

The Nordic countries were among the first in the world to develop into social welfare states. The welfare state model reflects strong values of solidarity and economic responsibility of the state for the needs of its citizens. Near the end of the 1800s, most functions within the fields of healthcare and education, which were previously performed by the family or the church, were already being taken over by the public sector. It became an important legislative policy to abolish all forms of unequal treatment on the basis of factors such as a person's sex or gender or birth within or out of marriage. Individual freedom and self-expression were upgraded into core values of family law. Through these developments the Scandinavian states came into the forefront of modernity[12] and gained the reputation of being among the most "secular" states in the world. With this in mind, it is not altogether surprising that the marriage-like institution of registered partnership for same-sex couples was first introduced in the Nordic legal environment and that the Scandinavian states were among the first in the world to extend the legal institution of marriage to same-sex couples.

III. From Registered Partnership to Same-Sex Marriage

A. Legally Recognizing the Couple as a Couple—Sweden

The legal recognition of same-sex couples is commonly seen as a revolutionary development. This applies to the Nordic states, too. In Sweden, for example, homosexual behavior was decriminalized as late as 1944, and homosexuality was classified as an illness until 1979. Yet, society was quickly adopting a more liberal attitude toward sexuality in general, as well as toward family life.

In Sweden (as elsewhere in Scandinavia), marriage rates declined dramatically toward the end of the 1960s as increasing numbers of young couples, in particular, chose to cohabit and even have children together without marrying. Politicians endorsed this development by adopting a so-called *ideology of neutrality* toward what they identified as "the various concepts of morality" in relation to the form of cohabitation chosen by couples. It was for individuals alone to decide how they wished to conduct their lives, including family life, and whether they wished to marry or not; legislation should not create unnecessary difficulties.

In Sweden, this policy contributed, among other things, to paring marriage obstacles down to a minimum, emancipating legislation from moral values such as "guilt" for failed marriages, and "elevating" divorce to the level of an unconditional legal right of each spouse, not dependent on the consent of the other spouse. Children's legal rights were made independent of the child's birth within or out of marriage. New legislation was adopted to provide certain basic economic protection for the weaker party upon termination of informal cohabitation, modeled on what applies to spouses upon divorce. In 1973, a Parliamentary committee stated that homosexual cohabitation should be regarded as fully acceptable from society's point of view.

These developments were in sharp contrast to traditional Christian values and outlooks, but surprisingly, opposition by the national church—the Evangelical Lutheran Church of Sweden—remained weak. In 1974, the Evangelical Lutheran Church of Sweden even conducted, on its own initiative, an internal investigation focusing on the situation of homosexual Christians. The investigation concluded by recommending that the Church confirm "genuine homosexuality," manifested in the form of a stable relationship, contrary to temporary lust-based relations. It also suggested that the Church offer a special blessing for stable homosexual relationships.

Shortly afterwards, the Swedish government initiated a comprehensive investigation on the situation of homosexual persons in Swedish society in general. In its report, finalized as late as in 1984, the law commission in charge proposed that homosexual couples should be legally protected in the same manner as heterosexual informally cohabiting couples.[13] But the commission also found that to extend marriage to same-sex couples, or to introduce any marriage-like institution to cover them, would lead to further stigmatization of homosexuals in society. This position turned out to be highly temporary, as demonstrated by the following developments.

Denmark's enactment of special legislation on registered partnerships (1989) for same-sex couples, soon followed by Norway (1992), created political pressure for similar legislation in Sweden, adopted in 1994. Registered partnership was introduced in Iceland in 1996 and in Finland in 2002.

B. The Developing Concept of Registered Partnership

In the original versions of Scandinavian registered partnerships, which were all modeled on Danish law, the institution was kept distinct from marriage (which remained reserved for opposite-sex couples).[14] Four important exceptions applied to registered partnerships as compared with what applied to traditional spouses. *First*, the applicability of all rules on parenthood and parental rights was excluded. *Second*, gender-specific provisions did not apply. *Third*, provisions of international treaties relating to marriage were excluded. *Fourth*, a legally valid registration of partnership had to take place in a civil ceremony. Through these restrictions, the state legislator signaled its concern to recognize (a) the (then) prevailing notion of the best interests of children; (b) the inapplicability of gender-specific provisions, such as the paternity presumption of a woman's husband to children born to her during the marriage; (c) the prevailing interpretation of Treaty law; and (d) the faith communities' reservations toward placing stable homosexual relationships on an equal footing with marriage.

In later legal reforms, these exceptions have been abolished, step by step, to the extent that has been politically feasible.[15] The situations in other European states[16] and judgments by the European Court of Human Rights affirming homosexual persons' rights to private life and, subsequently, to family life[17] have contributed to this development. A new ground of prohibition was incorporated in the states' anti-discriminatory legislation, namely, sexual orientation, on par with religious affinity. For example, according to the Swedish Constitution, society should counteract discrimination on the basis of a person's sex, color, national or ethnic origin, linguistic or *religious affinity*, handicap, *sexual orientation*, or age.[18] Society should also promote social inclusion and equality, as well as ethnic, linguistic, and religious minorities' right to develop their own cultures and communities. This parity in state law might explain why very few Swedes would be willing to publicly make any devaluing statements on homosexuality, in addition to the fact that in the Scandinavian societies such statements are labeled as expressions of homophobia and associated with national socialist and racist ideologies.[19]

C. Tensions with Freedom of Religion?

Importantly, in the investigations carried out by the Scandinavian states (usually by the government appointing a special law commission to evaluate arguments for and against a requested law reform), religion's impact on peoples' worldviews about homosexuality has been acknowledged and religiously motivated reservations have been addressed explicitly. Not only have these observations and reservations come from the law commissions in charge, but also from national governments, faith communities and other consulted bodies, and finally, from parliaments adopting a bill. But when religiously motivated counterarguments have been balanced against the main arguments in favor of the considered legal reform—that is, the social inclusion of homosexual persons and the importance of counteracting any inequality of treatment in law—legislators have considered the latter to weigh more heavily in any legislative context.

This outcome must, again, be understood against the Scandinavian states', and their constitutions', narrow notion of what freedom of religion can entail, in order to be protected (see above I.A). While the state cannot force churches to share the notions of state law and, for example, to oblige their ministers to marry same-sex couples, the churches cannot block state law from developing in the direction found necessary by the state legislature. Even still, the state may expect the churches—or at least its national Folks' Church—to adjust to the new developments, even if it cannot rule on this. Illustratively, the previously mentioned Swedish law commission (above III.A) stated in its 1984 report that "representatives of the various faith communities cannot avoid to be influenced by the increasingly open attitudes toward homosexuality in society. It would therefore be of great importance in particular for the many Christian homosexuals if the faith communities were willing to debate homosexuality and homosexuals not only within the communities but also externally."[20]

A later Swedish law commission, the 1993 commission on registered partnerships, identified different interpretations of the Bible, both against such partnerships (e.g., creation narrative, condemning of sin) and in favor of them (the commandment of love and tolerance), but abstained from taking an explicit position in matters of faith. In contrast, the commission found reason to explicitly state that all expressions of what the commission labeled as "moral panic" should be disregarded in any legislative context, such as allegations that the introduction of registered partnership would devalue marriage and deprive traditional family life of its moral worth, seduce youth to homosexuality, and lead to societal decadence.[21] This position means that from the state's point of view, the sex of a person's partner is irrelevant.

In 2007, an even later Swedish law commission (commission on registered partnership and same-sex marriage) justified its proposal to introduce same-sex marriage by reference to changing societal values, the need to eliminate the previous unfavorable treatment of homosexuals, and the need to counteract discrimination. The commission pointed out that the connotation of "marriage," for homosexual persons, apparently, has a higher value than "registered partnership." In the commission's opinion, this concern alone weighed more heavily in the legislative balance than any religious notions on homosexuality and religious communities' traditional outlook on marriage as a heterosexual union.[22] This was a radical position to take, considering that *all* legal differences of treatment between married spouses and registered partners had by then been abolished in Swedish law (above, III.B) and that the country's faith communities were opposed to this step.

D. Religion's Reduced Impact or Reinterpreting Faith?

What is perhaps most striking about the Scandinavian legal and religious milieu is that soon after the institution of registered partnership had been adopted in the form of legislation, the majority of society was prepared to accept same-sex couples, even families with parents of the same sex. The Scandinavian Evangelical Lutheran Folks' Churches have also been willing to follow along, but for different reasons and only to the extent that each of them has found it possible. The disparities can be explained, at least in part, by differences in political and lay influence within the Churches' organization and decision-making. This influence is broadest in Sweden, where lay members of the Church's decision-making bodies are largely nominated by the political parties active in the country among members of the Church.[23] In Norway, on the contrary, lay influence appears to be much more limited. In all of the national Folks' Churches, the particular issue of same-sex marriage has met opposition among the bishops,[24] whereas the ordinary ministers active in society are more open-minded. In Sweden, very few of the national Church's approximately 6,000 ministers refuse to solemnize same-sex marriages. Here, it is important to emphasize that the general principles of labor law, obliging a civil servant to perform an assigned task, cannot be applied. In Sweden, if a minister of the Church of Sweden refuses to solemnize the marriage of a same-sex couple, this position must be respected (see above, I.A). Religious marriage solemnization is a right but not a duty of the clergy. The Church's way out of the dilemma is by appointing another (willing) minister within the parish to conduct the marriage ceremony. In Norway, on the other hand, Church of Norway leadership continues to be strongly opposed to same-sex marriages. Ministers of the Church offer, in compensation, prayers as a supplement to the couple's civil marriage.

What explains the Folks' Churches' adjustment to the legal formalization of same-sex relationships, considering that all of them were initially opposed to registered partnerships, and later, to same-sex marriage? A general explanation would appear to be these Churches' historical role and position as national Folks' Churches to which the great majority of each state's population belongs. In order to be part of society at large, a national Folks' Church cannot cherish values that deviate too much from the prevailing mainstream values in society, irrespective of weakened ties with the state. For instance, when a bishop of the Church of Finland made critical statements about same-sex relationships in a published interview a few years ago, it drove thousands of members to leave the Church and made nationwide headlines in the Finnish media.

The national Churches are particularly vulnerable to public allegations of discrimination, due to their historical ties with the state and its organization. Losing members may also have a negative impact on church finances.[25] Minority churches are under much less pressure to review the interpretation of the content of their faith and their religious doctrines with respect to, for example, homosexuality and the notion and purpose of marriage. To belong to such a church is often an "active" choice, whereas one is "born" into the national Church and remains a member due to respect for old traditions.[26] In a secular environment, this implies a different kind of commitment. Correspondingly, the laws of the country reflect values that originate from, or are shared by, the national Church, and may have little in common with values of minority religions (or those of nonbelievers).[27]

Thus, following the introduction of the institution of registered partnership, Christian homosexual members of the national Folks' Churches publicly expressed their disappointment and resentment toward the lack of access to church ceremonies confirming the new union.[28] The Folks' Churches quickly responded by offering a symbolic ceremony of confirmation, in the form of a blessing (or a prayer) of their members' formalized registered partnerships, but subject to each individual priest's right to decline. Nevertheless, such blessings were not divine services of the Church and, according to state law, remained a symbolic supplement to a civil partnership registration.

Equally, once same-sex marriage was introduced by state law in Norway, Sweden, Iceland, and more recently in Denmark, there was an immediate demand to make church marriages available to same-sex couples on the same conditions as opposite-sex couples. Again, the Folks' Churches came under particular pressure by their members to follow suit. Only the Church of Norway has abstained from reforming its marriage liturgy accordingly, despite it being the first Scandinavian state to permit same-sex marriages (as of January 1, 2009). The marriage liturgy remains limited to opposite-sex couples and no priest of the Church can marry same-sex couples. Other Norwegian faith communities have responded similarly, whereas humanist life-stance communities solemnize same-sex marriages and, in a certain sense, replace churches in doing so. In Iceland, a revised marriage liturgy was in place when same-sex marriage reform entered into force in June 2010, enabling the country's prime minister to officiate her same-sex marriage in the Church of Iceland on the same day. In Sweden, since November 2009, six months after the new law's entry into force, a revised marriage liturgy enables same-sex couples to marry within the Church of Sweden. Of Sweden's approximately 40 faith communities with state authorization to solemnize marriages, only one additional faith community—the Mission

Church—has followed suit, equally leaving the final decision to each of its ministers. The Church of Denmark has adjusted its marriage liturgy to embrace same-sex marriages.

Of the Scandinavian Folks' Churches, the Church of Sweden was probably best prepared for the challenge of same-sex marriages. As pointed out in Section III.A., in the 1970s an internal investigation within the Church had recommended the endorsement of stable same-sex relationships. The Church returned to the topic once again in the 1990s by initiating a new internal investigation, which emphasized the necessity of not condemning but of providing pastoral care and spiritual assistance to homosexual Christians. In 2009, once the gender-neutral concept of marriage had been adopted by Swedish parliament, the Church assigned its theological committee to carry out an in-depth analysis of the new marriage concept from a biblical point of view. The following quote from this committee's final report serves as a summary of the conclusions:

> In the view of the Evangelical Lutheran Church, marriage is a social institution regulated by civil authorities. From a Creation theology perspective, the purpose of marriage is to support the mutual relationship between the spouses and provide a secure framework for bringing up children. These needs also exist in relationships between people of the same sex. From the perspective of biblical theology, the love commandment is superior to all other commandments and prohibitions in the Bible. The decisive factor where forms of cohabitation are concerned is therefore not the individual Bible passages but what is to the benefit or harm of people. This means that when the Church is to form an opinion on marriage for same-sex couples, the relevant question to ask is whether this harms or benefits people.[29]

In the theological committee's opinion, the numerous passages in the Bible condemning homosexual behavior should not be interpreted to prevent extending the notion of marriage to stable same-sex unions. It found that the issue could be approached from various theological perspectives, with various outcomes, depending on what was emphasized. In the theological committee's opinion, including same-sex couples could be seen as a good way of supporting people in line with the biblical commandment of love. On the other hand, with regard to the existing biblical interpretations also within the Church, it should be up to each minister to follow his or her personal conviction and conscience on the matter. These conclusions were of relevance for the following decisions within the Church. In September 2009, four months after the new concept of marriage had been introduced into Swedish legislation, the highest decision-making body of the Church of Sweden, the *General Synod*, voted by clear majority in favor of officiating same-sex marriages within the Church, following a corresponding proposal by the central Board of the Church. The marriage liturgy of the Church was revised accordingly.

In a later study carried out by Finnish professor of theology Jaana Hallamaa—apparently independently of the investigations carried out within the Church of Sweden—same-sex marriages were interpreted not to be in conflict with Evangelical Lutheran marriage ethics.[30] Of particular relevance according to Hallamaa is that, according to the Evangelical Lutheran doctrine, marriage is not a sacrament but a social institution. Contrary to Roman Catholicism, Lutheran social ethics do not directly support the thesis that the relationship between a man and a woman is special and complementary. Furthermore, each person is responsible for his or her own moral choices in front of both a worldly justice and a divine, while the purpose of morality is to serve those nearest to us, and to avoid doing them harm. The driving force of these acts is the love of God toward mankind.

The complexity of defining a certain faith's position on this issue is manifest when considering the fact that many Evangelical Lutheran communities in the United States are opposed to same-sex marriages.[31] The surrounding society's level of religious engagement has a clear impact on the chosen approach.

E. Marriage Solemnization within a Church and Freedom of Religion

In each of the Scandinavian states, a legal marriage can be validly performed, not only in a civil "secular" form, but alternatively within any faith community authorized by the state to solemnize (legal, fully valid, civil) marriages, in a religious ceremony. Although "secular" marriage ceremonies are increasing in popularity, the majority of marriages continue to be officiated in a religious form.

The origin of the Scandinavian double-track system of marriage lies in the special function of the Folks' Church in a (originally) united church-state system. Until the alternative of a civil marriage ceremony was introduced through legislative cooperation between the Scandinavian states around the year 1910, only marriages carried out within the national church were legally valid.[32] When freedom of religious affiliation was introduced as late as the early 1950s,[33] other faith communities could be granted (in each case, by special decision) a corresponding right, but only if the faith community fulfilled the requirements identified by state law. For example, the faith community might have been required to show that its activities are of a certain stability and vitality within the state in question, and that it can be expected to follow the laws of the state when making use of the marriage authorization. The marriage ceremony itself follows the rites of each faith community. To solemnize a marriage in the form of a religious ceremony is "a faith community's right but not its duty," according to state law. As pointed out by the Swedish law commission of 2007, "it would not be reasonable to require that a faith community would be willing to conduct wedding services that are alien to its belief."[34] The commission acknowledged that freedom of religion was at stake, since from the perspective of faith communities, religious marriage ceremonies are divine services.[35]

The fact that we, from the point of view of state law, are dealing with the delegation of public powers when faith communities are authorized by the state to solemnize marriages (establishing a civil law status of marriage) creates a dilemma of its own. Should every exercise of public power not carry with it the duty to treat everybody equally, and to accept state law's definition of what qualifies as marriage? How can the state justify the delegation of marriage solemnization powers to faith communities that do not share the state law's notion of marriage? In such instances, how can the state ensure respect for the underlying and fundamental concerns of counteracting discrimination?

In Sweden, as part of same-sex marriage reform an explicit provision was added to the Marriage Code (Ch. 4 § 3.2), stating that no minister of a faith community has a compulsory duty to solemnize any marriage.[36] According to critics, the state applies a double and contradictory standard here. But as has been pointed out earlier, the justification for this provision is the constitutionally protected freedom of religion. If the state's delegation of a "right" of exercising a public power had been combined with a "duty" to exercise it, critics suppose that faith communities could simply refrain from the "right."[37] In practice, however, for many seeking religious ceremonies, this would leave civil marriage as the only available option. This position was at odds with public opinion, which strongly supported the existing freedom of choice between a religious and civil ceremony, both producing legally valid marriages. It was recognized that if people were deprived of something they valued, the general attitude could turn against same-sex marriages and homosexual persons, which was not desirable.[38] Practical difficulties were also expected to arise. "For many people it would also entail repetition and possibly costs to first enter into a marriage by a civil procedure and thereafter have the marriage blessed in a separate religious ceremony," the Swedish law commission pointed out.[39]

IV. Toward Equal Rights of Parentage for Same-Sex Couples

In each Scandinavian state, a same-sex couple that has formalized its relationship (registered partnership or marriage) qualifies not only for shared parental rights but also for joint legal parental status (joint legal parentage), in full or in part.[40] The concerned rights have been introduced successively after about ten years of experience in each state with the formalization of same-sex relationships through registered partnership. In most cases, the first step taken has been permitting the same-sex registered partner of a parent to adopt the parent's child (biological or adopted), on the condition that the parent has full parental rights to the child and that the other parent (where there is another parent with parental responsibilities) agrees to the adoption. This step is commonly called "the right to adopt one's stepchild." The second step is permitting joint adoptions by a formalized same-sex couple. The third step is enabling the couple to acquire a joint legal parental status, when a child is born as a result of an assisted fertility treatment. In Scandinavia, this option is available for lesbian couples. In its recent, more radical version, the birth mother's female spouse or registered partner receives the legal status of a "co-mother." The fourth step is parenthood through surrogacy. Because of the monetary compensation that is normally involved in surrogacy, concern for exploitation of the birth mother, and concern for the child's best interests, this is the ethically most controversial step in the Scandinavian legal milieu. Current legislation does not confirm surrogacy arrangements in any of the Scandinavian states. The position taken in case law is more flexible, with reference to the already-born child's best interests. The intended father who is also the child's biological father can establish full parental rights through the confirmation of his paternity. Afterward, his spouse or registered partner, irrespective of his or her sex, may adopt the child (i.e., the first step identified in this paragraph). The Icelandic government has proposed permitting altruistic surrogacy; its bill will most likely result in legislation in 2015.

In Scandinavia, excluding parental rights on the basis of homosexuality has become politically and legally infeasible, primarily on the grounds that (a) society consists of a multitude of different kinds of families with children, including families where the parents are of the same sex; (b) there is no scientific proof that a child's development and best interests are negatively affected when growing up with parents of the same sex; and (c) the human right of equal dignity cannot be combined with any unfavorable treatment, when there are not convincing, objective arguments to justify such treatment.

Apparently, the Scandinavian approach to same-sex parentage is in deep contradiction with a traditional heterosexual and procreation-based notion of parentage. Interestingly, not a single same-sex couple in Sweden has been able to *jointly adopt* a child from abroad, even though, according to Swedish law since 2003, they may qualify for this.[41] Adoptions in Sweden outside the family consist of international adoptions, and so far no country has been willing to place children for adoption with a same-sex couple in Sweden. It follows that the impact of legal reform will remain a purely symbolic recognition of same-sex couples' equal worth as prospective adoptive parents. At the same time, the political ambition has also been to set an example for other states to follow, as illustrated by the following quote from the Swedish government bill of 2001 to Parliament: "A Swedish openness in this matter can in time also lead to a positive change in attitude toward homosexuals and adoption by registered partners, also in foreign countries."[42] With the exception of Finland, which does not permit joint adoptions by same-sex couples, all other Scandinavian states have followed the Swedish example.

V. Tensions in Light of Legal, Political, and Policy Controversies

A. Muslim Minorities

In 2010, an organization called the Swedish Muslim Social Democrats adopted a Manifesto for Muslim Social Democrats in Sweden. The manifesto sets forth eight points of relevance for those identifying themselves as Muslim Social Democrats. It reflects the values expressed in a corresponding manifesto by the Christian Swedish Social Democrats—an organization within Sweden's largest political party, The Social Democratic Party—but with one exception: equal rights for homosexual persons. This prompted a storm of criticism in the Swedish media. Many people in Sweden insisted that even socially vulnerable minority groups, such as Muslims, must stand behind the fundamental values of society, which includes respecting full rights for homosexual persons.[43] As is well known, however, the Muslim world disassociates itself strongly from homosexuality and homosexual relations. For example, contrary to all other invited faith communities, Sweden's Muslim faith communities declined an invitation to act as a "referee group" in the preparation of same-sex marriage reform (2007–2009).

B. Conditional State Funding of Faith Communities

The impact of such criticism has remained limited, however. For example, the Swedish state can by law fund faith communities active in Sweden (other than the Church of Sweden, which is funded in a special order) on condition that they, inter alia, are "committed to counteracting all forms of racism and other discrimination, violence and brutality," and "contribute to equality between men and women." Each funded faith community's staff is to "be guided by ethical principles which correspond with the fundamental democratic values of society."[44] If taken literally, it could be argued that these criteria require a commitment, from each state-funded faith community, to also counteract all forms of disadvantageous treatment of homosexuals. In that case, none of the hitherto subsidized faith communities would have qualified for state support.

A special state body consisting of representatives of the leading minority religions in Sweden is in charge of distributing this funding, which is intended to enable faith communities to pursue activities such as worship services, spiritual guidance, and education. Norway, which has a much more comprehensive system of state funding of faith communities, follows an equally cautious approach. The state funding of faith communities in both Sweden and Norway is driven by an ideology according to which faith communities form part of popular movements in civil society, perform functions that are advantageous to society, and in this manner contribute to strengthening fundamental societal values. In Sweden, many faith communities have abstained from applying for state funding, perhaps because of conditions attached to this funding.[45]

The following example from Norway illustrates possible tensions. A Norwegian state agency decided to withdraw its funding of the Salvation Army's youth activities because the Salvation Army, on its webpage, stated that people in homosexual partnerships could not become soldiers in uniform. All Christian youth organizations in Norway protested immediately against this decision, and it was eventually withdrawn.[46]

C. Freedom of Expression and Religion

1. The Pastor Green Case

In recent years, two cases heard by Sweden's highest court, the Supreme Court, have focused on how freedom of expression relates to criminal law protection against offensive statements on homosexuality and homosexuals. The first of them also touches upon religious freedom, namely, NJA 2005, p. 805, the so-called *Pastor Green Case*.

In a 2003 sermon delivered to a church audience of approximately fifty people, the Pentecostal pastor Åke Green described homosexuality as fornication and likened it to a cancerous tumor in society with catastrophic effects, spreading AIDS and other sexually transmitted illnesses, and directly contradicting the Bible's creation narrative and God's commandments.[47] The sermon, entitled "Is Homosexuality an Inborn Instinct or the Evil Forces' Trick upon People?," also insinuated that homosexuality was linked with sexual intercourse with children and animals. In support of his thesis, the pastor referred to numerous passages in the Bible. Afterwards, the pastor made a comprehensive effort to spread knowledge of his sermon to a broad public.[48]

Soon after, the public prosecutor brought criminal charges against him on the grounds that in his sermon he had disseminated statements of contempt for homosexuals on the basis of their sexual orientation and that his sermon had received extensive publicity. The pastor denied the charges and referred to his literal understanding of the word of the Bible. He claimed that his actions were intended, not to condemn or disgrace homosexuals, but to inform and guide people, particularly young people, about the Bible's and the free churches' outlook on homosexuality; to provide homosexual persons with pastoral care; and to add a new dimension to the Swedish debate on homosexuality.

From a legal point of view, the case came to focus, primarily, on how a specific provision in the Swedish Penal Code (Ch. 16 §8), which concerned an offence labeled *agitation against a national or ethnic group*, related to the pastor's sermon, the scope of the Swedish Constitution's protection for freedom of expression and religion, and the protection of these freedoms in the ECHR. In a Penal Code revision carried out at the time of Green's sermon in 2003, the Ch. 16 §8 provision was extended to include agitation against homosexuals,[49] on the basis that homosexuals are a particularly vulnerable group in society and are often victims of crime, perpetrated by extremist and racist groups, solely on the basis of their sexual orientation.[50] This criminalization was meant to be a limitation of the freedom of expression.

In the end, the pastor was acquitted by the Supreme Court (highest instance) and also by the Court of Appeals (second instance), but only after the district court (first instance) found him guilty of the alleged offence and sentenced him to one month in prison. The Court of Appeals emphasized that statements made during a sermon only qualify as agitation against a group under certain criteria; such criteria were not fulfilled in this case as the pastor's sermon was intended to explain and present his interpretation of the Bible regarding homosexuality, and to influence people's lifestyles. The Supreme Court paid special attention to the proportionality test of the ECHR, and to the European Court of Human Rights' case law, and concluded that a conviction of the pastor "probably" would not meet the intended "European standard." This Convention is implemented in Swedish positive law, on a constitutional level, obliging the courts to respect it as such.

Due to misunderstandings surrounding the legal assessment of this case, a few additional clarifications are necessary regarding the relevant Swedish legal context and how the Swedish courts argued. *First*, the government bill, preceding the enactment of the concerned provision of the Swedish Penal Code,

weighed the proposed criminalization against freedom of religion and freedom of expression, both constitutionally protected, and identified a potential
conflict of interests. Considering that these freedoms (in order to qualify for
protection) in a democratic society must be exercised in a manner respecting
other people's rights and equal dignity, and that the criminalization was not
intended to cover any objective discussion or criticism of homosexuality or
homosexual lifestyles and outlooks on life, the criminalization was regarded as
proportionate in relation to its aim. It follows that the scope of both freedom
of religion and freedom of expression was expressly addressed. According to
the Swedish Constitution, freedom of religion, within the constitutionally
envisaged scope, is an absolute right invulnerable to conflicting legislation.
What qualifies as freedom of religion cannot be limited by any other statutory
provisions, such as the Penal Code. Freedom of expression, on the other hand,
may be restricted by legislation. The ECHR, which also enjoys constitutional
status in Sweden, promotes a broader understanding of freedom of religion
but, on the other hand, permits certain limitations to be prescribed by law
(Article 9.2). Under the stipulated conditions, the states parties enjoy a margin of appreciation.

Second, as the government bill explicitly points out, quoting Bible passages
condemning homosexuality does not qualify as agitation toward homosexuals.[51] But when such quotations are supplemented with demeaning comparisons
or allegations (e.g., that homosexuality is a cancer or that it is tantamount to
sexual intercourse with animals or children) directed toward a group, drawing
the line is more difficult. In the opinion of the first-instance court, the pastor,
through such allegations, had deeply offended homosexuals as a group and his
statements were aimed at denigrating homosexuals as a group. In the opinion of
the (second-instance) Court of Appeal, on the other hand, it must be possible
to elucidate passages of the Bible, in a sermon, without being found guilty of
agitation.

Third, agitation against homosexuals is regarded as a serious crime in Sweden,
because it offends people on the basis of their sexual orientation and, in the long
run, undermines the values of a democratic society. Hence, in the first-instance
court's opinion, the right of homosexual persons not to be subjected to offensive
statements carried more weight than the pastor's right to make these statements
in the name of religion. However, the criteria for so-called hate speech are set
high, and according to the Supreme Court, they were not fulfilled in this case.

Fourth, the legal issue at stake was not the validity of the Penal Code provision
(that is, its compatibility with the constitution), but how the phrase "express
contempt" should be interpreted. Both the Court of Appeal and the Supreme
Court took a marginally more permissive view than the one expressed in the
government bill. Even if statements in a Swedish government bill are normally

followed by the courts, such statements do not have a binding legal force (see above, II.A).

2. *Vejdeland and Others v. Sweden*

In the next case reaching the Supreme Court, NJA 2006, p. 467, the Court this time found the defendants guilty of agitation against homosexuals. The facts of this case were, briefly, the following: A group of young men had distributed leaflets in a Swedish high school in which homosexuality was described as a "deviant sexual proclivity," with a "morally destructive effect on society," and the reason for HIV, AIDS, and pedophilia. The leaflets originated from an organization called "National Youth" with no links to the school. The public prosecutor raised charges against the men on the ground that they had agitated against homosexuals as a group, on the basis of sexual orientation. According to the defense, the action was intended only to encourage debate on the lack of objectivity in education regarding homosexuality in the Swedish school system. The defendants were convicted in the first-instance court, but acquitted by the Court of Appeal (second instance) with reference to the outcome in the *Pastor Green Case*, on the ground that a conviction would amount to a violation of their freedom of expression as guaranteed by the ECHR (Article 10). Finally, with a vote of 3-2, the defendants were found guilty of the offence by the Supreme Court. Of particular relevance for the conviction was that the offence had taken place in a school environment.

The defendants complained to the European Court of Human Rights, claiming that Sweden violated their conventionally protected freedom of expression (Article 10). In its judgment of February 9, 2012,[52] the court concluded unanimously that no such violation had taken place. The conviction by the Swedish Supreme Court was found to be reasonable, with regard to what is necessary in a democratic society *for the protection of the reputation and rights of others*. Of special relevance was the fact that the leaflets were distributed in a school environment not open to the public, without the students' consent.

This is the first judgment of the European Court where it applied principles related to expressions of contempt ("hate speech") in the context of sexual orientation. The Court also pointed out that "the situation was in part different from that in NJA 2005, p. 805, where [Pastor Green] made his statements before his congregation in a sermon based on certain biblical quotations." This is an important clarification. As I see it, the judgment in *Vejdeland and Others v. Sweden* is not in conflict with the Swedish Supreme Court's decision in the *Pastor Green Case*. Whereas the first situation took place in a religious setting, which qualifies for protection and a restrictive application of the Penal Code, the second does not. It will be interesting to see how this distinction plays out in future cases. The criteria of "protection of the reputation and rights of others" can prove useful also for religious communities, when their faith is subjected to expressions of contempt beyond objective criticism.

3. Hämäläinen v. Finland

In its judgment,[53] the European Court of Human Rights' Grand Chamber reiterated the Court's previous position that the ECHR does not impose any obligation on the contracting states to grant access to marriage to same-sex couples. In the Grand Chamber's opinion, this applies even when the change of a spouse's gender took place *within the context of a marriage*, which had been concluded in a legally valid manner. The applicant—Ms. Hämäläinen—who had changed her gender from male to female during the marriage, wished to receive a female identity number while remaining married to her (heterosexual) wife. Under (the current) Finnish law, the new identity number required the marriage to be converted into a registered partnership or to be dissolved by divorce. Ms. Hämäläinen and her wife were opposed to this condition, with reference to their strong religious belief on marriage as a lifelong union.[54] In the applicant's opinion, the Finnish authorities' refusal to grant her the requested new identity number was a violation of her right to private life and her right to family life, as protected by Article 8 of the ECHR. The Grand Chamber found no violation of the ECHR to have taken place. Of relevance was that the legal rights of the applicant under Finnish law, under the circumstances of the case, would not be affected by the conversion of the marriage into a registered partnership. Or alternatively, the applicant was free to remain married, but without a female identity number. The Court's assessment contributes to sense of predictability and legal certainty in Europe, considering that no European consensus exists on the disputed issues.

VI. Striking a Proper Balance— A Mission Impossible?

The various contributions in this volume illustrate considerable clashes of opinion on religious freedom and the legal recognition of homosexual relationships. On both sides, the other side's approach is accused of devaluing a superior common good, be it a traditional notion of marriage (as a part of religious freedom), or the recognition of each person's human worth and dignity, irrespective of sexual orientation, as a basis for equal access to family law rights and a fundamental value of democratic society. The depth of these clashes was surprising to me as a Scandinavian lawyer and academic. Evidently, in an international comparison, lawmakers in Scandinavia have often taken concerns of religion lightly. A change in this respect would require stronger constitutional protection for religious freedoms. It is an open question whether, in the future, the relatively new multi-faith presence in Scandinavia will give reason to strengthen the protection of religion. We should not forget, however, that a majority of the Scandinavian Folks' Churches have been willing to take part in the described societal developments and demonstrated their faith's adaptability.

In Scandinavia, anti-discrimination concerns dominate, with focus on homosexuals as a vulnerable group. It follows that Scandinavian legal norms have no room to accommodate, for example, the British couple that sought to qualify as foster parents, but were denied because of their anti-gay beliefs.[55] In Scandinavia, foster parents must be willing to teach children under their care the values that society considers fundamental, namely, equality and anti-discrimination.[56] Religious minorities in the population may feel uncomfortable with this development. But personally, as a mainstream Scandinavian and a mainstream member of a national Folks' Church, I feel equally uncomfortable about the manner in which religion can be used to dismiss the human dignity of homosexual persons, to devalue stable homosexual relationships, and to justify intolerance and a heterosexual superiority in society. The parallels drawn with polyamorous relationships do not fit into the mainstream Scandinavian outlook, acknowledged by law, according to which the only difference between homosexual and heterosexual love of a couple is the sex of the loved. As I explained earlier (section III.D), the Scandinavian Evangelical Lutheran Folks' Churches have found it possible to endorse stable same-sex relationships, on the basis of their interpretation of Jesus' commandment of love as the overriding virtue, even if the Churches remain divided on the issue of same-sex marriage. It follows that religious freedom and equal rights for same-sex couples can also be regarded as compatible with Christian faith.

Is it possible to identify recommendable solutions in the Scandinavian legal landscape, striking a reasonable balance between religious freedom and equality claims? In my opinion, not obliging faith communities or their ministers to solemnize any marriages to which they object, while maintaining their right according to state law to conduct legally valid marriage ceremonies, qualifies as an example of justifiably accommodating religion and religious freedom. Yet it cannot be denied that the gap between a religious understanding of marriage and the state's understanding of marriage has become so wide that the two should be kept separate. The transformation into multicultural, multi-faith societies widens this gap.[57] Consequently, there is a strong argument that now is the time for Scandinavian states to dissociate religion from legal marriage and to place marriage in the sphere of secular civil law. Faith communities' role in the performance of any marriage should be limited to the sphere of religion, without any legal implications. This would mean adopting the mainstream continental European approach, after a hundred years of hesitation in Scandinavia, following the introduction of the double-track system in the early 1900s (above, III.E).

Generally speaking, it appears quite difficult to achieve or maintain any good balance between the two concerns—religious freedom and gay equality—by any state or legal system *on its own*, on a purely national level. The *Pastor Green Case*, in which regard for the ECHR brought about a more respectful outcome for freedom of religious expression, illustrates this point well. There is always a risk of bias in favor of one side or the other. Internationally binding human rights instruments that go beyond any current mainstream national politics are, therefore, of crucial importance. In my opinion, human rights can be safeguarded and objectively balanced against each other only when there is a "superior legal power" that can apply strong pressure to national legislators and courts.

Afterword

ROGER TRIGG

Different Views of Religion

This volume was derived from a conference devoted to the conflicts emerging on both sides of the Atlantic between the claims of religious liberty and those of equality.[1] Differing historical traditions, particularly relating to the relation between church and state, have resulted in differing ways of dealing with issues that are causing the same perplexity for politics and law in many countries. The influence of the European Enlightenment has played out in varying ways. The early Enlightenment, as evidenced in the writings of John Locke, was imbued with a respect for human reason that nevertheless saw it firmly rooted in the rationality of the Creator. For Locke, as for the Cambridge Platonists who influenced him, reason was the "candle of the Lord."[2] Ideas such as those of equality were for him firmly rooted in their theological base.

Locke's thought was very influential in the "Glorious Revolution" of 1688 in England and the subsequent Bill of Rights in 1689. Yet his thought also proved important almost a century later in the nascent United States. Since Locke was greatly respected by, among others, Thomas Jefferson, his thought fed into the very founding of the United States, and lay at the roots of the struggle for religious freedom in a colony such as Virginia.

At the same time in France, where the Enlightenment had taken a very atheistic and materialist turn, rights and ideas related to equality were regarded as slogans with which to attack organized religion, in the guise of the traditional teaching of the Roman Catholic Church. Freedom and equality were somehow divorced from their previous theological grounding, and human reason was seen as "autonomous." The establishment in France of so-called "Temples of Reason" in the place of Churches (though short-lived) said it all. Traditional religion was seen as the enemy of progress.

This division between a vision of religion (particularly Christianity) as the guarantor of freedom and equality, and that of religion as the implacable opponent of both, has led to different conceptions of the place of religion in public life. It is particularly apparent in the way in which religion and religious symbols are driven out of the public sphere in France under its policy of *laïcité*. This contrasts with the way in which, even in an increasingly secular Britain, Christian rites and symbols still lie at the heart of national life. Although the so-called "separation of church and state" is a phrase much used in the United States, the wider question of the place of religion in society there is the subject of much dispute. It is not fanciful to see the "culture wars" of the last few years as a battle still being fought in contemporary American politics and law between Lockean and more atheistic versions of the Enlightenment. Does religion undergird our twin beliefs in freedom and equality, or is it intrinsically their enemy?

Is Religious Belief "Subjective"?

What part should avowedly religious views be allowed to play in public life? There is at present a definite tendency, seen in some legal judgments, to regard religious belief as inherently "subjective," and thus presumably as saying nothing about the nature of reality. Alarm bells were sounded for many by a judgment by Lord Justice Laws in the Court of Appeal in London in 2010, when he said: ". . . in the eye of everyone save the believer religious faith is necessarily subjective, being incommunicable by any kind of belief or evidence."[3] It is therefore not the kind of thing that can be dealt with in a court of law. Such beliefs appear to lie beyond the scope of human rationality, but are merely "subjective opinion."

Not only have these remarks been quoted with approval by other judges in subsequent cases, but the term "subjective" has been taken up in another case in a different context in the England and Wales Court of Appeal. The issue at stake was how far the competence of a court could extend in deciding cases that may go to the heart of the beliefs of particular religion. The particular case concerned a dispute within the Sikh religion about the governance of two Gurdwaras. The Court wisely decided that any decision would entangle it too much in particular matters in dispute of a theological nature. It accepted that "there will inevitably be disputes with a religious aspect which however controversial and profound to those involved, cannot exclude or limit the jurisdiction of the civil courts to determine civil rights."[4] That assertion of the rights of courts is important, as we shall see, in cases about equality. The case in question concerning the Sikhs was not, the Court thought, of that sort, and it felt that it did not lie within its competence to get involved with the religious issues at stake.

Yet the reasons given for its lack of competence are disturbing. Courts are certainly not competent to rule on matters that lie beyond the law. They should not determine questions of a scientific nature, such as issues at the frontiers of physics about an inflationary universe. Even suggesting the possibility of a court so doing is laughable. Judges are not scientists any more than they are theologians. They are simply not qualified. But that does not mean that the issues are "subjective" or do not concern truth, let alone that they are not matters to be dealt with rationally. Yet that is precisely the conclusion that the Court draws from its lack of competence to deal with religious issues. We are told that such questions are "not matters of law at all," but are "subjective inward matters incapable of proof by direct evidence or by inference." The question at issue was a "matter of professed subjective belief and faith on which secular municipal courts cannot possibly reach a decision, either as matter of law or fact."[5]

We had previously been told that "judicial method is equipped to deal in hard facts objectively ascertainable, directly or by inference, from probative evidence: it is not equipped to determine the truth, accuracy or sincerity of subjective religious beliefs about doctrine and practice."[6] One might question whether courts cannot test the sincerity of beliefs. They are often required to do so (for instance in cases of professed conscientious objection in time of war), but that is a peripheral point. The main question is the opposition being implicitly posited between faith and reason, between "objective" facts and "subjective" belief. The rationality of the legal process is portrayed in stark contrast with an implied lack of rationality of all religious belief. Yet if belief can be consigned like this to the realm of the subjective (in a manner congruent with the ideas of the later Enlightenment), religion can be removed not only from the purview of the courts, but from all public life. The subjective becomes the private, and law can thereby allow it to be marginalized. Thus, apparent judicial restraint may actually be the result of a deliberate downgrading of the relevance of all religion to legal process.

If religion is mere "subjective belief," its contribution to debates about the common good can be safely disregarded. Such belief will, it seems, tell us nothing about what is true, and everything about the person holding it. Any debate about public policy can, it seems, proceed without taking account of any claims that are perceived as "religious." The privatization of religion is in the process of being accepted by English judges. Its assimilation to personal belief of any kind is, in fact, encouraged by the European Convention on Human Rights, which refers in a broad way to the "right to freedom of thought, conscience and religion," and the freedom to manifest "one's religion or beliefs" (Article 9). The latter is immediately qualified by limitations, the most relevant of which is that it can be limited "for the protection of the rights and freedoms of others." The stage is immediately set for other rights to be allowed to "trump" religious freedom, and this is what is progressively happening.

It may be significant that, when the Gurdwara case came before the UK Supreme Court, the Court did not uphold the idea of non-justiciability in all cases involving religion. They gave as instances property disputes, and issues about disciplinary procedure, arising out of doctrinal disputes. They said: "The civil court does not resolve the religious dispute . . . its role is more modest: it keeps the parties to their contract."[7] Nevertheless doing that in ways that do not significantly affect the doctrinal issues is far from easy. Indeed in this case, the Supreme Court pointed out forcefully that it had to enforce English law on trusts, saying that, as a result, a court "may have to adjudicate upon matters of religious doctrine and practices in order to determine who are the trustees entitled to administer the trusts."[8] That is a sensitive and difficult area for any court. Indeed, there are contemporary church schisms in the United States, in states such as Virginia, that arise partly out of disputes about the recognition of homosexual practices. It is then a crucial task for the courts to make legal rulings about ownership of property that do not just support one side of a doctrinal dispute.

Discrimination on Grounds of Religion

Whether or not religion is seen as a purely subjective phenomenon, it was certainly seen in the later French Enlightenment as a positively malignant force, to be kept under strict control by the State. This is in sharp contrast to the explicit protection given in the First Amendment of the Constitution of the United States to the "free exercise of religion." There is no question of "religion" being attenuated by its connection with anything else. It is given explicit protection; indeed, as Richard Garnett mentions in Chapter 4, it has been seen as the "First Freedom" of crucial importance to the functioning of democracy.

Religion characteristically expresses what individuals see as what is most important in life. This is such a pervasive view that sometimes what someone sees as most important is automatically dubbed their "religion," even if it is just playing golf. The denial of religious truth is part of the same scenario, and freedom of religion is always taken to embody the freedom to dissent from any or all religion as well as to assent to it. A freedom to practice religion is not much of a freedom if we do not have the option to refuse to do so. John Finnis expresses this point well in his contribution to Chapter 1, this volume. After reaffirming the importance of people making a judgment about the nature of reality and of the place of humans in it, he writes: "A society which fails to acknowledge that duty" is "in a deep, implicit way . . . undercutting its own claim to be taken seriously and defended . . . against its enemies (28–29)."

It is clearly a crucial element of democracy that people should be allowed to express in public, and live by, what they consider most important in human life. So far from this being a subjective matter, it involves judgments about the nature of the world that may or may not be true. As such they deserve to receive proper discussion, and, if necessary, criticism, in the public arena. Indeed, an unlooked-for by-product of the privatization of religion is that all forms of religion are thereby removed from public scrutiny. While it is far too sweeping to assert that all religion is harmful, it is equally dangerous to assume that all is beneficent, without any adverse effects on society. There can be "pathologies" of religion, and if all religion is dismissed as non-rational "faith," that only means that they escape the scrutiny of reason that they deserve.

Article 14 of the European Convention on Human Rights prohibits discrimination on certain grounds, "such as sex, race, colour, language, religion, political or other opinion" and so on. Sexual orientation does not occur in the list but is generally accepted in law as also a prohibited ground. Yet religion is explicitly named, and discrimination on the grounds of religion ought therefore to be regarded as a serious matter, indeed just as serious as other grounds of discrimination.

This brings us fairly and squarely to the theme of this volume. The pursuit of equality involves, of its nature, the eradication of unfair discrimination. Racial discrimination is the paradigm case of such discrimination, but arbitrary discrimination on grounds of sex is also a clear abuse of enumerated rights. Employment law in western countries would normally prohibit it. Where then, to take an example, does that leave the restriction of the Roman Catholic priesthood to men? Should public policy dictate to the Roman Church what it should do? As Richard Garnett points out in his chapter, the US Supreme Court's 2012 *Hosanna-Tabor* decision[9] makes it absolutely clear that the so-called "ministerial exception" prohibits interference by law in the choice of clergy, those who "personify" particular set of beliefs. To allow otherwise would undermine religious freedom.

Things are not so clear in the United Kingdom, and we have already quoted the view of an English judge that courts may intervene to protect "civil rights." In other words, employment law can override the particular procedures of Churches, as successive employment cases concerning ministers of religion have made clear.[10] The outlawing of discrimination in one area can result in ignoring the problem of discrimination on grounds of religion. When public policy expressed in law can explicitly override even the internal disciplinary procedures of churches over their own clergy, they are no longer in control of the conduct of their own institutions and an important aspect of freedom of religion is being lost.

The "ministerial exception" in the United States provides an example of the way in which law can be adjusted to take account of religious freedom and to protect religious institutions from external interference. Exceptions can be built into the law of the land, and a reasonable accommodation arrived at to provide for conscientious objection. Yet all too often this is resisted, particularly when issues of religion are at the fore. The *Ladele* case, already described by John Finnis in Chapter 1, provides a classic example. Taken through the English courts and finally decided (against Ladele) by the European Court of Human Rights in 2013, it illustrates how other forms of discrimination—in this case concerning sexual orientation—simply trump any apparent religious discrimination. In addition, the idea of freedom of religion is narrowed so that it can carry little weight in a case such as this. Lillian Ladele was a civil registrar who refused to conduct civil partnership ceremonies because of her religious beliefs. She lost her job, even though other registrars could have taken those ceremonies so that she could have continued with the job she had always done before the law changed and civil partnerships for same-sex couples were introduced.

The view in this case was that a public servant must apply the law, and there is no room for any conscientious objection or accommodation of her beliefs. Otherwise, her employers, the London Borough of Islington, held, they would be condoning her discriminatory action against same-sex couples. Yet although European law explicitly limits the manifestation of "religion or beliefs" if it interferes with the rights and freedom of others, that does little to settle the issue of why discrimination of some kinds is fiercely opposed while discrimination on the grounds of religion appears to carry little weight.

One answer appears to be that while it is unlawful to discriminate against someone merely, say, because they are a Christian, acting in accordance with one's Christian beliefs is much less likely to be protected. There is, under European law, an absolute right to have a particular religion, or to believe something. When, though, it comes to action, different considerations become relevant. It is as if one can be a Christian without ever acting like one. Added to this, there are also disputes about what acting like a Christian amounts to. Christians are regularly told in English courts that certain actions are not part of their "core beliefs" as a Christian. Lillian Ladele was given precisely this answer by the Court of Appeal in London. It was said in the judgment that "Ms. Ladele's objection was based on her view of marriage, which was not a core part of her religion; and Islington's requirement in no way prevented her from worshipping as he wished."[11]

Similar remarks have been made in the context of wearing crosses. It is not an obligation of the Christian faith to wear one, and so no discrimination or breach of freedom of religion is allegedly involved when an employee is forbidden for whatever reason from wearing one. The submission of the British government to the European Court about two cases of wearing crosses at work (heard at the same time as that of Lillian Ladele) said: "The applicants' desire to wear a visible cross or crucifix may have been inspired or motivated by a sincere religious commitment. It was not, however, a recognized religious practice or commitment of the Christian faith."[12]

The trend of argument is always the same. Holding a religion such as that of Christianity, involves only the right to identify oneself as a Christian, and, it seems, also to worship. The right of Lillian Ladele to worship seemed to be regarded as the central feature of freedom of religion. Further manifestations of religious belief were regarded as of secondary importance. In the case of wearing a cross, one of the applicants to the European Court (Eweida) did win her case.[13] That, though, was just a matter of displaying a cross, with no obvious countervailing reason why she should not, apart from a ruling by her employers (British Airways). The second case considered, that of a nurse, was decided against the applicant, on the grounds that health and safety considerations must outweigh any matter of religious conscience.

There is a continuing tendency on both sides of the Atlantic to redefine freedom of religion in terms of the right to worship alone. That is certainly important, but for most Christians would comprise only an element in what it means to be a Christian and to behave like one. Belief and practice cannot so easily be prised apart.[14] The old adage "by their fruits shall you know them" sums up the traditional Christian view. Even so, even freedom to worship does not seem in practice to be held in very high esteem by the European Court of Human Rights. When employees ask that employers give them to time to worship on a Sunday or other day, such as a Friday for Muslims, the answer has been that freedom of contract gives the employee adequate protection to be free to worship.[15] They can give up their job or refuse to accept it in the first place if they do not like its requirements. In the days of increasing seven-day workweeks in shops and elsewhere, this, in effect, equates freedom of religion with the freedom to be unemployed. It suggests that religion as such is not given a high priority in the courts, and once again is trumped by other considerations, in this case the economic interests of employers. One of the most significant moments in the judgment of the European Court in *Eweida* did mark a possible turning away from such a stark view. The Court said that the possibility of changing one's job is only one aspect of the matter to be put in the balance.[16]

Reasonable Accommodation?

We quoted earlier the 2012 case in the England and Wales Court of Appeal in which the Court accepted a lack of competence on its part to deal with an internal dispute between Sikhs. The Court did not accept that "religious bodies or groups enjoy a spiritual independence or freedom that places them above, or exempts from, the law of the land, or that religion inhabits a 'civil-rights free zone.'" They said that was not the issue before them, which was what could or could not be properly decided in a court of law.[17]

Yet it also appears that issues about what are or are not "core" parts of Christian belief are not matters within the competence of secular judges to decide. A bench of bishops should not decide how the law is to be applied in particular case, and judges are not equipped to make theological decisions about the role of marriage in Christian belief. Many would hold that marriage is a central issue for Christian belief, and even the argument about what is or is not "core" is fraught with theological implications that judges should be wary of being involved in. Similarly, the issue of whether a Christian's wearing of a cross is positively required by faith seems far too strict. The display of a cross can clearly be a direct manifestation of Christian belief, as was evidenced by reactions to the discovery of the seventh-century burial site of an Anglo-Saxon girl near Cambridge in spring 2012. She was wearing a cross, and immediately that was taken to be a sign that she was a Christian and that this was an early Christian burial. It is also worth noting that being told that one cannot wear a cross takes one into new territory, even if it is an optional display of faith. Roman Catholics who were forbidden from going to Mass on Wednesdays might properly feel that their freedom of religion was being restricted, even if that is not a requirement of their faith.

In all of this, there is considerable pressure on religious people, both Christians and others, to restrict the manifestation of their faith and to conform to prevailing secular standards. This is considerably fueled by the idea that these are manifestations of a subjective, non-rational (even irrational) attitude that can say nothing of importance to those who do not share their faith. Matters such as "civil rights" are, by definition, beyond the scope of such idiosyncratic beliefs.

What though, are such rights themselves based on? If religion is turned into something subjective and beyond the scope of reason, it cannot itself provide any basis for legal principles. Where then do those principles come from? The issue of the basis of the very human rights so often appealed to in the current age is an acute one. It becomes even more pressing when rights conflict, as when the right not to be discriminated against in unfair ways, and the right to be treated equally with others and with proper human dignity, appear to cut across religious beliefs. Where does that leave religious freedom, which is itself, as we have seen, a basic right? How are we to resolve that kind of clash? How, likewise, are we to decide between discriminating against people on grounds of sexual orientation and on grounds of religious belief?

Many of the contributions to this volume have in fact been drawn to the incendiary issue of the equal recognition of homosexual and heterosexual relationships, and the current debates about same-sex marriage. In fact, the Oxford conference coincided with the beginning of a consultation by the British government on the issue of same-sex marriage. The consultation was somewhat flawed by the fact that the government already appeared to have made up its mind in favor of the principle. It then, despite widespread objections, proceeded to legislate for same-sex marriage in England and Wales, a law that came into force in March 2014. Scotland followed suit later in the year, but Northern Ireland proved much more reluctant. The issue remains controversial everywhere in the United Kingdom, and there is no doubt (as the *Ladele* case concerning the registration of civil partnerships already demonstrated) that the introduction of same-sex marriage in the country produces situations where people can easily find themselves at odds with the law because of conscientiously held beliefs about the nature of marriage. They can be, and are, at risk of losing their jobs because of their beliefs. For example, the issue of what can be taught about marriage in schools, even those that are faith based, such as those of the Church of England and the Roman Catholic Church, is extremely fraught.

There are, in fact, two issues at stake here. Is same-sex marriage to be accepted, or even welcomed, as an act of justice to those in homosexual relationships who want equal access to marriage? That is a major question, but although it is often advocated using the rhetoric of equality, it is not what is at issue. Everyone, of whatever sexual orientation, has always been equally able to marry, in the traditional sense of the word. It is just that those attracted to their own sex do not wish to. Instead they have wanted the institution of marriage to be changed in a significant manner. They want the meaning of "marriage" to be altered. One way of trying to accommodate all sides, though, should be resisted. Some suggest there should be a distinction between "civil marriage" and "religious marriage." Yet in society there can only be one institution of marriage that everyone can recognize. There may be different paths into it, and different ways of solemnizing marriage, both secular and religious, but marriage is marriage.

One general challenge raised in the conference on which this volume is based is whether the idea of what marriage is can be changed without opening a door for those who want a similar recognition for polygamy, or even incestuous relationships. There are such people waiting in the wings. Polygamy is a particularly tricky issue, as those advocating it as part of their religion could themselves claim that the demands of religious freedom support their case. In any case, however the debate proceeds, it is clearly about the meaning and purpose of marriage. As such, it does not directly engage the argument about conflicts between religious freedom and equality, with which this volume is primarily concerned, even though changes in our understanding of marriage can only exacerbate those conflicts.

How, though, when same-sex marriage is legally recognized, should those be treated who cannot accept such "marriage" and would want to have no part in facilitating it? The idea that we are all under the same law, which must apply to everyone equally, seems especially potent. The specter of *sharia* hovers in the background with a prevailing fear that any undue recognition given to religious differences could result in different laws for different groups. Surely, it will be said, we all have to live by the same legal standards, and recognize what the law of the land enjoins. It is at this point that the theme of this volume is particularly relevant. Can there be such a thing as "reasonable accommodation"? How far should those with conscientious objections be accommodated? Should they even obtain exemptions from a law, if they profoundly disagree with it? Put this way, it can be seen how some might perceive this as a challenge to democracy itself. We can only live together, it will be said, if we all accept the same system of law and the same system of deciding what the law should be. There can be no further provision for anyone opting out.

The plight of those who object to gay marriage but find themselves in a country that has agreed, through democratic procedures, to recognize it legally, is then the same as that of anyone who must obey laws to which they have strong objections. It may seem no different from other issues of "equality" enshrined in law, particularly those of or racial equality, and the outlawing of racial discrimination. Yet the idea that a democratic majority can ride roughshod over the consciences of a minority in any context remains troubling. There still remains the problem of why discrimination of one kind, over, say, sexual orientation, should be outlawed, while that of another kind explicitly mentioned in human rights documents, namely, religion, should be so ignored. Indeed, one of the motivations for enshrining basic principles of human rights in law is precisely to protect minorities of various kinds, whether racial, cultural, or religious, which may find themselves at odds with the will of the majority. The "tyranny of the majority" can be tyrannical indeed.

One of the problems with the way in which the argument is often couched is that there is a vague reference to "conscience." Whilst this may cover some of people's deepest motivations, it can also cover objections that may not be so important, and which may in the name of democracy have to be overridden. The views of a Labour party supporter under a Conservative administration, or a Republican under a Democratic one, may have to be ignored in the final instance if democracy is to function.

Special Privilege?

Stephen Law, in his contribution (Chapter 2), raises in an acute form the question of why religious people should receive any special privileges in the way of exemptions from a general law. He points out that those who want equal treatment for religious people may, in fact, want unwarranted special treatment. Yet that is not the view enshrined in the Constitution of the United States, which does single religion out for special protection. As we have seen, it does not merge it with a more general idea of "conscience" or "belief." This brings us back to the different legacies of the early and later Enlightenment, the former based on a theistic view of the universe. Is religion a mere idiosyncratic element in some people's belief, to be dismissed as "subjective?" Or is it, on the other hand, rooted much more deeply in human nature,[18] concerning matters of central importance to human life, particularly what counts as good and bad for human beings and contributes to their flourishing?

Richard Garnett maintains that the wrongfulness of discrimination rests on "pretty much the same reason that religious liberty is a fundamental human right: Every person is made in the image of and loved by God and as a consequence bears a dignity that should not be violated (81)." This is very much in tune with the sentiments of 1776, when the American Declaration of Independence said that: "all men are created equal" and "are endowed by their Creator with certain inalienable rights." In other words, the whole edifice of natural, or human rights, and our beliefs in equality and freedom depend on a theistic view of the dignity of human beings as being a reflection of their creation by God.

Can this view be sustained, or can rights be given some other basis? The present danger is that many countries are merely living off the spiritual capital of earlier generations. Having dispensed with religious belief, they take it for granted that all their other beliefs can remain the same. It is not clear how far their commitment to human dignity and human rights, and their belief in the fundamental equality of everyone, can still remain as the indispensable foundation of democratic societies. The issue is whether the fact that we happen to believe in such things at the present moment can be enough, when the original justification for them has been removed. It is perhaps no coincidence that even the certainties of the later Enlightenment, with its modernist commitment to rationality, has in recent decades fallen victim to the ravages of a postmodernist cynicism about the universality of reason, or of any particular "values." Universality has given way to the particularity of different traditions and sets of beliefs. Claims to objective truth have fallen victim to the apparent attractions of relativism. The idea of "human" rights must itself then be in jeopardy.

Even the future of democracy is at issue. What does it rest on? What principles can it appeal to? Does it rest on secure principles of equality and freedom, or merely the shifting beliefs of citizens? It is clearly an efficient mechanism for enabling people to live together in the midst of disagreement. The point, though, is that it can only work if each citizen is free to judge what is important and right, and then act accordingly. They can all bring their different judgments about this to public discussion. Different visions of the common good can be debated. Yet that can only mean that such different visions must be cherished in the first place. The very fact that religion has provided the basis for a belief by many in the foundational principles of democracy must mean that it has a particular claim to be cherished and respected. It does not have monopoly rights, but the fact that religion concerns what is most important in human life and society should prevent it from being sidelined. Of course, those who maintain that religion is subjective and non-rational in fact hold that it is not the kind of belief that can claim truth. It is merely a private attitude that may tell us something about the believer, but is not about anything real. Yet that rules out the place of religion in public life by an arbitrary definition (and one that would be fiercely contested in philosophy).[19]

Religious beliefs have helped form western societies. Paradoxically they have even created the conditions in which people are free to reject them. The imposition of a secularist orthodoxy, however, which refuses to give any recognition to religious belief, and its importance in the lives of believers, not only restricts the very freedom for individuals that lies at the root of a flourishing democracy, it removes one of the most powerful supports for the beliefs in freedom and equality that motivate those who seem ready to restrict the role of religious belief.

NOTES

Introduction

1. For a concise account of the intellectual underpinnings of religious freedom, see Timothy Samuel Shah, et al., *Religious Freedom: Why Now? Defending an Embattled Human Right* (Princeton: Witherspoon Institute, 2012).
2. See, e.g., Leo Strauss, *Natural Right and History* (Chicago: University of Chicago Press, 1953), 202–251; Stanley Rosen, "Benedict Spinoza," in *History of Political Philosophy*, 3rd ed., ed. Leo Strauss and Joseph Cropsey (Chicago: University of Chicago Press, 1987), 468–471.
3. See generally Timothy Samuel Shah and Allen Hertzke, eds., *Christianity and Freedom: Volume I, Historical Perspectives* (Cambridge: Cambridge University Press, 2016) and Larry Siedentop, *Inventing the Individual: The Origins of Western Liberalism* (Cambridge, MA: Belknap/Harvard University Press, 2014). For a compelling case for this view in brief compass, see Ronald Osborn, "The Great Subversion: The Scandalous Origins of Human Rights," *Hedgehog Review* 17, no. 2 (Summer 2015): 90–100.
4. Strauss, *Natural Right and History*, 81–119.
5. See Robert Louis Wilken, *The Christian Roots of Religious Freedom* (Milwaukee: Marquette University Press, 2014); Timothy Samuel Shah, "The First Enlightenment: The Patristic Roots of Religious Freedom," in Donald A. Yerxa, ed., *Religion and Innovation: Antagonists or Partners?* (New York: Bloomsbury Academic, 2015), 59–73; and see the essay by Timothy Samuel Shah, "The Roots of Religious Freedom in Early Christian Thought," and the essay by Robert Louis Wilken, "The Christian Roots of Religious Freedom," in Shah and Hertzke, eds., *Christianity and Freedom: Volume I, Historical Perspectives*.
6. Shah, et al., *Religious Freedom: Why Now?*, 6.
7. *United States v. Windsor*, 570 US ___, 133 S. Ct. 2675 (2013).
8. *Obergefell v. Hodges*, 576 US ___, S. Ct. 14-556 (2015).
9. *Bull & Anor v. Hall & Anor* [2013] UKSC 73, [2013] 1 WLR 3741 (November 27, 2013).
10. *Eweida and Others v. United Kingdom* [2013] IRLR 231, [2013] ECtHR 37 (January 15, 2013).
11. *X. and Others v. Austria* [2013] ECtHR 148 (February 19, 2013).
12. *Oliari and Others v. Italy* [2015] ECtHR 716 (July 21, 2015).
13. For the account that follows I am indebted to Kyle Harper, *From Shame to Sin: The Christian Transformation of Sexual Morality in Late Antiquity* (Cambridge, MA: Harvard University Press, 2013) and Kyle Harper, "Christianity and the Roots of Human Dignity in Late Antiquity," in Shah and Hertzke, eds., *Christianity and Freedom: Volume I, Historical Perspectives*.
14. This is evident since, strictly speaking, we discriminate all the time, from quotidian personal choices about where to dine and with whom to dine, to important political decisions

regarding to whom to grant asylum, where to distribute public funds, and whom to enfran-
chise (excluding, for example, minors, noncitizens, and in some states, convicted felons).

15. Osborn, "The Great Subversion," 96.
16. *Obergefell v. Hodges*, 576 US ___, S. Ct. 14-556 (2015), slip op. at 7 (Kennedy, J., for the
    Court). Available at http://www.supremecourt.gov/opinions/14pdf/14-556_3204.pdf.
    Accessed July 15, 2015.
17. Osborn, "The Great Subversion," 98.
18. *Obergefell*, 576 US ___, slip op. at 10.
19. Ibid., slip op. at 28.
20. Ibid., slip op. at 2 (Thomas, J., dissenting).
21. Ibid., slip op. at 16–17.
22. Ibid., slip op. at 27 (Roberts, C.J., dissenting).
23. Ibid., slip op. at 15 (Thomas, J., dissenting).
24. Ibid., slip op. at 6–7 (Alito, J., dissenting).

Chapter 1

1. See "Commission Launches Guidance on Managing Religious Belief in the Workplace," Notes
   to Editors, *Equality and Human Rights Commission*, http://www.equalityhumanrights.com/
   news/2013/february/commission-launches-guidance-on-managing-religion-or-belief-in-the-
   workplace. "[The Equality and Human Rights Commission] is the independent advocate for
   equality and human rights in Britain. It aims to reduce inequality, eliminate discrimination,
   strengthen good relations between people, and promote and protect human rights."
2. Equality and Human Rights Commission, "Commission Proposes 'Reasonable Accommodation'
   for Religion or Belief Is Needed," press release, July 11, 2011.
3. European Convention on Human Rights, Article 9: "(1) Everyone has the right to freedom of *thought, conscience and* religion; this right includes freedom to change his religion
   or belief, and freedom, either alone or in community with others and in public or private, to manifest his religion *or belief*, in worship, teaching, practice and observance. (2)
   Freedom to manifest one's religion *or beliefs* shall be subject only to such limitations as are
   prescribed by law and are necessary in a democratic society in the interests of public safety,
   for the protection of public order, health or morals, or the protection of the rights and
   freedoms of others." (emphasis added). This has effect in UK law by virtue of the Human
   Rights Act 1998.
4. *Eweida v. British Airways* [2010] EWCA Civ. 80, [2010] IRLR 322, [2010] ICR 890 (Sedley
   LJ), on appeal from [2009] ICR 303 (Employment Appeal Tribunal).
5. *Chaplin v. Royal Devon & Exeter NHS Foundation Trust* [2010] ET 1702886/2009 (unre-
   ported); see *Shirley Chaplin v. United Kingdom*, ECtHR application 59842/10. Chaplin was
   advised that appeals within England would be fruitless in view of the Court of Appeal decision
   in *Eweida*.
6. The Court of Appeal's *Eweida* judgment (note 4 above), by Sedley LJ, might fairly be described
   as a parade of technicalities in the service of evident antipathy to (such) claims of "freedom
   to manifest one's religion or beliefs"; it treats as decisive the fact that Eweida could produce
   no evidence that any other member of BA's staff had complained about the restriction, and it
   makes much of the fact that her litigation had some of the characteristics of a campaign (a matter normally studiously ignored by judges when considering proceedings to promote euthana-
   sia, assisted suicide, homosexual interests, abortion and the like). It finishes by remarking that
   in the list of categories protected against discrimination—i.e., "age, disability, gender reassignment, marriage and civil partnership, race, religion or belief, sex and sexual orientation"—"all of
   these apart from religion or belief are objective characteristics of individuals; religion and belief
   alone are matters of choice [!]" (para. 40).
7. *Ladele v. Islington London Borough Council* [2009] EWCA Civ 1357, [2010] 1 WLR 955.
8. *McFarlane v. Relate Avon Ltd* [2010] EWCA Civ 880, [2010] IRLR 872, 29 BHRC 249. The
   facts in the case are messy; McFarlane's dealings with his employer lacked frankness and consistency, his theological position lacks coherence, and above all he accepted the employment
   aware that it might involve such demands.

9. Civil partnerships cannot validly be entered into between persons within the degrees of consanguinity which invalidate marriages.

10. The Divisional Court in *Johns v. Derby County Council and Equality and Human Rights Commission* (intervening) [2011] EWHC 375 (Admin) (February 28, 2011) para. 83 noted that the American doctrine of reasonable accommodation of religious beliefs had been stressed by counsel for the applicants (citing the decision of Krieger J, sitting in the United States District Court for the District of Colorado, in *Buonanno v. A T & T Broadband LLC* (2004) 313 F Supp 2d 1069); but it disposed of the argument simply by citing the above-quoted passage from the leading Court of Appeal judgment in *Ladele*, quite unresponsive to the issue. (In *Johns*, as in *Ladele*, a central issue was whether the Council's enforcement of its sexual-orientation anti-discrimination policy amounted to unlawful indirect discrimination against persons—here, would-be foster parents for children under eight years of age—who were disproportionately affected by that policy or its enforcement—*disproportionately* because without sufficient reason.)

11. *Ladele*, para. 49 (emphasis added). Elias J's judgment said, more fully quoted: "They were entitled in these circumstances to say that the claimant could not pick and choose what duties she would perform depending upon whether they were in accordance with her religious views, at least in circumstances where her personal stance involved discrimination on grounds of sexual orientation. That stance was inconsistent with the non-discriminatory objectives, which the council thought it important to espouse both to their staff and the wider community. *It would necessarily undermine the council's clear commitment to that objective if it were to connive* [!] *in allowing the claimant to manifest her belief by refusing to do civil partnership duties*" (para. 111, emphasis added).

12. Ibid., para. 52 (emphases added).

13. See note 64 below.

14. See also paras. 46 and 51 of Neuberger MR's judgment: "Islington wished to ensure that all their registrars were designated to conduct, and did conduct, civil partnerships as they regarded this as consistent with their strong commitment to fighting discrimination, both externally, for the benefit of the residents of the borough, and internally in the sense of relations with and between their employees. I find it very hard to see how this could be challenged . . . as being a legitimate aim, in the light of Islington's Dignity for All policy, current legislation and mainstream thinking" (para. 46).

   Just as "discrimination" equivocally suggests unlawful discrimination, so "legitimate aim" equivocally suggests that the aim (of requiring *all* employees to perform certain acts regardless of their religious or other conscientious objections) is legitimate regardless of whether there are any or *no* means of pursuing it without violating human rights law. "[Ladele's counsel] argues that is not good enough, as, if Islington's aim was only achievable by disproportionate means, then it should not be justifiable, as '[t]o conclude otherwise would be to licence disproportionality'. . . . Accordingly, it is said, proportionality of means still ought to have been considered. In a case such as the present, it seems to me that argument might well be characterised as invoking the tail to wag the dog: the aim of the Dignity for All policy was of general, indeed overarching, policy significance to Islington, and it also had fundamental human rights, equality and diversity implications, whereas the effect on Ms Ladele of implementing the policy did not impinge on her religious beliefs: she remained free to hold those beliefs, and free to worship as she wished" (para. 51).

   But not free to manifest them, even though such manifestation could readily have been accommodated by an employer not determined from the outset to reject all accommodation of religious or other conscience rights in competition with sexual orientation non-discrimination (even though its published "Dignity for All Policy" also purportedly excluded all discrimination on grounds of religious belief: see para. 9).

15. *McFarlane v. Relate Avon Ltd* [2010] EWCA Civ 880, para. 25. In paras. 23–24, Laws LJ (sitting alone), reacting to an incautious affidavit by Lord Carey, a former Archbishop of Canterbury (who asked inter alia for some favor for Christian positions as distinct from other religious positions), assimilated protection of *religious* liberty of conscience to countenancing theocracy (or at least elided the two); he said: "[T]he conferment of *any legal protection . . .* upon a particular substantive moral position on the ground only that it is espoused by the

adherents of a particular faith . . . is deeply unprincipled. It imposes compulsory law, not to advance the general good on objective grounds, but to give effect to the force of subjective opinion. This must be so, since in the eye of everyone save the believer religious faith is necessarily subjective, being incommunicable by any kind of proof or evidence. It may of course be *true*; but the ascertainment of such a truth lies beyond the means by which laws are made in a reasonable society. Therefore it lies only in the heart of the believer, who is alone bound by it. No one else is or can be so bound, unless by his own free choice he accepts its claims" (para. 23, emphasis added).

This paragraph, from first to last, entails that freedom of religion, beyond belief and worship, was not properly included in the ECHR. Laws LJ goes on: "The promulgation of law *for the protection of a position held purely on religious grounds cannot therefore be justified*. It is irrational, as preferring the subjective over the objective. But it is also divisive, capricious and arbitrary. We do not live in a society where all the people share uniform religious beliefs. The precepts of any one religion—any belief system—cannot, by force of their religious origins, sound any louder in the general law than the precepts of any other. If they did, those out in the cold would be less than citizens; and our constitution would be on the way to a theocracy, which is of necessity autocratic. The law of a theocracy is dictated without option to the people, not made by their judges and governments. The individual conscience is free to accept such dictated law; but the State, if its people are to be free, has the burdensome duty of thinking for itself" (para. 24, emphasis added).

16. See Equality and Human Rights Commission, "Commission Proposes 'Reasonable Accommodation' for Religion or Belief Is Needed," July 11, 2011.
17. Submission of the Equality and Human Rights Commission in the European Court of Human Rights, *Eweida and Chaplin v. United Kingdom*, September 2011, para. 56, http://www.equalityhumanrights.com/sites/default/files/documents/legal/ehrc_submission_to_ecthr_sep_2011.pdf. This is close to the way the Court of Appeal ruled in *Ladele*: "It is clear that the rights protected by [Article 9 ECHR] are qualified, and that it is only beliefs which are 'worthy of respect in a democratic society and are not incompatible with human dignity' which are protected – *Campbell and Cosans v. United Kingdom* (1982) 4 EHRR 293, para. 36. As Lord Hoffmann put it in *R (SB) v. Governors of Denbigh High School* [2007] 1 AC 100, para. 50, 'Article 9 does not require that one should be allowed to manifest one's religion at any time and place of one's own choosing' " (para. 54).

"This appears to me [Neuberger MR] to support the view that Ms Ladele's proper and genuine desire to have her religious views relating to marriage respected should not be permitted to override Islington's concern to ensure that all its registrars manifest equal respect for the homosexual community as for the heterosexual community" (para. 55).

Neuberger MR's reasoning is loose, to the point (one may think) of irresponsibility. He offers two premises and fails to say which he is relying upon; if it is the first, he is saying that Ladele's Christian beliefs about marriage are simply incompatible with human dignity and unworthy of respect in a democratic society; if it is the second, he is saying, with respect absurdly, that any claim of conscientious objection to participation in a public ceremony entails a claim to be allowed to manifest one's religion at any time or place of one's choosing.
18. Submission of Equality and Human Rights Commission, para. 55 (emphasis added).
19. In *Ladele*, Lord Neuberger MR's reasoning on the justifiability of the Council's indirect discrimination against Ladele because of religion concluded: "Accordingly, in *Sahin v. Turkey* (2007) 44 EHRR 5, the Grand Chamber . . . . said that the need 'to maintain and promote the ideals and values of a democratic society', in that case 'the principle of secularism' . . . can properly lead to 'restrict[ing]' other rights and freedoms . . . set forth in the Convention' (in that case the wearing of beards and headscarves for religious reasons). In para. 105, the Grand Chamber endorsed the proposition that 'Article 9 does not protect every act motivated or inspired by a religion or belief. Moreover, in exercising his freedom to manifest his religion, an individual may need to take his specific situation into account.' " (para. 58).

"By contrast, decisions of the Strasbourg Court such as *Salguerio da Silva Mouta v Portugal* (2001) 31 EHRR 47 and *EB v France* (2008) 47 EHRR 21 emphasise that, to quote from para. 90 in the latter case, '[w]here sexual orientation is in issue, there is a need for particularly convincing and weighty reasons to justify a difference in treatment regarding rights falling within article 8.' It is not suggested that, by permitting Ms Ladele not to officiate at civil partnerships, Islington would have infringed anyone's rights under the Convention, but observations such as these demonstrate the importance which the Convention should be treated as ascribing to equality of treatment irrespective of sexual orientation" (para. 59, emphasis added).

The last sentence tacitly concedes that accommodation of Ladele's religious and conscientious interests or rights was possible without any impact at all on the treatment of persons entering or in civil partnerships, but treats such accommodation *as if* it were incompatible with such persons' interests—because of the now-overriding symbolic importance of upholding those interests. Knowledge that Ladele had those beliefs, and was being (for a time) accommodated, was alleged by two homosexual colleagues of hers in the registry to be *offensive* to them. It was this actual or purported taking of offence (by persons whose objective, non-symbolic interests were not affected) that prevailed with the Council and then with the courts.

20. In the context of her judgment in *Sahin v. Turkey* (2004) 41 EHRR 109, where she dissented from the other sixteen judges, Judge Tulkens's formulation follows a reference to the right to freedom of religion, which she sought to uphold (though she had no persuasive answer to the thesis of the majority that prohibition of wearing of religious headscarves could be justified as a proportionate means of preserving the *religious* and other freedoms of those who would otherwise be pressured by Islamic fundamentalists into wearing such scarves): see John Finnis, "Endorsing Discrimination between Faiths: A Case of Extreme Speech?," in *Extreme Speech and Democracy*, Ivan Hare and James Weinstein, eds. (Oxford: Oxford University Press, 2009), 433–439.

21. The spokesman for the Home Office, commenting on these reports, added, in relation to the *Ladele* and *McFarlane* cases, "The Equality Act makes very clear that people have the right to express their views in a legitimate way, as long as they do not discriminate against a particular group or individual." Steve Doughty and Nick Fagge, "Minister in Legal Battle to STOP Christians Being Able to Wear a Cross to Work," *Daily Mail (UK)*, March 12, 2012, http://www.dailymail.co.uk/news/article-2113639/Minister-launches-assault-right-wear-cross-instructs-government-lawyers-fight-claims-Christian-workers.html#ixzz1otMpdozS.

22. David Barrett, "Christians Have No Right to Wear Cross at Work, Says Government," *Telegraph (UK)*, March 10, 2012, http://www.telegraph.co.uk/news/religion/9136191/Christians-have-no-right-to-wear-cross-at-work-says-Government.html.

23. Ibid.

24. See Universal Declaration of Human Rights 1948, Article 26 (3): "Parents have a prior right to choose the kind of education that shall be given to their children."

25. This is acknowledged by the Supreme Court of the United States in *Boy Scouts of America v. Dale* 530 US 640 (2000). Note what the Court says at 653: "That is not to say that an expressive association can erect a shield against anti-discrimination laws simply by asserting that mere acceptance of a member from a particular group would impair its message. But here Dale, by his own admission, is one of a group of gay Scouts who have 'become leaders in their community and are open and honest about their sexual orientation.' Dale was the copresident of a gay and lesbian organization at college and remains a gay rights activist. Dale's presence in the Boy Scouts would, at the very least, force the organization to send a message, both to the youth members and the world, that the Boy Scouts accepts homosexual conduct as a legitimate form of behavior."

26. On chastity, see note 37 below.

27. Anti-Discrimination Act 1977 (New South Wales, Australia), s. 49ZH(3) provides [since 1994] that employment "(c) by a private educational authority" is not subject to the Act's provisions about discrimination against homosexuals in relation to employment; and s. 59A(1) provides [from 2010] that "Nothing in Part 3A [transgender] or 4C [homosexuality] affects any policy or practice of a faith-based organisation concerning the provision of adoption services under the Adoption Act 2000 or anything done to give effect to any such policy or practice."

28. Thus the British Prime Minister, responding in January 2007 to the request that certain faith-based adoption agencies be permitted to continue to decline to provide their services to same-sex couples, wrote: "I start from a very firm foundation: there is no place in our society

for discrimination. That is why I support the right of gay couples to apply to adopt like any other couple. And that is why there can be no exemptions for faith-based adoption agencies offering publicly-funded services from regulations which prevent discrimination." (Quoted in *Catholic Care [Diocese of Leeds] v. Charity Commission* [2010] EWHC 520 [Ch] [para. 7]). The reference to public funding was misleading; the prohibition imposed by the provisions then about to be imposed (Equality Act [Sexual Orientation] Regulations 2007) made it unlawful to discriminate on grounds of sexual orientation in the providing of a service "to the public or a section of the public," irrespective of the funding or otherwise of that providing of a service; likewise under the Equality Act 2010, s. 29, which supersedes the regulations. The "firm foundation" alleged by Mr. Blair is mushy and unstable, for the reason suggested by the judge, Briggs J., in *Catholic Care (Diocese of Leeds) v. Charity Commission*: "[W]hereas, under Article 14 [of the European Convention on Human Rights], justified differential treatment is not defined as discrimination at all, the Regulations contain a broader definition of discrimination, and then provide exceptions which mean that discrimination, thus defined, is not prohibited. Nonetheless that different use of the word discrimination does not mask the reality that the exceptions in the Regulations are designed to serve as a means of permitting justified differential treatment, as contemplated by Article 14" (para. 73).

The question is always whether differential treatment is justified, and that question is suppressed by conclusory use (such as the Prime Minister's) of the term "discrimination," use which treats the conclusion as a premise ("that is why . . ."). For similarly fallacious conclusory use of "discrimination/discriminatory" by courts that should know better and try harder, see text and notes throughout Section IV.

29. The effect of *Ladele* and *Johns* was summarized by the First-Tier Tribunal (Charity) of the General Regulatory Chamber in *Catholic Care (Diocese of Leeds) v. Charity Commission*, CA/2010/0007, decision of April 26, 2011, para. 14: "religious belief *cannot* provide a lawful justification for discrimination on grounds of sexual orientation in the delivery of a *public-facing service* such as the operation of a *voluntary* adoption agency" (emphases added; the law in no way turns on the provision or non-provision of public funds). The concept of accommodation is completely absent from the Tribunal's reasoning and approach.

30. Local Government Act 1988, c. 9, s. 28. *Pace* H.L.A. Hart: see John Finnis, "Hart as a Political Philosopher," in *Philosophy of Law*, vol. IV of *Collected Essays of John Finnis* (New York: Oxford University Press, 2011), 274, note 66 (hereafter *CEJF*).

31. The definitions of direct and indirect discrimination in the enactments (parliamentary or ministerial) discussed herein make it clear that even to count sexual orientation as a *negative*, though not in itself disqualifying, *factor* in decision-making about employment or selection of foster parents or adopters, etc., is now sufficient to constitute unlawful discrimination.

32. First, the Employment Equality (Sexual Orientation) Regulations 2003, s. 7(3) contained an exception in relation to "employment for purposes of an organised religion," where the employer applies a requirement related to sexual orientation either "so as to comply with the doctrines of the religion," or "because of the nature of the employment and the context in which it is carried out, so as to avoid conflicting with the strongly held religious convictions of a significant number of the religion's followers." This exception was immediately attacked as invalid in proceedings brought against the government in the High Court by various large unions of teachers and others. The judgment in *R (Amicus-MSF Section) v. Secretary of State for Trade and Industry* [2004] EWHC 860 (Admin), [2007] ICR 1176 upheld the validity of the exception. But the unions were essentially successful. For they elicited from the government and then from the Court itself an authoritative interpretation which (a) very severely limits the availability of the exception and holds that it has no application to schools, and (b) severely limits the scope of the legal "right to religious freedom" and of the legal "right to association" wherever either of those rights might affect the rights of privacy and equality insofar as the latter are the basis of the right not to undergo intentional (direct) or unintentional (indirect) discrimination or harassment as a result of sexual orientation.

Second, as thus interpreted, the exception is *not available at all to protect the self-regulation of any religious school*, or indeed of *any religious institution* other than the body that constitutes "the organised religion" itself. The ruling in *R (Amicus-MSF Section) v. Secretary of State for Trade and Industry* is that "Employment for the purposes of an organised religion clearly means [no more than] a job, such as a minister of religion, involving work for a church, synagogue or mosque" (para. 91, quoting Minister of State, Lord Sainsbury of Turville, in replying to the debate on the Regulations in the House of Lords on June 17, 2003) and does *not* include work for the purposes of any "religious organisation" such as a Church school or nursing home, etc. Moreover, the purposes of the organized religion itself, and even work for the Church itself, will not be within the scope of the exception unless the *doctrines* of the religion or the *strongly held religious convictions* of believers *require* that job to be restricted to (say) heterosexuals; so, in the view of the government and the Court, employment by the Conference of Bishops (or by a diocese or parish) as a secretary or altar server would not be within the scope of the exception (and so could not be withheld from an openly practicing homosexual or homosexual couple or bisexual triad).

Third, as the last sentence above indicates, the Court held that *the distinction (drawn by many Christian churches) between a homosexual "orientation" and homosexual "activity" is one that has no relevance or significance in law*. In the words of the Judge, Lord Justice Richards: "The protection against discrimination on grounds of sexual orientation relates as much to the manifestation of that orientation in the form of sexual behaviour as it does to sexuality as such" (para. 119). "As regards the protection conferred by the Convention . . . I do not consider there to be any material difference between [sexual *orientation* and sexual *behaviour*]. Sexual orientation and its manifestation in sexual behaviour are both inextricably connected with a person's private life and identity" (para. 29).

Moreover, in the case of the set of regulations dealing with *religious* discrimination in employment etc., Employment Equality (Religion or Belief) Regulations 2003, SI 1660/ 2003, issued simultaneously with the Employment Equality (Sexual Orientation) Regulations (SI 1661/2003), there was a provision that "(1) These [religious discrimination] regulations are without prejudice to—(a) sections 58–60 of the School Standards and Framework Act 1998." This preserved s. 60(5) of the School Standards and Framework Act 1998, whereby "(b) If [a] school is a [religious] voluntary aided school regard may be had, in connection with the termination of employment of any teacher at the school, to *any conduct on [the teacher's] part which is incompatible with the precepts,* or the upholding of the tenets, *of the religion* or religious denomination . . ." (emphasis added). *But there was no such saving clause in the simultaneously issued regulations prohibiting discrimination on grounds of sexual orientation.* It therefore had to be assumed that the courts would unhesitatingly hold that where a teacher's conduct was a manifestation of sexual orientation, the school had no right to dismiss the teacher for lawful homosexual conduct incompatible with precepts of the school's religion.

33. See the third paragraph of the preceding footnote ("Third, as the last sentence above indicates . . .").

34. *R (Amicus-MSF Section) v. Secretary of State for Trade and Industry* [2004] EWHC 860 (Admin), [2007] ICR 1176, para. 41.

35. An example of its fruitless deployment in argument is *Bull & Bull v. Hall & Preddy* [2012] EWCA Civ 83 (February 10, 2012), in which the Equality & Human Rights Commission instructed counsel appearing for the respondent homosexual civil partners, who successfully claimed damages for being discriminated against by being refused a double bed by the appellant hoteliers who, as a manifestation (as the trial court found) of their Christian belief in marriage, always refused double-bedded rooms to *unmarried* persons. (Being a private hotel, its operation was not subject to the traditional law of "common carriers," rules prohibiting most refusals to accommodate.) The Court of Appeal's decision rested principally on an accepted (though philosophically unsound) interpretation of what counts as *direct* discrimination (which in English law cannot, unlike indirect discrimination, be defended as justified), but it includes also a ruling that the regulation forbidding such discrimination (and by its terms rendering it direct, under the reigning doctrine) is not contrary to Article 9 ECHR. The leading judgment gratuitously observed that section 13 of the Human Rights Act 1998 is "a provision inserted into the legislation following representations from certain religious organisations" (para. 11). It also quoted para. 23 of Laws LJ's *dicta* in *McFarlane*. Concerning section 13 of the Human Rights Act 1998, it simply said: "it does not . . . on the facts of this case add to the requirements already set out in the Convention and, in any event, the present case is related not [sic] to a religious organization" (para. 53). Still, it attempted to distinguish,

rather than brush aside or ignore, the Ontario divisional court decision in *Ontario Human Rights Commission v. Brockie* [2002] 22 DLR (4th) 174, which counsel for the appellants had advanced in tandem with section 13 as supporting the case for a "reasonable balance" between religious and equality rights. Rafferty LJ said: "In that case [*Brockie*] a Christian printer was required to offer services to an homosexual group, but not required to print leaflets which actively promoted an homosexual lifestyle and which was [*sic*] dismissive of Christian beliefs. However, though in that case the printer was required positively to do something, here the Appellants were not. They were not put in a position which would have asked them so to behave as to suggest, wrongly, to an interested public that the views which apparently lay in their mouth were those they genuinely held. Far from it. All that happened here was the desire of the Respondents to rent a double-bedded room in a public hotel. I have no difficulty concluding that the discrimination here differs little from that in *Ladele*. The Appellants are able, as I have transposed the comments in *Pichon* [*v France*, ECtHR, Oct. 2, 2001], 'to manifest [their] beliefs in many ways outside the professional [commercial] sphere' " (*Bull*, para. 50).

As the bizarreness of the sentence beginning "all that happened here . . ." suggests, the judgment was implausibly evading the analogy: the respondents were indeed being required to do something—make available and service a double room in a private hotel—to persons of a class (the unmarried) which for decades they had declined to do lest by doing it they facilitate conduct contrary to their conscientious beliefs. The final sentence is rendered out of date by the ECtHR's subsequent cautious and limited move away from *Pichon* and toward accommodation in *Ladele* (see note 53 below).

36. "Chastity" sounds like a purely private virtue, but is of course a disposition (even among those who are not and may never be married) to respect and strengthen marriage—as an intrinsic human good and as the one institution inherently fit for creating and then protecting the rights, interests, and flourishing of a society's new generation—by reserving to faithful marriage the sexual acts that express, actualize, and enable spouses to experience and ratify their commitment to live (in substantial measure) with and for each other in that outward-looking commitment.

37. As to issue (i), these remarks supplement or revisit considerations advanced in John Finnis, "Darwin, Dewey, Religion, and the Public Domain," in *Religion and Public Reasons*, vol. V of *CEJF*, 17–41 (this essay was originally entitled "Does Free Exercise of Religion Deserve Constitutional Mention?" and was published in the *American Journal of Jurisprudence* 54 [2009]); as to issue (ii), in Finnis, "Part Six: Marriage, Justice, and the Common Good" (essays 20–22), in *Human Rights and Common Good*, vol. III of *CEJF*. See also note 45 below.

38. As to his contribution in general, I would suggest that it displays the distortion of reality, and some savor of anti-Catholic sentiment, characteristic of, for example, the newspaper it cites, *The Guardian*, and of the substantial sections of the British governing classes who share that journal's attitudes even when they subscribe to other newspapers such as the *Daily Mail* and the *Telegraph* (which themselves share important aspects of the *Guardian's* prejudice and unrealism). To go no further than the second and third sentences of his chapter: "One of the earliest beneficiaries of changes to the law to protect minorities from unfair discrimination was the Roman Catholic community. The Catholic Relief Act [*sic*] in 1829 aimed to protect Roman Catholics from such discrimination." If he were to consult the Act, Law would discover that it is the Roman Catholic Relief Act 1829 (10 Geo. IV, c. 7), and that its opening words, defining its purposes, are as follows: "Whereas *by various Acts of Parliament*, certain Restraints and Disabilities are imposed on the Roman Catholic subjects of His Majesty, to which other subjects of His Majesty are not liable: and whereas it is expedient that *such* restraints and disabilities shall be from henceforth discontinued: and whereas *by various Acts* certain Oaths and certain Declarations, commonly called the Declaration against Transubstantiation, and the Invocation of Saints, and the Sacrifice of the Mass, as practised in the Church of Rome, are or may be required to be taken, made and subscribed by the subjects of His Majesty, as qualifications for sitting and voting in Parliament, and for the enjoyment of certain offices, franchises, and civil rights" (emphases added).

The Act had nothing whatever to do with "protecting Catholics" against unfair discrimination; it merely removed *some* of the restraints, penalties, and disabilities that had been imposed *by previous Acts of Parliament* enacted from time to time over the centuries after 1558;

the reference to "civil rights" was simply to the hitherto-existing *statutory* prohibition on or impediments to acquisition of property by Catholics. Everyone in the Kingdom remained as legally free as ever before to discriminate against Catholics, in any otherwise lawful way they chose. The 1829 Act had a subsidary purpose, to renew and extend the law's severe prohibitions against being a Jesuit or a member of any other Catholic religious order (dedicated community) for men; the preamble to these prohibitions reads: "And whereas Jesuits and members of other religious orders, communities or societies, of the church of Rome, bound by monastic or religious vows, are resident within the United Kingdom; and it is expedient to make provision for the gradual suppression and final prohibition of the same therein." (The suppression was "gradual" just in the sense that it did not come into force until six full months from the enactment of the Act.)

The price exacted by the politico-religious establishment for its reluctant acquiescence in this whole Act was the simultaneous enactment of a change in voting laws in Ireland, to disenfranchise most of the Irish county electorate (non-urban, de facto almost entirely Catholic peasantry): the Irish Parliamentary Elections Act 1829 (10 Geo. IV, c. 8) raised the county freehold franchise from 40 shillings to £10, reducing the relevant electorate from 230,000 to approximately 14,000.

At the other end of his contribution, Law complains that it is discrimination for Catholics to maintain schools to which the state chooses to contribute financially but which, *when they are over-subscribed*, give preference to Catholics—which they do, of course, because it is a mission of those schools to assist Catholic parents in fulfilling their parental responsibilities to educate their children in their faith (including its authoritative teachings against religious coercion, against unjust discrimination, against e.g., homosexuals). At no point in his paper is there any explanation of his choice to focus his paper on Catholics and their schools, which are a minority of state-funded religious schools but whose selection practices are not unique or even peculiar in being mission-relative.

39. It is not possible to devise a fully neutral and universal principle of religious liberty, any more than it is possible to devise a neutral conception of public order. If Stephen Law or Linda McClain think that religious objections to anti-marital sex practices and their promotion are false because such practices are morally unobjectionable and/or their promotion is compatible with justice to children and the sustainability of society, and that the liberty of religious communities to promote such objections (as they were universally promoted in the western world in say 1960) can rightly be suppressed or discriminated against as if it were a religious teaching of black human inferiority or of the duty to commit suicide or of the legitimacy of killing apostates, their thought needs to be contested on its (de)merits as a (mis)judgment about the place of sex and marriage in human flourishing. As I put it in "Darwin, Dewey, Religion, and the Public Domain," *Religion and Public Reasons*, vol. V of *CEJF*, 37: "The mentality which regards same-sex marriage as conceivable, let alone desirable or reasonable, involves a truly radical break with human experience and reason. The consequent unjust impositions on religious or religiously motivated activities and associations are probably best resisted by pointing, not to religious liberty, but to the way these impositions infringe associational freedom and parental rights, while pointing in any case to their manifold wrong-headedness about sex and marriage, to their abuses of children's innocence, and to their recklessness about the common good and the nation's future."

40. See, e.g., my essays:
   (i) "Religion and State: Some Main Issues and Sources," *American Journal of Jurisprudence* 51 (2006): 107–130, http://ssrn.com/abstract=943420; subsequently published as "Political Neutrality and Religious Arguments," in *Religion and Public Reasons*, vol. V of *CEJF*, 103–112. See especially 91 and 97–99;
   (ii) "Nationality, Alienage and Constitutional Principle," *Law Quarterly Review* 123 (2007): 417–445; subsequently published as "Nationality and Alienage," *Human Rights and Common Good*, vol. III of *CEJF*, 133–150. See especially 149;
   (iii) "Discriminating between Faiths: A Case of Extreme Speech?," in *Extreme Speech and Democracy*, Ivan Hare and James Weinstein, eds. (New York: Oxford University Press, 2009), 440–441; also available at http://ssrn.com/abstract=1101522;

   (iv) "Discrimination between Religions: Some Thoughts on Reading Greenawalt's *Religion and the Constitution*," *Constitutional Commentary* 25 (2009): 265–271, http://con-servancy.umn.edu/bitstream/handle/11299/170486/25_02_Symposium_Finnis.pdf?sequence=1&isAllowed=y;

   (v) "Why Religious Liberty Is a Special, Important and Limited Right," *Notre Dame Legal Studies Paper* 09–11 (2009), http://ssrn.com/abstract=1392278;

   (vi) "Does Free Exercise of Religion Deserve Constitutional Mention?," *American Journal of Jurisprudence* 54 (2009): 41–66, http://scholarship.law.nd.edu/cgi/viewcontent.cgi?article=1867&context=law_faculty_scholarship; subsequently published as "Darwin, Dewey, Religion, and the Public Domain," in *Religion and Public Reasons*, vol. V of *CEJF*, 17–41. See especially 37–41.

41. Patrick Buisson, *1940–1945: Années Érotiques: L'Occupation Intime* (Paris: Albin Michel, 2011).

42. See the Accepting Schools Act 2012 (Ontario), requiring schools to acquiesce in—indeed, to favor—propaganda by pupils who wish to develop their "critical consciousness" by agitating (under the name of "Gay-Straight Alliance" or similar pupil-chosen name) in favor of accep-tance (legally and factually indistinguishable from approval of the desires and sex practices) of "lesbian, gay, bisexual, transgender, transsexual, two-spirited, intersex, queer and question-ing people."

43. Universal Declaration of Human Rights, adopted December 10, 1948, Article 16: "(1) Men and women of full age . . . have the right to marry and found a family . . . (3) The family is the natural and fundamental group unit of society and is entitled to protection by society and the State."

44. See Shekhar Bhatia, "Revealed: How More and More Britons Are Paying Indian Women to Become Surrogate Mothers," *Telegraph (UK)*, May 26, 2012, http://www.telegraph.co.uk/health/healthnews/9292343/Revealed-how-more-and-more-Britons-are-paying-Indian-women-to-become-surrogate-mothers.html: "One clinic in New Delhi, The Birthplace of Joy, said that their patients were '100 per cent foreign' and estimated that as many as half of them were homosexual couples wanting to become parents. At another clinic in New Delhi, Dr Shivani Gour, the director of Surrogacy Centre India, said her clients are overwhelmingly middle class, listing 'IT profession-als, Home Office staff, doctors from the NHS, people from multinationals, bankers, businessmen.' In March her clinic was responsible for 26 surrogate babies, one of whom went to Britain, eight to the United States, four to Australia, and the others to countries including Canada, Japan, and Spain. In other months the British figure has been much higher. 'Gay people are just so keen and so desperate to have a family,' she said. 'Many of the people say that as soon as they realised they were gay, the saddest thing was that they knew they would never have children.' "

    The article is illustrated with a photo of Indian babies, but more common is the practice of using eggs from European (e.g., Ukrainian or Estonian) women "donors" and only the wombs of Indian surrogate "mothers."

45. (i) John Finnis, "Law, Morality and 'Sexual Orientation'," in *Same Sex: Debating the Ethics, Science, and Culture of Homosexuality*, John Corvino, ed. (Lanham, MD: Rowman & Littlefield, 1997), 31–43; subsequently published as "Law, Morality, and Sexual Orientation," *Human Rights and Common Good*, vol. III of *CEJF*, 334–352; (ii) Finnis, "The Good of Marriage and the Morality of Sexual Relations: Some Philosophical and Historical Observations," *American Journal of Jurisprudence* 42 (1997) 97–134; subsequently published as "Sex and Marriage: Some Myths and Reasons," in *Human Rights and Common Good*, vol. III of *CEJF*, 353–388; (iii) Finnis, "Marriage: A Basic and Exigent Good," *Monist* 91 (2008) 388–406; subsequently published in *Human Rights and Common Good*, vol. III of *CEJF*, 317–332; (iv) John Finnis and Robert P. George, "Natural Law and the Unity and Truth of Sex: A Reply to Gary Gutting," *Public Discourse*, March 17, 2015, http://www.thepublicdiscourse.com/2015/03/14635/.

46. See Finnis, "The Profound Injustice of Judge Posner on Marriage," *Public Discourse*, October 9, 2014, http://www.thepublicdiscourse.com/2014/10/13896/.

47. *Bull & Bull v. Hall & Preddy* [2012] EWCA Civ 83 (February 10, 2012). See note 35 and Section IV.
48. See Finnis, "Judicial Law-Making and the 'Living' Instrumentalisation of the ECHR," in *Lord Sumption and the Limits of the Law*, Nicholas Barber, Richard Ekins and Paul Yowell, eds. (Oxford: Hart Publishing, 2016), 73–120.
49. I agree with Christopher McCrudden's view that a reasonable equivalent of the concept of reasonable accommodation can be found in the German constitutional concept of *practical concordancy*, articulated by (though doubtless misapplied by the majority of) the Federal Constitutional Court in the *Classrooms Crucifix Case (No. 2)* decision of August 10, 1995, BVerfGE 93, 1, Judgment C.II.3(a): "[C]onflict among various bearers of a fundamental right guaranteed without reservation, and between that fundamental right and other constitutionally protected objects, is to be resolved on the *principle of practical concordancy, which requires that no one of the conflicting legal positions be preferred and maximally asserted, but all given as protective as possible an arrangement* . . . Resolving the unavoidable tension between negative and positive religious freedom while taking account of the precept of tolerance is a matter for the Land legislature, which must through the public decision-making process seek a compromise acceptable to all. In its arrangements it may take as a guide the fact that on the one hand Art. 7 Basic Law allows religious and philosophical influences in the area of schooling, and on the other Art. 4 Basic Law commands the exclusion as far as at all possible of religious and philosophical compulsions when opting for a particular form of school. Both provisions have to be *seen together and reconciled with each other through interpretation, since it is only concordance of the objects of legal protection under both articles that can do justice to the decision contained in the Basic Law*" (emphases added).
    To say this is not to say that it is desirable for such accommodation or concordancy to be a matter for judicial rather than legislative decision, save in those jurisdictions which, by way of constitutional or quasi-constitutional provisions, have (regrettably, in most instances, I believe) imposed such a responsibility on courts. On this last point, see Finnis, "Human Rights and Their Enforcement," in *Human Rights and Common Good*, vol. III of *CEJF*, 19–46.
50. *Eweida and Others v. United Kingdom* [2013] IRLR 231, [2013] ECHR 37, para. 94.
51. Ibid., para. 99.
52. On the inconvenience of the ECHR's clumsy drafting, generating constant equivocation about "violations of a right" which are not violations at all (because fully justifiable and justified), see Finnis, "Human Rights and Their Enforcement," 39–41; and Finnis, "Judicial Law-Making and the 'Living' Instrumentalisation of the ECHR" at 80–82.
53. *Eweida and Others*, para. 83.
54. The Court in *Eweida* also rejected the UK government's deplorable argument (see text after note 21 above) that the only religious beliefs protected by Article 9 are those *mandated* by some religion: "In particular, there is no requirement on the applicant [relying upon Article 9] to establish that he or she acted in fulfilment of a duty mandated by the religion in question" (para. 82).
55. Of course, higher court decisions made originally by their judges' legislative choice then provide legal guidance to lower courts until some new act of legislation by the superior judiciary. Throughout, the terms of the ECtHR supply quite insufficient guidance, especially since the Convention has been subjected to a doctrine of "living instrument" judge-made revision to align and realign it with elite opinion. See Finnis, "Judicial Law-Making and the 'Living' Instrumentalisation of the ECHR" at 82–93.
56. As the Court notes: *Eweida and Others*, paras. 48–49.
57. *Eweida and Others*, paras 70–72.
58. Ibid., para. 104.
59. Ibid., para. 106.
60. This is rightly emphasized in the powerful judgment of Judges Gaetano and Vučinić, dissenting in *Ladele* but concurring in *McFarlane*: "If anything, both the law (the Civil Partnership Act 2004) and the practice of other local authorities allowed for the possibility of compromises which would not force registrars to act against their consciences (see § 25 [of the ECtHR judgment]). In [Ladele's] case, however, a combination of back-stabbing by her colleagues and the blinkered political correctness of the Borough of Islington (which clearly favoured

'gay rights' over fundamental human rights) eventually led to her dismissal. The *iter lamen-tabilis* right up to the Court of Appeal is described in §§ 26 to 29. We underscore these facts because [Ladele's] situation is substantially different from the situation in which [McFarlane] found himself, or, more precisely, placed himself. When Mr McFarlane joined Relate he must have known that he might be called upon to counsel same-sex couples. Therefore his position is, for the purposes of the instant case, not unlike that of a person who *volunteers* to join the army as a soldier and subsequently expects to be exempted from lawful combat duties on the grounds of conscientious objection" (joint partly dissenting opinion of Judges Vučinić and Gaetano, para. 5).

61. See text following note 10 above.
62. See among countless authoritative general statements of proportionality doctrine: *Recovery of Medical Costs for Asbestos Disease* [2015] UKSC 3 per Lord Mance para. 45, "There are four stages . . . involving consideration of (i) whether there is a legitimate aim which could justify a restriction of the relevant protected right, (ii) whether the measure adopted is rationally connected to that aim, (iii) whether the aim could have been achieved by a less intrusive measure and (iv) whether, on a fair balance, the benefits of achieving the aim by the measure outweigh the disbenefits resulting from the restriction of the relevant protected right."
63. *Eweida and Others*, paras. 109–110 (emphases added).
64. See note 41 above.
65. On conscience, see Finnis, "Faith, Morals and Thomas More," in *Religion and Public Reasons*, vol. V of *CEJF*, 169–170.
66. *Bull & Anor v. Hall & Anor* [2013] UKSC 73, [2013] 1 WLR 3741 (November 27, 2013). (Note that this case was heard before the UK Supreme Court, and should be distinguished from the earlier 2012 case decided by the England and Wales Court of Appeal in *Bull & Bull v. Hall & Preddy* [2012] EWCA Civ 83). That *Bull v. Hall* was reported in volume 1 of the *Weekly Law Reports* signals the editors' opinion that it, albeit a decision of the Supreme Court, is of minor importance, and entails that it will not be reported in the *Appeal Cases*; so we lack even a summary of the briefs and arguments of counsel. Thus we cannot readily discover whether the case for the Bulls was framed exclusively in terms of Article 9 by itself rather than also in combination with Article 14 (and thus as a religious discrimination claim), as in *Ladele*.
67. The hotel's online booking form read: "Here at Chymorvah we have few rules, but please note, that out of a deep regard for marriage we prefer to let double accommodation to heterosexual married couples only—thank you" (para. 9). It was pure accident, so far as the evidence went (see para. 10), that Hall and Preddy did not see the website, booked by phone, and by reason of Mr. Bull's illness were not given the verbal notice he otherwise always gave along the lines of the booking form.
68. As I do in "Equality and Differences," *American Journal of Jurisprudence* 56 (2011), 28–30; more fully, and with reference to the House of Lords decision discussed in this connection in *Bull v. Hall*, in my "Intention in Direct Discrimination" in *Intention and Identity*, vol. II of *CEJF*, 269–276 (originally published in *Law Quarterly Review* 126 (2010): 496).
69. But it is no laughing matter, for it reads into the legislation the harshest possible anti-"dis-crimination" meaning, widening greatly the class of actions that, despite the absence of any *intent* to discriminate against anyone in a protected class, are held—on the basis of a wholly fictitious intention—to be discriminatory acts incapable of being justified as a matter of rea-sonableness, self-defense, or any other justifying rationale.
70. In a context far removed from discrimination law, but concerning (homosexual) sexual orientation, see *HJ (Iran) v. Secretary of State for the Home Department* [2010] UKSC 31, [2011] 1 AC 596; see also Finnis, "Human Rights and Their Enforcement," in *Human Rights and Common Good*, vol. III of *CEJF*, 45–46, and "Marriage: A Basic and Exigent Good," in *Human Rights and Common Good*, vol. III of *CEJF*, 332–333, where I noted: "The sheer scale of the normative revolutions in our societies since the 1950s can be assessed by reading the judgments of each of the five Justices in *HJ (Iran) v. Secretary of State for the Home Department* [2010] UKSC 31. Set aside their proper concern with grossly persecu-tory acts (public hanging, castration by lynch mobs, and the like) and their argumentation about persecution and the Refugee Convention (on which see [pp. 45–46]). Set aside

also their particular concern with homosexual inclinations and activities. What is central, pervasive, and unchallenged in these judgments is this. Everyone has a sexual 'identity' defined, not just as hetero- or homo- but by any 'along a broad spectrum' of the types of sex acts and relationships he or she is inclined to, and by the strength of his or her inclinations. Though this identity or 'orientation' may change from time to time, it is 'so fundamental to identity or human dignity that it ought not to be required to be changed,' and open manifestation of it in search for, and activities with, numerous sexual partners ought positively to be allowed and facilitated, both by law and by social attitudes and opinion. Contrast this with the moral teachings and social traditions and laws all substantially overthrown by the normative revolutions. Central to them is and was a contrary proposition, with its corollary. Human dignity itself requires that one's inclinations be disciplined and reformed so as to be in line with marriage and marital paternity or maternity. And, for the sake of marriage as an institution essential to the survival of the group and its culture and freedom, and for the sake of justice to children whose true well-being depends on a marital upbringing, those whose inclinations unfit them for marriage, or who opt not to marry, or who cannot find anyone willing to marry them, or whose spouse becomes sexually disabled, can reasonably be publicly called upon to live in a way that at least openly does not defy these propositions."

71. *Bull & Anor v. Hall & Anor* [2013] UKSC 73, [2013] 1 WLR 3741 (November 27, 2013), paras. 36–37 (emphases added).
72. Ibid., para. 34 (emphasis added).
73. "They would have been prepared to let Mr Preddy and Mr Hall have a twin bedded room . . ." Ibid., para. 50. "Twin bedded and single rooms . . . would be let to any person regardless of marital status or sexual orientation." Ibid., para. 9.
74. Subject to the obscure implications of its restriction (why?) to "at least in some cases." Ibid., para. 47.
75. Ibid., paras. 45 and 47 (emphasis added).
76. Ibid., paras. 51–53 (emphasis added). Lady Hale adds only this: "There is no question of . . . replacing 'legal oppression of one community (homosexual couples) with legal oppression of another (those sharing the defendants' beliefs)'. . . . If Mr Preddy and Mr Hall ran a hotel which denied a double room to Mr and Mrs Bull, whether on the ground of their Christian beliefs or on the ground of their sexual orientation, they would find themselves in the same situation that Mr and Mrs Bull find themselves today" (para. 54).
      But the attempted parallel is absurd, because it again fails to acknowledge that the ground of the Bulls' refusal to let a double room was not the beliefs or the orientation of the homosexuals, but their concern that *their own provision* of a double bed would make them complicit in the *immoral conduct* (as they conscientiously judged it) of Preddy with Hall. What would be the imaginable counterpart in the Hall & Preddy hotel?

Chapter 2

1. Ipsos MORI and the Richard Dawkins Foundation, "Religious and Social Attitudes of UK Christians in 2011," poll, February 14, 2012, https://www.ipsos-mori.com/researchpublications/researcharchive/2921/Religious-and-Social-Attitudes-of-UK-Christians-in-2011.aspx.
2. *Bull & Bull v. Hall & Preddy* [2012] EWCA Civ 83 (February 10, 2012).
3. *Johns v. Derby County Council* [2011] EWHC 375 (Admin) (February 28, 2011).
4. This conference addressed the theme "Religious Freedom and Equality: Emerging Conflicts in North America and Europe" and was held at Magdalen College, Oxford University on April 11–13, 2012.
5. *Johns*, para. 33 (as quoted by Lord Justice Munby) (emphasis in original).
6. Ibid., para. 33 (as quoted by Lord Justice Munby) (emphasis in original).
7. Ibid., para. 33 (as quoted by Lord Justice Munby).
8. Ibid., para. 34 (as quoted by Lord Justice Munby).
9. Ibid., para. 34 (as quoted by Lord Justice Munby) (emphasis in original).
10. "High Court Judgment Suggests Christian Belief Harmful to Children. Fostering by Christians Now in Doubt," *Christian Concern*, February 28, 2011, Lorhttp://www.

christianconcern.com/our-concerns/religious-freedom/breaking-news-high-court-judgment-suggests-christian-beliefs-harmful-.

11. Quoted in "Court Rejects Foster Couple 'Christian Discrimination' Claim," *Ekklesia*, March 1, 2011, http://www.ekklesia.co.uk/node/14234.

12. Quoted in "BA Worker was not Discriminated against over Cross Ban" *Ekklesia*, January 9, 2008, http://www.ekklesia.co.uk/node/6550.

13. Peter Tatchell, "Christian Manager Fights Demotion over 'Homophobic' Facebook Comment," *The Huffington Post*, December 15, 2011, http://www.huffingtonpost.co.uk/peter-g-tatchell/adrian-smith-homophobic-comments_b_1147873.html.

14. David Wilkes, "Cancer Patient Left 'Traumatised' by Christian Teacher Sacked for Offering to Pray for Her," *Daily Mail (UK)*, December 21, 2009, http://www.dailymail.co.uk/news/article-1237601/Cancer-patient-left-traumatised-Christian-teacher-Olive-Joness-offer-pray-her.html.

15. "Teacher Suspended in Prayer Row," *BBC News*, December 20, 2009, http://news.bbc.co.uk/1/hi/england/bristol/8423265.stm.

16. Mail on Sunday Comment for the *Daily Mail*, "A Christian Who Fell Foul of Our New Religion," The Mail Comment, *Daily Mail*, December 20 2009, http://www.dailymail.co.uk/debate/article-1237206/MAIL-ON-SUNDAY-COMMENT-A-Christian-fell-foul-new-religion.html.

17. *Johns v. Derby County Council* [2011] EWHC 375 (Admin) (February 28, 2011).

18. *Eweida v. British Airways* [2010] EWCA Civ. 80, [2010] IRLR 322, [2010] ICR 890 (February 12, 2010).

19. *Bull & Bull v. Hall & Preddy* [2012] EWCA Civ 83 (February 10, 2012)

20. See, e.g., Jessica Shepherd and Simon Rogers, "Church Schools Shun Poorest Pupils," *Guardian (UK)*, March 5, 2012, http://www.guardian.co.uk/education/2012/mar/05/church-schools-shun-poorest-pupils?CMP=twt_gu.

21. Paper on file with author.

22. John Finnis, "Equality and Religious Liberty: Oppressing Conscientious Diversity in England," this volume, 28.

23. Ibid., 29.

24. Ibid., 29.

25. Interestingly, Finnis suggests that claiming that specifically *religious* freedoms are being trampled is probably *not* the best approach when it comes to defending the right of the religious to discriminate against those in same-sex relationships. In note 39, he says: "The mentality which regards same-sex marriage as conceivable, let alone desirable or reasonable, involves a truly radical break with human experience and reason. The consequent unjust impositions on religious or religiously motivated activities and associations are probably best resisted by pointing, not to religious liberty, but to the way these impositions infringe associational freedom and parental rights, while pointing in any case to their manifold wrong-headedness about sex and marriage, to their abuses of children's innocence, and to their recklessness about the common good and the nation's future" (quoting Finnis, "Darwin, Dewey, Religion, and the Public Domain," *Religion and Public Reasons*, vol. V of *Collected Essays of John Finnis* [New York: Oxford University Press, 2011], 37).

The thought here seems to be that the best way to defend the rights of the religious to discriminate if same-sex marriage is introduced is by (i) upholding their associational freedom and parental rights, and (ii) pointing out that the legislation is in any case wrongheaded and dangerous. Regarding (i): I have no problem with Finnis trying to mount a defense of discriminatory behavior on the basis of associational freedom or parental rights, as that defense would apply no less to non-religious people wanting to discriminate thus. The non-religious have (or should have) the same associational and parental rights as the religious. So let us see what sort of case Finnis can make and then let us assess that case on its merits. The point is, Finnis would *not* now be arguing for exemptions or exclusions on the basis of religiosity per se—which is the principle I have asked him and others to justify. Regarding (ii): by all means let Finnis argue against the legislation as such. What I am asking is why religiosity per se should qualify people for special exemptions or exclusions to such legislation if and when it is introduced. The wrongness of the legislation is a basis for repealing it. It is not a basis for giving some but not others special immunity to it.

26. Finnis devotes just 500 or so words to addressing the central question I raise in my essay. However, he produces a footnote of some 660 words dedicated to showing that my essay manifests a "distortion of reality, and some savor of anti-Catholic sentiment" (Finnis, this volume, note 38). On what evidence does Finnis base his suggestion of anti-Catholic sentiment? He points to just two passages. First, he quotes me as saying: "One of the earliest beneficiaries of changes to the law to protect minorities from unfair discrimination was the Roman Catholic community. The Catholic [sic] Relief Act [sic] in 1829 aimed to protect Roman Catholics from such discrimination."

The Act removed various forms of discrimination against Catholics, for example, allowing them to sit in Parliament and hold other official roles, and removing impediments to acquiring property. However, as Finnis points out, the Act did not protect Roman Catholics from being discriminated against by their fellow citizens. True. But then I did not suppose, or even state, otherwise. This is one for *Pedantry Corner*, surely? As to whether any ambiguity in my comment that Finnis here tries to exploit provides any sort of basis for suggesting I am guilty of anti-Catholic sentiment, I'll leave you to decide.

The only other evidence Finnis provides in support of the suggestion that I am guilty of a "some savor of anti-Catholic sentiment" is: "Law complains that it is discrimination for Catholics to maintain schools to which the state chooses to contribute financially but which, *when they are over-subscribed*, give preference to Catholics. . . . At no point in his paper is there any explanation of his choice to focus his paper on Catholics and their schools" (Finnis, this volume, note 38).

I will say first that Finnis appears to have misunderstood my intention in mentioning this complaint. My concern was not to endorse the complaint. Rather, I used the complaint to illustrate the point that other significant issues relating to religious freedom and equality are also at the forefront of public debate in the United Kingdom, and yet they have been entirely ignored by this conference, which has chosen to focus exclusively on cases in which, it is alleged, the *religious* are being unjustly treated. What I said about religious schools is accurate.

Now, Finnis suggests my comment is evidence of anti-Catholic sentiment because I chose, without explanation in the main text, to use state-funded Catholic schools as an illustration (rather than, say, state-funded Jewish schools, or state-funded religious schools more generally). So let me clarify: the reason I focused on Catholic schools to illustrate widespread public concerns about state funding and selection, is that, *as the article cited in note 20 of this chapter reveals*: "The Roman Catholic church, which has repeatedly insisted its schools are inclusive, comes out particularly badly in the examination of data published by the Department for Education (DfE) last month and in December. Three-quarters of Catholic primary and secondary schools have a more affluent mix of pupils than their local area." Jessica Shepherd and Simon Rogers, "Church Schools Shun Poorest Pupils."

Incidentally, there's some irony in Finnis's comment as he himself uses Catholic schools to illustrate a point without explaining why he has chosen a specifically Catholic example (". . . that we see being imposed, say, on the Catholic school system in Ontario" [Finnis, this volume, 30]).

So did I exhibit some savor of "anti-Catholic sentiment?" I don't think so, but even if I did, note that Finnis is here guilty of *ad hominem*—attacking my character rather than dealing with my argument. I suggest it would have been more constructive to have used these 660 words to bolster the mere 500 words Finnis spent addressing the issue I actually raised.

27. *Ladele v. Islington London Borough Council* [2009] EWCA Civ 1357, [2010] 1 WLR 955 (December 15, 2009).

Chapter 3

1. In the intervening years since this essay was first composed in 2012, the landscape in the United Kingdom has transformed dramatically. Most notably, same-sex marriage is now legal in England and Wales after the UK Parliament passed the Marriage (Same Sex Couples) Act

2013, and in Scotland after the Scottish Parliament passed the Marriage and Civil Partnership (Scotland) Act 2014.

2. *Bull & Anor v. Hall & Anor* [2013] UKSC 73, [2013] 1 WLR 3741 (November 27, 2013).

3. James Mills, "Foster Child to Be Taken Away because Christian Couple Refuse to Teach Him about Homosexuality," *Daily Mail Online*, last updated October 24, 2007, http://www.dailymail.co.uk/news/article-489285/Foster-child-taken-away-Christian-couple-refuse-teach-homosexuality.html#ixzz3fVCVanFx.

4. David Cameron, "Prime Minister's King James Bible Speech," *Official Website of the Government of the United Kingdom*, December 16, 2011, https://www.gov.uk/government/news/prime-ministers-king-james-bible-speech.

5. "Faith Rules 'End at Temple Door', Equalities Chief Says," *BBC*, February 17, 2012, http://www.bbc.com/news/uk-politics-17074114.

6. Pope Paul VI, Second Vatican Council, *Dignitatis humanae* (*Declaration on Religious Freedom*), "On the Right of the Person and of Communities to Social and Civil Freedom in Matters Religious," December 7, 1965, http://www.vatican.va/archive/hist_councils/ii_vatican_council/documents/vat-ii_decl_19651207_dignitatis-humanae_en.html.

7. Cardinal George Pell, "Varieties of Intolerance: Religious and Secular," (lecture, Divinity School, Oxford University, Oxford, United Kingdom, March 6, 2009), https://www.catholic-culture.org/culture/library/view.cfm?recnum=8812.

8. Pope Benedict XVI, "Address of His Holiness Benedict XVI to the Bishops of the United States of America on Their 'Ad Limina' Visit," January 19, 2012, http://w2.vatican.va/content/benedict-xvi/en/speeches/2012/january/documents/hf_ben-xvi_spe_20120119_bishops-usa.html.

9. Cardinal George Pell, "Varieties of Intolerance: Religious and Secular."

10. Ibid.

11. Ibid.

12. Ibid.

Chapter 4

1. Douglas Laycock, Anthony Picarello, and Robin Fretwell Wilson, eds., *Same-Sex Marriage and Religious Liberty: Emerging Conflicts* (Lanham, MD: Rowman & Littlefield, 2008).

2. At the time of this chapter's revision, the Supreme Court of the United States had heard arguments in, but not yet decided, *Obergefell v. Hodges*, 576 US ___, (2015), S. Ct. 14-556. On June 26, 2015, the Justices decided, by a 5-4 vote, that the Fourteenth Amendment requires a state to license a marriage between two people of the same sex and to recognize a marriage between two people of the same sex when their marriage was lawfully licensed and performed in another state. It is clear that, in the wake of this decision, the tension and the conflicts between claims of equal rights and claims of religious freedom will continue.

3. *Hosanna-Tabor Evangelical Lutheran Church & School v. Equal Employment Opportunity Commission*, 565 US ___, 132 S. Ct. 694 (2012).

4. I have developed this suggestion in other work. See Richard W. Garnett, "Religious Accommodations and—and among—Civil Rights: Separation, Toleration, and Accommodation," *Southern California Law Review* 88, published electronically February 23, 2015, http://papers.ssrn.com/sol3/papers.cfm?abstract_id=2568799; Richard W. Garnett, "Religious Freedom and the Nondiscrimination Norm," in *Legal Responses to Religious Practices in the United States: Accommodation and Its Limits*, Austin Sarat, ed. (New York: Cambridge University Press, 2012), 194–227.

5. See generally, e.g., Pope Benedict XVI, "Address to the Participants in the 56th National Study Congress Organized by the Union of Italian Catholic Jurists," Rome, December 9, 2006, http://w2.vatican.va/content/benedict-xvi/en/speeches/2006/december/documents/hf_ben_xvi_spe_20061209_giuristi-cattolici.html; Zachary R. Calo, "Human Rights and Healthy Secularity," *Journal of Catholic Social Thought* 7, no. 2 (2010): 231–251.

6. Kenneth Karst, "Foreword: Equal Citizenship under the Fourteenth Amendment," *Harvard Law Review* 91 (1977): 6 (quoting Robert Rodes, *The Legal Enterprise* [Port Washington, NY: Kennikat Press, 1976], 163).

7. Richard W. Garnett, "The Freedom of the Church," *Journal of Catholic Social Thought* 4, no. 1 (2007): 60 (quoting G. Weigel, *The Cube and the Cathedral: Europe, America, and Politics without God* [New York: Basic Books, 2005], 101).

8. Michael W. McConnell, "Why Is Religious Liberty the 'First Freedom'?" *Cardozo Law Review* 21, no. 4 (2000): 1244.

9. President Bill Clinton, address to James Madison High School, Vienna, Virginia, July 12, 1995, http://www.presidency.ucsb.edu/ws/?pid=51608. See also, e.g., Thomas J. Curry, *The First Freedoms: Church and State in America to the Passage of the First Amendment* (New York: Oxford University Press, 1986); McConnell, "The 'First Freedom'?"

10. See generally, e.g., John Witte, Jr., *Religion and the American Constitutional Experiment: Essential Rights and Liberties* (Boulder, CO: Westview Press, 2000); John T. Noonan, *The Lustre of Our Country: The American Experience of Religious Freedom* (Berkeley, CA: University of California Press, 1998).

11. For more on the Indiana proposal, see Doug Laycock, et al. to Hon. Brent Steele and members of the Senate Judiciary Committee, "RE: Religious Freedom Restoration Act," February 3, 2015, http://www.faithlafayette.org/uploads/Church/LetterSupportingReligiousFreedomRestoration.pdf (visited May 18, 2015).

12. More information about these and similar examples is available at, among other places, the website of the Institutional Religious Freedom Alliance: http://www.irfalliance.org/ (visited May 20, 2015).

13. See John Garvey, "State Putting Church Out of Adoption Business," *Boston Globe*, March 14, 2006, A15; Patricia Wen, "Catholic Charities Stuns State, Ends Adoptions," *Boston Globe*, March 11, 2006, A1.

14. See, e.g., "Illinois Catholic Charities Adoption Battle: Judge Rules against Church, Another Appeal Ahead," *Huffington Post*, September 27, 2011, http://www.huffingtonpost.com/2011/09/27/illinois-catholic-chariti_n_983517.html.

15. See, e.g., Riazat Butt, "Catholic Adoption Agency Loses Gay Adoption Fight," *The Guardian*, April 26, 2011, http://www.theguardian.com/society/2011/apr/26/catholic-adoption-agency-gay-lesbian.

16. "Center for Faith-Based and Neighborhood Partnerships," *US Department of Health and Human Services*, last reviewed July 1, 2014, http://www.hhs.gov/partnerships/.

17. Lauren Markoe, "Critics Push Obama to Change Faith-Based Hiring Rules," *USA Today*, June 22, 2011, http://usatoday30.usatoday.com/news/religion/2011-06-22-obama-religion-hiring_n.htm. The text of the president's remarks is available at the White House's website: http://www.whitehouse.gov/the-press-office/2011/07/22/remarks-president-university-maryland-town-hall.

18. The letter of September 19, 2011 is available at the website of Americans United for the Separation of Church and State: http://www.au.org/files/pdf_documents/letter-to-president-obama.pdf.

19. See generally, e.g., Douglas Laycock, Picarello, and Wilson, *Same-Sex Marriage and Religious Liberty*.

20. See generally, e.g., Micah Schwartzman, "What If Religion Is Not Special?" *University of Chicago Law Review* 79 (2012): 1351–1427.

21. See generally, e.g., Richard W. Garnett, "The Political (and Other) Safeguards of Religious Freedom," *Cardozo Law Review* 32 (2011): 1815–1829.

22. See Pope Paul VI, Second Vatican Council, *Dignitatis humanae* (*Declaration on Religious Freedom*), "On the Right of the Person and of Communities to Social and Civil Freedom in Matters Religious," Art. 2, December 7, 1965, http://www.vatican.va/archive/hist_councils/ii_vatican_council/documents/vat-ii_decl_19651207_dignitatis-humanae_en.html ("[Religious] freedom has its foundation" not in political convenience or indifference, but in "the very dignity of the human person[.]").

23. James Madison, "Memorial and Remonstrance against Religious Assessments," in *The Papers of James Madison*, vol. 8, *10 March 1784—28 March 1786*, Robert A. Rutland and William M. E. Rachal, eds. (Chicago: University of Chicago Press, 1973), 299.

24. *City of Boerne v. Flores*, 521 US 507, 553–554 (1997) (gathering examples).

25. European Convention on Human Rights, 1950, Art. 9, pp. 10–11, http://www.echr.coe.int/Documents/Convention_ENG.pdf.

26. Canadian Charter of Rights and Freedoms, section 2, Part 1 of the Constitution Act, 1982, being Schedule B to the Canada Act 1982 (UK), 1982 c 11.

27. *Dignitatis humanae*, Art. 4. See note 22 above.

28. Ibid., Art. 7.

29. Larry Alexander, "What Makes Wrongful Discrimination Wrong? Biases, Preferences, Stereotypes, and Proxies," *University of Pennsylvania Law Review* 141 (1992): 152.

30. Peter Westen, "The Empty Idea of Equality," *Harvard Law Review* 95 (1982): 537.

31. See generally, John E. Coons and Patrick M. Brennan, *By Nature Equal: The Anatomy of a Western Insight* (Princeton: Princeton University Press, 1999).

32. Cf. Jane Rutherford, "Equality as the Primary Constitutional Value: The Case for Applying Employment Discrimination Laws to Religion," *Cornell Law Review* 81 (1996): 1126–1128.

33. See, e.g., *Yick Wo v. Hopkins*, 118 US 356, 367 (1886).

34. See, e.g., *Hosanna-Tabor Evangelical Lutheran Church and School v. EEOC.*, 565 US ___, (2012).

35. *United States v. Stevens*, 559 US ___, 130 S.Ct. 1577 (2010).

36. *Snyder v. Phelps*, 131 S.Ct. 1207 (2011).

37. *Brown v. Entertainment Merchants Ass'n*, 131 S.Ct. 2729 (2011).

38. *Bob Jones University v. United States*, 461 US 574 (1983).

39. *Christian Legal Society v. Martinez*, 561 US ___, 130 S.Ct. 2971 (2010).

40. *Hosanna-Tabor Evangelical Lutheran Church and School v. EEOC.*, 565 US ___, (2012).

41. *Bob Jones*, 461 US at 579–580.

42. Ibid, 579 (quoting Revenue Ruling 71-447, 1971-2 Cum. Bull. 230).

43. *Bob Jones University v. United States*, 468 F.Supp. 890, 898 (D.S.C. 1978).

44. *Bob Jones University v. United States*, 639 F.2d 147, 153, 154 (4ᵗʰ Cir. 1980).

45. *Bob Jones University v. United States*, 461 US 574, 602 (1983).

46. Ibid., 592.

47. Ibid., 604.

48. I coauthored an *amicus curiae* brief, on behalf of a number of Christian student groups, which was filed with the Supreme Court in support of the Christian Legal Society. That brief is available here: http://www.americanbar.org/content/dam/aba/publishing/preview/publiced_preview_briefs_pdfs_09_10_08_1371_PetitionerAmCuCMDA_BYXandCLSchapters.authcheckdam.pdf (visited May 20, 2015).

49. *Christian Legal Society v. Martinez*, 561 US 661 (2010).

50. Ibid., 2980–2981.

51. Ibid., 2981.

52. *Christian Legal Society v. Kane*, 319 Fed.Appx. 645 (9ᵗʰ Cir. 2009).

53. Ibid., 2990 (internal citations and quotation marks omitted).

54. See, e.g., John Inazu, *Liberty's Refuge: The Forgotten Freedom of Assembly* (New Haven, CT: Yale University Press, 2012): 145–149; Corey Brettschneider, "Democratic Persuasion and Freedom of Speech: A Response to Four Critics and Two Allies," *Brooklyn Law Review* 79 (2014): 1059–1089; Linda C. McClain, "Religious and Political Virtues and Values in Congruence or Conflict? On *Smith, Bob Jones University*, and *Christian Legal Society*," *Cardozo Law Review* 32 (2011): 1959–2007; Michael Stokes Paulsen, "Disaster: The Worst Religious Freedom Case in Fifty Years," *Regent University Law Review* 24, no. 2 (2012): 283–309.

55. See generally, e.g., Richard W. Garnett and John M. Robinson, "*Hosanna-Tabor*, Religious Freedom, and the Constitutional Structure," *Cato Supreme Court Review* (2012): 307–330; Michael W. McConnell, "Reflections on *Hosanna-Tabor*," *Harvard Journal of Law & Public Policy* 35 (2012): 821–837; Christopher C. Lund, "In Defense of the Ministerial Exception," *North Carolina Law Review* 90 (2011): 1–72; Paul Horwitz, "Act III of the Ministerial Exception," *Northwestern University Law Review Colloquy* 106 (2011): 156–174.

56. *Hosanna-Tabor Evangelical Lutheran Church and School v. EEOC.*, 565 US ___, (2012), slip op. at 9 (quoting Letter from James Madison to Bishop Carroll [Nov. 20, 1806], reprinted in *Records of the American Catholic Historical Society*, vol. 20, [1909], 63–64).

57. *EEOC v. Hosanna-Tabor Evangelical Lutheran Church and School*, 582 F. Supp. 2d 881 (2008).

58. *EEOC v. Hosanna-Tabor Evangelical Lutheran Church and School*, 597 F.3d 769 (6ᵗʰ Cir. 2010).

59. See generally, e.g., Christopher C. Lund, "Free Exercise Reconceived: The Logic and Limits of *Hosanna-Tabor,*" *Northwestern University Law Review* 108 (2014): 1183–1233; Brian M. Murray, "The Elephant in *Hosanna-Tabor,*" *Georgetown Journal of Law and Public Policy* 10 (2012): 493–528.

60. See Richard W. Garnett, "Hosanna-Tabor Ruling a Win for Religious Freedom," *USA Today,* January 11, 2012.

61. Diana B. Henriques, "Where Faith Abides, Employees Have Few Rights," *New York Times,* October 9, 2006.

62. Vivian Berger, "Can Civil Rights Be Ordained Wrongs?" *The National Law Journal,* September 19, 2011.

63. Leslie C. Griffin, "Ordained Discrimination: The Cases against the Ministerial Exception," *University of Houston Law Center* No. 2011-A-9. See generally Caroline Mala Corbin, "Above the Law? The Constitutionality of the Ministerial Exemption from Antidiscrimination Law," *Fordham Law Review* 75 (2007): 1965–2038.

64. In an earlier work, I referred to a discriminatory practice's or act's "social meaning" as determining whether it is or is not wrongful. It now seems to me that the notion of "social meaning" is not helpful for this purpose. See generally, e.g., Richard Ekins, "Equal Protection and Social Meaning," *American Journal Jurisprudence* 57 (2012): 21–48.

65. Paul Woodruff, "What's Wrong with Discrimination?" *Analysis* 36 (1976): 158.

66. Deborah Hellman, "The Expressive Dimension of Equal Protection," *Minnesota Law Review* 85 (2000): 1–70.

67. Deborah Hellman, *When Is Discrimination Wrong?* (Cambridge, MA: Harvard University Press, 2008): 8.

68. Robert Rodes, *The Legal Enterprise* (Port Washington, NY: Kennikat Press, 1976), 163.

69. *Runyon v. McCrary,* 427 US 160 (1976).

70. *Christian Legal Society v. Martinez,* 561 US ___, 130 S.Ct. 2971, 2990 (2010).

71. See generally Richard W. Garnett, "A Hands-Off Approach to Religious Doctrine: What Are We Talking About?" *Notre Dame Law Review* 84 (2009): 837–864.

72. Pope Benedict XVI, "I Go to the United States with Joy," Press Conference aboard Papal Flight to United States, *Zenit,* April 16, 2008, http://www.zenit.org/en/articles/press-conference-aboard-papal-flight. For a compelling account of how this "healthy" or "positive" form of secularity helps to promote democratization and secure protections for human rights, see Monica Duffy Toft, Daniel Philpott, and Timothy Samuel Shah, *God's Century: Resurgent Religion and Global Politics* (New York: W.W. Norton & Company, 2011).

73. Pope Benedict XVI, Address to French Politicians, Paris, September 12, 2008, http://w2.vatican.va/content/benedict-xvi/en/speeches/2008/september/documents/hf_ben-xvi_spe_20080912_parigi-cultura.html.

74. See generally, e.g., John D. Inazu, "A Confident Pluralism," *Southern California Law Review* 88 (2015): 587–617.

75. Immanuel Kant famously insisted, "Out of timber so crooked as that from which man is made nothing entirely straight can be built." Isaiah Berlin, *The Crooked Timber of Humanity: Chapters in the History of Ideas,* 2nd ed., Henry Hardy, ed. (Princeton: Princeton University Press, 1991), xxii. (quoting Immanuel Kant, *Idee zu einer allgemeinen Geschichte in weltbürgerlicher Absicht* [1784]).

76. Mark DeWolfe Howe, "Foreword: Political Theory and the Nature of Liberty," *Harvard Law Review* 67 (1953): 91.

77. *Kedroff v. St. Nicholas Cathedral* 344 US 94 (1952). See generally, Richard W. Garnett, "'Things That Are Not Caesar's': The Story of *Kedroff v. St. Nicholas Cathedral,*" in *First Amendment Stories,* Richard W. Garnett and Andrew Koppelman, eds. (New York: Foundation Press, 2011), 171–198.

78. See generally, Richard W. Garnett, "The Story of Henry Adams's Soul: Education and the Expression of Associations," *Minnesota Law Review* 85 (2001): 1841–1883.

79. See Abner S. Greene, "Government of the Good," *Vanderbilt Law Review* 53 (2000): 7 ("[The Constitution's] combination of structure and rights prevents the concentration of power that is the harbinger of despotism").

80. Gary Lawson, "Prolegomenon to Any Future Administrative Law Course: Separation of Powers and the Transcendental Deduction," *St. Louis University Law Journal* 49 (2005): 885.
81. *Roberts v. US Jaycees*, 468 US 609, 619 (1984).
82. *Hosanna-Tabor Evangelical Lutheran Church & School v. EEOC*, 565 US at ___, slip op. at 1 (Thomas, J., concurring).

Chapter 5

1. *United States v. Windsor*, 570 US ___, 133 S. Ct. 2675 (2013).
2. *Obergefell v. Hodges*, 576 US ___, 135 S. Ct. 2584, 2597, 2604–2605, 2608 (2015). Appendix A to Justice Kennedy's opinion, "State and Federal Judicial Decisions Addressing Same-Sex Marriage," provides a list of these federal appellate and district court opinions. Ibid., 2608. In *DeBoer v. Snyder*, 772 F.3d 388 (6th Cir. 2014), the Sixth Circuit reversed federal district court rulings that struck down as unconstitutional state laws in Kentucky (*Bourke v. Beshear*, 996 F. Supp. 2d 542 [W.D. Ky 2014]), Michigan (*DeBoer v. Snyder*, 973 F. Supp. 2d 757 [E.D. Mich. 2014]), Ohio (*Obergefell v. Wymslo*, 962 F. Supp. 2d 968 [S.D. Ohio 2013]), and Tennessee (*Tanco v. Haslam*, 7 F. Supp. 3d 759 [M.D. Tenn. 2014]) that barred same-sex couples from marrying and/or barred recognition of their out-of-state marriages. These several cases were consolidated before the Supreme Court under the name *Obergefell v. Hodges*.
3. See Most Rev. William E. Lori, "Address on Religious Liberty," (presented at the general assembly of the United States Conference of Catholic Bishops, Baltimore, Maryland, November 14–16, 2011), http://www.usccb.org/about/leadership/usccb-general-assembly/2011-november-meeting/archbishop-lori-religious-liberty-november-2011-address.cfm; Rev. John Flynn, "The End of Religious Liberty?" *Crisis Magazine*, November 7, 2011, http://www.crisismagazine.com/2011/the-end-of-religious-liberty (reporting Archbishop Dolan's examples of the New York marriage law and the Justice Department's "attack on DOMA"); Joan Frawley Desmond, "Bishops Fight Threats to Religious Liberty," *National Catholic Register*, October 17, 2011, http://www.ncregister.com/site/article/bishops-fight-threats-to-religious-liberty; also see Archbishop Timothy Dolan's letter to US Bishops, September 29, 2011, http://www.usccb.org/issues-and-action/religious-liberty/upload/dolan-letter-on-religious-liberty.pdf.
4. Lori, "Address on Religious Liberty."
5. *United States v. Windsor*, 570 US ___, 133 S. Ct. 2675, 2702–2711 (2013) (Scalia, J., dissenting); 2717–2718 (Alito, J., dissenting); 2696 (Roberts, C.J., dissenting).
6. *Perry v. Schwarzenegger*, 704 F. Supp. 2d 921 (N.D. Cal. 2010).
7. For a criticism of Indiana's law, see "In Indiana, Using Religion as a Cover for Bigotry," *New York Times*, March 31, 2015, http://www.nytimes.com/2015/03/31/opinion/in-indiana-using-religion-as-a-cover-for-bigotry.html?_r=0; also see Monica Davey and Mitch Smith, "Indiana Governor, Feeling Backlash from Law's Opponents, Promises a 'Fix,'" *New York Times*, March 31, 2015, http://www.nytimes.com/2015/04/01/us/politics/indiana-governor-mike-pence-feeling-backlash-from-religious-laws-opponents-promises-a-fix.html.
8. Charles J. Chaput, et al., "Now Is the Time to Talk about Religious Liberty," *Public Discourse*, April 3, 2015, http://www.thepublicdiscourse.com/2015/04/14748/.
9. Ibid.
10. *Obergefell v. Hodges*, 135 S. Ct. 2584, 2642 (2015) (Alito, J., dissenting). For example on October 8, 2015, the American Principles Project (founded by Professor Robert P. George) quoted Justice Alito's prediction about vilification in its "Statement Calling for Constitutional Resistance to Obergefell v. Hodges." https://americanprinciplesproject.org/founding-principles/statement-calling-for-constitutional-resistance-to-obergefell-v-hodges%E2%80%AF/.
11. Nancy L. Rosenblum, *Membership and Morals: The Personal Uses of Pluralism in America* (Princeton: Princeton University Press, 1998), 41. On congruence, again see Rosenblum, *Membership and Morals*, 36–41. For an often-cited account of civil society as mediating institutions, see Peter Berger and Richard John Neuhaus, *To Empower People: The Role of Mediating Structures in Public Policy* (Washington, DC: American Enterprise Institute, 1977). I have discussed this idea of civil society as "seedbeds of civic virtue" extensively in my own work, but for a useful introduction, see Mary Ann Glendon and David Blankenhorn, eds., *Seedbeds*

of Virtue: Sources of Competence, Character, and Citizenship in American Society (Lanham, MD: Madison Books, 1995).

12. Robert P. George, Timothy George, and Chuck Colson, "Manhattan Declaration: A Call of Christian Conscience," November 20, 2009, http://www.manhattandeclaration.org/man_dec_resources/Manhattan_Declaration_full_text.pdf.

13. Robert P. George, et al., "Manhattan Declaration," 4.

14. For reference to "prejudice," see *Goodridge v. Department of Public Health*, 798 N.E.2d 941, 968 (Mass. 2003). For reference to "animus," see *Baker v. State*, 744 A.2d 864, 885 (Vt. 1999).

15. Brief for Manhattan Declaration as Amicus Curiae Supporting Respondent Bipartisan Legal Advisory Group, *United States v. Windsor*, 133 S. Ct. 2675 (2013).

16. Robert George, Sherif Girgis, and Ryan Anderson, *What Is Marriage? Man and Woman: A Defense* (New York: Encounter Books, 2012).

17. Brief for Robert P. George, Sherif Girgis, and Ryan T. Anderson as Amici Curiae Supporting Hollingsworth and Bipartisan Legal Advisory Group (Addressing the Merits and Supporting Reversal), *Hollingsworth v. Perry*, 570 US ___, 133 S. Ct. 2652 (2013) & *Windsor*, 133 S. Ct. (Nos. 12-144 & 12-307).

18. See Douglas E. Abrams, et al., *Contemporary Family Law*, 4th ed. (St. Paul, MN: West Academic Publishing, 2015).

19. *Goodridge*, 798 N.E.2d at 954.

20. See *In Re Marriage Cases*, 183 P.3d 384 (Cal. 2008); *Hernandez v. Robles*, 855 N.E.2d 1 (N.Y. 2006).

21. See generally John Witte, Jr., *From Sacrament to Contract: Marriage, Religion, and Law in the Western Tradition* (Louisville, KY: Westminster John Knox Press, 1997).

22. See Perry Dane, "A Holy Secular Institution?" *Emory Law Journal* 58 (2009): 1123–1194 (challenging the notion that marriage is a "wholly secular institution").

23. See Lee E. Teitelbaum, "Religion and Modernity in American Family Law," in *American Religions and the Family: How Faith Traditions Cope with Modernization and Democracy*, Don S. Browning and David A. Clairmont, eds. (New York: Columbia University Press, 2007), 229.

24. Douglas Laycock, "Religious Liberty and the Culture Wars," *University of Illinois Law Review* 2014, no. 3 (2014): 851.

25. Brief for United States Catholic Bishops as Amicus Curiae Supporting Petitioners and Supporting Reversal at 6, *Hollingsworth v. Perry*, 570 US ___, 133 S. Ct. 2652 (2013).

26. Katherine Shaw Spaht, "Louisiana's Covenant Marriage: Social Commentary and Legal Implications," *Louisiana Law Review* 59 (1998): 63–130.

27. Ibid., 76 n. 49 (describing a statement from The Catholic Bishops of Louisiana recognizing that the required divorce instruction under Covenant Marriage would "confuse or obscure the integrity of the Church's teaching and disciple" because it is "contradictory to Church teaching and mandated by this state law").

28. Brief for Robert P. George, et al., 5.

29. Ibid., 6.

30. Laycock, "Religious Liberty," 848.

31. Ibid.

32. Ibid.

33. Michael Sandel, *Justice: What's the Right Thing to Do?* (New York: Farrar, Straus and Giroux, 2009), 253–254.

34. James E. Fleming and Linda C. McClain, *Ordered Liberty: Rights, Responsibilities, and Virtues* (Cambridge, MA: Harvard University Press, 2013), 176–204.

35. *Bowers v. Hardwick*, 478 US 186, 196 (1986).

36. For a more thorough treatment of the Court's evolving jurisprudence on the role of moral disapproval, see Linda C. McClain, "From *Romer v. Evans* to *United States v. Windsor*: Law as a Vehicle for Moral Disapproval in Amendment 2 and the Defense of Marriage Act," *Duke Journal of Gender Law & Policy* 20 (2013): 351–478.

37. *Romer v. Evans*, 517 US 620, 628 (1996) (quoting the Colorado Supreme Court's construction of Amendment 2 in *Evans v. Romer*, 854 P. 2d 1280, 1284–1285 [Colo. 1993]).

38. Quoting *Department of Agriculture v. Moreno*, 413 US 528, 534 (1973).

39. Quoting *Louisville Gas & Electric Co. v. Coleman*, 277 US 32, 37–38 (1928).

40. Charles W. Colson, "Kingdoms in Conflict," *First Things*, November 1996, http://www.firstthings.com/article/1996/11/006-the-end-of-democracy-kingdoms-in-conflict. The symposium is called "The End of Democracy? The Judicial Usurpation of Politics."

41. Charles W. Colson, "Kingdoms in Conflict."

42. Ibid.

43. Hadley Arkes, "A Culture Corrupted," *First Things*, November 1996, http://www.firstthings.com/article/1996/11/005-the-end-of-democracy-a-culture-corrupted.

44. Ibid.

45. Ibid.

46. *Lawrence v. Texas*, 539 US 558, 578 (2003).

47. McClain, "From *Romer v. Evans* to *United States v. Windsor*," 432–436, 440–441.

48. *Bowers v. Hardwick*, 478 US 186, 196 (1986).

49. *Lawrence*, 539 US at 601.

50. Ibid., 604–605.

51. Peter Sprigg, "Does *Lawrence v. Texas* Imply a Right to Same-Sex Marriage?" *Family Research Council Blog*, August 6, 2010 (reprinting 2004 column), http://www.frcblog.com/2010/08/does-ilawrence-v-texasi-imply-a-right-to-same-sex-marriage/.

52. Sprigg, "Does *Lawrence v. Texas* Imply a Right to Same-Sex Marriage?"

53. The New York Marriage Equality Act, A8354, 2011–2012 Sess. (N.Y. 2011) is codified as Marriage Equality Act, NY Domestic Relations §10-a (2011).

54. *Hernandez v. Robles*, 855 N.E. 2d 1 (N.Y. 2006).

55. This analysis draws on my discussion in Fleming and McClain, *Ordered Liberty*, 199–205.

56. Remarks by Senator Saland, New York Senate Transcript, June 24, 2011, 6100, http://open.nysenate.gov/legislation/transcript/regular-session-06-24-2011.

57. Remarks by Senator Saland, 6107.

58. Stephen Saland, "Senator Saland's Statement on Marriage Equality," June 25, 2011, http://www.nysenate.gov/print/105811 (accessed January 24, 2015).

59. Remarks by Senator Grisanti, New York Senate Transcript, June 24, 2011, 6128, http://open.nysenate.gov/transcripts/floor-transcript-062411v1txt.

60. Remarks by Senator Grisanti, 6129–6130.

61. Deborah Glick, Remarks on Marriage Equality Vote, June 15, 2011 (my transcription from video clip), http://assembly.state.ny.us/mem/?ad=066&sh=video (accessed October 5, 2011).

62. Richard Gottfried, Remarks on Marriage Equality Legislation, June 15, 2011 (my transcription from video clip), http://assembly.state.ny.us/mem/Richard-N-Gottfried/video/ (accessed October 5, 2011).

63. Remarks by Senator Diaz, New York Senate Transcript, June 24, 2011, 6113, http://open.nysenate.gov/legislation/transcript/regular-session-06-24-2011 (accessed January 24, 2015).

64. Ruben Diaz and Michael Long, "If the NY Senate Passes Gay Marriage, It's Republicans Who Will Take the Heat," *National Review*, June 22, 2011, http://www.nationalreview.com/corner/270218/if-ny-senate-passes-gay-marriage-its-republicans-who-will-take-heat-ruben-diaz-michael (accessed January 27, 2015).

65. "Statement of the Bishops of New York State on Same-Sex 'Marriage' Vote," June 24, 2011, http://www.nyscatholic.org/2011/06/statement-of-the-bishops-of-new-york-state-on-same-sex-marriage-vote/ (accessed January 27, 2015).

66. Laycock, "Religious Liberty," 848.

67. United States Conference of Catholic Bishops, "Bishop Corlieone Expresses Grave Disappointment over NY Bill Redefining Marriage," press release, June 28, 2011, http://www.usccb.org/news/2011/11-131.cfm.

68. Samuel G. Freedman, "How Clergy Helped a Same-Sex Marriage Law Pass," *New York Times*, July 16, 2011, http://www.nytimes.com/2011/07/16/us/16religion.html?_r=0 (describing personal journey and organizing efforts of Ms. Taylor Sweringen).

69. Ibid. (quoting Julian E. Zelizer, history professor at Princeton).

70. Ibid.

71. New York Marriage Equality Act, A08354, Memorandum (2011), http://assembly.state.ny.us/leg/?default_fld=&bn=A08354&term=2011&Memo=Y (accessed January 24, 2015).

72. A08354 Memo, "Purpose."
73. A08354 Memo, "Statement in Support."
74. New York Marriage Equality Act, § 10-B, http://www.assembly.state.ny.us/leg/?default_fld= &bn=A08354&term=2011&Summary=Y&Text=Y.
75. Danny Hakim, "Exemptions Were Key to Vote on Gay Marriage," *New York Times*, June 26, 2011, http://www.nytimes.com/2011/06/26/nyregion/religious-exemptions-were-key-to-new-york-gay-marriage-vote.html; also see Christopher W. Dickson, "Inseverability, Religious Exemptions, and New York's Same-Sex Marriage Law," *Cornell Law Review* 98 (2014):181, 182–186 (discussing the importance of the religious exemptions to securing the necessary votes to pass the Marriage Equality Act).
76. See Public Rights/Private Conscience Project of the Columbia School of Law to Interested Parties, "Proposed Conscience or Religion-Based Exemptions for Public Officials Authorized to Solemnize Marriages," memorandum, November 5, 2014 (on file with author). The memo explores the constitutionality of proposed conscience or religion-based exemptions for public officials authorized to solemnize marriages.
77. For elaboration, see Fleming and McClain, *Ordered Liberty*, Chapter 6.
78. Robert D. Putnam and David E. Campbell, *American Grace: How Religion Divides and Unites Us* (New York: Simon and Shuster Paperbacks, 2012), 401–406.
79. Laycock, "Religious Liberty," 867.
80. These letters are available at the *Mirror of Justice* blog, http://mirrorofjustice.blogs.com/mir-rorofjustice/2009/08/memosletters-on-religious-liberty-and-samesex-marriage.html; see also Robin Fretwell Wilson, "The Calculus of Accommodation: Contraception, Abortion, Same-Sex Marriage and Other Clashes between Religion and the State," *Boston College Law Review* 53 (2012): 1417, 1484–1486.
81. "Marriage and Religious Freedom: Fundamental Goods That Stand or Fall Together: An Open Letter from Religious Leaders in the United States to All Americans," January 12, 2012, http://www.usccb.org/issues-and-action/marriage-and-family/marriage/promotion-and-defense-of-marriage/upload/Marriage-and-Religious-Freedom-Letter-Jan-12-2012-4.pdf.
82. USCCB, "Questions and Answers on 'Marriage and Religious Freedom,'" January 12, 2012, http://www.usccb.org/issues-and-action/marriage-and-family/marriage/promotion-and-defense-of-marriage/questions-and-answers-on-marriage-and-religious-freedom-letter-jan-12-2012.cfm; see also Timothy M. Dolan, et al., "Statement of the Bishops of New York State on Same-Sex 'Marriage' Vote," June 24, 2011, http://www.nyscatholic.org/2011/06/statement-of-the-bishops-of-new-york-state-on-same-sex-marriage-vote/. A few years ago, I had the experience of being on a panel with a religious opponent of same-sex marriage who, when I characterized the New York exemptions as "robust," audibly snorted and lifted out of his chair!
83. Laycock, "Religious Liberty," 879.
84. Thomas Kaplan, "Rights Collide as Town Clerk Sidesteps Role in Gay Marriages," *New York Times*, September 27, 2011, http://www.nytimes.com/2011/09/28/nyregion/rights-clash-as-town-clerk-rejects-her-role-in-gay-marriages.html (quoting Governor Cuomo).
85. See New York State Department of Health Office of Vital Records to New York State Town and City Clerks, "Amendment to Domestic Relations Law—'The Marriage Equality Act,'" informational memorandum, July 13, 2011 ("No application for a marriage license shall be denied on the ground that the parties are of the same or a different sex"); Kaplan, "Rights Collide"; Robert Harding, "Ledyard Clerk Controversy Headed for Courts?" *Citizen* (Auburn, NY), November 13, 2011, http://auburnpub.com/news/local/article_6922ee6c-0da6-11e1-b3ed-001cc4c03286.html (accessed January 24, 2015) (reporting that the couple, Katie Carmichael and Dierdre DiBaggio, were considering legal action and that the Courage Fund would support the newly re-elected clerk, Rose Marie Belforti, in such a challenge); Lori, "Address on Religious Liberty," 5 (listing as threat to religious liberty "a county clerk in New York State who faces legal action because she refuses to take part in same-sex marriages").
86. See Wilson, "The Calculus of Accommodation," 1426, 1440–1442; Wilson, "Insubstantial Burdens: The Case for Government Employee Exemptions to Same-Sex Marriage Laws," *Northwestern Journal of Law and Social Policy* 5 (2010): 318, 323–326.
87. See Robin Fretwell Wilson's chapter in this volume.

88. Alan Blinder and Richard Fausset, "Clerk Who Said 'No' Won't Be Alone in Court," *New York Times*, September 2, 2015, http://www.nytimes.com/2015/09/03/us/kentucky-rowan-county-clerk-kim-davis-denies-marriage-license.html?_r=0 (reporting that Liberty Counsel is representing Kim Davis pro bono).

89. Alan Blinder and Richard Pérez-Peña, "Kentucky Clerk Denies Same-Sex Marriage Licenses, Defying Court," *New York Times*, September 1, 2015, http://www.nytimes.com/2015/09/02/us/same-sex-marriage-kentucky-kim-davis.html.

90. Blinder and Fausset, "Clerk Who Said 'No' Won't Be Alone" (quoting Molly Criner, clerk in Irion County, Texas).

91. "North Carolina: Suit Filed Over Marriage Recusal Law," *New York Times*, December 10, 2015, at A26.

92. Ibid.

93. *McCarthy v. Liberty Ridge Farm*, Recommended Findings of Fact, Opinion and Decision and Order, Case No. 10157952 (N.Y. Division of Human Rights).

94. Ibid. See *Gifford v. McCarthy*, No. 520410, ___ N.Y.S.3d ___, 2016 WL 155543 (N.Y. App. Div. January 14, 2016) (affirming ALJ). For press coverage, see Sarah Pullam Bailey, "Farm Owners Fined for Saying No to Lesbian Wedding," *Religious News Service*, August 19, 2014, http://www.washingtonpost.com/national/religion/farm-owners-fined-for-saying-no-to-lesbian-wedding/2014/08/19/1cfe5ca2-27dd-11e4-8b10-7db129976abb_story.html.

95. Laycock, "Religious Liberty," 879. Also see Robin Fretwell Wilson, et al. to Gov. John Baldacci, "Religious Liberty Implications of S.P. 384," May 1, 2009, http://mirrorofjustice.blogs.com/files/sp-384-me-letter-to-governor.pdf (in which the authors seek "marriage conscience protection").

96. *McCarthy v. Liberty Ridge Farm*, 11.

97. See, e.g., "NYCLU Victory: Wedding Venues Cannot Discriminate against Same-Sex Couples," *NYCLU*, August 14, 2014, http://www.nyclu.org/news/nyclu-victory-wedding-venues-cannot-discriminate-against-same-sex-couples (quoting NYCLU director Donna Lieberman); Bailey, "Farm Owners Fined" (quoting Adam Winkler).

98. Davey and Smith, "Indiana Governor, Feeling Backlash."

99. Lori, "Address on Religious Liberty," 5.

100. Defense of Marriage Act, H.R. Rep. 104-664, 104th Cong. 2d Sess, at 2.

101. *Goodridge v. Department of Public Health*, 798 N.E.2d 941 (Mass. 2003).

102. Ibid., 958–959.

103. At the time the US Supreme Court reviewed Edith Windsor's challenge to DOMA, the majority opinion noted that eleven states and the District of Columbia allowed same-sex couples to marry. *United States v. Windsor*, 133 S. Ct. 2675 (2013).

104. See *Windsor v. United States*, 833 F. Supp. 2d 394, 398–400 (S.D.N.Y. 2012), aff'd, 699 F.3d 169 (2d Cir. 2012) (concluding that New York, "through its executive agencies and appellate courts, uniformly recognized Windsor's [out of state] marriage" in 2009, when she paid federal estate taxes).

105. See, e.g., *Massachusetts v. US Dept. of Health and Human Services*, 682 F.3d 1, 6–7, 15–16 (1st Cir. 2012) (detailing lawsuits challenging Section 3 brought by Massachusetts couples and by the Commonwealth of Massachusetts; affirming lower court ruling finding Section 3 unconstitutional).

106. John Flynn, "The End of Religious Liberty."

107. Attorney General Eric Holder to Rep. John Boehner, "Letter from the Attorney General to Congress on Litigation Involving the Defense of Marriage Act," February 23, 2011, 1.

108. This is a bit of a misnomer since the two Democrats in this five-member group declined to participate in defending DOMA.

109. The four factors are: "(1) whether the group in question has suffered a history of discrimination; (2) whether individuals 'exhibit obvious, immutable, or distinguishing characteristics that define them as a discrete group'; (3) whether the group is a minority or is politically powerless; and (4) whether the characteristics distinguishing the group have little relation to legitimate policy objectives or to an individual's 'ability to perform or contribute to society.'" Ibid., 2.

110. Quoting *Lawrence v. Texas*, 539 US 558, 578 (2003).

111. Quoting *Bowen v. Gilliard*, 438 US 587, 602–603 [1987]; *City of Cleburne v. Cleburne Living Center*, 473 US 432, 441–442 (1985).
112. Quoting *Frontiero v. Richardson*, 411 US 677, 686 (1973).
113. Quoting H.R. Rep. No. 104-664, at 13.
114. Quoting *Romer v. Evans*, 517 US 620, 635 (1996); *Cleburne*, 473 US at 448, *Palmore v. Sidoti*, 466 US 429, 433 (1984).
115. *Windsor v. United States*, 833 F. Supp. 2d 394, 397 (S.D.N.Y. 2012).
116. They registered as domestic partners in New York City in 1993, "as soon as that option became available." Ibid.
117. *Windsor v. United States*, 699 F.3d 169, 176 (2d Cir. 2012). The judge was Chief Judge Dennis Jacobs.
118. Ibid., 181.
119. Ibid., 180–181.
120. There were 80 amicus curiae briefs filed in *Windsor*: 32 in support of respondent BLAG, 46 in support of respondent Windsor, and 2 in support of neither party. Some organizations filed the identical brief in both the *Windsor* and *Hollingsworth* cases. For more information, see Preview of the United States Supreme Court Cases, *US v. Edith Schlain Windsor*, Docket No. 12-307, www.americanbar.org/publications/preview_home/12-307.html; also see Supreme Court Information, *US v. Windsor*, www.supremecourt.gov/Search.aspx?Filename=/docketfiles/12-307.htm. I joined an amicus brief filed in support of *Windsor*, Brief of Amici Curiae Family and Child Welfare Law Professors Supporting Respondents, *United States v. Windsor*, 133 S. Ct. 2675 (2013), as well as amicus briefs filed by this group in lower court proceedings in the DOMA litigations.
121. McClain, "From *Romer v. Evans* to *United States v. Windsor*," 430–460. This section of the chapter incorporates some of that analysis.
122. Brief for Robert P. George, et al. as Amici Curiae Supporting Hollingsworth and Bipartisan Legal Advisory Group (Addressing the Merits and Supporting Reversal) at 5–6, *Hollingsworth v. Perry*, 570 US __, 133 S. Ct. 2652 (2013) and *Windsor*, 133 S. Ct. 2675 (2013) (Nos. 12-144 & 12-307).
123. Ibid., 5.
124. Ibid., 15.
125. See Brief for National Association of Evangelicals, et al., as Amici Curiae Supporting Bipartisan Legal Advisory Group of the United States House of Representatives (Addressing the Merits), *Windsor*, 133 S. Ct.
126. NAE brief is quoting *Board of Education of Westside County Schools (Dist. 66) v. Mergens*, 496 US 226, 248 (1990), which is in turn quoting *McDaniel v. Paty*, 435 US 618, 641 (1978) (Brennan, J., concurring in judgment).
127. See, e.g., Brief for Liberty Counsel Brief as Amici Curiae Supporting Respondent Bipartisan Liberty Advisory Group at 36, *Windsor*, 133 S. Ct. (quoting O'Connor, J., concurring, *Lawrence v. Texas*, 539 US 558, 585 [2003]); Brief for Manhattan Declaration as Amicus Curiae Supporting Respondent Bipartisan Legal Advisory Group at n. 15, *Windsor*, 133 S. Ct. (quoting ibid.).
128. Brief for Manhattan Declaration at 3, *Windsor*, 133 S. Ct.
129. Brief for the Coalition for the Protection of Marriage as Amicus Curiae Supporting Hollingsworth and Bipartisan Legal Advisory Group (Addressing the Merits and Supporting Reversal) at 35, *Hollingsworth v. Perry*, 570 US __, 133 S. Ct. 2652 (2013) (quoting Brief for Judge Georg Ress and the Marriage Law Foundation as Amici Curiae Supporting Petitioners at 2, *Hollingsworth*, 133 S. Ct. 2652).
130. Brief for the Coalition for the Protection of Marriage at 6–7, *Hollingsworth*, 133 S. Ct.
131. Brief for Manhattan Declaration at 6–7, *Windsor*, 133 S. Ct.
132. See Brief for Westboro Baptist Church as Amicus Curiae Supporting Neither Party (Suggesting Reversal) at 13–20, *Windsor*, 133 S. Ct.
133. Brief for Foundation for Moral Law as Amicus Curiae Supporting Respondent Bipartisan Legal Advisory Group at 3, *Windsor*, 133 S. Ct.
134. Ibid.

135. Brief for the Becket Fund for Religious Liberty as Amicus Curiae Supporting Hollingsworth and the Bipartisan Legal Advisory Group (On the Merits) at 29, *Windsor*, 133 S. Ct.
136. Brief for Catholic Answers, Christian Legal Society, and Catholic Vote Education as Amici Curiae Supporting Respondent Bipartisan Legal Advisory Group (Addressing the Merits and Supporting Reversal) at 4, *Windsor*, 133 S. Ct.
137. Ibid.
138. Brief for Chaplain Alliance for Religious Liberty, et al. as Amici Curiae Supporting the Bipartisan Legal Advisory Group (Addressing the Merits & Supporting Reversal) at 3–4, *Windsor*, 133 S. Ct.
139. Ibid., 4–5.
140. Brief for Manhattan Declaration at 3–4, *Windsor*, 133 S. Ct.
141. Brief for Liberty, Life, and Law Foundation and North Carolina Values Coalition as Amici Curiae Supporting Hollingsworth and Respondent Bipartisan Legal Advisory Group (Addressing the Merits and Supporting Reversal) at 16, *Windsor*, 133 S. Ct.
142. Ibid., 17.
143. Ibid., 15–16.
144. Brief for the Bishops of the Episcopal Church in the States of California, Connecticut, Iowa, Maine, Maryland, Massachusetts, New Hampshire, New York, Vermont, and Washington and the District of Columbia, et al. as Amici Curiae Supporting Respondent Edith Schlain Windsor at 3, *Windsor*, 133 S. Ct.
145. Brief for the American Humanist Association and American Atheists, Inc., et al. as Amici Curiae Supporting Respondents (Addressing the Merits) at 4, *Windsor*, 133 S. Ct.
146. Ibid.
147. Brief for the Anti-Defamation League, et al. as Amici Curiae Supporting Respondent Edith Windsor at 19, *Windsor*, 133 S. Ct. (citing *Lawrence v. Texas*, 539 US 558, 574–575 [2003]).
148. Brief for Utah Pride Center, Campaign for Southern Equality, Equality Federation and Twenty-Five State-Wide Equality Organizations as Amici Curiae at 30, *Windsor*, 133 S. Ct.
149. Ibid.
150. Ibid.
151. See Brief for the American Jewish Committee as Amicus Curiae Supporting Individual Respondents (On the Merits) at 3–4, *Windsor*, 133 S. Ct.
152. *Windsor*, 133 S. Ct. at 2693.
153. Quoting H.R. Rep. No. 104-664, 12–13 (1996).
154. See Fleming and McClain, *Ordered Liberty*, 190–205 (elaborating a view of marriage as securing rights and responsibilities and allowing various substantive moral goods).
155. Citing *Lawrence v. Texas*, 539 US 558, 558 (2003).
156. Steven D. Smith, "The Jurisprudence of Denigration," *UC Davis Law Review* 48 (2014): 677, 700.
157. *Obergefell v. Hodges*, 135 S. Ct. 2584, 2602 (2015).
158. Justice Kennedy identifies four relevant "principles and traditions" that "demonstrate that the reasons marriage is fundamental under the Constitution apply with equal force to same-sex couples. Ibid., 2599.
159. *Hollingsworth v. Perry*, 570 US ___, 133 S. Ct. 2652 (2013).
160. Ibid., 2674.
161. Prop 22 (codified as Cal. Fam. Code § 308.5 [2000], and held unconstitutional by *In re Marriage Cases* 183 P.3d 384, 453 [Cal. 2008]).
162. *In re Marriage Cases* at 413, 414–416.
163. Ibid., 446, 452.
164. For an analysis of this case, see Fleming and McClain, *Ordered Liberty*, 190–199.
165. See Cal. Const. Art. I, § 7.5 ("Only marriage between a man and a woman is valid or recognized in California").
166. Nicholas Riccardi, "Mormons Feel the Backlash over Their Support of Prop. 8," *Los Angeles Times*, November 17, 2008 (accessed January 27, 2015), http://articles.latimes.com/2008/nov/17/nation/na-mormons17.
167. Robert D. Putnam and David E. Campbell, *American Grace: How Religion Divides and Unites Us*, pbbk. ed. (New York: Simon and Schuster, 2012), 365.

168. First Presidency of the Church of Jesus Christ of Latter-day Saints, "Preserving Traditional Marriage and Strengthening Families," letter to Church leaders in California, June 29, 2008, http://www.mormonnewsroom.org/article/california-and-same-sex-marriage.

169. Putnam and Campbell, *American Grace*, 365.

170. Ibid.

171. *Perry v. Schwarzenegger*, 704 F. Supp. 2d 921, 930–932 (N.D. Cal. 2010). Also ibid., 991.

172. "Honest Answers to Questions Many Californians Are Asking about Proposition 8," ProtectMarriage.com, advertisement, November 2, 2008, https://ecf.cand.uscourts.gov/cand/09cv2292/evidence/PX2153.pdf.

173. *Perry*, 704 F. Supp. at 1002.

174. Indeed, in his *Obergefell* dissent (2613), Chief Justice Roberts explains the origin and purpose of marriage as "ensuring that children are conceived by a mother and father committed to raising them in the stable conditions of a lifelong relationships."

175. *Perry*, 704 F. Supp. at 932, 935, 956, 963.

176. Richard Garnett, "Wrongful Discrimination? Religious Freedom, Pluralism, and Equality" (this volume).

177. *Perry*, 704 F. Supp. at 1001.

178. Quoting *Romer v. Evans*, 517 US 620, 634 (1996).

179. Quoting *Palmore v. Sidoti*, 466 US 429, 433 (1984).

180. *Perry v. Brown*, 671 F. 3d 1052, 1092 (9th Cir. 2012) (quoting *Strauss v. Horton*, 207 P. 3d at 76 [2009]).

181. Quoting *Lawrence v. Texas*, 539 US 558, 577–578 (2003) and citing *Loving v. Virginia*, 388 US 1 (1967).

182. See, e.g., *Bishop v. U.S.*, 962 F. Supp. 2d 1252, 1279 (N.D. Okla. 2014), *aff'd*, *Bishop v. Smith*, 760 F.3d 1070 (10th Cir. 2014); *Bostic v. Rainey*, 970 F. Supp. 2d 456, 476 (E.D. Va. 2014), *aff'd*, *Bostic v. Schaefer*, 760 F. 3d 352 (4th Cir. 2014) (quoting *Bishop*).

183. Daniel Burke, "Mormon Church Backs LGBT Rights—With One Condition," CNN.com, February 23, 2015, http://www.cnn.com/2015/01/27/us/mormon-church-lgbt-laws/.

184. Ross Douhat, "The Terms of Our Surrender," *New York Times*, March 1, 2014, http://www.nytimes.com/2014/03/02/opinion/sunday/the-terms-of-our-surrender.html?_r=0 (urging compromise).

185. Ibid. See also Terry Kleeman, letter to the editor, *New York Times*, March 7, 2014, http://www.nytimes.com/2014/03/08/opinion/the-holdouts-on-same-sex-marriage.html (critiquing Douhat; asking if Jim Crow laws were "an acceptable accommodation to the religious beliefs of white supremacy" and asserting that "fortunately, by the time we got around to legalizing interracial marriage, we had had enough" and "no one was permitted to discriminate against interracial couples" lest they face a civil rights prosecution).

186. Ryan T. Anderson, "We Don't Need Kim Davis to Be in Jail," *New York Times*, September 7, 2015, http://www.nytimes.com/2015/09/07/opinion/we-dont-need-kim-davis-to-be-in-jail.html.

187. See, e.g., Jeremy Grey, "Is Kim Davis the New Rosa Parks or George Wallace," http://www.al.com/news/index.ssf/2015/09/is_kim_davis_the_new_rosa_park.html.

188. "Statement Calling for Constitutional Resistance."

189. *Employment Division v. Smith*, 494 U.S. 872, 879 (1990). In view of Justice Scalia's repeated critiques of *Obergefell* as anti-democratic and trampling the religious beliefs of the majority, some commentators have recently argued that Justice Scalia supported a "majoritarian theocracy." Richard J. Posner and Eric J. Segall, "Justice Scalia's Majoritarian Theocracy," *New York Times*, December 2, 2015, http://www.nytimes.com/2015/12/03/opinion/justice-scalias-majoritarian-theocracy.html.

190. *Brenner v. Scott*, 999 F. Supp. 2d 1278 (N.D. Fla. 2014).

Chapter 6

1. See Jana Singer, "Balancing Away Marriage Equality," *SCOTUSblog*, August 29, 2011, http://www.scotusblog.com/2011/08/balancing-away-marriage-equality. She suggests that "broad-based exemptions are both constitutionally problematic and politically unwise." If Professor Singer's over-accommodation argument were correct, thousands of state and federal religious

statutory accommodations would be invalidated—from military conscientious objection provisions to Native American peyote use, which received statutory exemption in response to *Employment Division v. Smith*, 494 US 872, 890 (1990). See generally Michael W. McConnell, "The Problem of Singling Out Religion," *DePaul Law Review* 50 (2010): 1–47 (discussing the extent of existing religious liberty accommodations).

2. Matthew J. Franck, "Is Sex Just Like Race?" *The Public Discourse*, July 8, 2011, http://www.thepublicdiscourse.com/2011/07/3520 ("Today it is those claiming a specious 'freedom to marry'" who make a claim at odds with the institution's nature and alien to its purposes. It is they who would instrumentalize it by a redefinition, a destroying and remaking, that puts marriage to a new kind of work in the service of state policy.").

3. *United States v. Windsor*, 133 S. Ct. 2675, 2696 (2013) (holding that the Fifth Amendment requires the federal government to recognize same-sex marriages that are valid under state law). See also *Hollingsworth v. Perry*, 133 S. Ct. 2652, 2668 (2013) (reinstating the federal district court decision invalidating Proposition 8).

4. When this chapter was first written, the Supreme Court had agreed to review the constitutionality of same-sex marriage—on January 16, 2015, it granted certiorari in the case of *Obergefell v. Hodges*, 576 US ___, (2015), 135 S. Ct. 1039 (2015), which concerned two questions: first, whether the 14th Amendment requires states to license a marriage between two people of the same sex; and second, whether the 14th Amendment requires states to recognize a marriage between two people of the same sex that was lawfully performed in another state—but had not yet released its decision. As is widely known, on June 26, 2015 the Court declared same-sex marriage a constitutional right. Due to timing, however, this chapter does not fully address the broad implications that this ruling will undoubtedly have on American culture, politics, and law.

5. See Appendix 6.B; see generally Wilson, "Marriage of Necessity," supra note *.

6. Robin Fretwell Wilson, "Symposium: The Human Costs of Staying Out of the Marriage Debate," *SCOTUSblog*, October 7, 2014, http://www.scotusblog.com/2014/10/symposium-the-human-costs-of-staying-out-of-the-marriage-debate/ [hereinafter "Human Costs"].

7. See *Obergefell v. Hodges*, 135 S. Ct. 2584 (2015); Robert Barnes, "Supreme Court Agrees to Hear Gay Marriage Issue," *Washington Post*, January 16, 2015, http://www.washingtonpost.com/politics/courts_law/supreme-court-agrees-to-hear-gay-marriage-issue/2015/01/16/865149ec-9d96-11e4-a7ee-526210d665b4_story.html. See also Adam Liptak, "Supreme Court to Decide Marriage Rights for Gay Couples Nationwide," *New York Times*, January 16, 2015, http://www.nytimes.com/2015/01/17/us/supreme-court-to-decide-whether-gays-nationwide-can-marry.html.

8. A January 2015 nationwide poll found that "44 percent of Americans favor . . . legal same-sex marriage in their own states." See GfK Public Affairs and Corporate Communications, "The AP-GfK Poll: January, 2015," (2015), http://ap-gfkpoll.com/main/wp-content/uploads/2015/02/AP-GfK_Poll_January_2015_Topline_marriage.pdf (conducting a web-based survey of a representative sample of the United States, in which households with computers and Internet services participated with their own equipment and those that did not have such equipment and access received the needed equipment); Emily Swanson and Brady McCombs, "AP-GfK Poll: Support of Gay Marriage Comes with Caveats," *Associated Press*, February 5, 2015, http://ap-gfkpoll.com/featured/findings-from-our-latest-poll-13 (reporting that "39 percent oppose legal same-sex marriage in their own states") [hereinafter "AP-GfK Poll"].

9. See Part I.B.1.

10. See Part I.B.1.

11. AP-GfK Poll, supra note 9.

12. See Anthony Kreis and Robin Fretwell Wilson, "Embracing Compromise: Marriage Equality and Religious Liberty in the Political Process," *Georgetown Journal of Gender and the Law* 15, no. 2 (2014): 485–542 [hereinafter "Embracing Compromise"] (summarizing interviews with legislators about the role of religious liberty protections in enacting marriage equality legislation and presenting close vote counts in numerous jurisdictions).

13. See infra Appendix 6.C for states that recognized same-sex marriage as of November 11, 2014.

14. See Judy Harrison, "Mainers Approve Gay Marriage Referendum," *Bangor Daily News* (ME), November 6, 2012, http://bangordailynews.com/2012/11/06/politics/both-sides-of-gay-marriage-question-optimistic-as-polls-close/. In 2009, the Maine legislature passed a same-sex marriage bill later repealed by voter referendum. Maine voters enacted same-sex marriage by ballot initiative in 2012. See Appendix 6.C.

15. David Eggert, "Michigan's Balking at Anti-Gay Discrimination Law," *Crux*, September 19, 2014, http://www.cruxnow.com/life/2014/09/19/barring-anti-gay-discrimination-tenuous-in-capitol/. For a listing of sexual orientation non-discrimination laws, see "Marriage of Necessity," Tbls. A2, A4 supra note *.

16. David Callahan, "No One Left Behind: Tim Gill and the New Quest for Full LGBT Equality," *InsidePhilanthropy*, November 19, 2015, http://www.insidephilanthropy.com/home/2015/8/25/no-one-left-behind-tim-gill-and-the-new-quest-for-full-lgbt.html.

17. Rachel Zoll, "Next Gay Marriage Fight: Religious Exemptions," *Associated Press*, October 14, 2014, http://bigstory.ap.org/article/de029a0e8b7145e1bd84e15a9ff91a1c/next-gay-marriage-fight-religious-exemptions (discussing Utah State Rep. Jacob Anderegg's plan to reintroduce a religious exemptions bill allowing anyone authorized to solemnize marriages to refuse same-sex couples on religious grounds).

18. S.B. 296 Antidiscrimination and Religious Freedom Amendments, Utah St. Legislature, http://le.utah.gov/~2015/bills/static/SB0296.html (accessed March 22, 2015); S.B. 297 Second Substitute Protections for Religious Expression and Beliefs About Marriage, Family, or Sexuality, Utah St. Legislature, http://le.utah.gov/~2015/bills/static/SB0297.html (accessed March 22, 2015).

19. LB586—Prohibit Discrimination Based Upon Sexual Orientation and Gender Identity, Nebraska St. Legislature, http://nebraskalegislature.gov/bills/view_bill.php?DocumentID=24833 (accessed March 22, 2015).

20. For a discussion of how legislative behavior is governed by powerful, vocal (and sometimes minority) constituent groups, see Cindy Handler, "Friends Don't Let Friends Discriminate," *Huffington Post*, May 9, 2011, http://www.huffingtonpost.com/cindy-handler/friendfactor-gay-marriage-legislation_b_858857.html.

21. See Appendix 6.A.

22. *Obergefell v. Hodges*, 135 S. Ct. 2584, 2626 (2015) ("Unfortunately, people of faith can take no comfort in the treatment they receive from the majority today.").

23. Whether the LGBT community can secure non-discrimination protections through litigation is a live question. For competing views on whether LGBT status will or can be recognized as a suspect classification, see generally William N. Eskridge, Jr., "Is Political Powerlessness a Requirement for Heightened Equal Protection Scrutiny?" *Washburn Law Journal* 50 (2010): 1–32 (noting the arguments against considering sexual orientation a suspect classification); Courtney A. Powers, "Finding LGBTs a Suspect Class: Assessing the Political Power of LGBTs as a Basis for the Court's Application of Heightened Scrutiny," *Duke Journal of Gender Law and Policy* 17 (2010): 385–398 (2010) (arguing that LGBT persons should be considered a suspect class).

24. See supra notes 14 and 15.

25. See Wilson, "Human Costs," supra note 6.

26. E.g., Christine Mai-Duc, "Florist Who Rejected Same-Sex Wedding Job Broke Washington Law, Judge Rules," *Los Angeles Times*, February 18, 2015, http://www.latimes.com/nation/nationnow/la-na-nn-florist-same-sex-wedding-20150218-story.html; Abby Ohlheiser, "This Colorado Baker Refused to Put an Anti-Gay Message on Cakes. Now She Is Facing a Civil Rights Complaint," *Washington Post*, January 28, 2015, http://www.washingtonpost.com/news/post-nation/wp/2015/01/22/this-colorado-baker-refused-to-put-an-anti-gay-message-on-cakes-now-she-is-facing-a-civil-rights-complaint/; Samuel Smith, "Four More North Carolina Judges Resign over Refusal to Conduct Same-Sex Weddings," *Christian Post*, October 30, 2014, http://www.christianpost.com/news/four-more-north-carolina-judges-resign-over-refusal-to-conduct-same-sex-weddings-128890/.

27. Joel Benenson and Amy Levin to Interested Parties, "Recent Utah Poll Results," memorandum, September 26, 2014, http://freemarry.3cdn.net/f24d394cb3c9bdb591_8gm6bxgau.pdf (finding that 49% of Utahans favored and 48% were against same-sex marriage without

religious protections, but 60% of Utahans supported, and only 34% opposed, same-sex marriage with religious protections).

28. AP-GfK Poll, supra note 9.

29. Kathleen Gray, "Religious Freedom Bill Passes out of Michigan House," *Detroit Free Press*, December 7, 2014, http://www.freep.com/story/news/local/michigan/2014/12/04/michigan-religious-freedom-bill-moves-house/19889979/.

30. See Sam Stein, "Obama Backs Gay Marriage," *Huffington Post*, May 9, 2012, http://www.huffingtonpost.com/2012/05/09/obama-gay-marriage_n_1503245.html.

31. The *National Journal* excluded California and Hawaii when it tallied 29 states with constitutional amendments banning same-sex marriage. See Julie Sobel, "North Carolina Voters Approve Same-Sex Marriage Ban," *National Journal*, May 8, 2012, http://www.nationaljournal.com/politics/north-carolina-voters-approve-same-sex-marriage-ban-20120508. California and Hawaii both now recognize same-sex marriage. See Appendix 6.C.

32. See Melissa Rogers, "Obama and the Two Types of Marriage," *Huffington Post*, May 17, 2012, http://www.huffingtonpost.com/melissa-rogers/civil-and-religious-marriage-and-obama_b_1521981.html.

33. See Will Brooks, "NC Speaker Visits Campus," *Technician Online*, March 25, 2012, http://www.technicianonline.com/article_1e7f2d15-68d8-5671-a44f-1c57f539c724.html (describing same-sex marriage as "a generational issue"). North Carolina voters approved Amendment 1 on May 8, 2012, by a margin of 61% to 39%. See Rachel Weiner, "North Carolina Passes Gay Marriage Ban Amendment One," *Washington Post*, May 8, 2012, http://www.washingtonpost.com/blogs/the-fix/post/north-carolina-passes-gay-marriage-ban-amendment-one/2012/05/08/gIQAHYpfBU_blog.html. On October 10, 2014, a federal judge struck down Amendment 1, bringing same-sex marriage to North Carolina. See Appendix 6.C.

34. See supra note 9.

35. This tally does not count Oregon, which began allowing same-sex marriages after Judge Michael McShane struck Oregon's constitutional ban on May 19, 2014, without issuing a stay. Rebecca Nelson, "How 2014 Was the Beginning of the End for the Gay-Marriage Fight," *National Journal*, December 17, 2014, http://www.national journal.com/domesticpolicy/how-2014-was-the-beginning-of-the-end-for-the-gay-marriage-fight-20141217.

36. See "Human Costs," supra note 6 (explaining how the Court's November 2014 refusal to review a same-sex marriage case left in place now-authoritative last words on the issue by three federal Circuit Courts of Appeals).

37. See Appendix 6.B. Connecticut's law followed the Connecticut Supreme Court decision in *Kerrigan et al. v. Commissioner of Public Health*, 957 A.2d 407 (2008), requiring the state to recognize same-sex marriage. Maine's 2009 same-sex marriage law, which contained a clergy-only exemption, was repealed in a "people's referendum." See Appendix 6.C. Maine later recognized same-sex marriage by ballot with religious liberty protections. See Appendix 6.B.

38. See supra note 32.

39. At the end of 2012, eight states still had state Defense of Marriage Acts ("DOMA"). See "Same-Sex Marriage, State by State," *Pew Research Center*, June 26, 2015, http://www.pewforum.org/2015/06/26/same-sex-marriage-state-by-state/ (select 2012 as the year on the interactive map).

40. Nelson, supra note 36; Figure 6.1; Appendix 6.C.

41. See Appendix 6.B; Appendix 6.C.

42. See Appendix 6.C.

43. See Appendix 6.C for Massachusetts, Iowa, New Jersey, and New Mexico. In Connecticut, following the *Kerrigan* decision, the legislature enacted same-sex marriage legislation.

44. See Joel Connelly, "Gregoire Signs Same-Sex Marriage Bill," *Seattle Post-Intelligencer* (WA), February 13, 2012, http://www.seattlepi.com/local/connelly/article/Make-History-Gregoire-signs-same-sex-marriage-3312315.php; Aaron Davis, "Maryland Senate Passes Same-Sex Marriage Bill," *Washington Post*, February 24, 2012, http://www.washingtonpost.com/local/md-politics/maryland-senate-passes-same-sex-marriage-bill/2012/02/23/gIQAfbakWR_story.html.

45. Davis, supra note 47, "Maryland Senate Passes Same-Sex Marriage Bill."

46. Rachel La Corte, "Gay Marriage Opponents Closer to Qualifying R-74," *Seattle Times*, May 9, 2012, http://www.seattletimes.com/seattle-news/gay-marriage-opponents-closer-to-qualifying-r-74/; Annie Linskey, "Same-Sex Marriage Opponents Gather Twice the Signatures Needed for Referendum," *Baltimore Sun*, May 29, 2012, http://articles.baltimoresun.com/2012-05-29/news/bs-md-same-sex-signatures-submitted-20120529_1_marriage-law-tuition-law-marriage-opponents.

47. Maryland's legislation survived by a 52% to 48% margin of support, while Washington's enjoyed a 53% to 47% margin of support. See "Minnesota Amendment 1 Same-Sex Marriage Ballot Measure Fails," *Huffington Post*, November 7, 2012, http://www.huffingtonpost.com/2012/11/07/minnesota-amendment-1-results-2012_n_2050310.html.

48. See infra notes 60–68.

49. David Eggert, supra note 16, "Michigan's Balking at Anti-Gay Discrimination Law." For a listing of sexual orientation non-discrimination laws, see "Marriage of Necessity," Tbls. A2, A4, supra note *.

50. Andrew R. Flores, "National Trends in Public Opinion on LGBT Rights in the United States," *The Williams Institute*, 6, http://williamsinstitute.law.ucla.edu/wp-content/uploads/POP-natl-trends-nov-2014.pdf (aggregating results from over 300 surveys over 37 years).

51. In 1978, only 30% of Americans thought lesbians and gays faced "a lot of discrimination." Today, 71% of Americans believe transgender individuals face a great deal of discrimination. Ibid.

52. Human Rights Campaign and Greenberg Quinlan Rosner Research to Interested Parties, "A Giant Step Forward on the Road to Equality, But Still Progress to Be Made" memorandum, July 26, 2011, http://hrc-assets.s3-website-us-east-1.amazonaws.com//files/assets/resources/HRCsummer2011pollmemo.pdf (79% in 2011 favored protections).

53. Flores, "National Trends in Public Opinion on LGBT Rights in the United States," 6–7; Robert P. Jones, Daniel Cox, and Juhem Navarro-Rivera, "A Shifting Landscape: A Decade of Change in American Attitudes about Same-Sex Marriage and LGBT Issues," *Public Religion Research Institute*, February 26, 2014, 34, http://publicreligion.org/site/wp-content/uploads/2014/02/2014.LGBT_79% in 2011REPORT.pdf. High levels of support may reflect the mistaken supposition held by 75% of Americans that federal law presently bans an employer from firing or refusing to hire an LGBT individual because of their sexual orientation.

54. It is unclear that LGBT individuals will be able to secure non-discrimination protections through litigation if courts do not consider them a suspect class under equal protection doctrine. See generally Bertrall L. Ross II and Su Li, "Measuring Political Power: Suspect Class Determinations and the Poor," *California Law Review* 104 (2016), published electronically February 25, 2015, http://poseidon01.ssrn.com/delivery.php?ID= 8380690700930670800 28103111005016 (providing an empirical assessment of group political power as it relates to suspect class determinations); supra note 244.

55. Rachel Zoll, "Next Gay Marriage Fight: Religious Exemptions," *Associated Press*, October 14, 2014, http://bigstory.ap.org/article/de029a0e8b7145e1bd84e15a9ff91a1c/next-gay-marriage-fight-religious-exemptions.

56. The Church of Jesus Christ of Latter-day Saints, "Transcript of News Conference on Religious Freedom and Nondiscrimination," Official Statement, January 27, 2015, http://www.mormonnewsroom.org/article/publicstatement-on-religious-freedom-and-nondiscrimination.

57. Ben Winslow, "There Could Be One Big Bill in Utah on Gay Rights and Religious Liberties," *Fox 13 Salt Lake City*, February 11, 2015, http://fox13now.com/2015/02/11/there-could-be-one-big-bill-in-utah-on-gay-rights-and-religious-liberties/.

58. William A. Galston, "Utah Shows the Way on Gay Rights," *Wall Street Journal*, March 17, 2015, http://www.wsj.com/articles/william-a-galston-utah-shows-the-way-on-gay-rights-1426633856.

59. S.B. 296, 61st Leg., 2015 Gen. Sess. (Utah 2015).

60. Utah Code Ann. § 63G-20-201; Utah Code Ann. § 17-20-4; SB297, lines 195–198, 73–79; Galston, supra note 62. For a high profile refusal, see Ryan Felton, "Kentucky Clerk Kim Davis Released from Jail After Judge Lifts Contempt Ruling," September 8, 2015, GUARDIAN; Eyder Peralta, "Just Before Big Rally, Kim Davis is Released from Jail," September

8, 2015, NPR, http://www.npr.org/sections/thetwo-way/2015/09/08/438587612/hours-before-big-rally-judge-orders-kim-davis-released.

61. Utah Code Ann. § 63G-20-203; Utah Code Ann. § 63G-20-204; SB297, lines 209–219.

62. Utah Code Ann. § 34A-5_112; SB 296, lines 700–706.

63. Utah Code Ann. § 34A-5-112; SB 296, lines 695–699.

64. Galston, supra note 62.

65. Harry Bruinius, "Hoston's Angry Debate Over Gay Rights Can Be Avoided. Here's How," *Christian Science Monitor* November 5, 2015, http://www.csmonitor.com/USA/Politics/2015/1105/Houston-s-angry-debate-over-gay-rights-can-be-avoided.-Here-s-how.

66. Robin Fretwell Wilson, "Op-ed: SB296 Comes in the American Tradition of Live and Let Live," *Salt Lake Tribune (UT)*, March 7, 2015, http://www.sltrib.com/opinion/2255002-155/op-ed-sb296-comes-in-the-american.

67. Editorial Board, "Expanding Gay Rights: Utah's Smart Compromise," *Boston Globe*, March 20, 2015, http://www.bostonglobe.com/opinion/editorials/2015/03/20/expanding-gay-rights-utah-smart-compromise/9mq0WnK1Axcten5Bc5bXTJ/story.html.

68. Michigan's paired bills to enact a state RFRA and ban discrimination based on one's status as lesbian, gay or bisexual individual came apart over the failure to protect transgender individuals. See Kathleen Gray, "Michigan Religious Freedom Bill Stalls in Lame-Duck Session," *Detroit Free Press (IL)*, December 17, 2014, http://www.freep.com/story/news/local/michigan/2014/12/17/religious-freedom-bill-likely-dies-year/20561539/; James Chilton, "Anti-Discrimination Bill Passes Second Reading in Wyoming Senate," *Casper Star (WY) Tribune*, February 10, 2015, http://trib.com/news/state-and-regional/govt-and-politics/anti-discrimination-bill-passes-second-reading-in-wyoming-senate/article_d89bb369-0755-5bf4-8c1d-3266be685eed.html. In Wyoming, the Wyoming House killed the bill.

69. LB586—Prohibit Discrimination Based Upon Sexual Orientation and Gender Identity, Nebraska Legislature, http://nebraskalegislature.gov/bills/view_bill.php?DocumentID=24833 (last visited November 19, 2015); Legislative Journal—February 12, 2015, http://nebraskalegis-lature.gov/FloorDocs/104/PDF/Journal/r1journal.pdf#page=521 (last visited November 19, 2015) (quoting committee amendment to LB586); Joe Duggan, "Sen. Bob Krist Flips on Anti-Bias Bill, Seeks Religious Exemptions," Omaha.com, February 11, 2015, http://www.omaha.com/news/legislature/sen-bob-krist-flips-on-anti-bias-bill-seeks-religious/article_04be61f5-c151-5bf7-b9ee-97ccc3925e8a.html; Joe Duggan, "LGBT Employment Discrimination Ban Advances out of Committee," Omaha.com, February 12, 2015, http://www.omaha.com/news/legislature/lgbt-employment-discrimination-ban-advances-out-of-committee/article_5cbefee5-dbda-545b-9d23-c7d49504eaf2.html?mode=jqm.

70. An Act to Amend the Indiana Code Concerning Civil Rights, 119th 2d. Reg. Sess. Gen. Assemb. (Ind. 2016), http://www.indianasenaterepublicans.com/clientuploads/Documents/2016%20Session/SB100_LS6175.pdf; Tony Cook, Stephanie Wang & Chelsea Schneider, "Republicans' LGBT Protections Bill Draws Criticism on Both Sides," *Indy Star* November 17, 2015, http://www.indystar.com/story/news/politics/2015/11/17/republicans-unveil-sexual-orientation-gender-identity-bill/75942498/; Tony Cook, Stephanie Wang & Chelsea Schneider, "Who's Protected—And Who's Not—in Indiana's LGBT, Religious Rights Bill," *Indy Star* November 18, 2015, http://www.indystar.com/story/news/politics/2015/11/18/whos-protected----and-whos-not----indianas-lgbt-religious-rights-bill/75996984/; Stphaine Wang, Tony Cook & Chelsea Schnieder, "Lawmaker Proposes Alternative Civil Rights Bill," *Indy Star* January 7, 2016, http://www.indystar.com/story/news/politics/2016/01/07/lawmaker-proposes-alternative-civil-rights-bill/78403942/.

71. See Kreis and Wilson, "Embracing Compromise," supra note 13 (noting that in all jurisdictions to enact same-sex marriage by legislation or referendum [with the exception of Minnesota and Delaware], the successful legislation resulted after unsuccessful attempts to enact same-sex marriage with purely symbolic religious liberty protection limited only to the clergy).

72. Marc Stern, "Same-Sex Marriage and the Churches," in *Same-Sex Marriage and Religious Liberty: Emerging Conflicts*, Douglas Laycock, Anthony R. Picarello, Jr., and Robin Fretwell Wilson, eds. (Lanham, MD: Rowan and Littlefield, 2008), 1–58 [hereinafter "Same-Sex Marriage and Religious Liberty"].

73. See Wilson, "Calculus of Accommodation," supra note *. This is not to say that all same-sex marriage bills that included some robust exemptions succeeded. See Kreis and Wilson, "Embracing Compromise," n. 90, supra note 13 (charting the evolution of Maryland's protections).

74. Maine's same-sex marriage law provided "protection" that was coterminous with constitutional guarantees. Me. Rev. Stat. Ann. tit. 19-A, § 650 (repealed November 3, 2009, by "people's veto"). It also provided protections for authorized celebrants, as the voluntary same-sex marriage states uniformly do. See Appendix 6.B.

75. Dale Carpenter, "There's Always Next Year," *The Volokh Conspiracy*, November 4, 2009, http://volokh.com/2009/11/04/theres-always-next-year/. Others chalk up the demise of Maine's same-sex marriage law to the vitriol in the referendum. Jeff Jacoby, "Wedded to Vitriol, Backers of Gay Marriage Stumble," *Boston Globe*, November 11, 2009, www.boston.com/bostonglobe/editorial_opinion/oped/articles/2009/11/11/wedded_to_vitriol_backers_of_gay_marriage_stumble/.

76. The strength of preference matters, of course. A voter could tend to favor religious liberty over LGBT rights, but not know how to weigh or evaluate evidence of a religious liberty impact. See supra notes 28 and 29. The real assay of whether religious liberty concerns move undecided citizens occurs when a referendum considers a bill with robust religious liberty protection, as occurred in Maryland and Washington. See supra note 50.

77. See "2012 General Election Results for Maine," *Bangor Daily News (ME)*, http://maineelections.bangordailynews.com/.

78. An Act to Allow Marriage Licenses for Same-Sex Couples and Protect Religious Freedom, LR 2840, 125th Leg., 2d Reg. Sess. (Ma. 2012), http://www.mainelegislature.org/legis/bills/bills_125th/billtexts/IB000301.asp.

79. Ibid.

80. Ibid.

81. Compare Robyn Burnham and Kristen Schulze Muszynski, "Is Same-Sex Marriage the Right Choice for Maine? A Look at the 'Yes on 1' and 'No on 1' Campaigns," *Journal Tribune (ME)*, November 5, 2012, http://www.journaltribune.com/articles/2012/11/03/features/doc509469d639361287963751.txt (reporting on the contours of the religious protections) with Judy Harrison, "Supporters Want a Wordier Same-Sex Marriage Question on November's Ballot," *Bangor Daily News (ME)*, June 20, 2012, http://bangordailynews.com/2012/06/20/politics/more-words-needed-in-same-sex-marriage-ballot-question-supporters-say/ (noting efforts to expand the ballot text to emphasize religious liberty protections and concerns, including discussion of possible risks to an objector's tax-exemption).

82. See "Yes On 1: Mainers United For Marriage—Pastor Michael Gray & Robyn Gray," YouTube Video, :30, posted by MainersUnited.org, September 11, 2012, https://www.youtube.com/watch?v=OIY_Hj72YWU (Mainers United advertisement explaining the religious protections in the proposed act); Adam Polaski, "Draft of Maine Ballot Question Fails to Convey True Mission of Initiative," Freedom to Marry, June 20, 2012, http://www.freedomtomarry.org/blog/entry/draft-of-maine-ballot-question-fails-to-convey-true-mission-of-initiative.

83. See Appendix 6.B. Maine's same-sex marriage law, which contained a clergy-only exemption, was repealed in a "people's referendum," while a similar measure passed the New Hampshire legislature only to be vetoed by Governor Lynch. See Kreis and Wilson, "Embracing Compromise," Part II.B1, supra note 13. The New Hampshire legislature subsequently amended the bill to include more robust exemptions and Governor Lynch then signed it into law.

84. See Appendix 6.B.

85. See Stern, supra note 76. In *Smith*, the United States Supreme Court concluded that neutral and generally applicable laws do not violate Free Exercise guarantees, no matter how much they burden an individual's or organization's exercise of religion. *Employment Division v. Smith*, 494 US 872, 890 (1990), *superseded by statute*, Religious Freedom Restoration Act, 42 U.S.C. § 2000bb(a)(4) (2006).

86. See Appendix 6.B.

87. See infra note 98.

88. See Central Conference of American Rabbis, "American Reform Responsa: 146. Reform Judaism and Mixed Marriage," XC (1980): 86–102. https://ccarnet.org/responsa/arr-445-465/.

89. These protections encompass "all" marriages, including interfaith marriages, second marriages, and same-sex marriages. See, e.g., N.Y. Dom. Rel. § 10-b ("Religious corporations . . . shall *not be required* to provide services, accommodations, advantages, facilities, goods, or privileges for the solemnization or celebration of *a marriage*"); Appendix 6.B.

90. Vt. Stat. Ann. tit. 9 § 4502(l) (2011). Some statutes also require "such solemnization, celebration, or promotion of marriage is in violation of his or her religious beliefs and faith." N.H. Rev. Stat. Ann. § 457:37(III) (2013). See Appendix 6.B.

91. See, e.g., Vt. Stat. Ann. tit. 9 § 4502(l) (2013); Vermont provides an exemption without specifying more. Also see Appendix 6.B.

92. See Appendix 6.B.

93. See Appendix 6.B.

94. See N.Y. Dom. Rel. § 10-b (1). See also N.H. Rev. Stat. Ann. § 457:37(III); Md. Code Ann. Fam. Law § 202-3(b); Minn. Stat. Ann. § 517.09(3)(b) (West Supp. 2013); R.I. Gen. Laws Ann. § 15-3-6.1(c)(2)(e) (LexisNexis 2013); Wash. Rev. Code § 7(a)(i).

95. See Del. Code Ann. tit. 13 § 106 (2013), http://delcode.delaware.gov/ title13/c001/sc01/index.shtml.

96. Wilson, "Calculus of Accommodation," 1480, supra note * (criticizing an "exemption for government employees or officials—unqualified by hardship—[as possibly] erect[ing] a roadblock to marriage").

97. *Employment Division v. Smith*, 494 US 872 (1990). The model accommodations in Appendix 6.A would also protect marriage license clerks and individuals in ordinary commerce—like bakers, photographers, caterers, musicians—who prefer for religious reasons to step aside from facilitating same-sex marriages when no hardship would result to same-sex couples.

98. See supra note 50.

99. See Don Lattin, "Charities Balk at Domestic Partner, Open Meeting Laws," *San Francisco Chronicle*, July 10, 1998, A-1, http://www.sfgate.com/news/article/Charities-Balk-at-Domestic-Partner-Open-Meeting-3001593.php.

100. See *Bernstein v. Ocean Grove Camp Meeting Ass'n*, Dkt. No. PN34XB-03008 (N.J. Dep't of Law & Pub. Safety, Notice of Probable Cause, December 29, 2008). The association rented "space at the Pavilion for weddings," had rented "wedding space to heterosexual couples irrespective of their tradition," and had never "inquire[d] into religious beliefs or practice because it did not sponsor, or otherwise control, these weddings," and thus violated New Jersey's Law Against Discrimination "when it refused to conduct a civil-union ceremony for" a same-sex couple. *Bernstein v. Ocean Grove Camp Meeting Ass'n*, O.A.L. Dkt. No. CRT 6145-09, at 6 (January 12, 2012). The federal courts refused to intervene. *Ocean Grove Camp Meeting Ass'n of the United Methodist Church v. Vespa-Papaleo*, 2007 WL 3349787 (November 7, 2007 D. N.J.); *aff'd*, 339 Fed. Appx. 232 (3rd Cir. 2009).

101. See Kreis and Wilson, "Embracing Compromise," supra note 13; Bill Bowman, "$20G Due in Tax on Boardwalk Pavilion," *Asbury Park (NJ) Press*, February 23, 2008. Although the loss of a tax exemption expressly conditioned upon "public access" to a parcel of land hardly seems unfair, tax-exempt religious groups fear that they may lose valuable benefits if their views of marriage become "disfavored."

    The exchange during oral arguments for *Obergefell* between, Justice Alito and Solicitor General Donald Verrilli about whether the tax exemption of a university opposed same-sex marriage might be revoked, as occurred in *Bob Jones University v. United States*, 461 U.S. 574 (1983), as a result of the University's ban on interracial dating, has only fueled fears. Sarah Pulliman Bailey, *Could Religious Institutions Lose Tax-Exempt Status Over Supreme Court's Gay Marriage Case?*, WASH. POST (Apr. 28, 2015), https://www.washingtonpost.com/news/acts-of-faith/wp/2015/04/28/could-religious-institutions-lose-tax-exempt-status-over-supreme-courts-gay-marriage-case/.

    IRS Commissioner John Koskinen's pledge that, as long as he is commissioner, he would not take any such action has done little to allay fears. *See* David Badash, *IRS: Religious*

Colleges Can Still Keep Tax-Exempt Status While Discriminating Against Gays, NEW CIVIL RIGHTS MOVEMENT (Aug. 3, 2015), http://www.thenewcivilrightsmovement.com/david-badash/irs_commits_to_allowing_religious_colleges_keep_tax_exempt_status_while_discriminating_against_gays. Professor Douglas Laycock believes that no "administration of either party would try to deny a tax exemption ... based on [a religious institution's] views on homosexuality" until "gay rights looks like race does today, where you have a handful of crackpots still resisting." Laurie Goodstein & Adam Liptak, *Schools Fear Gay Marriage Ruling Could End Tax Exemptions*, N.Y. TIMES (June 24, 2015), http://www.nytimes.com/2015/06/25/us/schools-fear-impact-of-gay-marriage-ruling-on-tax-status.html.

102. Paul Horwitz, Op-Ed., "Hobby Lobby Is Only the Beginning," *New York Times*, July 1, 2014, http://www.nytimes.com/2014/07/02/opinion/for-the-supreme-court-hobby-lobby-is-only-the-beginning.html.

103. See Robin Fretwell Wilson, "Bargaining for Religious Accommodations: What Hobby Lobby Portends for Same-Sex Marriage and LGBT Rights," in *The New Religious Institutionalism*, Zoë Robinson, Chad Flanders, and Micah Schwartzman, eds. (2016), 257–284.

104. See "Artist Hit for Refusal on Beliefs," *Washington Times*, February 25, 2008, http://www.washingtontimes.com/news/2008/feb/25/artist-hit-for-refusal-on-beliefs/.

105. See Appendix 6.C. New Mexico also did not recognize same-sex civil unions. See Christine Vestal, "California Gay Marriage Ruling Sparks New Debate," *Stateline*, May 16, 2008, http://www.stateline.org/live/ViewPage.action?siteNodeId=136&languageId=1&contentId=15576.

106. See *Elane Photography v. Willock*, 309 P.3d 53 (N.M. 2013).

107. George Rede, "Sweet Cakes Final Order: Gresham Bakery Must Pay $135,000 for Denying Service to Same-Sex Couple," July 2, 2015, Oregonian, *available at* http://www.oregonlive.com/business/index.ssf/2015/07/sweet_cakes_final_order_gresha.html.

108. Wayne T. Price, "Businesses walk fine line when accommodating disabilities," August 9, 2015, *Florida Today*, August 9, 2015, *available at* http://www.floridatoday.com/story/money/business/2015/08/09/businesses-walk-fine-line-accommodating-disabilities/31162465/.

109. *Goodridge v. Dep't of Pub. Health*, 798 N.E.2d 941 (Mass. 2003).

110. See Katie Zezima, "Obey Same-Sex Marriage Law, Officials Told," *New York Times*, April 26, 2004, A15, http://www.nytimes.com/2004/04/26/us/obey-same-sex-marriage-law-officials-told.html. Some Massachusetts Justices of the Peace had previously announced they would resign if forced to perform same-sex marriages. See Kathleen Burge, "Justices of the Peace Confront Gay Marriage," *Boston Globe*, April 18, 2004, B1, http://www.boston.com/news/local/articles/2004/04/18/wedding_quandaries?pg=full.

111. See infra note 237.

112. See Iowa Department of Justice, Office Attorney General, "Statement of Iowa Attorney General Tom Miller—County Recorders Must Comply with Supreme Court's Varnum Decision," press release, April 21, 2009; New York State Office of Vital Records to New York State Town and City Clerks, "Amendment to Domestic Relations Law—'The Marriage Equality Act,'" informational memorandum, June 13, 2011; Kilian Melloy, "Iowa Magistrate to Stop Performing Marriages," *EdgeBoston*, April 23, 2009, http://www.edgeboston.com/index.php?ch=news&sc=&sc2=news&sc3=&id=90310.

113. See Thomas Kaplan, "Rights Collide as Town Clerk Sidesteps Role in Gay Marriages," *New York Times*, September 27, 2011, http://www.nytimes.com/2011/09/28/nyregion/rights-clash-as-town-clerk-rejects-her-role-in-gay-marriages.html; People for the American Way, "PFAW Foundation Demands That NY Town Clerks End Marriage Discrimination," press release, September 12, 2011, http://www.pfaw.org/press-releases/2011/09/pfaw-foundation-demands-ny-town-clerks-end-marriage-discrimination (quoting the president of People for the American Way Foundation). For a discussion of the permissibility of that process, see Wilson, "Calculus of Accommodations," 1472–1474, supra note *.

114. The two exceptions to this pattern are Connecticut and Maine. In 2007, Connecticut considered and failed to pass same-sex marriage legislation containing clergy-only protections. On October 28, 2008, the Connecticut Supreme Court held in *Kerrigan et al. v. Comm'r of Pub. Health*, 957 A.2d 407, 412 (2008) that "the state has failed to provide sufficient justification

for excluding same-sex couples from the institution of marriage. . . ." With the judiciary's thumb on the scales, legislators then introduced a same-sex marriage bill with substantial protections that ultimately passed in 2009. See Appendix 6.C.

In Maine, legislation containing a clergy-only exemption attained overwhelming legislative support before being repealed in a popular referendum. See supra notes 78–86.

115. S.B. 5884, 2007 Leg., Reg. Sess. (N.Y. 2007), http://assembly.state.ny.us/leg/?term=2007&bn=S05884 ("[N]o clergyman, minster or Society for Ethical Culture leader shall be required to solemnize any marriage when acting in his or her capacity under this subdivision."); S.B. 4401, 2009 Leg., Reg. Sess. (N.Y. 2009) (same). Both stripped-down measures died in the New York Senate. See Dwyer Acre, "New York Senate Rejects Same-Sex Marriage Legislation," Jurist, December 2, 2009; Danny Hakim, "Bruno Says 'We're Not Doing Gay Marriage,'" New York Times, June 19, 2007, http://cityroom.blogs.nytimes.com/2007/06/19/bruno-says-were-not-doing-gay-marriage.

116. Bill A08354, N.Y. St. Assembly, http://assembly.state.ny.us/leg/?default_fld=&bn=A08354&term=2011&Summary=Y&Votes=Y (last visited April 22, 2014).

117. See Robin Fretwell Wilson, "Cuomo Marriage Bill Fails—Inexplicably—To Protect Ordinary Religious Individuals," New York Sun, June 16, 2011, http://www.nysun.com/opinion/cuomo-marriage-bill-fails-inexplicitly-to-protect/87397/.

118. See Nicholas Confessore and Michael Barbaro, "New York Allows Same-Sex Marriage, Becoming Largest State to Pass Law," New York Times, June 24, 2011, http://www.nytimes.com/2011/06/25/nyregion/gay-marriage-approved-by-new-york-senate.html.

119. See Danny Hakim, "Exemptions Were Key to Vote on Gay Marriage," New York Times, June 25, 2011, http://www.nytimes.com/2011/06/26/nyregion/religious-exemptions-were-key-to-new-york-gay-marriage-vote.html. Strenuous lobbying by Governor Cuomo and New York City Mayor Michael Bloomberg persuaded Senate Majority Leader Dean Skelos not to block the vote and may have persuaded some Republican members of the Senate to support the final bill. See Michael Barbaro, "Cuomo Strategy Shepherds Gay Marriage into N.Y.," Boston Globe, June 26, 2011, http://www.boston.com/news/politics/articles/2011/06/26/cuomo_strategy_shepherds_gay_marriage_into_ny/ (outlining the role of money in passing the legislation).

120. See Andrew Garber, "Gay Marriage Bill Passes House, Awaits Gregoire's Signature," Seattle Times, February 8, 2012, http://www.seattletimes.com/seattle-news/gay-marriage-bill-passes-house-awaits-gregoires-signature/; Connelly, supra note 47, "Gregoire Signs Same-Sex Marriage Bill; Wilson, "Marriage of Necessity," 1190–1192 and Fig. 3, supra note *; "Md. Gay Marriage Bill to Become Law Thursday Afternoon, Opponents Begin Referendum Effort," Washington Post, February 24, 2011.

121. See Annie Linskey, "Soul Searching, Swing Votes Make Difference for Same-Sex Marriage: Measure That Put Md. in National Spotlight Moves to Senate," Baltimore Sun, February 18, 2012, http://www.baltimoresun.com/news/maryland/politics/bs-md-same-sex-sunday-20120217,0,232363.story (noting that one of the votes needed "to pass the measure" came from Del. Olszewski, a "devoted Methodist," who said the governor's measure "goes above and beyond" to protect the "right of religious institutions to decide what is right for them"); John Wagner and Aaron C. Davis, "O'Malley Unveils Agenda, Including Same-Sex Marriage Bill," Washington Post, January 23, 2012, http://www.washingtonpost.com/local/dc-politics/omalley-unveils-agenda-including-same-sex-marriage-bill/2012/01/23/gIQAV8gMMQ_story.html (explaining that O'Malley's "[r]eligious-exemption language" was "intended to pick up additional support in the House of Delegates, where a bill fell unexpectedly short last year after clearing the Senate").

122. Telephone Interview by Anthony Kreis with Michael Busch, Speaker, Md. House of Delegates (July 3, 2012) (on file with author). The Maryland legislation passed the House with a 72-67 vote and the Senate with 25-22. Wilson, "Marriage of Necessity," 373, supra note *.

123. Kreis and Wilson, "Embracing Compromise," supra note 13 (recounting telephone interview with Christine Gregoire, Governor of Wash., July 27, 2012).

124. Concededly, other things may contribute to this legislative track record. For example, Rhode Island's 2011 same-sex marriage bill contained a clergy-only exemption while its successful

bill contained arguably the most robust protections in the nation to date. See Kreis and Wilson, "Embracing Compromise," Part II.B, supra note 13; Appendix 6.B. Nonetheless, the pattern of failure is almost surely attributable to the refusal to embrace meaningful concessions, while the pattern of success likely stems from "a 'perfect storm' of characteristics favoring marriage equality in jurisdictions that voluntarily embraced same-sex marriage, together with extensive bargaining around religious liberty." Wilson, "Marriage of Necessity," 1163, supra note * (providing empirical data). Although it is impossible to say definitively that robust protections proved decisive in enacting same-sex marriage, the number of narrowly defeated bills that later succeeded with thicker protections is suggestive. Also suggestive is Maine's 2009 experience: even where a same-sex marriage bill passed both chambers of the legislature by substantial majorities, voters rejected a law protecting only the clergy.

125. Jonathan Rauch, "The Majority Report," *Advocate*, November 19, 2010, http://www.advocate.com/politics/commentary/2010/11/19/majority-report.

126. Eggert, "Michigan's Balking at Anti-Gay Discrimination Law," supra note 16. For a listing of sexual orientation non-discrimination laws, see "Marriage of Necessity," Tbls.A2, A4, supra note *.

127. Tom Dart and Molly Redden, "Transgender Advocates Lament Backlash Against Failed Houston Equal Rights Bill," *Gaurdian*, November 4, 2015, http://www.theguardian.com/us-news/2015/nov/04/houston-equal-rights-ordinance-transgender-lgbt-discrimination.

128. "Rev. Wilson Reed: Houston's Equal Rights Ordinance Protects Everyone," *Houston Unites*, https://soundcloud.com/user-390132883-859756609/rev-will-reed-houstons-equal-rights-ordinance-protects-everyone (quoting Rev. Will Reed). *Manny Fernandex v. Mitch Smith*, "Houston Voters Reject Broad Anti-Discrimination Ordinance," *New York Times*, November 3, 2015, http://www.nytimes.com/2015/11/04/us/houston-voters-repeal-anti-bias-measure.html?_r=0.

129. Harry Bruinius, "Houston's Angry Debate Over Gay Rights Can Be Avoided. Here's How," *Christian Science Monitor*, November 5, 2015, http://www.csmonitor.com/USA/Politics/2015/1105/Houston-s-angry-debate-over-gay-rights-can-be-avoided.-Here-s-how.

130. Ibid.

131. For instance, in 2012, nine couples filed suit in Illinois state court trying to invalidate the state's statutory same-sex marriage ban. "Couples Challenge Illinois Law Denying Same-Sex Marriage," *CNN*, May 30, 2012, http://articles.cnn.com/2012-05-30/us/us_illinois-same-sex-marriage_1_civil-unions-lesbian-couples-recognition-of-such-marriages?_s=PM:US.

132. Ryan T. Anderson, "In Illinois, Redefining Marriage Threatens Marriage and Religious Freedom," *Daily Signal*, January 4, 2013, http://blog.heritage.org/2013/01/04/in-illinois-redefining-marriage-threatens-marriage-and-religious-freedom/.

133. See Jeffrey M. Jones, "Same-Sex Marriage Support Solidifies above 50% in U.S.," *Gallup Politics*, May 13, 2013, http://www.gallup.com/poll/162398/sex-marriage-support-solidifies-above.aspx.

134. Justin McCarthy, "Same-Sex Marriage Support Reaches New High at 55%," *Gallup Politics*, May 21, 2014, http://www.gallup.com/poll/169640/sex-marriage-support-reaches-new-high.aspx.

135. Jeffrey R. Lax and Justin H. Phillips, "Gay Rights in the States: Public Opinion and Policy Responsiveness," *American Political Science Review* 103 (2009): 367–386, Fig. 8 (online appendix only), http://www.columbia.edu/~jrl2124/Lax_Phillips_Gay_Policy_Responsiveness_2009.pdf (reproduced with permission of authors).

136. See "Changing Attitudes on Gay Marriage," *Pew Research Center Forum on Religion & Public Life*, June 8, 2015, slide 2 ("Attitudes by Generation"), http://www.pewforum.org/2014/09/24/graphics-slideshow-changing-attitudes-on-gay-marriage/.

137. Ibid.

138. Ibid.

139. See Wilson, "Marriage of Necessity," Fig. 10, supra note *.

140. See Andrew Kohut, "The Electorate Changes, and Politics Follows," *New York Times*, April 16, 2012, http://www.nytimes.com/roomfordebate/2012/04/16/is-support-for-gay-rights-still-controversial/the-electorate-changes-and-politics-follow?scp=4&sq=kohut%20marriage&st=cse.

141. Bryan P. Wilson, "State Constitutional Environmental Rights and Judicial Activism: Is the Big Sky Falling?" *Emory Law Journal* 53 (2004): 639.

142. Ibid.

143. See supra note 32.

144. See Ga. Const. Art. X, § 1, para. 1–6; Idaho Const. Art. XX, § 1–3; Kan. Const. Art. XIV, § 1–2; La. Const. Art. XIII, § 1–3; N.C. Const. Art. XIII, § 1–4; S.C. Const. Art. XVI, § 1–3; Tex. Const. Art. XVII, §; infra note 152 (summarizing Utah's process).

145. See infra Appendix 6.C.

146. See Utah Const. Art. XXIII, § 1–3.

147. See Ala. Const. Art. XVIII, § 284–287; Alaska Const. Art. XIII, § 1–3; Ky. Const. § 256–263; Nev. Const. Art. 16, § 1–2; Ore. Const. Art. XVII, § 1–2; Tenn. Const. Art. XI, § 3; Wis. Const. Art. 12, § 1; infra note 154.

148. Va. Const. Art. XII, § 1–2.

149. Ariz. Const. Art. XXI, § 1–2; Ark. Const. Art. XIX, § 22; Colo. Const. Art. XIX, § 1–2; Fla. Const. Art. XI, § 1–5; Mich. Const. Art. XII, § 1–3; Miss. Const. Art. XV, § 273; Mo. Const. Art. XII, § 2–3; Mont. Const. Art. XIV, § 1–9; Neb. Const. Art. XVI, § 1–2; N.D. Const. Art. III, § 1–9; Ohio Const. Art. XVI, § 1–2; 2; Okla. Const. Art. XXIV, § 1–3; S.D. Const. Art. XXIII, § 1–3.

150. See N.D. Const. Art. III, § 1–9 (2 %); Ariz. Const. Art. XXI, § 1–2 (15 %).

151. Ariz. Const. Art. XXI, § 1–2.

152. The 1994–1996 support data are taken from the *New York Times*. Andrew Gelman, Jeffrey Lax, and Justin Phillips, "Over Time, a Gay Marriage Groundswell," Week in Review, *New York Times*, August 22, 2010, http://www.nytimes.com/2010/08/22/weekinreview/22gay.html. Actual support at the time of the state bans appear in Wilson, "Marriage of Necessity,"Tbl. 6, supra note *. The 2012 and 2016 statistics are taken from Nate Silver, "The Future of Same-Sex Marriage Ballot Measures," *FiveThirtyEight*, June 29, 2011, http://fivethirtyeight.com/features/the-future-of-same-sex-marriage-ballot-measures/.

153. See Wilson, "Marriage of Necessity," Tbl. 6, supra note *.

154. See infra Appendix 6.C.

155. See Wilson, "Marriage of Necessity," Tbl. 6, supra note *.

156. See infra Appendix 6.C.

157. See Wilson, "Marriage of Necessity," Tbl. 6, supra note *.

158. Ibid.

159. See infra Appendix 6.C. On March 21, 2014, the District Court for the Eastern District of Michigan struck Michigan's same-sex marriage ban, but the Sixth Circuit Court of Appeals reversed; the US Supreme Court then granted certiorari. *DeBoer v. Snyder*, 973 F. Supp. 2d 757, 759 (E.D. Mich.), *rev'd*, 772 F.3d 388 (6th Cir. 2014), *cert. granted sub nom.*, *Obergefell v. Hodges*, 576 US __, (2015), 135 S. Ct. 1039 (2015), *cert. granted sub nom.*, *Tanco v. Haslam*, 135 S. Ct. 1040 (2015), *cert. granted*, 135 S. Ct. 1040 (2015), *cert. granted sub nom.*, *Bourke v. Beshear*, 135 S. Ct. 1041 (2015).

160. See Silver, "The Future of Same-Sex Marriage Ballot Measures," supra note 158.

161. Wilson, "Marriage of Necessity," 1235, Fig. 24, supra note *.

162. See "Ted Cruz Calls Gay Marriage Ruling The 'Very Definition of Tyranny.'" *Huffington Post*, July 22, 2015, http://www.huffingtonpost.com/entry/ted-cruz-gay-marriage_55b00157e4b07af29d57677c.

163. See "Article 4, Arizona Constitution," *Ballotpedia*, http://ballotpedia.org/Article_4,_Arizona_Constitution#Part_1.

164. See Robin Fretwell Wilson, "Indiana law won't erase protections against bias," *Chicago Sun-Times*, April 1, 2015, http://chicago.suntimes.com/politics/7/71/489503/xxxxxxx; Robert King, "RFRA: Boycotts, Bans and a Growing Backlash," *USA Today*, April 2, 2015, http://www.indystar.com/story/news/politics/2015/04/01/rfra-boycotts-bans-growing-backlash/70810178/.

165. See Douglas Laycock, afterword to *Same-Sex Marriage and Religious Liberty*, 195, supra note 73 [hereinafter "Afterword"]; Robin Fretwell Wilson, "Insubstantial Burdens: The Case for Government Employee Exemptions to Same-Sex Marriage Laws," *Northwestern*

Journal of Law and Social Policy 5 (2010): 318–368, http://papers.ssrn.com/sol3/papers.cfm?abstract_id=2027942 [hereinafter "Insubstantial Burdens"].

166. See "Religious Liberty Implications of D.C.'s Same-Sex Marriage Bill (18-482)," transcript of D.C. Council Hearings, November 2, 2009, http://dccarchive.oct.dc.gov/services/on_demand_video/on_demand_November_2009_week_1.shtm [hereinafter "D.C. Council Transcript"].

167. See infra Part II.D. Other points of resistance have also been articulated, including whether one can avoid hardship in the especially difficult context of insurance benefits. For a response, see Wilson, "Calculus of Accommodation," supra note *.

168. See, e.g., Erwin Chemerinsky, *Constitutional Law: Principles and Policies*, 3rd ed. (New York: Aspen Publishers, 2006), 1189–1190; *United States v. Kuch*, 288 F.Supp. 429, 445 (D.D.C. 1968).

169. See, e.g., *Doswell v. Smith*, 139 F.3d 888, 1998 WL 110161, at *1–2, 5–6 (4th Cir. 1998) (unpublished table decision).

170. See, e.g., *Cruzan v. Miss. Dep't of Health*, 497 US 261 (1990). Some religious believers assert claims of faith to avoid healthcare for their children. See generally John DeWitt Gregory, Peter N. Swisher, and Robin Fretwell Wilson, *Understanding Family Law*, 4th ed. (New Providence: Matthew Bender & Co., 2013), § 7.05, 212–215. These protections have been roundly criticized. See Robin Fretwell Wilson, "The Perils of Privatized Marriage," in *Marriage and Divorce in a Multicultural Context: Reconsidering the Boundaries of Civil Law and Religion*, Joel A. Nichols, ed. (New York: Cambridge: Cambridge University Press, 2011), 253–283, http://papers.ssrn.com/sol3/papers.cfm?abstract_id=2016231.

171. See Kent Greenawalt, "Religious Toleration and Claims of Conscience," *Journal of Law and Politics* 28 (2013):104.

172. Federal conscience protections contemporaneous with the US Supreme Court's landmark 1973 decision in *Roe v. Wade* provide that "No individual shall be required to perform or assist in the performance of any part of a health service program or research activity funded in whole or in part under a program administered by the Secretary of Health and Human Services if his performance or assistance in the performance of such part of such program or activity would be contrary to his religious beliefs or moral convictions." See 42 U.S.C. § 300a-7(d) (2012) (popularly known as the "Church Amendment"). Twenty states similarly provide conscientious objectors with an absolute exemption from participating in sterilizations and abortions. See Robin Fretwell Wilson, "The Erupting Clash between Religion and the State over Contraception, Sterilization, and Abortion," in *Religious Freedom in America: Constitutional Roots and Contemporary Challenges*, Allen Hertzke, ed. (Norman, OK: University of Oklahoma Press, 2015), 135–169 [hereinafter "Erupting Clash"].

173. Wilson, "Erupting Clash," 145, supra note 182 (allegation in complaint).

174. See Tina Susman, "N.J. Bridal Salon Slammed for Refusing to Sell Gown to Lesbian," *Los Angeles Times*, August 22, 2011, http://latimesblogs.latimes.com/nationnow/2011/08/bridal-salon-slammed-for-refusing-gown-to-lesbian.html.

175. Greenawalt, "Religious Toleration and Claims of Conscience," 25, supra note 181.

176. 42 U.S.C. § 2000cc-1(a) (2012).

177. Tony Barboza, "Inmate Claims Fictitious 'Festivus' Religious Holiday to Score Better Food," *Los Angeles Times*, December 14, 2010, http://latimesblogs.latimes.com/lanow/2010/12/oc-inmate-claims-religious-ties-to-festivus-to-score-better-food.html.

178. See, e.g., *Grayson v. Schuler*, 666 F.3d 450, 455 (7th Cir. 2012) (reversing summary judgment against a pro se Rastafarian inmate suing under RLUIPA after prison officials cut plaintiff's dreadlocks).

179. 544 US 709, 725 n.13 (internal citations and quotation marks omitted).

180. 134 S. Ct. 2751 (2014).

181. 42 U.S.C. § 2000bb (2012).

182. *Burwell v. Hobby Lobby*, 573 US ___, (2014), 134 S. Ct. 2751, 2759–2780 (2014).

183. Ibid., 2779.

184. See *Aguayo v. Harvey*, 476 F.3d 971, 973, 979–981 (D.C. Cir. 2007).

185. See *McDonnell Douglas Corp. v. Green*, 411 US 792, 804 (1973).

186. *United States v. Ballard*, 322 US 78 (1944); Chemerinsky, *Constitutional Law: Principles and Policies*, 1190, supra note 178.
187. Ibid.
188. Greenawalt, "Religious Toleration and Claims of Conscience," 26, supra note 181 (discussing moral objections versus religious objections).
189. Ibid.
190. See Wilson, "Erupting Clash," supra note 182 (describing threats against abortion objectors).
191. See, e.g., D.C. Code § 46-406(e) (2010).
192. Kent Greenawalt, *Religion and the Constitution: Free Exercise and Fairness* (Princeton: Princeton University Press, 2006), 110.
193. Wilson, "Calculus of Accommodation," 1461, supra note *.
194. See, e.g., US Const. amend. I; Anthony R. Picarello, Jr. to Deborah Kelly in regards to D.C. Bill No. 18-0482, "Religious Freedom and Civil Marriage Equality Amendment Act of 2009," letter, November 9, 2009, 4.
195. See, e.g., D.C. Council Transcript, 7:00:32, supra note 176 (statement of Councilmember Mendelson).
196. John Corvino, "The Slippery Slope of Religious Exemptions," November 22, 2009, http://johncorvino.com/2009/11/the-slippery-slope-of-religious-exemptions/.
197. See ibid. Also implicit is the assumption that social services provided by religious organizations are not as inherently "religious" as other activities. Yet religious organizations may view these services as part of a larger ministry to which the group is called. For more on this point, see Thomas C. Berg, "Taking Exception: Gay Marriage Legislation," *Christian Century* 126, no. 13 (July 2009).
198. Laycock "Afterword," 195, supra note 173.
199. Ibid.
200. Ibid., 195–196.
201. Ibid., 196.
202. As noted above, absent such protections, the decision to celebrate only marriages recognized by one's faith may subject one to civil liability. See supra notes 95 and 96.
203. See supra note 89.
204. To date, all states but one have provided protection to religious institutions and nonprofits when providing space for a reception or otherwise facilitating or celebrating a marriage. See Appendix 6.B.
205. 42 U.S.C. § 300a-7(b) (2012).
206. See Robin Fretwell Wilson, "The Limits of Conscience: Moral Clashes over Deeply Divisive Healthcare Procedures," *American Journal of Law and Medicine* 34 (2008): 53 (discussing extensive network of abortion clinics across the country).
207. Robin Fretwell Wilson, "When Governments Insulate Dissenters from Social Change: What Hobby Lobby and Abortion Conscience Clauses Teach about Specific Exemptions," *UC Davis Law Review* 48 (2014): 703–790.
208. See, e.g. Ariz. Rev. Stat. Ann § 36-2154(A) (Supp. 2011)) ("[A]ny other person"); Ark. Code Ann. § 20-16-601(a) (2005) ("No person shall be required"); N.M. Stat. Ann. § 30-5-2 (2004) ("A person who is a member of, or associated with, the staff of a hospital, or any employee of a hospital"); Robin Fretwell Wilson, "Matters of Conscience: Lessons for Same-Sex Marriage from the Healthcare Context," in *Same-Sex Marriage and Religious Liberty*, supra note 67, Appendix.
209. See, e.g., 42 U.S.C. § 300a-7(d) (2012) ("No individual").
210. See, e.g., 42 U.S.C. § 238n (2012).
211. See, e.g., 42 U.S.C. § 300a-7(d) ("No individual shall be required to perform or assist in the performance of any part of a health service program or research activity . . . if his performance or assistance . . . would be contrary to his religious beliefs or moral convictions."). This protection arose after the Public Health Service's infamous "Tuskegee Study of Untreated Syphilis in the Male Negro" became public in 1973. See Wilson, "When Governments Insulate Dissenters," 759, 759, supra note 197.
212. See 42 U.S.C. §§ 2000e(j), 2000e-2(a)(1) (2012).

213. *Trans World Airlines, Inc. v. Hardison* narrowly interpreted Title VII's requirement that employers accommodate an employee's religious belief or practice to mean that required accommodations not impose more than a de minimis burden on employers or coworkers. See *Trans World Airlines, Inc. v. Hardison*, 432 US 63, 84 (1977).

214. For example, in *Shelton v. University of Medicine & Dentistry of New Jersey*, the US Court of Appeals for the Third Circuit considered staff nurse Yvonne Shelton's Title VII religious discrimination claim that she should not be required to perform emergency abortions. *Shelton v. University of Medicine & Dentistry of New Jersey* 223 F.3d 220, 222 (3d. Cir, 2000). Although the court ultimately granted summary judgment in favor of Shelton's employer, a state hospital, it concluded that Shelton had established a prima facie case of religious discrimination, which shifted the burden "to the Hospital to show either that it offered Shelton a reasonable accommodation, or that it could not do so because of a resulting undue hardship." *Shelton*, 225, 228. The hospital offered to transfer Shelton elsewhere without a loss of pay or benefits, doing work that would not be "religiously untenable." *Shelton*, 226. Shelton's steadfast refusal to "cooperate in attempting to find an acceptable religious liberty accommodation" ultimately doomed her claim. See *Shelton*, 228.

   Title VII creates an important workplace norm to accommodate religious practices if possible. As with Shelton, the proffered accommodation may not be acceptable to the employee. See *Walden v. Centers for Disease Control & Prevention*, 669 F.3d 1277 (11th Cir. 2012).

215. See Wilson, "Insubstantial Burdens," 354–355, supra note 175.

216. Ibid., 355–357 (discussing *Haring v. Blumenthal*, 471 F. Supp. 1172 [D.D.C. 1979]).

217. 41 Iowa Op. Att'y Gen. 474, 478 (March 1, 1976).

218. Vt. Stat. Ann. tit. 9 § 4502(l) (2011). New Hampshire requires that "such solemnization, celebration, or promotion of marriage [be] in violation of his or her religious beliefs and faith." N.H. Rev. Stat. Ann. § 457:37(III) (2011). Compare Appendix 6.B.

219. See Appendix 6.A. In the case of government employees, the couple must be able to receive the requested service immediately, while for commercial vendors, the couple must be able to secure the desired service without substantial hardship. Thus, these exemptions would *not* allow religious individuals in commerce or government employment to act as a roadblock on the path to marriage.

220. E.g., D.C. Council Transcript, 7:29:55, supra note 176 (statement of Councilmember Jim Graham).

221. See supra note 115.

222. See supra note 117.

223. See Dan Wiessner, "New York Town Clerk Quits over Gay Marriage License," *Reuters*, July 11, 2011, http://www.reuters.com/article/2011/07/12/us-gaymarriage-newyork-resignation-idUSTRE76B7BJ20110712.

224. Gavin Off, "NC Magistrates Resign over Gay Marriage Rulings," *Charlotte (NC) Observer*, October 25, 2014, http://www.charlotteobserver.com/2014/10/25/5266424/nc-magistrates-resign-over-gay.html#.VKB6cl4AKA. North Carolina enacted a clunky measure permitting magistrates and registrars recuse themselves from performing all lawful marriages, provided that they give notice and do no other marriage for six months. SB 2, Reg. Sess. 2015 (N.C. 2015), http://www.ncleg.net/Applications/BillLookUp/LoadBillDocument.aspx?SessionCode=2015&DocNum=459&SeqNum=0. Unfortunately, the measure would permit government officials to act on an objection when the first same-sex couple presents, causing harm to that couple and inviting unnecessary conflict with the public. See Robin Fretwell Wilson, "Real Religious Liberty Risks and Misplaced Fears," *Cornerstone, Religious Freedom Project, Berkley Center for Religion, Peace & World Affairs*, July 2, 2015, http://berkleycenter.georgetown.edu/cornerstone/obergefell-v-hodges-the-ruling-and-its-implications-for-religious-freedom/responses/real-religious-liberty-risks-and-misplaced-fears.

225. See Wilson, "Marriage of Necessity," Tbl.A2, supra note *.

226. For a discussion of objectors' exposure to sexual orientation or marital status discrimination claims, see Thomas C. Berg, et al. to Hawaii State Senator Rosalyn H. Baker, "Religious Liberty Implications of Proposed Hawaii Marriage Equality Act of 2013," letter, May 2, 2013, http://mirrorofjustice.blogs.com/files/hawaii-special-session-letter-10-17-13.pdf

[hereinafter "Berg Letter"]. See generally Wilson, "Marriage of Necessity," 734, n. 156, supra note * (explaining that "[w]hile certain nondiscrimination bans literally applied to wedding services before the recognition of same-sex marriage, objectors were simply not asked to facilitate or celebrate a marriage that they could not recognize consistent with their faith—until the law actually established marriage equality").

227. See Mass. Gen. Laws ch. 272, § 98; ch. 151B, § 5(c) (2015).

228. Conn. Gen. Stat. § 46a–81d(b) (2011). A public accommodation is "any establishment which caters or offers its services or facilities or goods to the general public." Also see § 46a-63.

229. See, e.g., Taylor Flynn, "Clarion Call or False Alarm: Why Proposed Exemptions to Equal Marriage Statutes Return Us to a Religious Understanding of the Public Marketplace," *Northwestern Journal of Law and Social Policy* 5 (2010): 251–254.

230. The Netherlands first recognized same-sex marriage in 2001, but same-sex marriage was not recognized in any US jurisdiction until 2004, when Massachusetts began issuing marriage licenses to same-sex couples. *Goodridge v. Dep't of Pub. Health*, 798 N.E.2d 941 (Mass. 2003); Carolyn Lochhead, "Pivotal Day for Gay Marriage in U.S. Nears," *San Francisco Chronicle*, May 2, 2004, http://www.sfgate.com/news/article/Pivotal-day-for-gay-marriage-in-U-S-nears-2762513.php. Many state laws banning discrimination based on sexual orientation predate 2004. See Wilson, "Marriage of Necessity," Tbl.A2, supra note *.

231. This is not to say that every objection will be made in good faith. Although some faith traditions object to homosexual sex, an objection to facilitating a marriage on this ground alone would not be protected under the model provision in Appendix 6.A. It would protect refusals to "solemniz[e] or celebrat[e] [] any marriage" only when doing so would force one to "violate their sincerely held religious beliefs." See Appendix 6.A.

   All civil rights laws prohibit covered entities from discriminating on certain bases yet allow them to act on others. Thus, courts must parse legitimate, permitted grounds from illegitimate ones, considering all circumstances. See *Ash v. Tyson Foods*, 664 F.3d 883, 898 (11th Cir. 2011). Although exemptions seek to protect bona fide objections, individuals may claim exemptions for malign reasons. The possibility of misuse by some does not condone such misuse. More importantly, sincerity tests serve an important screening function and should discourage bad faith claims.

232. See Charles Reid, "Marriage: Its Relationship to Religion, Law, and the State," in *Same-Sex Marriage and Religious Liberty*, 157–188, supra note 76.

233. Mccrory vetoes NC Religious Objection Bill On Gay Marriage," *ABC11*, May 29, 2015, http://abc11.com/politics/mccrory-vetoes-nc-religious-objection-bill-on-gay-marriage/746406/. Badly constructed accommodations may give a religious objector a platform for telling taxpayers what she thinks of their lawful marriages, much as Kim Davis relentless did in Kentucky. Such cluncky measures harm same-sex couples, coarsen public dialogue, and set back the entire enterprise of finding ways to live together in peace.

234. See Laycock, "Afterword," 200, supra note 175 ("If the dissenters want complete moral autonomy on this issue, they must refrain from occupying such a choke point").

235. See Laycock, "Afterword," 200, supra note 175 ("If the dissenters want complete moral autonomy on this issue, they must refrain from occupying such a choke point"); History Channel, Integration of Central High School, http://www.history.com/topics/black-history/central-high-school-integration.

236. See Appendix 6.B; "Marriage of Necessity," Tbl.A2, supra note *.

237. See Utah Code Ann. § 17-20-4; SB 297, lines 73–79.

238. Personal communication, Utah Senate Majority Whip Senator J. Stuart Adams, September 30, 2015.

239. See supra note 64; Robin Fretwell Wilson, "Accommodate without bias," *The Charlotte Observer*, June 3, 2015, http://www.charlotteobserver.com/opinion/op-ed/article23032926.html.

240. See Wilson, "Insubstantial Burdens," 335–339, supra note 175.

241. Rachel E. Gross, "Gay Rights & Religious Freedom: Can We Find Common Ground?" *Moment*, July/August 2014, http://www.momentmag.com/gay-rights-religious-freedom-common-ground/ (last visited January 3, 2014).

242. *Obergefell v. Hodges*, 135 S. Ct. 2584, 2625 (2015) (Roberts, J., dissenting).

243. See supra note 89 (discussing *Smith*).

244. See Laycock, "Afterword," 200, supra note 175 ("If the dissenters want complete moral autonomy on this issue, they must refrain from occupying such a choke point").

245. See Wilson, "Calculus of Accommodation," supra note *.

246. See Douglas Laycock to Gov John Baldacci, "Religious Liberty Implications of SP 0384, LD 1020," letter dated April 30, 2009, in Shannon Gilreath, *The End of Straight Supremacy: Realizing Gay Liberation* (New York: Cambridge University Press, 2011), 260 [hereinafter "Baldacci Letter"].

247. See Susman, "N.J. Bridal Salon Slammed for Refusing to Sell Gown to Lesbian," supra note 184.

248. See reviews of Here Comes the Bride, *Yelp*, http://www.yelp.com/biz/here-comes-the-bride-somers-point (last visited February 28, 2012).

249. See Wilson, "Calculus of Accommodation," supra note *.

250. James E. Gregory to Mark Jordan, Ledyard Town Supervisor, and Rose Marie Belforti, Ledyard Town Clerk, letter, September 9, 2011, 2, http://site.pfaw.org/pdf/Jordan_Belforti_NY_Marriage.PDF.

251. See Wilson, "Insubstantial Burdens," supra note 175. See also *Am. Postal Workers Union v. Postmaster Gen'l*, 781 F.2d 772, 776 (9th Cir. 1986) (noting that employment status includes compensation, conditions, terms, and privileges of employment).

252. See Wilson, "Insubstantial Burdens," 350–353, supra note 175. Religious liberty accommodations for objecting marriage clerks and justices pose far less difficulty than accommodating police and firefighters because clerks perform routine, predictable, easily staffed-around assignments. "Insubstantial Burdens," 349. Even with police and firefighters, public employers can and routinely do offer new assignments, transfers, and low-level work-arounds, allowing the religious objector to step aside from services that violate deeply held religious beliefs. "Insubstantial Burdens," 354.

    Speculative predictions regarding possible future disruptions are not to be considered. Employers are to be guided by the facts on the ground. See *McGinnis v. U.S.P.S.*, 512 F. Supp. 517 (N.D. Cal. 1980); *Haring v. Blumenthal*, 471 F. Supp. 1172 (D.D.C. 1979) ("'[U]ndue hardship' must mean present undue hardship, as distinguished from anticipated or multiplied hardship. Were the law otherwise, any accommodation, however slight, would rise to the level of an undue hardship. . . .").

253. See Wilson, "Insubstantial Burdens," 354–357, supra note 175; *Am. Postal Workers Union*, supra note 267.

254. See Wilson, "Insubstantial Burdens," 322–331, supra note 175.

255. See supra Figure 6.6.

256. See "Baldacci Letter," 260, supra note 257.

257. Laycock, "Afterword," 198, supra note 175.

258. Tennessee hardware store puts up 'No Gays Allowed' sign, *USA Today*, July 1, 2015, http://www.usatoday.com/story/news/nation-now/2015/07/01/tennessee-hardware-store-no-gays-allowed-sign/29552615/.

259. Federal Election Commission, Federal Elections 2012, Election Results for the U.S. President, the U.S. Senate and the U.S. House of Representatives 39 (July 2013). New York provides no explicit protections for transgender people in its housing and hiring nondiscrimination laws, although New York's protections extend to public accommodations. *See* Office of N.Y. State Office of the Attorney Gen. Eric T. Schneiderman, The Sexual Orientation Non-Discrimination Act (SONDA), http://www.ag.ny.gov/civil-rights/sonda-brochure.

260. See supra note 111 (Sweet Cakes by Melissa); Tom Coyne, "Memories Pizza Reopens after Gay Wedding Comments Flap," *The Washington Times*, April 9, 2015, http://www.washingtontimes.com/news/2015/apr/9/memories-pizza-walkerton-indiana-reopens-after-gay/.

261. See supra Figures 6.7–6.9.

262. Laycock, "Afterword," 261, supra note 175.

263. Wilson, "Calculus of Accommodation," supra note *.

264. Non-discrimination laws provide protection in a range of contexts other than housing, hiring, and public accommodations. See "Marriage of Necessity," Tbls. A2, A4, supra note *.

265. Harry Bruinius, "Houston's Angry Debate Over Gay Rights Can Be Avoided. Here's How," *Christian Science Monitor*, November 5, 2015, http://www.csmonitor.com/USA/Politics/ 2015/1105/Houston-s-angry-debate-over-gay-rights-can-be-avoided.-Here-s-how.

266. Berg et al., "Berg Letter," supra note 227.

267. Some have expressed concern that the proposed text would have permitted objections to interracial marriage. Although such objections are likely to be rare, if not nonexistent, this concern is readily addressed by a simple proviso that would read: "Notwithstanding any of the foregoing provisions, this section does not change any provision of law with respect to discrimination on the basis of race."

Chapter 7

1. See James Davison Hunter, *Culture Wars: The Struggle to Define America* (New York: Basic Books, 1991). Writing in the 1990s, Hunter described the competing positions with the terms "orthodox" and "progressive." The "orthodox" camp, reflecting a "biblical the-ism" that includes many Catholics, Protestants, and Jews, is defined by "the commit-ment on the part of adherents to an external, definable, and transcendent authority." This authority "tells us what is good, what is true, how we should live, and *who we are*" (44; emphasis omitted, added). By contrast, the progressive camp is composed both of "secularists" who adhere to no religion and also of persons who, though counting themselves religious, place their trust in "personal experience or scientific rationality" over "the traditional sources of moral authority, whether scripture, papal pronounce-ments, or Jewish law" (44–45). The conflict between these contrasting perspectives, Hunter thought, "amounts to a fairly comprehensive and momentous struggle to define *the meaning of America*—of how and on what terms will Americans live together, of what comprises the good society" (51; emphasis added). For an update and debate, see James Davison Hunter and Alan Wolfe, *Is There a Culture War?* (Washington, DC: Brookings Institution Press, 2006); "Political Polarization in the American Public," *Pew Research Center*, June 12, 2014, http://www.people-press.org/2014/06/ 12/political-polarization-in-the-american-public/.

2. As noted above, supra note *, in *Obergefell v. Hodges* the Supreme Court interpreted the Constitution to require recognition of same-sex marriage.

3. For exploration of the conflict, see the essays in Douglas Laycock, Anthony R. Picarello, Jr., and Robin Fretwell Wilson, eds., *Same-Sex Marriage and Religious Liberty: Emerging Conflicts* (Lanham, MD: Rowan and Littlefield, 2008).

4. The term is rhetorically powerful—who after all wants to come out against either "mar-riage" or "equality"?—but also (or perhaps because) tendentious and question-begging. See Steven D. Smith, "The Red Herring of 'Marriage Equality,'" *Public Discourse*, March 27, 2013, http://www.thepublicdiscourse.com/2013/03/7912/.

5. See, e.g., Laura S. Underkuffler, "Odious Discrimination and the Religious Exemption Question," *Cardozo Law Review* 32 (2011): 2069–2091; Chai R. Feldblum, "Moral Conflict and Conflicting Liberties," in *Same-Sex Marriage and Religious Liberty*, 123, supra note 3.

6. See Thomas C. Berg, "Progressive Amendments for Religious Organizational Freedom: Reflections on the HHS Mandate," *Journal of Contemporary Legal Issues* 21 (2013): 279–333; Thomas C. Berg, "What Same-Sex Marriage and Religious-Liberty Claims Have in Common," *Northwestern Journal of Law and Social Policy* 5, no. 2 (2010): 206–235; Douglas Laycock and Thomas C. Berg, "Protecting Same-Sex Marriage and Religious Liberty," *Virginia Law Review* 99 (2013): 1–9.

7. See Alan Brownstein, "Gays, Jews, and Other Strangers in a Strange Land: The Case for Reciprocal Accommodation of Religious Liberty and the Right of Same-Sex Couples to Marry," *University of San Francisco Law Review* 45 (Fall 2010): 389–436.

8. See Laycock and Berg, "Protecting Same-Sex Marriage and Religious Liberty," supra note 6; Douglas Laycock, "Religious Liberty and the Culture Wars," *University of Illinois Law Review* (2014): 839–880; Douglas Laycock, "Sex, Atheism, and the Free Exercise of Religion," *University of Detroit Mercy Law Review* 88 (Spring 2011): 407–431 (see espe-cially 429–430).

9. See, e.g., Robin Fretwell Wilson, "The Calculus of Accommodation: Contraception, Abortion, Same-Sex Marriage, and Other Clashes between Religion and the State," *Boston College Law Review* 53, no. 4 (2012): 1417–1513.

10. See, e.g., Brownstein, "Gays, Jews, and Other Strangers in a Strange Land: The Case for Reciprocal Accommodation of Religious Liberty and the Right of Same-Sex Couples to Marry," 390, 416, supra note 7; Berg, "What Same-Sex Marriage and Religious-Liberty Claims Have in Common," 208, 226, 228, supra note 6; Laycock, "Religious Liberty and the Culture Wars," 852, 878–879, supra note 8; Laycock, "Sex, Atheism, and the Free Exercise of Religion" 429, supra note 8.

11. See supra notes 6, 8.

12. See Laycock and Berg, "Protecting Same-Sex Marriage and Religious Liberty," 3–5, supra note 6.

13. Laycock, "Religious Liberty and the Culture Wars," 879, supra note 8.

14. See, e.g., Laycock and Berg, "Protecting Same-Sex Marriage and Religious Liberty," 9, supra note 8 ("Of course, no same-sex couple would ever want to be counseled by such a counselor. Demanding a commitment to counsel same-sex couple does not obtain counseling for those couples, but it does threaten to drive from the helping professions all those who adhere to other religious understandings of marriage.").

15. Laycock, "Religious Liberty and the Culture Wars," 879, supra note 8.

16. The position is a "compromise" both for traditionalists who oppose same-sex marriage and for proponents of same-sex marriage who would prefer narrower or no exceptions or qualifications. It is not a compromise for the moderators themselves: they get pretty much everything they want, so to speak.

17. These are rough and underinclusive descriptions of the competing sides. Plainly there are non-Christians on the more traditional side, and religious liberals or (as they often prefer) "progressives" on the "egalitarian" side. Hunter's more deliberate sociological study defined the camps more inclusively. See supra note 1. Laycock's articles focus mostly on Christian traditionalists and their secular opponents, however, and for the limited purposes of this essay that focus seems acceptable.

18. Laycock and Berg, "Protecting Same-Sex Marriage and Religious Liberty," 5, supra note 6.

19. I have elsewhere described Laycock as "the preeminent lawyer-scholar of religious liberty over the last quarter-century." Steven D. Smith, "Lawyering Religious Liberty," *Texas Law Review* 89 (2011): 917.

20. Laycock, "Sex, Atheism and the Free Exercise of Religion," 418, supra note 8.

21. Since the Supreme Court's decision in *Obergefell v. Hodges*, 576 US ___, (2015), of course, the first part of this supposition is no longer hypothetical; the second part has been to some extent foreclosed, at least as part of a compromise accepting the legalization of same-sex marriage.

22. Martha C. Nussbaum, *Liberty of Conscience: In Defense of America's Tradition of Religious Equality* (New York: Basic Books, 2009), 28.

23. *In re Marriage Cases*, 183 P.3d 384, 399–401 (Cal. S. Ct. 2008).

24. See, e.g., Michael C. Dorf, "Same-Sex Marriage, Second-Class Citizenship, and Law's Social Meanings," *Virginia Law Review* 97 (2011): 1267–1346; Nelson Tebbe and Deborah A. Widiss, "Equal Access and the Right to Marry," *University of Pennsylvania Law Review* 158 (2010): 1375–1449.

25. Laycock and Berg may understand themselves to be addressing this problem—I am not sure—when they argue that we need to disentangle the religious from the legal dimension of marriage. The conflation of these dimensions, they suggest, is a—or is perhaps *the*—principal source of conflict: "Advocates of marriage equality tend to see the legal relationship as primary; most opponents see the religious dimension as primary" (Laycock and Berg, "Protecting Same-Sex Marriage and Religious Liberty," 6, supra note 6). This seems to me a dubious diagnosis. It is true that some Christians—not all—understand marriage to be a sacrament (see John Witte, Jr., *From Sacrament to Contract: Marriage, Religion, and Law in the Western Tradition* [Louisville, KY: Westminster John Knox Press, 1997]). And it is true that some—Mormons, for example—believe it is possible to be legally but not religiously married. But it seems quite unlikely that the contentious disagreement is mainly over religious

versus legal marriage, or that a more publicly explicit distinction would do much at all to dissolve the disagreements.

26. Michael Perry points out to me that a judicial decision striking down a traditional marriage law need not assert that traditional views are false; the decision might instead assert that the law is based on religious rationales that are not necessarily false but that are deemed inadmissible as a basis for secular law. See, e.g., *Varnum v. Brien*, 763 N.W.2d 862, 897–904 (Iowa 2009). I think Perry is right (although I also think this judicial rationale is misguided). Both in popular debate and in the US Supreme Court, however, opponents of traditional marriage laws routinely equate support for such laws with hatred or "animus." E.g., *United States v. Windsor*, 133 S. Ct. 1675 (2013). This argument may be criticized, to be sure. See Steven D. Smith, "The Jurisprudence of Disparagement," *U.C. Davis Law Review* 48 (2014): 675–701. Even so, given this pervasive feature of the cultural debate, it seems virtually certain that rejection of traditional marriage laws in favor of the legalization of same-sex marriage will be perceived and mostly intended as indicating that the traditional laws are archaic and wrongheaded. And many Christians surely do perceive the legalization of same-sex marriage as a rejection of Christian values and views. See, e.g., Rod Dreher, "Sex after Christianity," *Maggie Gallagher* (blog), April 11, 2013, http://maggiegallagher.com/2013/04/rod-drehers-sex-after-christianity/.

27. For diverging analyses of this concern, compare Allison Fetter-Harrott, "Recognition of Same-Sex Marriage and Public Schools: Implications, Challenges, and Opportunities," *B.Y.U. Education and Law Journal* 2011, no. 2 (2011): 237–262, with E. Vance Randall, "Same Sex Marriage and Education: Implications for Schools, Parents, and Students," *B.Y.U. Education and Law Journal* 2011, no. 2 (2011): 385–420.

28. It is true, to be sure, that anti-discrimination laws can be interpreted aggressively against, say, photographers and others even in states that do not recognize same-sex marriage—see, e.g., *Elane Photography v. Willcock*, 309 P.3d 53 (N.M. 2013)—and vice versa. Even so, it would be naive, I think, to pretend that legalization of same-sex marriage will not over time have effects on the scope and application of anti-discrimination laws.

29. See T. Alexander Aleinikoff, "Constitutional Law in the Age of Balancing," *Yale Law Journal* 96 (1987): 943–1005.

30. See, e.g., *Bob Jones University v. US*, 461 US 574, 593–595 (1983).

31. Cf. Thomas Paine, "The Rights of Man," in *Reflections on the Revolution in France and The Rights of Man* (Garden City, NY: Anchor Books, 1973), 267, 324 ("Toleration is not the *opposite* of intoleration, but is the *counterfeit* of it. Both are despotisms.") (emphasis in original).

32. Laycock, "Religious Liberty and the Culture Wars," 879, supra note 13. See also Laycock, "Sex, Atheism, and the Free Exercise of Religion," 418, supra note 8 ("The pro-life and traditional marriage side wants to eliminate abortions and restrict the personal lives of gays and lesbians.").

33. Laycock, "Religious Liberty and the Culture Wars," 867, supra note 8.

34. Ibid., 878.

35. Ibid., 879.

36. Laycock acknowledges that religious conservatives would restrict abortion because they "see[] it as killing innocent human beings." Ibid., 878.

37. See Laycock, "Sex, Atheism and the Free Exercise of Religion," 418, supra note 8 ("The pro-choice and gay rights groups want conservative believers not just to leave them alone, but to affirmatively assist with abortions and same-sex relationships—or else leave any occupation that might ever be relevant.").

38. For discussion of this dilemma in the area of adoption services, see Robin Fretwell Wilson, "A Matter of Conviction: Moral Clashes over Same-Sex Adoption," *B.Y.U. Journal of Public Law* 22, no. 2 (2008) 475–497. More generally, discussing cases in the United States, Canada, and Germany in which anti-discrimination laws were held to override claims of religious freedom, Brett Scharffs observes "a much deeper pattern of equality trumping liberty, both within the United States and beyond. Indeed, in surveying law and religion trends around the world over the past twenty years, one of the most notable patterns is the systematic preferences of equality over liberty interests." Brett G. Scharffs, "Equality in Sheep's Clothing: The Implications of Anti-Discrimination Norms for Religious Autonomy," *Santa Clara Journal of*

International Law 10, no. 1 (2012): 128. For skepticism about this claim, see Asifa Quraishi-Landes, "Comment on Brett G. Scharffs' *Equality in Sheep's Clothing: The Implications of Anti-Discrimination Norms for Religious Autonomy*," *Santa Clara Journal of International Law* 10, no. 1 (2012): 139–146.

39. *Bob Jones University v. US*, 461 US 574 (1983).
40. See, e.g. Corey Brettschneider, "How Should Liberal Democracies Respond to Faith-Based Groups That Advocate Discrimination? State Funding and Nonprofit Status," in *Legal Responses to Religious Practices in the United States: Accommodation and Its Limits*, Austin Sarat, ed. (Cambridge: Cambridge University Press, 2012), 72–114; Caroline Mala Corbin, "Expanding the *Bob Jones* Compromise," in ibid., 123–167.
41. *Christian Legal Society v. Martinez*, 130 S. Ct. 2971 (2010).
42. See, e.g., the cases listed in Timothy J. Tracey, "Christian Legal Society v. Martinez: In Hindsight," *University of Hawaii Law Review* 34 (2012): 84 n. 106.
43. In this vein, arguing against any exemption of religious objectors from general laws, Brian Barry compares this policy to "a course of chemotherapy" that "holds out the hope of destroying the malignant features of religion." Barry acknowledges that this treatment will be "experienced as debilitating by believers," but he regards this as a good thing, given his opposition to that sort of strong religion. Brian Barry, *Culture and Equality: An Egalitarian Critique of Multiculturalism* (Cambridge, MA: Harvard University Press, 2001).
44. Cf. Caroline Mala Corbin, "The Contraception Mandate," *Northwestern University Law Review* 107, no. 3 (2013): 1469–1483 (arguing that contraception mandate does not substantially burden Catholic religion because most American Catholics do not oppose contraception anyway).
45. See supra note 14 and accompanying text.
46. See Paul Horwitz, "Freedom of the Church without Romance," *Journal of Contemporary Legal Issues* 21 (2013): 89–95.
47. See, e.g., *Town of Greece v. Galloway*, 572 US ___, (2014), 134 S. Ct. 1811 (official prayer); *Elk Grove School District v. Newdow*, 542 US 1 (2004) (Pledge of Allegiance); *Salazar v. Buono*, 559 US 700 (2010) (cross on federal property).
48. *Lynch v. Donnelly*, 465 US 668, 688 (1984) (O'Connor, J., concurring).
49. For further discussion, see Steven D. Smith, "Symbols, Perceptions, and Doctrinal Illusions: Establishment Neutrality and the "No Endorsement" Test," *Michigan Law Review* 86 (1987): 310–312.
50. This proposition has been defended, debated, refined, and resisted by now in a vast scholarly literature. For one careful and insightful treatment, see Christopher J. Eberle, *Religious Conviction in Liberal Politics* (Cambridge: Cambridge University Press, 2002).
51. *Perry v. Schwarzenegger*, 704 F.Supp. 2d 921, 930–931 (N.D. Cal. 2010).
52. Ibid., 952.
53. I have elsewhere criticized this classification. See Steven D. Smith, "The Constitution and the Goods of Religion," in *Dimensions of Goodness*, Vittorio Hosle, ed. (Newcastle upon Tyne: Cambridge Scholars Publishing, 2013), 319–338.
54. For discussion, see Steven D. Smith, "Toleration and Liberal Commitments," in *Toleration and its Limits*, NOMOS XLVIII, Melissa S. Williams and Jeremy Waldron, eds. (New York: New York University Press, 2008), 259–264.
55. See Michael J. Perry, *Love and Power: The Role of Religion and Morality in American Politics* (New York: Oxford University Press, 1991), 10. In some contexts, particular beliefs or commitments—racist commitments, for example—may be deemed politically inadmissible for *all* citizens, secular or religious. And theorists such as John Rawls sometimes favor a norm discouraging citizens from acting on "comprehensive doctrines," religious or not. These more general prohibitions, however, have not been implemented in actual constitutional law.
56. Rodney O. Davis and Douglas L. Wilson, eds., *The Lincoln-Douglas Debates: The Lincoln Studies Center Edition* (Urbana: University of Illinois Press, 2008), 100, 242, 276.
57. For skepticism about such claims, see Steven D. Smith, "Recovering (from) Enlightenment?" *San Diego Law Review* 41 (2004): 1263–1310.
58. Thomas Jefferson, "Notes on the State of Virginia," in *Thomas Jefferson: Writings*, Library of America Series (Book 17), Merrill D. Peterson, ed. (New York: Library of America, 1984), 285.

59. See Douglas Laycock, "Religious Liberty as Liberty," *Journal of Contemporary Legal Issues* 7 (1996): 317 (contending that "beliefs at the heart of religion—beliefs about theology, liturgy, and church governance—are of little importance to the civil government").

60. It would also be easy enough to articulate different background assumptions—assumptions that have in fact prevailed in many times and places—under which Jefferson's complacent comment would seem uncompelling, or even obtuse.

     From either a religious or more anti-religious perspective, for example, it may seem that religion has a powerful effect, for good or ill, on culture and politics. See, e.g., Ross Koppel, "Public Policy in Pursuit of Private Happiness," *Contemporary Sociology* 41 (2012): 49–52 (asserting that "on a macro level, the net effects of religion and faith are . . . a few thousand years of horrible wars, genocide, slavery's ideology, sexual exploitation, torture, devaluing others as not human, terrorism, and organized hatred."). If you hold Koppel's view, it would seem odd and even reprehensible to adopt Jefferson's nonchalant attitude toward something that has had such catastrophic social consequences.

61. In this vein, Martha Nussbaum associates what she perceives as the intolerance of the religious right with "fear and insecurity," "sheer selfishness," and a desire to "lord it over" others. Nussbaum, *Liberty of Conscience: In Defense of America's Tradition of Religious Equality*, 8, 28, supra note 22.

62. *Abrams v. United States*, 250 US 616, 630 (1919) (Holmes, J., dissenting).

63. Holmes's rationale has been much debated. See, e.g., Steven D. Smith, "Skepticism, Tolerance, and Truth in the Theory of Free Expression," *Southern California Law Review* 60 (1987): 649–731.

64. I have developed this point at much greater length in Smith, "Toleration and Liberal Commitments," supra note 54; Smith, "Skepticism, Tolerance, and Truth in the Theory of Free Expression," supra note 63.

65. See generally Alexandra Walsham, *Charitable Hatred: Tolerance and Intolerance in England, 1500-1700* (Manchester: Manchester University Press, 2006). Ethan Shagan observes that "[b]efore the 1640s, the state's prerogative to punish religious deviance was almost unanimously praised as moderate, while broad claims for religious toleration were almost unanimously condemned as extremist." Ethan H. Shagan, *The Rule of Moderation: Violence, Religion and the Politics of Restraint in Early Modern England* (New York: Cambridge University Press, 2011), 288.

66. Roger Williams and John Milton would be notable exceptions to this generalization.

67. See, e.g., Ramsay MacMullen, *Christianity and Paganism in the Fourth to Eighth Centuries* (New Haven, CT: Yale University Press, 1997), 2 (describing ancient paganism as a "spongy mass of tolerance and tradition"); Edward Gibbon, *The History of the Decline and Fall of the Roman Empire*, David Womersley, ed., Vols. 1 and 2 (London: Penguin Books, 1994), 57, 447.

68. See Steven D. Smith, *The Rise and Decline of American Religious Freedom* (Cambridge, MA: Harvard University Press, 2014) 19, 28.

69. See, e.g., *Edwards v. Aguillard*, 482 US 578 (1987).

70. Cf. Lee C. Bollinger, *The Tolerant Society* (New York: Oxford University Press, 1986), 106–113 (acknowledging and discussing "the impulse to excessive intolerance").

71. See Smith, *The Rise and Decline of American Religious Freedom*, 14–47, supra note 68.

72. J. A. North explains: "[I]f there was tolerance it was not tolerance born of principle. So far as we know, there was no fixed belief that a state or individual ought to tolerate different forms of religion; that is the idea of far later periods of history. The truth seems to be that the Romans tolerated what seemed to them harmless and drew the line whenever there seemed to be a threat of possible harm; only, they saw no great harm in many of the cults of their contemporary world." J. A. North, *Roman Religion* (Cambridge: Cambridge University Press, 2000), 63.

73. See Louis Pojman, "On Equal Human Worth: A Critique of Contemporary Egalitarianism," in *Equality: Selected Readings*, Louis P. Pojman and Robert Westmoreland, ed. (New York: Cambridge University Press, 1997), 295 ("The argument implicit in the Judeo-Christian tradition seems to be that God is the ultimate value and that humans derive their value by being created in his image and likeness.").

74. See, e.g., Jeremy Waldron, *God, Locke, and Equality: Christian Foundations in Locke's Political Thought* (Cambridge: Cambridge University Press, 2002), 243; Michael J. Perry, *The Idea of Human Rights: Four Inquiries* (New York: Oxford University Press, 1998) 11–41; Pojman, "On Equal Human Worth: A Critique of Contemporary Egalitarianism," 282–298, supra note 73.

75. John Locke, "A Letter Concerning Toleration," in *John Locke, The Second Treatise of Government and A Letter Concerning Toleration*, Tom Crawford, ed. (New York: Dover, 2002), 113.

76. Ibid., 119.

77. Thus, Lactantius, advisor to Constantine and tutor of his children, wrote that "[l]iberty has chosen to dwell in religion. For nothing is so much a matter of free will as religion, and no one can be required to worship what he does not will to worship." Quoted in Brian Tierney, "Religious Rights: A Historical Perspective," in *Religious Liberty in Western Thought*, Noel B. Reynolds and W. Cole Durham, Jr., eds. (Grand Rapids, MI: Wm. B. Eerdmans Publishing Co., 1996), 32. See also Paul Veyne, *When Our World Became Christian, 312-394*, Janet Lloyd, trans., (Cambridge: Polity, 2010), 90 ("Throughout the fourth century, it was repeated that it was not possible to compel consciences or to force people to believe.").

78. Such objections are of course the basis of the numerous current cases typified by *Burwell v. Hobby Lobby*, 573 US ___, (2014), 134 S. Ct. 2751.

79. See supra notes 32–37 and accompanying text.

80. For a review of the situation in the 1950s, see Robert E. Rodes, Jr., *On Law and Chastity* (Durham, NC: Carolina Academic Press, 2006), 9–24.

81. In this respect, it may be helpful to distinguish contemporary secular egalitarianism from traditional mainstream liberalism, which *does* have considerable experience with toleration as well as the intellectual resources to justify it: think of John Stuart Mill. I would classify Professor Laycock and his fellow moderators within the broad tent of traditional mainstream liberalism.

82. See generally, Smith, "Recovering (from) Enlightenment," supra note 57.

83. Peter Westen, "The Empty Idea of Equality," *Harvard Law Review* 95 (1982): 537–596.

84. Overwhelming evidence for this assertion is marshaled in Daniel Boorstin, *The Lost World of Thomas Jefferson* (Chicago: Chicago University Press, 1993 [first published 1948]).

85. See Alexis de Tocqueville, *Democracy in America*, George Lawrence, trans., J. P. Meyer, ed. (New York: Harper & Row, 1966), 12, 18, 37, 56, 60, 277, 281, 282, 301, 370, 378, 397, 405, 413, 446, 486, 704, 705.

86. More generally, modern secular society itself seems to be a new thing—different, as Charles Taylor argues, from "anything else in human history." Charles Taylor, *A Secular Age* (Cambridge, MA: Harvard University Press, 2007), 1.

87. Robert Nisbet, *Twilight of Authority* (New York: Oxford University Press, 1975), 180–193.

88. Ibid., 184.

89. Ibid. Cf. Tocqueville, *Democracy in America*, 538, supra note 85: "When inequality is the general rule in society the greatest inequalities attract no attention. When everything is more or less level, the slightest variation is noticed. Hence the more equal men are, the more insatiable will be their longing for equality."

90. Jeremy Waldron argues that John Locke's commitment to equality was grounded in religious assumptions, and that modern efforts to support the commitment have to this point proven unavailing. See generally Jeremy Waldron, *God, Locke, and Equality: Christian Foundations in Locke's Political Thought* (Cambridge: Cambridge University Press, 2002): "[M]aybe the notion of humans as one another's equals will begin to fall apart, under pressure, without the presence of the religious conception that shaped it. . . . Locke believed this general acceptance [of equality] was impossible apart from the principle's foundation in religious teaching. We believe otherwise. Locke, I suspect, would have thought we were taking a risk. And I am afraid it is not entirely clear, given our experience of a world and a century in which politics and public reason have cut loose from these foundations, that his cautions and suspicions were unjustified." (243).

91. The classic law review article is Charles R. Lawrence III, "The Id, the Ego, and Equal Protection: Reckoning with Unconscious Racism," *Stanford Law Review* 39 (1987): 317–388.

92. See Robert Louis Wilken, *The Christians as the Romans Saw Them*, 2nd ed. (New Haven, CT: Yale University Press, 2003), 165–166. H. A. Drake contends that imperial policy under Constantine and his son Constantius was broadly tolerant and inclusive. However, the effort of the emperor Julian ("the Apostate") in the mid-fourth century to restore paganism by legally marginalizing Christianity revived memories and fears of the persecutions under Diocletian earlier in the century, thereby provoking a repressive backlash following Julian's death. H. A. Drake, *Constantine and the Bishops: The Politics of Intolerance* (Baltimore, MD: Johns Hopkins University Press, 2000).

93. See *Elane Photography v. Willcock*, 309 P.3d 53 (N.M. 2013); *Craig v. Masterpiece Cakeshop, Inc.*, CR 2013-0008 (Colo. Office of Admin. Cts. 2013) (initial decision).

94. Laycock, "Religious Liberty and the Culture Wars," 863–869, supra note 8.

95. Ibid., 869.

96. In fact, the church's attitude toward the revolution was complex. Many clerics supported many of the revolution's objectives. Moreover, it seems a bit harsh to fault the church for being less than enthusiastic about a movement that essentially nationalized the church and coerced clergy to swear allegiance to the state, confiscated and sold vast amounts of church property, and executed thousands of priests deemed not sufficiently supportive of the revolution. See generally John McManners, *The French Revolution and the Church* (London: S.P.C.K., 1969).

97. See Laycock, "Sex, Atheism and the Free Exercise of Religion," 418, supra note 8.

98. For a history of the conflict in France, see Mack P. Holt, *The French Wars of Religion, 1562–1629*, 2nd ed. (New York: Cambridge University Press, 2005).

99. Ibid., 110–111.

100. Cf. Tocqueville, *Democracy in America*, 691, 694, supra note 85 (observing "the trivial nature of men's passions now" and suggesting that democratic egalitarianism becomes a kind of soft despotism that "slowly stifles [men's] spirits and enervates their souls").

101. Stephen Macedo, "Transformative Constitutionalism and the Case of Religion: Defending the Moderate Hegemony of Liberalism," *Political Theory* 26 (1998): 61, 63.

102. Brad S. Gregory, *Salvation at Stake: Christian Martyrdom in Early Modern Europe* (Cambridge, MA: Harvard University Press, 2001), 352. Gregory further explains that to early modern Christians "[t]he prospect of doctrinal pluralism horrified and disgusted them. They *preferred* a world in which truth did battle, come what may, to one swarming with ever-proliferating heresies" (346; emphasis original).

103. 576 US ___, (2015).

104. For my commentary on this aspect of the opinion, see Steven D. Smith, "'Liberty,' 'Marriage,' and Religious Freedom," *Cornerstone* (blog), June 29, 2015, http://berkleycenter.george-town.edu/cornerstone/obergefell-v-hodges-the-ruling-and-its-implications-for-religious-freedom/responses/liberty-marriage-and-religious-freedom.

105. See Robin Fretwell Wilson, "A Closing Window," *Library of Law and Religion* (blog) http://www.libertylawsite.org/2014/06/11/a-closing-window/.

106. Compare, e.g., Jonathan Rauch, "The Landmark LGBT-Mormon Compromise in Utah," *FixGov* (blog), Brookings Institution, March 25, 2015, http://www.brookings.edu/blogs/fixgov/posts/2015/03/17-mormon-lgbt-rights-utah-rauch (praising compromise) and J. Stuart Adams and Robin Fretwell Wilson, "Protecting Religious Liberty Requires Protections for All," Cornerstone (blog), April 30, 2015, http://berkleycenter.george-town.edu/cornerstone/indiana-rfra-and-beyond/responses/protecting-religious-liberty-requires-protections-for-all (recommending Utah measure as example for other states to follow) with Walter Olson, "Why Utah's Mormon/LGBT Compromise Is Just Awful," Daily Beast, March 20, 2015, http://www.thedailybeast.com/articles/2015/03/20/why-utah-s-mormon-lgbt-compromise-is-just-awful.html (criticizing measure from libertarian perspective) and Nelson Tebbe, Richard Schragger, and Micah Schwartzman, "Utah 'Compromise' to Protect LGBT Citizens from Discrimination Is No Model for the Nation," http://www.slate.com/blogs/outward/2015/03/18/gay_rights_the_utah_compromise_is_no_model_for_the_nation.html (criticizing compromise from egalitarian perspective).

107. See Ross Douthat, "Op-ed; The Case of Brendan Eich," *New York Times*, April 8, 2014, http://douthat.blogs.nytimes.com/2014/04/08/the-case-of-brendan-eich/.

108. See Editors, "Why Law Professor Douglas Laycock Supports Same-Sex Marriage and Indiana's Religious Freedom Law," interview with Douglas Laycock, *Religion & Politics*, April 1, 2015, http://religionandpolitics.org/2015/04/01/why-law-professor-douglas-laycock-supports-same-sex-marriage-and-indianas-religious-freedom-law/.

109. The controversy generated extensive commentary. For my own small contribution, see Steven D. Smith, "Indiana Among the Pagans?," *Cornerstone* (blog), April 28, 2015, http://berkleycenter.georgetown.edu/responses/indiana-among-the-pagans-c9a78c67-5e56-4371-b46d-0d7d207ad752.

110. See, e.g., Frederick Mark Gedicks and Rebecca G. Van Tassell, "RFRA Exemptions from the Contraception Mandate: An Unconstitutional Accommodation of Religion," *Harvard Civil Rights-Civil Liberties Law Review* 49 (2014): 343–384.

111. *Burwell v. Hobby Lobby*, 573 US ___, (2014), 134 S. Ct. 2751.

112. Douglas NeJaime and Reva B. Seigel, "Conscience Wars: Complicity-Based Conscience Claims in Religion and Politics," *Yale Law Journal* 124, no. 7 (2015): 2516–2591.

113. For powerful criticism of both arguments, see Marc O. DeGirolami, "Free Exercise by Moonlight," *San Diego Law Review* (forthcoming 2015), published electronically March 30, 2015, http://papers.ssrn.com/sol3/papers.cfm?abstract_id=2587216##.

114. For a more accommodating stance from a leading egalitarian, see Andrew Koppelman, "Gay Rights, Religious Accommodations, and the Purposes of Antidiscrimination Laws," *Southern California Law Review* 88 (2015): 619–660.

Chapter 8

1. See, e.g., T. W. Adorno, *Against Epistemology: A Metacritique; Studies in Husserl and the Phenomenological Antimonies* (1956), W. Domingo, trans. (Cambridge, MA: MIT Press, 1982).

2. See, for instance, Jacques Derrida, "Interview with Jean Louis Houdebine and Guy Scarpetta," in *Positions*, Alan Bass, trans. (Chicago: University of Chicago Press, 1981).

3. Dean H. Hamer, et. al., "A Linkage between DNA Markers on the X Chromosome and Male Sexual Orientation," *Science* 261, no. 5119 (1993): 321–327.

4. George Rice, et. al., "Male Homosexuality: Absence of Linkage to Microsatellite Markers at X 28," *Science* 284, no. 5414 (1999): 665–667.

5. To tell the whole truth we must say that the author of the alleged discovery never pretended that the gene he discovered could be the only cause of male homosexuality. See Dean Hamer and Peter Copeland, *The Science of Desire: The Search for the Gay Gene and the Biology of the Future* (New York: Simon and Schuster, 1994).

6. Bruce S. Thornton, *Eros: The Myth of Ancient Greek Sexuality* (Boulder: Westview Press, 1997).

7. Plato, *Symposium*, sec. 192(a).

8. Craig Williams, *Roman Homosexuality: Ideologies of Masculinity in Classical Antiquity* (Oxford: Oxford University Press, 1999).

9. Sigmund Freud, *Three Essays on the Theory of Sexuality* (1905), James Strachey, trans. (New York: Basic Books, 1975).

10. St. Paul for instance. See Romans 1:18–27.

11. For Christians this should be read also on the background of the doctrine of original sin. All men are sinners and stand in need of mercy, homosexuals as well as heterosexuals. A negative moral judgment on homosexuality does not entail a presumption of superiority. Ibid.

12. Immanuel Kant, *Critique of Pure Reason*, para. 16.

13. Immanuel Kant, *Groundwork of the Metaphysics of Morals*), B52.

14. Ibid., BA 67.

15. Max Horkheimer, "Authoritarianism and the Family Today," in *The Family: Its Function and Destiny*, Ruth Nanda Anshen, ed. (New York: Harper, 1949), 359–374.

16. Aristotle, *Nichomachean Ethics*, 1130b–1132b.

17. See *Costituzione della Repubblica Italiana*, Art. 3.

18. See also Arts. 22–27 of the Universal Declaration of Human Rights.

19. For a critique of second-generation rights, see Maurice Cranston, "Human Rights, Real and Supposed" in *Political Theory and the Rights of Man*, D. D. Raphael, ed. (Bloomington, IN: Indiana University Press, 1967).

20. J. D. Skrentny, *The Ironies of Affirmative Action* (Chicago: University of Chicago Press, 1996).

21. You will look in vain for this sentence in Voltaire's *Traitéèè de la Tolerance* (1763), or in any other of his works. This quote was first attributed to him by Evelyn Beatrice Hall in the book *The Friends of Voltaire* published under the pseudonym S. G. Tallentyre in 1906. Despite this, it has become the most frequent of Voltaire's "quotes."

22. See Richard Vernon, ed., *Locke on Toleration* (New York: Cambridge University Press, 2010). Locke's first Letter on Toleration was written in 1689.

23. Pope Paul VI, Second Vatican Council, *Dignitatis humanae (Declaration on Religious Freedom)*, "On the Right of the Person and of Communities to Social and Civil Freedom in Matters Religious," December 7, 1965, http://www.vatican.va/archive/hist_councils/ii_vatican_council/documents/vat-ii_decl_19651207_dignitatis-humanae_en.html.

24. Toleration presupposes the difference between God's possession of truth and the human grasp of truth. See G. B. Vico, "De Antiquissima Italorum Sapientia," in *Opere Filosofiche*, P. Cristofolini, ed. (Sansoni, 1971), 55–131.

25. The *Two Treatises on Government* of John Locke were published in 1689 and contain the ideal basis of the revolution of 1689. See also the *Bill of Rights* (1689), although the exact relation of historical and natural rights in the Glorious Revolution remains a matter of discussion. For the American Revolution, see US Declaration of Independence (1776), Virginia Declaration of Rights (1776). See also M. P. Zuckert, *The Natural Rights Republic: Studies in the Foundation of the American Political Tradition* (Notre Dame: University of Notre Dame Press, 1996).

26. See Ralph McInerny, "Natural Law and Human Rights," *American Journal of Jurisprudence* 36, no. 1 (1991): 1–14.

27. Plato, *The State*, 336b–354c.

28. Perhaps, however, it is simply impossible, and not even desirable, to completely disentangle ourselves from all presuppositions. After all, they help us to categorize the flux of experience. It may be that we would not be able to orient ourselves in the world we live in if we had to develop an original cognitive contact with reality with each new experience. Yet it is nevertheless important that we call into question what we think, what we suppose we know, and let it undergo new scrutiny.

29. Josef Seifert, *Back to "Things in Themselves": A Phenomenological Foundation for Classical Realism* (New York and London: Routledge and Kegan Paul, 1987).

30. Edmund Husserl, *The Crisis of European Sciences and Transcendental Phenomenology: An Introduction to Phenomenological Philosophy* (1954), David Carr, trans. (Evanston, IL: Northwestern University Press, 1970).

31. Andrew Sullivan, ed., *Same-Sex Marriage: Pro and Con—A Reader* (New York: Vintage Books, 2004).

32. *Costituzione Della Repubblica Italiana* Arts. 29–31.

33. Karol Wojtyla, "Rodzicielstwo jako Communio Personarum," in *Atheneum Kaplanskie* 83, no. 3 (1974): 347–371.

34. Carl Jung, "Die psychologischen Aspekte des Mutterarchetypus (Psychological Aspects of the Mother Archetype)," *Eranos* 6 (1938): 405–409.

35. William Marsiglio, et. al., "Scholarship on Fatherhood in 1990s and Beyond," *Journal of Marriage and Family* 62, no. 4 (November 2000): 1173–1191.

36. John Bowlby, *Child Care and the Growth of Love* (Baltimore: Penguin Books, 1953).

37. Sigmund Freud, *The Ego and the Id* (1923) (Seattle, WA: Pacific Publishing, 2010).

38. *Quod plerumque accidit*, in the language of St. Thomas Aquinas.

39. *X. and Others v. Austria* [2013] ECHR 148 (February 19, 2013).

Chapter 9

1. C. Saracino, "Le Unioni Civili in Europa: Modelli a Confronto," *Diritto di Famiglia* 33 (2011): 1471. For recent snapshot of the diversity of solutions across Europe,

see Michael Lipka, "Where Europe Stands on Gay Marriage and Civil Unions," *Pew Research Center*, June 9, 2015, http://www.pewresearch.org/fact-tank/2015/06/09/where-europe-stands-on-gay-marriage-and-civil-unions/.

2. See the cases enlisted in M. Bonini Baraldi, "Le Famiglie Omosessuali nel Prisma della Realizzazione Personale," *Quaderni Costituzionali* 4 (2009): 895.

3. As to the European Court of Human Rights approach to same-sex partnerships as legitimate private life relationships, see *Karner v. Austria* [2003] ECHR 395 (July 24, 2003); *Kozak v. Poland* [2010] ECHR 280 (March 2, 2010); *P.B. and J.S. v. Austria* [2010] ECHR 1146 (July 22, 2010).

4. *Schalk and Kopf v. Austria* [2010] ECHR 1996 (November 22, 2010).

5. N. Melehi, "The Right to Family Life Free from Discrimination on the Basis of Sexual Orientation: The European and Inter-American Perspectives," *American University International Law Review* 29, no. 4 (2014): 986.

6. *Vallianatos and Others v. Greece*, [2013] ECHR 1110 (November 7, 2013).

7. *Oliari and Others v. Italy*, [2015] ECHR 716 (July 21, 2015).

8. European Parliament Resolution, "On Equality Between Women and Men in the European Union—2011," March 13, 2012 (2011/2244 [INI]), point 7, http://www.europarl.europa.eu/sides/getDoc.do?pubRef=-//EP//TEXT+TA+P7-TA-2012-0069+0+DOC+XML+V0//EN.

9. Ibid., point 6.

10. It has become increasingly difficult for EU states that have not introduced same-sex marriage to accommodate the status of same-sex couples that are legally married according to other EU states' laws. See A. Schuster, *Il Matrimonio e la Famiglia Omosessuale in Due Recenti Sentenze. Prime Note in Forma di Soliloquio*, www.forumcostituzionale.it (visited May 25, 2012).

11. A clear example of this can be found in the recent Reggio Emilia Civil Tribunal decision (February 13, 2012), which recognized the right of a non-European citizen to live in Italy since he in Spain had married an Italian man living in Italy.

12. *Schalk and Kopf v. Austria* [2010] ECHR 1996 (November 22, 2010).

13. Ibid., para. 93.

14. See M. Bonini Baraldi, "Le Famiglie Omosessuali nel Prisma della Realizzazione Personale," *Quaderni Costituzionali* 4 (2009): 882 and 888.

15. All Constitutional Court's judgments can be retrieved at: www.cortecostituzionale.it

16. Art. 93, 96, 98, 107, 108, 143, 143-bis, and 156-bis, Civil Code.

17. Among many, see R. Romboli, "Il Diritto 'Consentito' al Matrimonio ed il Diritto 'Garantito' alla Vita Familiare per le Coppie Omosessuali in una Pronuncia in cui la Corte dice 'Troppo' e 'Troppo Poco,'" *Giurisprudenza Costituzionale* 2 (2010): 1629.

18. Art. 29, 2nd paragraph.

19. P. A. Capotosti, "Matrimonio tra Persone dello Stesso Sesso: Infondatezza Versus Inammissibilità nella Sentenza n. 138 del 2010," *Quaderni Costituzionali* 2 (2010): 363.

20. See E. Crivelli, "Il Caso Schalk v. Austria in Tema di Rapporti Omosessuali," in *Dieci Casi sui Diritti in Europa*, M. Cartabia, ed. (Bologna: il Mulino, 2011) 67, where the author contrasts the decision of the Italian Constitutional Court with the European Court of Human Rights' decision *Schalk and Kopf v. Austria*, which reflected on the extension of the marriage to same-sex couples.

21. See, notably, the speech of the then–President of the Constitutional Court Franco Gallo, April 12, 2013, available at http://www.cortecostituzionale.it/documenti/relazioni_annuali/RelazioneGallo_20130412.pdf.

22. Court of Cassation, I Civil Law session, decision November 4, 2011–March 15, 2012, no. 4184, available at http://www.giurcost.org/casi_scelti/Cassazione/Cass.sent.4184-2012

23. Art. 17, decree of the President of the Republic no. 396, 2000.

24. Italian Constitutional Court, Judgment no. 170, 2014.

25. Art. 4, law n. 164, 1982.

26. See Italian Constitutional Court, Judgment no. 170, 2014, para. 5.6.

27. *Schalk and Kopf v. Austria* [2010] ECHR 1996 (November 22, 2010), para. 105 (emphasis added).

28. Ibid. (emphasis added).

29. *Oliari and Others v. Italy*, [2015] ECHR 716 (July 21, 2015).
30. Ibid., para. 169.
31. Ibid., para 178.
32. Ibid., para. 179.
33. M. Cartabia, "Avventure Giuridiche della Differenza Sessuale," *Iustitia* 3 (2001): 303.
34. As to the individualistic approach that contemporary law takes, see J. H. H. Weiler, "Individuals and Rights—The Sour Grapes," *European Journal of International Law* 21, no. 2 (2010): 277.
35. Along these lines, see R. Dworkin, *Justice for Hedgehogs* (Cambridge: Belknap Press, 2011), 369 and 377.
36. See decision no. 387, delivered in 2007.
37. M. Cartabia, "The European Court of Human Rights: Judging Nondiscrimination," *International Journal of Constitutional Law* 9, no. 3–4 (2011): 809.
38. A. Panebianco, *Il Potere, lo Stato, la Libertà. La Gracile Costituzione della Società Libera* (Bologna: il Mulino, 2004).
39. A. Scola, *Una Nuova Laicità. Temi per una Società Plurale* (Venezia: Marcianum Press, 2007).
40. F. Viola, "L'obiezione di Coscienza come Diritto," in *Diritto & Questioni Pubbliche* 9 (2009): 174.
41. See the French "Report by the Commission on the Measurement of Economic Performance and Social Progress," 151 and 204. The report was drafted under the supervision of J. P. Fitoussi, J. E. Stiglitz, and A. Sen, http://www.stiglitz-sen-fitoussi.fr/documents/rapport_anglais.pdf (visited May 26, 2012).
42. A. Shachar, "State, Religion, and the Family: The New Dilemmas of Multicultural Accommodation," in *Shari'a in the West*, R. Ahdar and N. Aroney, eds. (Oxford: Oxford University Press, 2010), 128.
43. C. A. Anderson, "Can Beauty Save the World?" in *Sufficit Gratia Tua*, G. Marengo, J. Prades Lopez, and G. Richi Alberti, eds. (Venice: Marcianum Press, 2012), 61.
44. S. Sileoni, "La Corte di Strasburgo e i Matrimoni Omosessuali: il Consenso Europeo, un Criterio Fragile ma Necessario," *Quaderni Costituzionali* 4 (2010): 870. Sileoni highlights the artificial divide between culture and law in several episodes of legal reasoning on this subject. See also C. Cardia, *Le Sfide Della Laicità. Etica, Multiculturalismo, Islam* (Milano: San Paolo, 2007), 186.
45. Several decisions of the Italian Constitutional Court stressed that the Constitution and the Parliament have gradually updated the marriage institution and freed it from the patriarchal, discriminating features by which it had been characterized. See, for instance, decisions no. 170 (released in 1999) and 166 (released in 1998).
46. B. Pezzini, *Il Matrimonio Same Sex si Potrà Fare*. "La Qualificazione della Discrezionalità del Legislatore nella Sent. n. 138 del 2010 della Corte Costituzionale," *Giurisprudenza Costituzionale* 3 (2010): 2715.
47. European Parliament Resolution, "On Equality Between Women and Men in the European Union—2011," March 13, 2012 (2011/2244 [INI]), point 7. See note 8 above.
48. See, more recently, R. Dworkin, *Justice for Hedgehogs* (Cambridge: Belknap Press, 2011), 196.
49. L. Violini and S. Ninatti, "Nel Labirinto del Principio di Nondiscriminazione: Adozione, Fecondazione Eterologa e Coppia Omosessuale Davanti alla Corte di Strasburgo," in *Studi in Onore di Loiodice* (Bari, Italy: Cacucci Editore, 2012), 11–14, http://www.forumcostituzionale.it/wordpress/images/stories/pdf/documenti_forum/paper/0318_ninatti_violini.pdf.
50. Law no. 40, 2014.
51. N. Rao, "Three Concepts of Dignity in Constitutional Law," *Notre Dame Law Review* 86, no. 1 (2011): 262.
52. F. Viola, "L'obiezione di Coscienza Come Diritto," *Diritto & Questioni Pubbliche* 9 (2009): 170.
53. Davide Paris, *L'obiezione di Coscienza. Studio Sull'ammissibilità di un'eccezione dal Servizio Militare alla Bioetica* (Bagno a Ripoli, Italy: Passigli, 2011), 38.
54. In *Eweida & Others v. United Kingdom* [2013] ECHR 37 (January 15, 2013), the European Court of Human Rights maintained that, to fall under the religious freedom provision, the "act in question must be *intimately* linked to the religion or belief." See para. 82.
55. *Eweida & Others v. The United Kingdom*, para. 84.

56. *Ladele* case, in *Eweida & Others v. United Kingdom*, para. 23ff.
57. R. Bertolino, *L'obiezione di Coscienza Moderna per una Fondazione Costituzionale del Diritto di Obiezione* (Torino: Giappichelli, 1994), 90.
58. Judgment no. 2, 2014, para. 3.1.
59. G. Rossi, "Verso un Nuovo Femminismo Della Dignità," in *Sufficit Gratia Tua*, G. Marengo, J. Prades Lopez, and G. Richi Alberti, eds. (Venice: Marcianum Press, 2012), 620.
60. One can see the analogies between this way of thinking and the traditionalism that was criticized by J. Pelikan, *The Vindication of Tradition* (New Haven: Yale University Press, 1984), in which he advocated the role of tradition but opposed traditionalism.

Chapter 10

1. See, for example, Ninna Edgardh and Per Pettersson, "The Church of Sweden: A Church for All, Especially the Most Vulnerable," in *Welfare and Religion in 21st Century Europe*, vol. 1, *Configuring the Connections*, Anders Bäckström and Grace Davie, eds. (Farnham: Ashgate Publishing Limited, 2010), 55.
2. Certain other continental European countries, on the contrary, made the new institution of registered partnership available also to opposite-sex couples, such as the Netherlands.
3. Interestingly enough, the decision by parliament followed a so-called citizens' initiative whereby more than 166,000 Finnish citizens in December 2013 requested the law reform, following the government's inability to reach an agreement on a bill.
4. In a strict geographic sense, Iceland and large parts of Finland are not a part of Scandinavia. The other often-used term "Nordic states" appears, however, too vague in a contribution aimed for an international public.
5. NJA 2005, p. 805.
6. *Vejdeland & Ors v. Sweden* [2012] ECHR 242 (February 9, 2012).
7. *Hämäläinen v. Finland* [2014] ECHR 787 (July 16, 2014).
8. See, for example, Peter Lödrup, "The Reharmonisation of Nordic Family Law," in *European Challenges in Contemporary Family Law*, K. Boele-Woelki and T. Sverdrup, eds. (Portland, OR: Intersentia, 2008), 17–26.
9. The trend in all the states is to loosen the legal ties with the state. In Sweden, the legal separation of the Church from the state was carried out in 2000 and in Norway in 2013.
10. See Anders Bäckström, Ninna Edgardh Beckman, and Per Pettersson, *Religious Change in Northern Europe: The Case of Sweden* (Stockholm: Verbum, 2004), 88–90 and 139f. See also Maarit Jänterä-Jareborg, "On the Cooperation between Religious and State Institutions in Family Matters: Nordic Experiences," in *Family, Religion and Law: Cultural Encounters in Europe*, Prakash Shah, Marie-Claire Foblets, and Mathias Rohe, eds. (Burlington: Ashgate Publishing, 2014), 80–85.
11. Olav Helge Angell, "Sacred Welfare Agents in Secular Welfare Space: The Church of Norway in Drammen," in *Welfare and Religion in 21st Century Europe*, vol. 1, *Configuring the Connections*, Anders Bäckström and Grace Davie, eds., 72.
12. See Rolf Nygren, "Legal Culture and World Value Mapping," in *Europäische Rechtsgechichte und europäische Integration, Heinz Mohnhaupt von seinen skandinavischen Kollegen gewidmet* (Stockholm: Rönnels Förlag, 2002), 117. See also Kjell Åke Modeer, "Secularization, Liberalization and Modernization: Family Law in Scandinavian Welfare States in the 1960s and 1970s," in *Japanese Family Law in Comparative Perspective*, H. N. Schneider and L. Mayali, eds. (Berkeley: University of California, 2009), 215.
13. See *Statens Offentliga Utredningar* (SOU) 1984:83 (Homosexuella och samhället, Homosexuals and Society). This resulted in the 1987 enactment by parliament, called Homosexual Cohabitees' Joint Homes Act.
14. See further, e.g., Caroline Sörgjerd, *Reconstructing Marriage: The Legal Status of Relationships in a Changing Society* (Portland, OR: Intersentia, 2012); Ingrid Lund-Andersen, "The Nordic Countries: Same Direction—Different Speeds," in *Legal Recognition of Same-Sex Relationships in Europe: National, Cross-Border and European Perspectives*, K. Boele-Woelki and A. Fuchs, eds. (Portland, OR: Intersentia, 2012), 3–17.

15. See Maarit Jänterä-Jareborg, "Parenthood for Same-Sex Couples:—Scandinavian Developments," in *Legal Recognition of Same-Sex Relationships in Europe: National, Cross-Border and European Perspectives*, 91–122.

16. For developments within member states of the European Union, see Katharina Boele-Woelki, "The Legal Recognition of Same-Sex Relationships within the European Union," *Tulane Law Review* 82 (2008): 1949–1981. See also Frederik Swennen and Sven Eggermont, "Same-Sex Couples in Central Europe: Hop, Step and Jump," 19–39; Cristina González Beilfuss, "All or Nothing: The Dilemma of Southern Jurisdictions," 41–53; and Monika Jagielska, "Eastern European Countries: From Penalisation to Cohabitation or Further?," 55–69 all in *Legal Recognition of Same-Sex Relationships in Europe, National, Cross-Border and European Perspectives*. The data provided by Lynn D. Wardle, "Marriage and Religious Liberty: Comparative Law Problems and Conflict of Laws Solutions," *Journal of Law and Family Studies* 12 (2010): 328–329 (and Appendix I) demonstrate, nevertheless, that contrary to Europe, these institutions have met the approval of only a very small minority of the world nations.

17. Important judgments include the cases of *Schalk and Kopf v. Austria*, [2010] ECHR 995 (June 24, 2010); *E.B. v. France* [2008] ECHR 55 (January 22, 2008); and *Fretté v. France* [2002] ECHR 156 (February 26, 2002).

18. Swedish Ordinance of Government (*Regeringsformen*), Ch. 1 § 2.

19. This was "the ideological milieu" of the "agitators" in the case of *Vejdeland and Others v. Sweden*. See section V.C.

20. SOU 1984:63, p. 59.

21. SOU 1993:98 (Betänkande av Partnerskapskommittén, Committee Report on Partnership), 86–88.

22. SOU (Äktenskap för par med samma kön, vigselfrågor, Marriage for same-sex couples) 2007:17, pp. 32–33 and 220–221.

23. Church elections take place in Sweden every four years, focusing on choosing the lay representation to the Church of Sweden on both a national and a diocesan level. Although nonpolitical groups also may draw up special lists of candidates, such lists are a minority.

24. In Norway, the majority of the bishops of the Church of Norway have condemned the reform, not only as an infringement of the notion of marriage in Christianity and most other religions, but also as a social, cultural, and ecological experiment with unforeseeable consequences. See Ot. Prp. Nr. 33 (2007–2008) (n. 4), p. 19. Also in Sweden, several bishops of the Church of Sweden have publicly opposed the reform. Also the Church of Iceland had doubts, but not as strong as in the other two national churches. See further, Maarit Jänterä-Jareborg, "When 'Marriage' Becomes a Religious Battleground—Swedish and Scandinavian Experiences at the Dawn of Same-Sex Marriages," in *Private Law, National—Global—Comparative, Festschrift für Ingeborg Schwenzer zum 60. Geburtstag* (Bern: Stämpfli Verlag AG, 2011), 859–865.

25. Each member of the Church of Sweden, for example, contributes in the form of paying a church fee, approximately 1% of the person's income. This fee is levied by the state, in connection with state taxation.

26. Until 1996, all citizens of Sweden, upon birth, automatically became members of the Church of Sweden, on condition that at least one of the parents belonged to the Church. Since then, but not retroactively, one must be baptized to become a Church member. Approximately 60% of newborn children are baptized in Sweden. Approximately 70% of Sweden's population belongs as members to the Church of Sweden, which is the lowest membership rate among the Scandinavian national Churches.

27. See Martin Scheinin, "Secular Human Rights Perspectives As a Challenge to Nordic Law & Religious Solutions," in *Law and Religion in the 21st Century*, L. Christoffersen, K. Å. Modéer, and S. Andersen, eds. (Copenhagen: Djøf Publishing, 2010), 547–548; Maarit Jänterä-Jareborg, "The Legal Scope for Religious Identity in Family Matters: The Paradoxes of the Swedish Approach," in *The Place of Religion in Family Law: A Comparative Search*, J. Mair and E. Örücü, eds. (Portland, OR: Intersentia, 2011), 79–80 and 95–96. Similarly, Lynn D. Wardle, "Marriage and Religious Liberty: Comparative Law Problems and Conflict of Laws Solutions," 317.

28. See Maarit Jänterä-Jareborg and Caroline Sörgjerd, "The Experiences with Registered Partnership in Scandinavia," in *Die Praxis des Familienrechts* 5 (2001): 577–597 (see esp. 585–587).
29. See The Church of Sweden, "Information on a Possible Decision by the Church of Sweden Regarding Same-Sex Marriages," September 17, 2009, 14 (available in English).
30. Jaana Hallamaa, "Parisuhde ja sen sääntely uskonnollisena kysymyksenä," in *Lakimies* 109 (2011): 1232–1248.
31. Wardle mentions the Evangelical Lutheran Church in America and the Lutheran Church-Missouri Synod among the US churches opposed to same-sex marriages. Lynn D. Wardle, "Marriage and Religious Liberty: Comparative Law Problems and Conflict of Laws Solutions," 315–364, 332, n. 71.
32. Certain exceptions applied, e.g., in relation to the states' Jewish communities.
33. In Sweden, a decisive event was the adoption of the Freedom of Religion Act (*Religionsfrihetslagen*) in 1951. See M. Jänterä-Jareborg, "Religion and the Secular State in Sweden," in *Religion and the Secular State: National Reports*, under the direction of J. Martinez-Torrón and W. C. Durham, Jr., The International Center for Law and Religion Studies (Provo, 2010), 671.
34. SOU 2007:17, p. 43 (summary in English).
35. The right to conscientious objections does not include civil marriage authorities, who are bound by state law to perform all the functions of their office.
36. The right of refusal is a general one. A priest can refuse to marry a couple, for example, because they belong to different faiths or are divorced.
37. See SOU 2007:17, p. 279f.
38. SOU 2007:17, p. 41 (summary in English).
39. See SOU 2007:17, p. 41 (summary in English).
40. See Maarit Jänterä-Jareborg, "Parenthood for Same-Sex Couples: Scandinavian Developments," 91–122.
41. On the other hand, in a few purely domestic cases a married or registered same-sex couple could jointly adopt a child in Sweden.
42. Government Bill, Prop. 2001/02:123, p. 29.
43. See, e.g., *Upsala Nya Tidning*, January 9, 2011 (Editorial).
44. See Maarit Jänterä-Jareborg, "On the Cooperation between Religious and State Institutions in Family Matters: Nordic Experiences," 86–89. See above note 10.
45. According to critics, the conditions imposed qualify as an "instrumental definition of religion." See Anders Jarlert, "Individuell eller institutionell religionsfrihet?" in *Familj—Religion—Rätt, En antologi om kulturella spänningar inom familjen—med Sverige och Turkiet som exempel*, A. Singer, M. Jänterä-Jareborg, and A. Schlytter, eds. (Uppsala: Iustus Förlag, 2010), 117. Critically also, SOU 2009:52 (Staten och imamerna, The State and Imams), p. 89–90.
46. Example given by Oddbjörn Leirvik, Oslo University, Norway, Conference on Welfare and Values, Uppsala University, March 2009.
47. In his picturesque language, the pastor refers to parliament and government as the fools governing the country, drafting and enacting laws contradictory to the creation order.
48. The pastor had invited the media to his sermon (but they did not attend). He tape recorded it and sent it to various newspapers. It was only when the local paper published an account of the sermon that news of it spread and received national coverage in Sweden.
49. According to this provision, "a person who in a disseminated statement or communication threatens or expresses contempt for a national, ethnic or other such group of persons with allusion to race, color, national or ethnic origin or religious belief or sexual orientation, shall be sentenced for agitation against a national or ethnic group to imprisonment for at most two years, or if the crime is petty, to a fine."
50. See Government Bill, Prop. 2001/02:59, p. 33, emphasizing the link between agitation against homosexuals and crimes against homosexuals.
51. See, in particular, Government Bill, Prop. 2001/02:59, pp. 41–42, drawing up guidelines, upon request by Sweden's Council for Free Churches.
52. *Vejdeland & Ors v. Sweden* [2012] ECHR 242 (February 9, 2012).
53. *Hämäläinen v. Finland* [2014] ECHR 787 (July 16, 2014).

54. The spouses were of the Evangelical Lutheran faith.
55. *Johns v. Derby County Council and Equality and Human Rights Commission* (intervening) [2011] EWHC 375 (Admin) (February 28, 2011).
56. I find it misleading to equate *applicants* interested to qualify as foster parents with parents of children. Foster parents exercise special functions under strict public control, and special criteria apply with respect to who can qualify according to state law. Parents (biological and adoptive) have a totally different kind of autonomy in their educational and child-bringing functions, with which the state may intervene only in the case of serious abuse.
57. Evasion of state law and its impediments to marriage, such as the husband's existing marriage or the required marriage age, take place in a religious marriage setting and have become an increasing public concern in the Scandinavian states. See Maarit Jänterä-Jareborg, "On the Cooperation between Religious and State Institutions in Family Matters: Nordic Experiences," 93–99. See above note 10.

Afterword

1. For more on religious freedom in the face of diverse beliefs see Roger Trigg, *Religious Diversity: Philosophical and Political Dimensions* (Cambridge: Cambridge University Press, 2014).
2. See John Locke, *Essay Concerning Human Understanding*, Andrew S. Pringle-Pattison, ed. (Oxford: Clarendon Press, 1924), bk. I, ch. 1, sec. 5, p. 13 and bk. IV, ch. 3, sec. 20, p. 280.
3. *McFarlane v. Relate Avon Ltd* (2010) EWCA Civ 880 (April 29, 2010), para. 23.
4. *Khaira v. Shergill* (2012) EWCA Civ 983 (July 17, 2012), para. 69.
5. *Khaira v. Shergill*, paras. 70, 72.
6. *Khaira v. Shergill*, para. 5.
7. *Shergill and Others v. Khaira and Others* [2014] UKSC 33 (June 11, 2014), para. 48.
8. *Shergill v. Khaira*, para. 59.
9. *Hosanna-Tabor Evangelical Lutheran Church and School v. Equal Employment Opportunity Commission* 565 US ___, (2012), 132 S. Ct. 694.
10. See, for example, *Percy v. Church of Scotland Board of National Mission (Scotland)* [2005] UKHL 73 (December 15, 2005).
11. *Ladele v. London Borough of Islington* (2009) EWCA Civ 1357 (December 15, 2009), para. 52.
12. *Eweida and Chaplin v. United Kingdom*, Application Nos. 484/10 and 59842/10, Respondent's Observations, October 14, 2011, para. 10.
13. *Eweida and Others v. United Kingdom* [2013] IRLR 231, [2013] ECHR 37 (January 15, 2013).
14. See Roger Trigg, "Belief and Practice," in *Equality, Freedom and Religion* (Oxford: Oxford University Press, 2012), 97–110.
15. See Roger Trigg, *Religion in Public Life* (Oxford: Oxford University Press, 2007), 153ff.
16. *Eweida and Others*, para. 83.
17. *Khaira v. Shergill*, para. 25.
18. See Roger Trigg, *Equality, Freedom and Religion*, 18–26; Roger Trigg and Justin L. Barrett, eds., *The Roots of Religion: Exploring the Cognitive Science of Religion* (Burlington, VT: Ashgate Publishing, 2014).
19. See Roger Trigg, *Rationality and Religion: Does Faith Need Reason?* (Oxford: Basil Blackwell, 1998).

INDEX

CPSIA information can be obtained
at www.ICGtesting.com
Printed in the USA
BVOW00s2025011216
469535BV00002B/48/P